An Account of the Most Important and Interesting Religious Events, Which Have Transpired From the Commencement of the Christian Era to the Present Time;

Tom Beach,
Centerville
Conn,

Christianity

descending from Heaven - holds in her right hand, the crown of Immortality; in her left, the New Testament.—Asia is represented prostrate; Europe in a bending posture;—Africa by a figure kneeling; and America by an Indian with the Calumet, or pipe of peace.—The broken chains &c. represent the effects of Christianity in the destruction of Slavery and Idolatry. The dark sky in the back ground, shows the state of the world when Christianity first appeared. A few twinkling stars show that a measure of light shined in the darkest period of time.

AN ACCOUNT

OF THE

MOST IMPORTANT AND INTERESTING

RELIGIOUS EVENTS,

WHICH HAVE TRANSPIRED

FROM THE COMMENCEMENT OF THE CHRISTIAN ERA TO THE PRESENT TIME

WITH A

SHORT BIOGRAPHICAL SKETCH OF PERSONS DISTINGUISHED IN RELIGIOUS HISTORY.

COLLECTED AND COMPILED FROM THE MOST APPROVED AUTHORITIES,

BY J. W. BARBER.

NEW HAVEN:

PUBLISHED BY L. H. YOUNG.

1834.

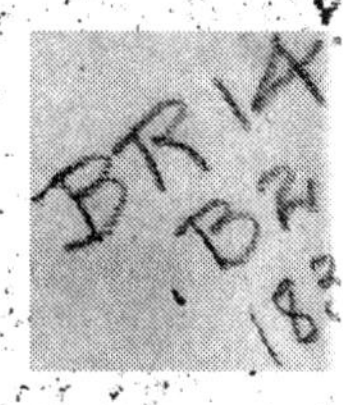

STEREOTYPED BY L. JOHNSON,
PHILADELPHIA.

PREFACE.

"The course of Religious Events embraces a more interesting history than all the secular achievements of man, since the Christian era commenced; and it is believed the cases are rare, where even those who are professedly interested in Religious History are sufficiently acquainted with its various and highly interesting details." The reason for this has been, in many instances, that works on Religious History have generally been voluminous and expensive. To remedy this defect, in some measure, has been one object of this work. It is, it will be perceived, arranged upon a new plan; the account of each event, or fact, is in some respects insulated; not being necessarily connected with any other. The object of the compiler was to give the reader a comprehensive view of each subject introduced. He has generally confined himself to the bare relation of facts as he found them, leaving his readers to draw their own inferences and conclusions. A short biographical sketch is given of persons distinguished in Religious History; and a chronological table of Religious Events is added: these, with the other part of the work, it is believed, will be found valuable as a book of reference, for facts which have been recorded in Church History.

"No apology is necessary for the free use which has been made of the labours of others, for the plan of this book is so essentially different from that of any which has preceded it, that the author has not encroached upon the objects which others have had in view. He has had no hesitation in using their very language, whenever it suited him. Compilers seem to be licensed pillagers. Like the youth of Sparta, they may lay their hands upon plunder without a crime, if they will but seize it with adroitness."* The numerous engravings interspersed through the book, it is thought, will be of utility in making the work interesting, and assist in preserving in the mind the events which they represent. J. W. B.

NEW HAVEN, 1834.

---

* Preface to Allen's American Biographical Dictionary.

CONTENTS.

AN

OUTLINE SKETCH

OF

CHURCH HISTORY,

FROM THE CHRISTIAN ERA.

FIRST CENTURY.

When Jesus Christ made his appearance on earth, a great part of the world was subject to the Roman empire. This empire was much the largest temporal monarchy that had ever existed; so that it was called all the world, Luke ii. 1. The time when the Romans first subjugated the land of Judea was between sixty and seventy years before Christ was born; and soon after this, the Roman empire rose to its greatest extent and splendour. To this government the world continued subject till Christ came, and many hundred years afterwards. The remote nations, that had submitted to the yoke of this mighty empire, were ruled either by Roman governors, invested with temporary commissions, or by their own princes and laws, in subordination to the republic, whose sovereignty was acknowledged, and to which the conquered kings, who were continued in their own dominions, owed their borrowed majesty. At the same time, the Roman people, and their venerable senate, though they had not lost all shadow of liberty, were yet in reality reduced to a state of servile submission to Augustus Cæsar, who, by artifice, perfidy and bloodshed, attained an enormous degree of power, and united, in his own person, the pompous titles of *emperor*, *pontiff*, *censor*, *tribune of the people*; in a word, all the great offices of the state.

As most of those valuable documents which could be depended upon, concerning the success and extent of the gospel among the Gentiles, in this early age of Christianity, were destroyed either by the pagan persecutors, or Gothic barbarians, it is impossible to ascertain the precise limits of the kingdom of Christ. It is quite certain, however, that through the instrumentality of St. Paul, the Christian religion was received both in Athens and Rome; the former of which beheld his triumph in their seats of learning and justice, and the latter saw the banner of the cross on the palace gates of their emperor.

From the Acts of the Apostles, which is the only account that can be relied upon, it appears that by the preaching of Christ crucified, the worship of heathen deities in many parts of Asia and Europe was entirely abolished. In the year 64, *Nero*, the Emperor of Rome, a cruel and bloody tyrant, commenced a furious persecution against the church of God. It is probable that this persecution raged as far as the Roman authority itself extended; the number of the victims, therefore, must have been immense.

After this tyrant had lived for some time under the horrors of his guilty conscience, he was condemned, by the senate, to be put into the pillory, there to be scourged to death; but in the year 68, after several pusillanimous efforts, he put an end to his life.

During the reign of *Vespasian*, the year 70, Jerusalem was taken by his son *Titus*.

Domitian, who was nearly equal to Nero in cruelty, renewed the persecution in the year 94; but it was of short duration, as he was put to death by his own soldiers. In the reign of Domitian, St. John the Apostle was banished to the isle of Patmos.

It is a melancholy reflection, that error soon reared its hundred heads in the church of God, and the Epistles of St. John were particularly directed against those heretics, who may be classed under the general term of *Gnostics*, and who, with their many absurdities, denied the Godhead of our blessed Lord. They likewise denied that he was clothed with a real body, asserting that this, together with his sufferings and trials, as stated in the Scriptures, were only in appearance. They also held, that the world was created by a malevolent being, and that rational souls were imprisoned in corrupt matter by the power of malignant spirits, contrary to the Supreme Will, who, they expected, would send a messenger to rescue miserable mortals from the chains of these usurpers. Perceiving Christ's miracles, and therefore concluding him to be the expected messenger, they were induced to embrace Christianity; or rather, to corrupt the doctrines and precepts of Christ, to reconcile them with their own tenets.

SECOND CENTURY.

As it is well known, that at this time the greatest part of the world had been subjugated to the Roman authority, the circumstances of the church of God must consequently have been materially affected by the disposition of the Roman emperors towards it. It appears necessary, therefore, to take a view of the respective reigns of those persons into whose hands the government of the world fell.

This century began with the emperor *Trajan*, who can only be reproached with persecuting the Christians, on whom he had been prevailed to look with an evil eye. But this persecution was of short duration; for Pliny, the younger, who was then consul of Bythinia, where a great number of Christians resided, having written to the emperor a very elegant letter, in which he bears witness to the innocence of the first Christians' lives, Trajan stopped the proceedings against them. During his reign, Ignatius, bishop of Antioch, suffered martyrdom.

He died Anno Domini 117, after a reign of nineteen years, and was succeeded by *Adrian*, during whose reign the ruin of the Jews was completed. Rufus, President of Judea, having engaged them under a mad leader, named Barchobebas, (or the son of the star,) slew many thousands, not sparing even women and children; and forbade the survivors from coming within sight of Jerusalem. This Barchobebas asserted that he was the Messiah of the Jews, and the star predicted by the Prophet Balaam. The Jews flocked to him in crowds, verifying the prediction of our Lord Jesus Christ, "I am come in my Father's name, and ye receive me not; if another shall come in his own name, him ye will receive."

Adrian, after having reigned upwards of twenty years, was succeeded by *Antoninus*, during whose reign Christianity continued to spread in the surrounding countries, notwithstanding persecutions were very frequent throughout the whole Roman empire. Justin Martyr, a celebrated philosopher, who had embraced Christianity, became their advocate; and, in an apology which he presented to the emperor, so affectingly represented their case, that a rescript was issued, forbidding their punishment, unless for crimes against the state; nor was the profession of Christianity to be considered as such. This holy man, whose works are still extant, was at last burnt alive at Rome, for the faith of our Lord Jesus Christ.

Antoninus had chosen two successors, who, after his death, reigned jointly; viz. *Marcus Aurelius Antoninus* and *Lucius Ælius Verus*, which was the first instance of two emperors reigning at the same time. Ælius Verus was fond of ease and voluptuousness; but by nature averse to cruelty and injustice. After a reign of little more than eight years, he died of an apoplexy, leaving the empire to Marcus Aurelius, who countenanced accusations against Christians, under any form. During his reign, Polycarp, Bishop of Smyrna, added new credit to the cause of Christ, by his triumphant martyrdom. The renowned apologist, Justin Pothenus, Bishop of Lyons, and many other eminent men, suffered martyrdom in this reign. A learned Christian, named Athenagorias, addressed to him a masterly apology for the Christian religion; and it is presumed that his remonstrances had the desired effect, and convinced the emperor of the innocence of the unjustly persecuted Christians. The next emperor was *Commodus*, during whose reign the churches increased, and many characters of the first consequence were added to the Lord, particularly at Rome. But here, Apollonius, a senator, was accused of Christianity, and with much eloquence and boldness defended his profession before the senate; for which he was condemned to death.

Severus, who was the last emperor of this century, was an implacable enemy to Christianity. During his reign, seas of sacred blood were shed in Asia and Egypt; but at Alexandria (which Eusebius calls the noblest stadium of God) the greater number of victims fell. Some were fastened to crosses; others torn to pieces with nails of iron; others were exposed to wild beasts; and others burned alive.

Amongst a great number of renowned sufferers, are to be reckoned Leonides, the father of Origen, Irenæus, Bishop of Lyons, and a celebrated Christian lady, named Potamiaena, who gained immortal dignity by her sufferings.

Tertullian, a native of Carthage, stood up as an apologist for the Christians at this time, and essentially contributed to the advancement of the best of causes.

The second century closed amidst the infernal triumphs of persecution.

THIRD CENTURY.

The respite which the death of Severus afforded to the church, was but partial. Under the reign of his son, *Caracalla*, the Christians in Africa suffered greatly, by the instigation of Scapula, the proconsul of that province, whose cruelties roused the spirit of Tertullian: he, regardless of consequences, boldly addressed the proconsul in behalf of the cause of Christ, and referring to some late calamities with which the empire had been visited, declared them to be nothing but the judgments of Heaven, for shedding the innocent blood of its righteous servants; and entreated Scapula to exercise moderation and clemency towards those who had ever proved themselves deserving subjects of the state.

However dead the hearts of their enemies were to their pathetic remonstrances, their sufferings were in a great measure alleviated. The emperor marked out new objects for his infernal passion. His friends, his counsellors, and his wife, indiscriminately fell by the command of this overgrown savage; till heaven, wearied with forbearance, sent him to his own place by the hand of an assassin, in the year 217.

Under the reign of the two succeeding emperors, *Macrinus* and *Avitus*, the state of the church was in no particular manner affected; but under the reign of *Alexander Severus*, it received considerable acquisitions.

Whether from false politics or want of light, cannot be said, but it is certain that this emperor made a strange mixture of Christianity and paganism. He had a chapel in his palace, where he paid honors to the images of Apollonius of Tyanus, the celebrated Pythagorean philosopher; to those of Jesus Christ, Abraham and Orpheus.

His mother, Mamea, however, having had a conference with the famous Origen, became considerably attached to Christianity; and is reported to have entered into a profession of the same, at which the pagan priests were particularly alarmed, and perceiving the rapid progress of Christianity, declared, "*That if the Christians were allowed to have temples of their own, the temples of the Roman deities would be forsaken, and the empire would soon embrace Christianity.*" Though the emperor was hereby deterred from building churches to the name of Christ, yet he forbade those already built to be injured.

To Alexander succeeded *Maximin*, a man of monstrous body, and no less monstrous mind. His villanies were most eminently exemplified where he himself resided. The bishops, and principal men among the Christians, were those that he selected for his own vengeance; and in consequence of his example, the heathen priests, the magistrates, and the common people, were animated in persecuting all those who bore the Christian name. Having waded in blood for three years, Heaven caused this gigantic wretch to be slain by his own soldiers; and his execrable body to be cast out, and devoured by dogs and birds.

To the tempest raised by Maximin, a happy calm ensued to the church of God; which may be attributed to two causes—the inroads of different nations upon the empire (which diverted their attention from the concerns of the Christians), and the pacific virtues of the emperors themselves.

Gordian, a man of learning, and heathen virtue, knew how to value merit wherever he discovered it; and therefore was mild towards the Christians from principle.

Philip, who succeeded Gordian, though a wicked man, yet, if not professedly a Christian, certainly wished to be so. The emperor and empress, being at Antioch, attempted to enter the church during divine service; upon which Babylas (the worthy bishop of that church), laying his hand upon his heart, declared, that he was unworthy to enter into the fold of Christ; and that he should have no admittance, unless he were brought to repentance for his sins, and made a public acknowledgment of the same.

Decius was next raised to the throne: he was a violent persecutor of the Christians, and formed the dreadful project of extirpating all who professed that faith. To give effect to his design, he issued edicts conveying the most unlimited powers to the governors of all the provinces. The heathens emulated each other in promoting the execution of the imperial edicts. Hence, rocks, sharp stakes, fire, burning pincers, wild beasts, scalding pitch, and tortures in a thousand forms, and of the most exquisite kinds, were heaped upon these innocent men.

Here the weakness of human nature was lamentably evinced. Those amongst the Christians who were not dismayed at death itself, were nevertheless appalled at the tremendous forms which it now assumed; to evade which, unwarrantable means were used, such as bribing the heathen priests to give them certificates, certifying that they were not Christians, offering sacrifices, or burning incense before the images of false gods. Notwithstanding, however, the injury which the best of causes sustained by the defection of some of its avowed friends, the multitude of those who loved not their lives to the death, was truly great. Many, who before this trying period had not been known as favourers of Christianity, now came boldly forward, declaring themselves the servants of Christ, and exulting at an opportunity of sealing their testimony with their blood. This wicked emperor perished miserably, and it is a fact worthy of observation, that almost all the princes who persecuted the Christians came to an untimely end.

Gallus, who succeeded to the empire, carried on the dreadful work of Decius, and made the Christians groan under his persecuting hand. A terrible pestilence having desolated the Roman provinces, the pagan priests improved the occasion, industriously attributing the calamity to the anger of the gods, for the lenity shown to the Christians; and hereby reanimated the rage of persecution.

The death of Gallus, who was slain in battle, afforded a release to the suffering church of Christ, by the accession of *Valerian* to the throne, who, for the first five years of his reign, exercised a considerable degree of clemency towards the Christians; but in the last two years he was influenced by Macrianus, an Egyptian magician, his chief counsellor, to renew the persecution. The Christian churches were ordered to be shut, and no age, sex, or character, was spared. Many eminent men gave illustrious proofs of the invincible nature of divine grace, by the heroism of their conduct in the presence of their adversaries. Under this emperor's reign, the great St. Cyprian, in obedience to his orders, suffered martyrdom at Carthage.

The time, however, arrived, when the just judgment of God reached Valerian. He was taken prisoner by *Sapor*, king of Persia, who reduced him to the vilest situation, using him as a footstool to mount his horse; plucked out his eyes; flayed his body when alive; and when dead, had it preserved and hung up in one of his temples.

Under the reigns of *Gallienus, Aurelian, Tacitus, Probus* and *Carus*, the Christians enjoyed perfect peace from their public enemies.

FOURTH CENTURY.

Diocletian, who came to the empire, A. D. 284, for the first twenty years of his reign, was far from being an enemy of Christians. But in the beginning of this century, he became their most cruel foe, and marked all his footsteps with the blood of saints. For a length of time, from a natural love of ease, and aversion to bloodshed, he withstood the solicitations of the pagan priests, who urged him to employ his power and authority in saving their threatened cause from impending ruin. Galerius, one of the censors, a man of ferocious mind, by the use of every diabolical art, finally excited him to loose the demon of persecution upon the defenceless flock of Christ.

The dreadful scene commenced in Nicomedia, the residence of Diocletian and Galerius, on the 23d of February, 303, in presence of the emperor and his censor. The officers of the city entered the Christian churches, brought forth the sacred books and utensils, and threw them into the fire. The next day, an edict was published, excluding the Christians from the protection of the laws; commanding their churches to be demolished, and subjecting their persons to death. Every species of torture which malice could invent, was put into operation; but religion, as usual, acquired additional splendour from the fury of its adversaries, and evinced its divine nature amidst the sufferings of its illustrious confessors. Human nature, however, always frail, lamentably evinced its weakness, in the conduct of some, who, in order to evade the imputation of Christianity, and thereby shun the sufferings to which they were exposed, delivered up their religious books. Their conduct was strongly condemned by the real friends of the gospel, who marked them with the name of *Traditores*. Galerius, the source of all this cruelty, was, by the hand of God, called to give an account of his unparalleled wickedness, after having endured in this life the most grievous afflictions; having his insides preyed upon by vermin, and the whole mass of his body turned into rottenness. In addition to the pains occasioned by his disorder, he felt all the horrors of a most guilty conscience, for his conduct to the Christians. Hoping that his miseries might be alleviated by their intercessions with God, he published an edict in their favour, and after lingering under the violence of his disorder a considerable time, this impious wretch expired in the year 311.

Diocletian, who had been compelled by Galerius to resign his imperial dignity, died a miserable death in the year 312.

Constantius Clorus, was peculiarly beloved by his subjects, and deservedly esteemed as a friend of the Christians: he was succeeded by his son.

Constantine, who for near seven years had shown no attachment to any religious principles; but in the year 312 he appeared a favourer of Christianity, and after some time proved himself a professed disciple of the Lord Jesus, being converted to the Christian faith, it is said by a remarkable vision of a cross, while marching at the head of his army.

During Constantine's reign, a priest of Alexandria, named Arius, introduced new opinions concerning the divinity of Jesus Christ, which occasioned great troubles. The emperor assembled a council of bishops from all parts of the Roman empire, at Nice, where they declared the principles of Arius contrary to holy writ, and to the faith maintained by all the churches. Arianism subsisted, however, in several places, till towards the close of the sixth century, when it was entirely abolished.

Constantine, Constantius, and *Constans*, succeeded their father Constantine in the empire, and like him, proceeded in the demolition of pagan superstition and idolatry.

Julian, the Apostate, nephew to Constantine the first, upon the death of the three brothers, was declared emperor. He had been educated in the Christian religion, but apostatized from it, and exercised all his power to restore the faded glory of expiring polytheism. He attempted to rebuild the temple of Jerusalem, apparently to disprove the prophecies of Jesus Christ; but God sending forth flames of fire from the earth and destroying his workmen, defeated his wicked intention. He was mortally wounded in a battle with the Persians, when catching the blood which issued from the wound, he threw it up towards heaven, exclaiming, "Vicisti, O Galilea!" O Galilean, thou hast conquered.

Jovian, Valentinian, &c. &c., succeeded Julian: they all professed Christianity, and employed themselves in eradicating paganism, so that towards the close of this century, the splendor of superstition, by its lengthened shadows, indicated its irrecoverable decline.

FIFTH CENTURY.

This century was distinguished by the famous Pelagian and semi-Pelagian controversies; also for the persecutions of Huneric and Arian, who, among other acts of barbarity, ordered the tongues of a number of those pious men, who adhered to the doctrine of the true divinity of our Lord Jesus Christ, to be cut out.

In the year 496, *Clovis*, king of France, embraced the Christian religion, and was baptized at Rheims in Champaigne.

At the beginning of this century the Roman empire fell into the hands of Theodosius, who at his death left it to his two sons, Arcadius and Honorius. The former had the eastern empire for his portion, and the latter the western; and in the year 410, the city of Rome was taken from him by Alaric, and pillaged.

The eastern empire, during the reign of Theodosius, enjoyed peace; but the church was much disturbed by the factions of the prelates of Alexandria. Under the reign of Arcadius, Theophilus, patriarch of that city, had cruelly persecuted St. John Chrysostom, one of the most pious prelates of the east, and sent him into exile; and these factions raged with still greater violence under the feeble government of Theodosius the younger, the son of Arcadius.

SIXTH CENTURY.

In the sixth century, the ambition of the Roman pontiff distinguished itself in a violent struggle for absolute supremacy, with John, surnamed the foster bishop of Constantinople. Long had the man of sin, in the persons of the bishops of Rome, aimed at every possible degree of accession to his impious domination. In the language of the apostle, "hitherto there had been one who let;" which was none other than the Roman civil power, exercised by the emperors.

But in the year 534, the emperor Justinian gave supreme power to the beast, by declaring him "*Head of all the churches; the Judge of all others—himself to be judged by none.*" In the east his pretensions were disregarded, and his authority rejected: but in the west his design too well succeeded.

Ennodius, bishop of Ticinum, in a fulsome panegyric, asserted that the bishop of Rome was constituted *judge in the place of God.* Although this supremacy was disputed and resisted, and the surrounding princes exercised their authority independent of the ghostly dominion of the Roman pontiff, yet the foundation of his antichristian greatness was so firmly laid, that, at future periods, princes, kings, and emperors, submitted to his orders, expressing the most servile subjection to his authority, and performing the most degrading acts of humiliation at his command.

Theodoric (a Roman emperor) put to death the illustrious Christian philosophers, *Boethius* and *Symmachus*, his father-in-law, on a false accusation of attempting to re-establish the liberties of Rome. He also killed *John*, bishop of Rome, and committed other cruel and unjust actions.

He died in 526, after a reign of thirty-five years. It is said, that seeing the head of a large fish served at his table, he fancied he beheld the head of Symmachus, and it is supposed the agitation of his conscience hastened his death.

Justinian erected at Constantinople the church of St. Sophia, which passes for one of the wonders of the world. This edifice, which was commenced Anno Domini 537, is now converted into a Turkish mosque.

In 596, Pope Gregory, surnamed the Great, sent into Great Britian some monks, the chief of whom was named Augustine, for the purpose of preaching the Christian religion.

SEVENTH CENTURY.

THIS century is distinguished by the *rise of Mahometanism*. *Mahomet*, the founder of this religion, was a native of Mecca, in Arabia, a man who wanted neither abilities nor address to insinuate his dogmas, which he did partly by force and partly by persuasion. The unhappy divisions which at this period prevailed among the Christians, contributed greatly to the advancement of his religion.

The tenets of this deceiver are contained in the *Koran*, which is a confused mixture of some of the truths of Judaism and Christianity, with a variety of absurd fables.

His religion began in the year 622, which is called the first of the *Hegira* or flight of Mahomet, when he was driven from Mecca by his fellow citizens. Mahomet died Anno Domini 631.

In the year 690, *Willibrod*, an English monk, preached the gospel in the Netherlands.

EIGHTH CENTURY.

WHILST the grand Impostor of the East, with incredible celerity, traversed the earth, and incalculable myriads of the human race, either compelled by the terror of his arms, or allured by the hope of sensual gratifications, acknowledged him as the prophet of God; Christianity, which had been planted by apostolic hands, languished in a state of melancholy decay; and although the eighth century of the Christian era had commenced, several parts of Europe yet remained in a state of pagan darkness.

The Saracens, followers of Mahomet, availed themselves of the distractions which prevailed in the east, ravaged the provinces of Asia and Africa, and heaped upon the Christian the heaviest calamities. Crossing the Mediterranean, they entered Spain, became victorious, overthrew its empire, obtained a considerable extent of territory, and made that country, and part of France, groan under their oppressive yoke.

In this century, the worship of images, the remains of paganism, was established in almost every part of the eastern empire.. This abuse the emperor Leo endeavoured to prevent, by causing them to be taken out of the churches from the year 726, and by prohibiting the use of them in 730 by a solemn edict. This drew upon him the hatred of the ignorant and superstitious ecclesiastics, and occasioned the loss of all that the em pire possessed in Italy. Gregory II., Pope of Rome, undertook the defence of the images, and in a council of bishops, dependent on him, condemned the edict of the emperor. By virtue of this seditious communication, he caused Rome and the rest of Italy to revolt, having forbidden the people thenceforth to acknowledge the emperor of Rome, or to pay him any tribute.

In the year 744, the emperor Constantine assembled at Constantinople a council of three hundred and thirty-eight bishops, in which the worship of images was declared contrary to the word of God, and absolutely forbidden throughout the empire. It would now have ceased, had it not been for the obstinacy of the monks, who, supported by certain bishops, and the ignorant populace, continued it in secret, and thus kept up one of the first sources of corruption in the church.

The emperor *Charlemagne*, one of the greatest princes of the western empire, subdued the Saxons in 785, and obliged Witekind, their prince, to embrace the Christian religion.

The same emperor, having in 794 entirely subdued the Frisi, stipulated that they should embrace Christianity; in which case he permitted them to preserve the title of a free people, and exempted them from paying any tribute. From that time the gospel was generally received among them.

The empress Irene, who was a very superstitious and wicked woman, in the year 787 assembled at Nice a council of two hundred and eighty very ignorant bishops. Here the worship of images was established, which the council held at Constantinople, under Constantine, had condemned; and those who refused adoration to the images, were declared heretics, and anathematized.

In the year 794, the emperor Charlemagne assembled another council at Frankfort, where that held by Irene, and the worship of images, were condemned.

NINTH CENTURY.

The emperor *Charlemagne* died the 28th of January, 814, at the age of 71, in the 47th year of his reign and the 14th of his empire. In this century, a furious contest arose between the patriarchs of Constantinople and the pontiffs of Rome, which produced a rupture between the Greek and Latin churches, and terminated in their final separation.

The isle of Great Britain in this century produced the truly great *Alfred*, during whose reign learning was in a great measure advanced, which was before so reduced, that among the clergy there was not a man to be found in the kingdom of Wessex, who understood the Latin service. Christianity, which had been languishing to a state of the most extreme wretchedness, experienced the fostering care of the worthy Alfred, and its dying embers soon began to revive.

TENTH CENTURY.

In this century, *Otho the Great*, emperor of Germany, extended the Christian religion throughout the empire, and founded the bishopricks of Brandenburg, Havelburg, Meisen, Zeitz, and Magdeburg. But the doctrine and manners of its professors were so corrupt, that, on account of the prevailing ignorance and depravity, historians have given the tenth the appellation of the *iron century.*

The Russians, till this period, were pagans, but were, about the year 924, converted to Christianity by the Greeks of Constantinople. *Alba*, their duchess, and Woldomir, her son, were baptized. Micislaus, king of Poland, was also converted in the year 965; and Stephen, the first Christian king of Hungary, was baptized in 969.

ELEVENTH CENTURY.

The bishops of Rome, availing themselves of the negligence of the emperors, and of the people's ignorance, now began to erect themselves into primates and sovereigns of all christendom. Having ruled despotic in the spiritual, they presumed to extend their authority over the temporal affairs of emperors and kings.

At this time, the see of Rome was occupied by *Gregory* VII., who, in the year 1074, prohibited the marriage of priests; and although at first he found difficulties in establishing this decree, in the end he prevailed, and his successor finished what he begun.

From the seventh century, the city of Jerusalem had been subject to the Mahometans; but Pope Urban II. having caused a crusade against them to be preached in all the kingdoms of christendom, raised an army of two hundred and sixty thousand men in France, Germany, and other countries. In the year 1096, this army, led on by *Peter the Hermit*, went into Palestine, where they did not arrive till the year 1099. The Christians took Jerusalem that year, and having erected it into a kingdom, proclaimed *Godfrey de Bouillon* first king of Jerusalem and Palestine.

Godfrey was not, however, crowned, owing to his refusal of that honor. "God forbid," said he, "that I should appear crowned with gold in a place where Jesus Christ, my master, wore a crown of thorns."

TWELFTH CENTURY.

The Christians retained possession of Jerusalem eighty-five years, at the end of which it was retaken by Saladin.

Frederic Barbarossa, one of the greatest princes of Germany, after having been engaged in a long war with the popes, was finally forced to enter into an irksome treaty, one of the conditions of which was, that he should engage in the crusade.

Frederic, having arrived in Palestine, learnt that Jerusalem had been retaken by the famous Saladin, Sultan of Egypt. This, however, did not prevent his performing many gallant actions in that country, where he continued till his death, which took place in the year 1190.

THIRTEENTH CENTURY.

This century was distinguished by the founding of the *inquisition*, a tribunal erected by the popes, for the examination and punishment of heretics.

In 1215, Pope *Innocent* III. held at Rome a council, in which, by order of that pontiff, *transubstantiation* was ranked among the articles of the church of Rome's faith. This was called the *Council of Lateran*. This council consisted of 412 bishops, 800 abbots and priors, and ambassadors from almost every court in Christendom. At this time, *auricular confession* was introduced into the Romish church.. The power of the pope was increased at this period, immense donations being given him.

FOURTEENTH CENTURY.

In this century the dominion of the Roman church appeared rapidly to decline, owing to the contentions between the pope and the king of France.

The popes now laboured only to increase their authority, and corrupt the pure doctrines of religion. *Boniface* VIII., a detestable character, established the jubilee in the year 1300.

Under false pretences he excommunicated *Philip the Fair*; but that prince sent troops into Italy and took him prisoner at Arrania, from whence he was sent to Rome, where he died of rage and despair. At this time *Wickliffe*, the great English reformer, opposing the errors of the church of Rome, was brought before the bishop in St. Paul's, and finally silenced. His followers were distinguished by the name of Lollards. He died in 1385, at Lutterworth, and owing to the hatred which was entertained by the Romish church against him and his doctrines, his remains many years after his death were dug up, burnt to ashes, and thrown into the river.

FIFTEENTH CENTURY.

The ignorance and ambition of the ecclesiastics, at this period, created a general disorder. There were no less than three popes, who mutually excommunicated each other, and who, supported by princes of their respective parties, stirred up dreadful dissensions and troubles in all the states of Europe.

The emperor *Sigismond*, with the consent of the other princes of the empire, assembled a council at Constance, when the two surviving popes, Benedict XII. and John XXIII. were deposed, and Cardinal *Odo Colonne*, who took the name of Martin V., elected in their room.

It was at this council, that *John Huss* and *Jerome of Prague*, his disciple, were condemned to be burnt for having written and preached against the flagrant abuses of the Roman church. Sigismond had granted them safe conduct to Constance, where, contrary to all public faith, they were put to a cruel death. Their death was, however, avenged by *John Ziska*, a man of noble family, and in high repute for his wisdom and courage. This person declared war against *Sigismond*, and in several engagements defeated his armies.

This century was distinguished by the discovery of the new world, by *Columbus*, and also by the noble art of printing; which was invented in 1440.

Learning was now cultivated with incredible ardour, and the family of the Medici was raised up to patronize science; and towards the end of this century, *Erasmus* arose, whose good sense, taste, and industry, were uncommonly serviceable to the reformation. By his labours, monastic superstition received a wound, which has never been healed; and learned men were furnished with critical skill and ingenuity, of which they failed not to avail themselves in the instruction of mankind to a degree beyond what Erasmus himself had ever conceived.

Thus, under the care of Divine Providence, materials were collected for the diffusion of that light, which appeared in the next century.

About the year 1487, Innocent VIII. invested Albert, archdeacon of Cremona, with power to persecute the Waldenses in the south of France, and in the vallies of Piedmont. This persecution was marked with the most savage barbarity, and continued till the reformation, by Luther.

Constantinople, during the reign of Constantine VIII., was taken by Mahomet II., emperor of the *Turks*, in 1453. In 1491, the Spaniards took Grenada from the Mahometans, being the only city that they then possessed in Spain.

SIXTEENTH CENTURY.

THIS century is distinguished for the great *Reformation* under the instrumentality of *Martin Luther*. The reformed religion, although greatly opposed by the pope and his adherents, was received in Sweden, Denmark, Hungary, Prussia, and, to some extent, even in France.

In England, the papal power was overthrown in consequence of difficulties occurring between the reigning monarch, Henry VIII. and the pope, which finally resulted in a separation of England from the Romish church.

In 1546, the same year that terminated the life of Luther, the famous *council of Trent* was convened, and began to publish its decrees in favour of the doctrines and discipline of the church of Rome.

In 1517, the reformation was begun by Luther in Germany. In 1540, the order of Jesuits was established, and *Ignatius Loyola* appointed first general of the order. In 1560, the reformation was completed in Scotland by John Knox, and the papal authority abolished. In 1572, the massacre of St. Bartholomews took place, the object of which was the destruction of all protestants in France; and in 1598 the edict of Nantes was issued, tolerating the protestant religion in France. Towards the conclusion of the reign of Henry VIII. parliament had passed an act, commonly known by the name of the '*bloody statute*,' consisting of six articles, designed to favour the cause of popery. By these articles it was enacted, that in the sacrament, the bread and wine are changed to the body and blood of Christ; that communion in both kinds is not essential to the common people; and that priests may not marry; with other sentiments of a similar character.

In consequence of these articles, many were persecuted and compelled to flee the country; but at the accession of Edward to the English throne, this statute was repealed.

During this prince's reign, the Liturgy, or Church Service Book of England was composed. About this time also, articles of religion to the number of forty-two, were agreed upon by the bishops and clergy, to which subscription was required, by all who held ecclesiastical offices. These articles were the basis of the celebrated thirty-nine articles of the church of England, which form at present the code of faith and discipline in that church.

Edward died in 1553, and at his death gave the crown to Lady Jane Grey; but the same year the princess Mary, a bigoted papist, claimed the throne as her right, and succeeded in taking possession of it, August, 1553.

Mary now united herself in marriage with Philip, of Spain, and in 1554 Cardinal Pole arrived from Rome, with authority from the pope to receive the submission of the king and queen, which was offered on their knees. When this was done, the cardinal pronounced the kingdom absolved from all censures, and once more returned to the bosom of the Catholic church.

Soon after this reconciliation was effected, an act was passed in parliament for the burning of heretics, and in less than two years above four hundred were publicly executed. Among the distinguished men who suffered were Rogers, Saunders, Hooper, Taylor, Ridley, Latimer, and Cranmer.

At a meeting of parliament in January, 1559, a majority were found in favour of the reformation, at which time several acts were passed in favour of the protestant cause.

In this century, the sect called *Puritans* were formed, being dissenters from the church of England.

SEVENTEENTH CENTURY.

In the year 1602, the puritans separated from the established church, and organized themselves into two churches; the history of one, after a short time, is lost. Of the other, Mr. John Robinson was elected pastor, and in 1608, owing to the persecution they received in England, they removed to Holland, and on the 6th of September, 1620, a portion of this church, under the charge of Elder *Brewer*, set sail for America, and landed at Plymouth, New England, the 22d of December.

In 1605, a scheme was formed by the Roman Catholics, the object of which was to cut off at one blow the king, lords, and commons, at a meeting of parliament. This was called the *gunpowder plot*. Happily, the design was discovered in time to prevent its execution. In 1613, a translation of the Bible into the English tongue was made, being the same which is now in use.

In 1685, the famous edict of Nantes was revoked by Lewis XIV. In 1646, Mr. Eliot, a distinguished minister of New England, applied himself to the improvement of the Indians in that quarter, and met with great success. He laboured till his death in 1690.

EIGHTEENTH CENTURY.

In the course of this century, the light of Christianity was gradually extended in various parts of the world. The spirit of Christianity appeared to receive a new impulse from the labours of Mr. Whitfield and the Wesleys, both in England and America.

The first protestant nation who engaged in Foreign Missions, for the conversion of the heathen, were the *Danes*. Their missionary efforts were commenced about the year 1705, and were directed, in the first place, to the inhabitants on the coast of Malabar, in the East Indies; and a few years after, to the people dwelling in Greenland.

The Moravians, stimulated by the example of the Danes, commenced their missionary operations about the year 1732. Though a small people, they for a time exceeded all others in their missionary enterprise.

It deserves to be recorded, to the honour of Dr. Coke, that as early as 1786, he commenced a mission to the blacks in the West Indies, which was undertaken on his own responsibility, and sustained for some time by his individual exertions. Other missionaries, however, followed him in his labours, who have succeeded in adding great numbers to the Methodist connexion.

The Baptists first effectually commenced their missionary operations in 1792, about which time a society in England was formed through the instrumentality of the Rev. Mr. Carey, of Leicester.

The principal missionary enterprises of the British at this time were conducted under the auspices of three societies, viz. London Missionary Society, formed in 1795; Edinburgh Missionary Society, in 1796; and the Church Missionary Society, formed about the same period.

CRUCIFIXION.

MARTYRDOM OF ST. PETER

St. Peter was crucified with his head downwards,- deeming himself not worthy to suffer in the same posture with our Lord.

RELIGIOUS EVENTS, &c.

---

1. State of the Jews at the coming of Christ.

The state of the Jews was not much better than that of other nations, at the time of Christ's appearance on earth. They were governed by Herod, who was himself tributary to the Roman people. His government was of the most vexatious and oppressive kind. By a cruel, suspicious, and overbearing temper, he drew upon himself the aversion of all, not excepting those who lived upon his bounty.

Under his administration, and through his influence, the luxury of the Romans was introduced into Palestine, accompanied with the vices of that licentious people. In a word, Judea, governed by Herod, groaned under all the corruption which might be expected from the authority and example of a prince who, though a Jew in outward profession, was, in point of morals and practice, a contemner of all laws, human and divine. After the death of this tyrant, the Romans divided the government of Judea between his sons. In this division, one half of the kingdom was given to Archelaus, under the title of Exarch. Archelaus was so corrupt and wicked a prince, that, at last both Jews and Samaritans joined in a petition against him to Augustus, who banished him from his dominions about ten years after the death of Herod the Great. Judea was by this sentence reduced to a Roman province, and ordered to be taxed.

The governors whom the Romans appointed over Judea were frequently changed, but seldom for the better. About the sixteenth year of Christ, *Pontius Pilate* was appointed governor, the whole of whose administration, according to Josephus, was one continual scene of venality, rapine, and every kind of savage cruelty. Such a governor was ill calculated to appease the ferments occasioned by the late tax. Indeed, Pilate was so far from attempting to appease, that he greatly inflamed them, by taking every occasion of introducing his standards, with images, pictures, and consecrated shields, into the city ; and at last, by attempting to drain the treasury of the temple, under pretence of bringing an aqueduct into Jerusalem. The most remarkable transaction of his government, however, was his condemnation of Jesus Christ ; seven years after which he was removed from Judea.

About the time of Christ's appearance, the Jews of that age concluded the period pre-determined by God to be then completed; and that the promised Messiah would suddenly appear. Devout persons waited day and night for the consolation of Israel ; and the whole nation, groaning under the Roman yoke, and stimulated by the desire of liberty or of vengeance, expected their deliverer with the most anxious impatience.

Two religions flourished at this time in Palestin the *Jewish* and *Samaritan*. The Samaritans blended the errors of paganism with the doctrines of the Jews. The learned among the Jews were divided into a great variety of sects. The *Pharisees*, the *Sadducees*, and *Essenes* eclipsed the other denominations.

The most celebrated of the Jewish sects was that of the Pharisees. It is supposed by some, that this denomination existed about a century and a half before the appearance of our Saviour. They separated themselves not only from pagans, but from all such Jews as complied not with their peculiarities. Their separation consisted chiefly in certain distinctions respecting food and relegious ceremonies. It does not appear to have interrupted the uniformity of religious worship, in which the Jews of every sect seem to have always united. This denomination, by their apparent sanctity of manners, had rendered themselves extremely popular. The multitude, for the most part, espoused their interests ; and the great, who feared their artifice, were frequently obliged to court their favor. Hence, they obtained the highest offices in the state and priesthood;

and had great weight, both in public and private affairs. It appears from the frequent mention made by the evangelists of the Scribes and Pharisees in conjunction, that the greatest number of Jewish teachers, or doctors of the law (for those were expressions equivalent to scribe), were at that time of the pharisaical sect. The principal doctrines of the Pharisees were as follows:—that the *oral law*, which they suppose God delivered to Moses by an archangel on Mount Sinai, and which is preserved by tradition, is of equal authority with the written law; that by observing both these laws, a man may not only obtain justification with God, but perform meritorious works of supererogation; that fasting, alms-giving, ablutions, and confessions are sufficient atonements for sin; that thoughts and desires are not sinful, unless they are carried into action. This denomination acknowledged the immortality of the soul, future rewards and punishments, the existence of good and evil angels, and the resurrection of the body. They maintained both the freedom of the will and absolute predestination; and adopted the Pythagorean doctrine of the transmigration of souls, excepting the notoriously wicked, whom they supposed consigned to eternal punishments.

The sect of the Sadducees derived its origin and name from one *Sadoc*, who flourished in the reign of Ptolemy Philadelphus, about two hundred and sixty-three years before Christ. The chief heads of the Sadducean doctrine are as follow:—That all laws and traditions, not comprehended in the written law, are to be rejected as merely human inventions; neither angels nor spirits have a distinct existence separate from their corporeal vestment; the soul of man, therefore, expires with the body; there will be no resurrection of the dead, nor rewards and punishments after this life; man is not subject to irresistible fate, but has the framing of his condition chiefly within his power; and that polygamy ought to be allowed.

The practices of the Pharisees and Sadducees were both perfectly suitable to their sentiments. The former were notorious hypocrites; the latter, scandalous libertines.

The Essenes were a Jewish sect; some suppose they took their rise from that dispersion of their nation which took place after the Babylonian captivity. They maintained that rewards and punishments extended to the soul alone, and considered the body as a mass of malignant matter, and the poison of the immortal spirit. The greatest part of this sect considered the laws of Moses as an allegorical system of spiritual and mysterious truth, and renounced all regard to the outward letter in its explanation.

Besides these eminent Jewish sects, there were several of inferior note at the time of Christ's appearance: the *Herodians*, mentioned by the sacred writers, and the *Gaulonites*, mentioned by Josephus.

The Herodians derived their names from Herod the Great. Their distinguishing tenet appears to be, that it is lawful, when constrained by superiors, to comply with idolatry, and with a false religion.

---

2. Gentile Philosophy.

At the important era of Christ's appearance in the world, two kinds of philosophy prevailed among the civilized nations. One was the philosophy of the Greeks, adopted also by the Romans; and the other, that of the Orientals, which had a great number of votaries in Persia, Syria, Chaldea, Egypt, and even among the Jews. The former was distinguished by the simple title of *philosophy*; the latter was honoured by the more pompous appellation of *science* or *knowledge*; since those who adhered to the latter sect pretended to be the restorers of the knowledge of God, which was lost to the world.*

Amongst the Grecian sects, there were some who declaimed openly against religion, and denied the immortality of the soul; and others, who acknowledged a

* Hannah Adams' Dict. of Religions.

Deity, and a state of future rewards and punishments. Of the former kind were the *Epicureans* and *Academics*; of the latter, the *Platonists* and *Stoics*.

The Epicureans derived their name from *Epicurus*, who was born 242 years before Christ. He accounted for the formation of the world in the following manner:—a finite number of that infinite multitude of atoms, which, with infinite space, constitutes the universe, falling fortuitously into the region of the world, were, in consequence of their innate motion, collected into one rude and undigested mass. All the various parts of nature were formed by those atoms which were best fitted to produce them. The fiery particles formed themselves into air; and from those which subsided, the earth was produced. The mind, or intellect, was formed of particles in their nature, and capable of the most rapid motion. The world is preserved by the same mechanical causes by which it was framed; and from the same cause it will at last be dissolved.

The followers of *Aristotle* were another famous Grecian sect. That philosopher was born in the ninety-ninth Olympiad, about 384 years before the birth of Christ.

Aristotle supposed the universe to have existed from eternity. He admitted, however, the existence of a Deity, whom he styled the *first mover*, and whose nature, as explained by him, is something like the principle which gives motion to a machine. It is a nature wholly separated from matter, immutable, and far superior to all other intelligent natures. The celestial sphere, which is the region of his residence, is also immutable; and residing in his first sphere, he possesses neither immensity nor omnipresence. Happy in the contemplation of himself, he is entirely regardless of human affairs. In producing motion, the Deity acts not voluntarily, but necessarily; not for the sake of other beings, but for his own pleasure.

Nothing occurs in the writings of Aristotle, which decisively determines whether he supposed the soul of man mortal, or immortal. Respecting ethics, he taught, that happiness consisted in the virtuous exercise of the mind, and that virtue consists in preserving that mean in all things, which reason and prudence prescribe. It is the middle path between two extremes, one of which is vicious through excess, the other through defect.

The stoics were a sect of heathen philosophers, of which *Zeno*, who flourished about two hundred and fifty years before Christ, was the original founder. They received their name *Stoics* from a place in which Zeno delivered his lectures, which was a portico in Athens. Their distinguishing tenets were as follows:—that God is underived and eternal, and by the powerful energy of the Deity, impressed with motion and form; that though God and matter existed from eternity, the present regular frame of nature had a beginning, and will have an end; that the element of fire will at last, by an universal conflagration, reduce the world to its pristine state; that at this period all material forms are lost in one chaotic mass, all animated nature is reunited to the Deity, and matter returns to its original form: that from this chaotic state, however, it again emerges, by the energy of the efficient principle; and gods and men, and all forms of regulated nature, are renewed, to be again dissolved and renewed in endless succession; that at the restoration of all things, the race of men will return to life. Some imagined that each individual would return to its former body; while others supposed, that after the revolution of the great *year*, similar souls would be placed in similar bodies.

According to the doctrine of the Stoics, all things are subject to an irresistible and irreversible fatality; and there is a necessary chain of causes and effects, arising from the action of a power which is itself a part of the machine it regulates, and which, equally with the machine, is subject to the immutable law of necessity.

The *Platonic* philosophy is denominated from Plato, who was born in the eighty-seventh Olympiad, 426 years before Christ. He founded the old academy on the opinions of *Heraclitus*, *Pythagoras*, and *Socrates;* and by adding the information he had acquired to their discoveries, he established a sect of philosophers, who were esteemed more perfect than those who had before appeared in the world.

The outlines of Plato's philosophical system were as follows: That there is one God, an eternal, immutable, and immaterial Being, perfect in wisdom and goodness, omniscient and omnipresent; that this all-wise and perfect Being formed the universe from a mass of pre-existing matter to which he gave form and arrangement; that there is in matter a necessary, but blind and refractory force, which resists the will of the Supreme Artificer, so that he cannot perfectly execute his designs; and this is the cause of the mixture of good and evil, which is found in the material world; that the soul of man was derived by emanation from God; but this emanation was not immediate, but through the intervention of the soul of the world, which was itself debased by some material admixture; that the relation which the human soul, in its original constitution, bears to matter, is the source of moral evil; that when God formed the universe, he separated from the soul of the world inferior souls, equal in number to the stars, and assigned to each its proper celestial abode; that these souls were sent down to earth, to be imprisoned in mortal bodies; hence proceed the depravity and misery to which human nature is liable; that the soul is immortal, and by disengaging itself from all animal passions, and rising above sensible objects to the contemplation of the world of intelligence, it may be prepared to return to its original habitation; that matter never suffered annihilation, but that the world will remain for ever, but that the action of its animating principle accomplishes certain periods, within which every thing returns to its ancient place and state. This periodical revolution of nature is called the *Platonic* or *great year*.

3. Crucifixion of Christ.

The coming of our Lord and Saviour Jesus Christ, his sufferings and death, are the greatest and most important events which have ever taken place in our world.

Jesus Christ, the only begotten Son of the Father, came into our world, took upon him our nature, and suffered the penalties of the divine law in our stead. By his sufferings, and death by crucifixion, he hath brought "life and immortality to light;" he hath opened a glorious way whereby fallen and depraved man can be reconciled and received into the favour of God.

"In the hour of Christ's death," says an elegant writer, "the long series of prophecies, visions, types, and figures was accomplished. This was the centre in which they all met; this the point towards which they had tended and verged, throughout the course of so many generations. By that one sacrifice which he now offered, he abolished sacrifices for ever. Altars on which the fire had blazed for ages, were now to smoke no more. Victims were no more to bleed. 'Not with the blood of bulls and goats, but with his own blood, he now entered into the Holy Place, there to appear in the presence of God for us.'

"This was the hour of association and union to all the worshippers of God. When Christ said 'It is finished,' he threw down the wall of partition, which had so long divided the Gentile and Jew. He proclaimed the hour to be come, when the knowledge of the true God should be no longer confined to one nation, nor his worship to one temple; but over all the earth, the worshippers of the Father should 'serve him in spirit and in truth.' From that hour, they who dwelt in the 'uttermost ends of the earth, strangers to the covenant of promise, began to be brought nigh.' In that hour, the foundation of every pagan temple shook; the statue of every false god tottered on its base; the priest fled from his falling shrine; and the heathen oracles became dumb for ever.

"In the hour when Christ expiated guilt, he disarmed death, by securing the resurrection of the just. When he said to his penitent fellow-sufferer, 'To-day shalt thou be with me in Paradise,' he announced to all his followers the certainty of heavenly bliss. From the hill of Calvary, the first clear and certain view was given to the world of the everlasting mansions."

The manner of crucifixion by which our Saviour suffered, was considered the most dreadful of all punishments, both for the shame and pain of it; and so scandalous, that it was inflicted as the last mark of detestation upon the vilest of people. The cross was made of two beams, one of which crossed the other at the top at right angles, thus, †, or in the middle of their length, thus, ×, and the criminal's hands and feet were nailed thereon. The cross to which our Saviour was fastened, and on which he died, was of the former kind; being thus represented by old monuments, coins, and crosses.

---

4. Martyrdom of the Apostles.

After the crucifixion of our Lord, the apostles were scattered abroad in various parts of the world. They preached the gospel wherever they went, and the most of them were called to seal their testimony with their blood.

St. James the Great was by trade a fisherman, and partner with Simon Peter, and related to our Lord, his mother and the Virgin Mary being kinswomen.

When Herod Agrippa was made governor of Judea by the emperor Caligula, he raised a persecution against the Christians, and particularly singled out James, as an object of his vengeance. This martyr, on being condemned to death, showed such an intrepidity of spirit, and constancy of mind, that even his accuser was struck with admiration, and became a convert to Christianity. This transaction so enraged the people in power, that they condemned him to death likewise; when James the Apostle, and his penitent accuser were both beheaded on the same day, with the same sword. These events took place in the year of our Lord 44.

St. Philip was employed in several important commissions by Christ, and being deputed to preach in Upper Asia, laboured very diligently in his apostleship. He then travelled into Phrygia, and arriving at Heliopolis, found the inhabitants so sunk in idolatry as to worship a large serpent. St. Philip, however, was the means of converting many of them to Christianity, and even procured the death of the serpent. This so enraged the magistrates, that they committed him to prison, had him severely scourged, and afterwards hanged him up against a pillar till he died, A. D. 52.

St. Matthew. This evangelist, apostle, and martyr, after our Saviour's ascension, travelled into Ethiopia and Parthia, where he preached the gospel with great success. He suffered martyrdom in the city of Nadabar, being slain by a halberd, about A. D. 60.

St. Mark. After writing his gospel, he went to Egypt and founded a church. When Mark was preaching in his church at Alexandria, some of the idolatrous inhabitants broke in upon him, and dragged him by his feet through the streets, till his flesh was torn off his bones, and he expired under their hands; they afterwards burned his body.

St. James the Less suffered martyrdom at Jerusalem, in the ninety-fourth year of his age. He was thrown headlong from the temple, stoned, and his brains dashed out by a fuller's club.

St. Matthias, the apostle, who was appointed to supply the vacant place of Judas Iscariot, suffered martyrdom at Jerusalem, being first stoned, and then beheaded.

St. Andrew, the brother of St. Peter, preached the gospel to many Asiatic nations. On arriving at Edessa, the governor of the country ordered him to be crucified on a cross, two ends of which were transversely fixed in the ground; he lived two days after he was tied to the cross, preaching the most of the time to the people.

St. Peter was crucified at Rome, by order of the tyrant Nero; he was led up to the top of a mount, and was crucified with his head downwards (according to his request), thinking it too high an honour to die in the same posture with his Lord and Master. Peter and Paul suffered martyrdom on the same day. St. Paul, being a Roman citizen, was beheaded.

St. Jude went to Edessa, where many were converted to Christianity by his preaching, which, stirring up the resentment of the people in power, he was crucified, A. D. 72.

St. Bartholomew translated St. Matthew's gospel in the Indian tongue, and propagated it in that country; but at length the idolaters, growing impatient with his doctrines, severely beat, crucified, and slew him, and then cut off his head.

St. Thomas preached the gospel in Parthia and India, where, displeasing the pagan priests, he was martyred, by being thrust through with a spear.

St. Luke. This apostle and evangelist had the advantage of a liberal education, and was by profession a physician. He travelled with St. Paul to Rome, and preached to many barbarous nations, till the priests of Greece hanged him on an olive-tree.

St. Simon was distinguished for his zeal by the name of Zelotes. He preached with great success in Africa, and it is asserted that he came into the island of Great Britain. He was crucified, A. D. 74.

St. John is said to be the only apostle who escaped a violent death, and lived the longest of any of them, being nearly one hundred years of age at the time of his death.

---

5. Signs and Appearances preceding the Destruction of Jerusalem.

After our Lord had foretold the ruin and desolation coming upon the Jewish people, their city and temple, his disciples came to him privately, saying, tell us when shall these things be, and what shall be the sign of thy coming? &c. Our Lord then informs them of five signs which shall precede the destruction of Jerusalem. The first sign is false Christs; "*for many shall come in my name, saying, I am Christ; and shall deceive many.*" The second, wars and commotions; "*nation shall rise against nation.*" The third, pestilence and famine; "*there shall be famines and pestilences.*" The fourth is "*earthquakes in divers places.*" All of these events took place according to our Lord's prediction, as may be fully seen in the history of the Jews, by Josephus (the Jewish historian), and also by other writers who lived at the time. The fifth sign is, "*there shall be fearful sights and great signs from heaven.* (Luke chapter xxi: 11.) Josephus, in his preface to the Jewish war, enumerates these—1st. A star hung over the city like a sword; and a comet continued a whole year. 2d. The people being assembled at the feast of unleavened bread, at the ninth hour of the night, a great light shone about the altar and the temple, and this continued for half an hour. 3d. At the same feast, a cow, led to the sacrifice, brought forth a lamb in the midst of the temple! 4th. The eastern gate of the temple, which was of solid brass, and very heavy, and could hardly be shut by twenty men, and was fastened by strong bars and bolts, was seen, at the sixth hour of the night, to open of its own accord! 5th. Before sun-setting, there was seen, all over the country, chariots and armies fighting in the clouds, and besieging cities. 6th. At the feast of Pentecost, when the priests were going into the inner temple by night, to attend their service, they heard first a motion and noise, and then a voice as of a multitude, saying, LET US DEPART HENCE. 7th: What Josephus reckons one of the most terrible signs of all was, that one *Jesus*, a country fellow, *four years before the war began*, and when the city was in peace and plenty, came to the feast of tabernacles, and ran up and down the streets day and night, crying, "A voice from the east! a voice from the west! a voice from the four winds! a voice against Jerusalem and the temple! a voice against the bridegrooms and brides! and a voice against all the people!" Though the magistrates endeavoured by stripes and tortures to restrain him, yet he still cried with a mournful voice, "Wo, wo to Jerusalem!" and this he continued to do for several years together, going about the walls and crying with a loud voice, "Wo, wo to the city, and to the people, and to the temple;" and as he added, "*wo, wo to myself!*" a stone, sent by the Romans from some sling or engine, struck him dead upon the spot! It is worthy of remark, that Josephus appeals to the testimony of others, who saw and heard these fearful things. *Tacitus*, a Roman historian, gives nearly the same account with that of Josephus.—*Clarke's Commentary.*

---

6. Destruction of Jerusalem.

The siege and destruction of the city and temple of Jerusalem, and the subversion of the whole political constitution of the Jews, is one of the most striking incidents of the divine vengeance on a wicked people, that we have recorded in history. Our Lord, who foresaw the desolation and calamities coming upon the city, wept over it, declaring his willingness to gather them under his protection: but they would not accept of his salvation; therefore destruction came upon them, and their "house was left unto them desolate."

About forty years after our Lord had foretold the destruction of Jerusalem, the Roman government sent an army under Cestius Gallius against the Jews, in order to quell their rebellious and factious spirit. Gallius came and invested Jerusalem with a powerful army. Our Lord declared to his disciples, that "*when ye shall see Jerusalem compassed with armies, then know that the desolation thereof is nigh.*" And then, in order that his followers might be preserved in safety, he adds, "*Then let them that are in Judea flee to the mountains; and let them that are in the midst of it depart out,*" &c. This counsel was remembered and wisely followed by the Christians; and it is mentioned as a remarkable fact by *Eusebius* and other ancient historians, that not a single Christian perished in the destruction of Jerusalem, though many of them were there when Gallius invested the city; and had he persevered in the siege, he would have soon rendered himself master of it; but when he unexpectedly and unaccountably raised the siege, all who believed in Christ took that opportunity and fled to Pella, and other places beyond Jordan.

Vespasian was appointed to succeed Gallius in prosecuting the war against the Jews; he accordingly subdued the country, and prepared to besiege Jerusalem, but being appointed emperor, he returned to Rome, and gave the command of his forces to his son *Titus*. Titus, having made several assaults without success, resolved to surround the city (which was nearly four English miles in circumference) with a wall; which was, with incredible speed, completed in three days! The wall was strengthened with forts at proper distances, so that all hope of safety was cut off; none could make his escape from the city, and no provisions could be brought into it; thus fulfilling our Lord's words, "*thine enemies shall cast a trench about thee, and compass thee round, and keep thee in on every side.*" Titus now prosecuted the siege with vigour. In addition to this, the Jews were divided into factions among themselves, murdered each other with a blind fury, and burnt their provisions. No history can furnish us with a parallel to the calamities and miseries of the Jews; rapine, murder, famine, and pestilence *within*, fire and sword, and all the horrors of war *without*. While the famine prevailed, the house of a Jewish lady named Miriam, was repeatedly plundered of provisions. Her sufferings became so extreme, that she entreated, and sometimes attempted to provoke those who plundered her, to put an end to her miserable life. At length, frantic with despair, she snatched her infant son from her breast, cut its throat, and boiled it; and having satisfied present hunger, concealed the remainder. The smell of it soon brought the voracious soldiers to her house; they threatened her with the most excruciating tortures, if she did not discover her provisions to them. Being compelled in this manner, she set before them the mangled remains of her son. At this horrid spectacle, the soldiers, inhuman as they were, stood aghast, struck with horror, and at length rushed from the house. The report of this transaction having spread through the city, the horror and consternation of the Jews was universal: they now for the first time began to think themselves forsaken of God. Titus, on hearing this account, was filled with surprise and indignation. "Soon," said he, "shall the sun never more dart his beams on a city where mothers feed on their children; and where fathers, no less guilty, choose to drive them to such extremities, rather than lay down their arms."

Titus now pushed the siege with still greater vigour, and endeavoured to obtain possession of the temple, the preservation of which was strongly desired by him. A Roman soldier, urged on, as he said, *by a divine impulse*, seized a firebrand, and getting on his comrades' shoulders, threw it into a window of the temple, and immediately set this noble edifice, the pride and glory of the Jewish nation, in flames. Titus immediately gave orders to extinguish the fire; he threatened, he entreated his soldiers, and used every exertion to stop the progress of the fire, but all in vain. The exasperated soldiery, bent on destroying the city and all it contained, either did not hear or did not regard him.

"These were the days of vengeance, that all things which were written might be fulfilled." These were the days in which all the calamities predicted by Moses, Joel, Daniel, and other prophets, as well as those predicted by our Saviour, met in one common centre, and were fulfilled in the most terrible manner on that generation. It is remarkable that the temple was burnt by the Romans in the same month, and the same day of the month, on which it had been burned by the Babylonians.

Josephus computes the number of those who perished in the siege at *eleven hundred thousand*, besides those who were slain in other places. When Titus was viewing the fortifications, after the taking of the city, he could not help ascribing his success to God. "We have fought," said he, "with God on our side; and it is God who pulled the Jews out of these strongholds; for what could *machines* or the *hands of men* avail against such towers as these?" Our Lord says, "They shall fall by the edge of the sword, and shall be led away captive into all nations; and Jerusalem shall be trodden down by the Gentiles, till the times of the Gentiles be fulfilled."

The Jews were miserably tormented, and distributed over the Roman provinces; and continue to be distressed and dispersed over all the nations of the world to this present day. Jerusalem also continues to be "*trodden down by the Gentiles*." Since its destruction by Titus it never has been in the possession of the Jews. It was first in subjection to the *Romans*, afterwards to the *Saracens*, then to the *Franks*, next to the *Mamelukes*, and now to the *Turks*.

"Thus has the prophecy of Christ been most literally and terribly fulfilled, on a people who are still preserved as continued monuments of the truth of our Lord's prediction, and of the truth of the Christian religion."

---

7. Faith and Practice of Christians in the first Century.

The following account of the first Christians is taken from Dr. Mosheim's celebrated Church History:—"The apostles and their disciples took all possible care that in the earliest times of the church, the Holy Scriptures might be in the hands of all Christians, that they might be read and explained in the assemblies of the faithful, and thus contribute, both in private and in public, to excite and nourish, in the minds of Christians,

THE CITY AND TEMPLE OF JERUSALEM,

Were taken and destroyed by Titus the son of Vespasian, the Roman Emperor, in the year 70.

MARTYRDOM OF ST. IGNATIUS.

Ignatus bishop of Antioch, by the order of Trajan, was sent to Rome and being thrown to the wild beasts suffered martyrdom, about the year 108.

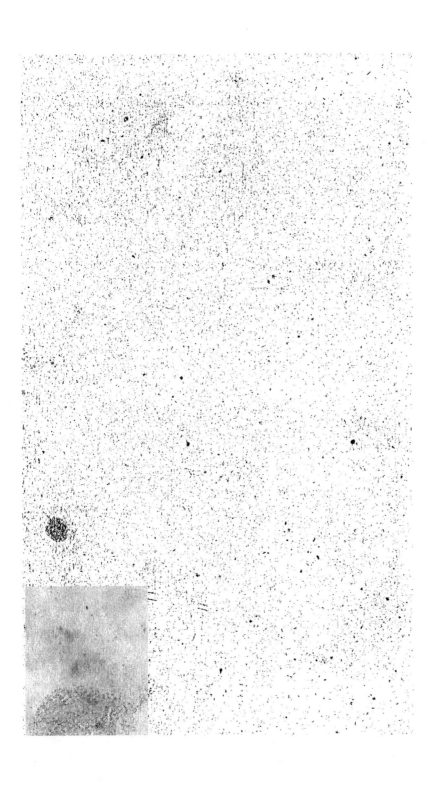

a fervent zeal for the truth, and a firm attachment to the ways of piety and virtue. Those who performed the office of interpreters studied above all things plainness and perspicuity. At the same time, it must be acknowledged that, even in this century, several Christians adopted that absurd and corrupt custom, used among the Jews, of darkening the plain words of the Holy Scriptures by insipid and forced allegories, and of drawing them violently from their proper and natural signification, in order to extort from them certain mysteries and hidden significations. For a proof of this, we need go no further than the *Epistle of Barnabas*, which is still extant.

"The method of teaching the sacred doctrines of religion was, at this time, most simple, far removed from all the subtle rules of philosophy, and all the precepts of human art. This appears abundantly, not only in the writings of the apostles, but also in all those of the second century which have survived the ruins of time. Neither did the apostles or their disciples ever think of collecting into a regular system the principal doctrines of the Christian religion, or of demonstrating them in a scientific and geometrical order. The beautiful and candid simplicity of these early ages rendered such philosophical niceties unnecessary; and the great study of those who embraced the gospel, was rather to express its divine influence in their dispositions and actions, than to examine its doctrines with an excessive curiosity, or to explain them by the rules of human wisdom.

"There is indeed extant a brief summary of the principal doctrines of Christianity in that form, which bears the name of the *Apostles' Creed*, and which, from the fourth century downwards, was almost generally considered as a production of the apostles. There is much more reason and judgment in the opinion of those who think that this creed was not all composed at once, but, from small beginnings was imperceptibly augmented in proportion to the growth of heresy, and according to the exigences and circumstances of the church, from whence it was designed to banish the errors that daily arose.

"In the earliest times of the church all who professed firmly to believe that *Jesus* was the only Redeemer of the world, and who, in consequence of this profession, promised to live in a manner conformable to the purity of his holy religion, were immediately received among the disciples of *Christ.* This was all the preparation for *baptism* then required; and a more accurate instruction in the doctrines of Christianity was to be administered to them after their receiving the sacrament. But when Christianity had acquired more consistence, and churches rose to the true God and his eternal Son almost in every nation, this custom was changed for the wisest and most solid reasons. Then none were admitted to baptism but such as had been previously instructed in the principal points of Christianity, and had also given satisfactory proofs of pious dispositions and upright intentions. Hence arose the distinction between *catechumens,* who were in a state of probation, and under the instruction of persons appointed for that purpose, and *believers,* who were consecrated by baptism, and thus initiated into all the mysteries of the Christian faith.

"The methods of instructing the *catechumens* differed according to their various capacities. Those in whom the natural force of reason was small, were taught no more than the fundamental principles and truths, which are, as it were, the basis of Christianity. Those, on the contrary, whom their instructers judged capable of comprehending, in some measure, the whole system of divine truth, were furnished with superior degrees of knowledge; and nothing was concealed from them which could have any tendency to render them firm in their profession, and assist them in arriving at Christian perfection. The care of instructing such was committed to persons who were distinguished by their gravity and wisdom, and also by their learning and judgment. From hence it comes, that the ancient doctors generally divide their flock into two classes,—the one comprehending such as were solidly and thoroughly instructed; the other, those who were acquainted with little more than the first principles of religion. Nor do they deny that the methods of instruction applied to these two sorts of persons were extremely different.

"The Christians took all possible care to accustom their children to the study of the Scriptures, and to instruct them in the doctrines of their holy religion; and schools were every where erected for this purpose, even from the very commencement of the Christian church. We must not, however, confound the *schools* designed only for children, with the *gymnasia*, or academies of the ancient Christians, erected in several large cities, in which persons of riper years, especially such as aspire to be public teachers, were instructed in the different branches, both of human learning and of sacred erudition. We may, undoubtedly, attribute to the apostles themselves, and their injunctions to their disciples, the excellent establishments in which the youth destined to the holy ministry received an education suitable to the solemn office they were to undertake. St. John erected a school of this kind at *Ephesus*, and one of the same nature was founded by *Polycarp* at *Smyrna*. But none of these were in greater repute than that which was established at *Alexandria*, which was commonly called the *catechetical school*, and is generally supposed to have been erected by *St. Mark*.

"One of the circumstances which contributed chiefly to preserve, at least, an external appearance of sanctity in the Christian church, was the right of excluding from thence, and from all participation of the sacred rites and ordinances of the gospel, such as had been guilty of enormous transgressions, and to whom repeated exhortations to repentance and amendment had been administered in vain. This right was vested in the church, from the earliest period of its existence, by the apostles themselves, and was exercised by each Christian assembly upon its respective members. The rulers or doctors denounced the persons whom they thought unworthy of the privileges of church-communion; and the people, freely rejecting or approving their judgment, pronounced the decisive sentence. It was not, however, irrevocable; for such as gave undoubted signs of their sincere repentance, and declared their solemn resolutions of future reformation, were readmitted into the church, however enormous their crimes had been; but, in case of a relapse, their second exclusion became irreversible.

"The rites instituted by *Christ* himself were only two in number, and these designed to continue to the end of the church here below, without any variation. These rites were *baptism* and the *holy supper*, which are not to be considered as mere ceremonies, nor yet as symbolic representations only, but also as ordinances accompanied with a sanctifying influence upon the heart and affections of true Christians; and we cannot help observing here, that since the divine Saviour thought fit to appoint no more than two plain institutions in his church, this shows us that a number of ceremonies is not essential to his religion, and that he left it to the free and prudent choice of Christians to establish such rites as the circumstances of the times, or the exigences of the church might require.

"There are several circumstances which incline us to think that the friends and the apostles of our blessed Lord either tolerated through necessity, or appointed for wise reasons, many other external rites in various places. At the same time, we are not to imagine that they ever conferred upon any person a perpetual, indelible, pontifical authority, or that they enjoined the same rites in all churches. We learn, on the contrary, from authentic records, that the Christian worship was, from the beginning, celebrated in a different manner in different places, and that, no doubt, by the orders, or at least with the approbation, of the apostles and their disciples. In these early times, it was both wise and necessary to show, in the establishment of outward forms of worship, some indulgence to the ancient opinions, manners, and laws of the respective nations to whom the gospel was preached.

"In those Christian societies which were totally or principally composed of Jewish converts, it was natural to retain as much of the Jewish ritual as the genius of Christianity would suffer; and a multitude of examples testify that this was actually done. But that the same translation of Jewish rites should take place in Christian churches, where there were no Jews, or a very small and inconsiderable number, is utterly incredible; because such an event was morally impossible. In a word, the external forms of worship used in the times of old, must necessarily have been regulated and modified according to the character, genius, and manners of the different nations on which the light of the gospel arose."

---

8. Regard paid to the Scriptures by the early Christians.

The following interesting account of the regard paid to the Holy Scriptures by the early Christians, is extracted from Cave's Primitive Christianity.

"Their next care was diligently and seriously to read the Scriptures, to be mighty in the Divine Oracles, as, indeed, they had an invaluable esteem of, and reverence for, the word of God, as the book which they infinitely prized above all others; upon which account Nazianzen very severely chides his dear friend Gregory Nyssen, then having laid aside the Holy Scriptures (the most excellent writings in the world), which he was wont to read privately to himself, and publicly to the people, he had given up himself to the study of foreign and profane authors, desirous rather to be accounted an orator than a Christian. St. Augustine tells us, that after his conversion, how meanly soever he had before thought of them, the Scriptures were become the matter of his pure and chaste delight, in respect of which all other books (even of Cicero himself, which once he had so much doated on), became dry and unsavory to him. It was in the study of this book that Christians then mainly exercised themselves, as thinking they could never fully enough understand it, or deeply enough imprint it upon their hearts and memories. Of the younger Theodosius, they tell us, that rising early every morning, he, together with his sisters, interchangeably sung psalms of praise to God; the Holy Scriptures he could repeat, in any part of them, with the bishops that were at court, as readily as if he had been an old bishop himself. We read of Origen, though then a child, that when his father commanded him to commit some places of Scripture to memory, he most willingly set himself to it, and not content with the bare reading, he began to inquire into the more profound and recondite meaning of it, often asking his father (to his no less joy than admiration) what the sense of this or that place of Scripture was; and his thirst after divine knowledge still continued and increased in him all his life. St. Jerome reports it out of a letter of one who was his great companion and benefactor, that he never went to his meals without some part of Scripture being read, never to sleep till some about him had read them to him, and that, both by night and by day, no sooner had he done praying but he betook himself to reading, and after reading returned again to prayer. Valens, deacon of the church of Jerusalem, a venerable old man, had so entirely given up himself to the study of the Scriptures, that it was all one to him to read or to repeat whole pages together. The like we find of John, an Egyptian confessor (whom Eusebius saw and heard), that though both his eyes were put out, and his body mangled with unheard-of cruelty, yet he was able at any time to repeat any places or passages, either out of the Old or New Testament; which, when I first heard him do in the public congregation, I supposed him (says Eusebius) to have been reading in a book; till coming near, and finding how it was, I was struck with great admiration at it. Certainly, Christians then had no mean esteem of, and took no small delight in these sacred volumes. For the sake of this book (which he had chosen to be the companion and counsellor of his life), Nazianzen professes he had willingly undervalued and relinquished all other things; this was the mine where they enriched themselves with divine treasures, a book where they furnished themselves with a true stock of knowledge: as St. Jerome speaks of Nepotian, that by daily reading and meditation he had made his soul a library of Christ, and he tells us of Blesilla, a devout widow, that though she was so far overrun with weakness and sickness, that her foot would scarce bear her body, or her neck sustain the burden of her head, yet she was never found without a Bible in her hand."

---

9. Greek and Latin Fathers.

The term *Father* is applied to those ancient authors who have preserved in their writings traditions of the church. No author who wrote later than the twelfth century is dignified with this title. The most distinguished of the fathers were the following characters:

1. *Clemens Romanus*, who was born at Rome, and was the fellow labourer of Paul, was distinguished both as a minister, and a zealous defender of the faith. He sustained a truly apostolic character. There is remaining of his writings a very fine epistle to the church of Corinth, which (next to holy writ) has been esteemed one of the most valuable monuments which have come down to us from ecclesiastical antiquity. He died at the advanced age of one hundred.

2. *Ignatius* was bishop of Antioch. In the year 107, Trajan, being on his way to the Parthian war, came to Antioch. Ignatius, hoping to avert any storm which might be arising against the Christians there, presented himself before the emperor, and offered to suffer in their stead. Trajan, being exasperated at the frankness and independence of Ignatius, ordered him to be sent to Rome, and thrown to the wild beasts. Being detained at Smyrna, while on his way to Rome, he had the pleasure of visiting Polycarp, who had been

a fellow-disciple with him of St. John. Their mingled emotions of joy and grief can scarcely be imagined. While at Smyrna, he addressed four epistles to various churches. At length he arrived at Rome, was thrown to the wild beasts, and devoured. A few bones were left, which were collected by the deacons, his attendants, and buried at Antioch.

3. *Polycarp* lived in the reign of Marcus A. Antonius, and was a companion of Ignatius. He was pastor of a church in Smyrna eighty years. Being marked as the victim of persecution, he was persuaded by his friends to retire for a season from the fury of his enemies; upon which, they proceeded to torture some of his friends, to extort from them a disclosure of the place of his retreat. This was too much for Polycarp to bear, who accordingly surrendered himself, a prey to his enemies. Being brought before the proconsul, efforts were made to induce him to abjure his faith, and swear by the fortune of Cæsar. Refusing, he was threatened with being made a prey to wild beasts. "Call for them," said he; "it does not well become us to turn from good to evil." The consul rejoined, "Seeing you make so light of wild beasts, I will tame you with the more terrible punishment of fire." To this he replied, "You threaten me with a fire that is quickly extinguished, but are ignorant of the eternal fire of God's judgment, reserved for the wicked in another world." As they were about to *nail* him to the stake, he said, "Let me remain as I am; for he who giveth me strength to sustain the fire, will enable me to remain unmoved." The fire was kindled; but after a while, fearing he might not certainly be despatched, an officer drew a sword, and plunged it into his body. His bones were afterwards gathered up by his friends, and buried.

4. *Justin Martyr*, so called from his being a martyr, was born at Neapolis, in Palestine, and became a convert to Christianity in the sixteenth year of Trajan. From this time, he employed his pen in defence of Christianity. He drew up two apologies, addressed

to the emperor Marcus, and the Roman senate, which very much irritated the temper of the times. He was accordingly, with six others, apprehended, whipped, and beheaded. Thus fell Justin Martyr, a man of distinguished powers, and the first who had adorned the church with his learning, since the apostle Paul.

5. *Irenæus*, by birth a Greek, was born at or near Smyrna. He was a disciple of Polycarp, and for about forty years he was the bishop of Lyons; in which office he suffered much from foes without and heretics within. Against the latter, he employed his pen. Five of his books are now extant. He suffered martyrdom, in the reign of Severus, A. D. 202.

6. *Clemens Alexandrinus*, so called to distinguish him from *Clemens Romanus*, was born at Alexandria, in the second century. He was distinguished for his literature, and exact and enlarged views of the Christian religion. Three of his works remain.

7. *Tertullian*, by birth a Carthagenian, was bred up at the bar; but afterwards became a Christian. He possessed great abilities and learning, which he vigorously employed in the Christian cause; but toward the latter part of his life, being naturally credulous and superstitious, he became a heretic. Eusebius says that he was one of the ablest Latin writers which had existed.

8. *Origen*, one of the most conspicuous characters belonging to the age in which he lived, was born at Alexandria, A. D. 185. In his youth, he saw his father beheaded for the profession of Christianity, and the family estate confiscated. Being taken under the patronage of a rich lady, he applied himself to study, and soon acquired great stores of learning. At the age of forty-five, he was ordained, and delivered theological lectures in Palestine. He was the author of the *Hexapla*, which filled fifty large volumes. This work was mostly destroyed in the capture of Tyre, in 653. He maintained that the Scriptures were not to be explained in a *literal*, but in an *allegorical* manner; that is, it had a *hidden* or *figurative* meaning. This

sense he endeavoured to give, but often at the expense of the truth. He first introduced the practice of selecting a single text, as the subject of discourse. He suffered martyrdom under Decius, about 254.

9. *Cyprian* was bred a lawyer, received a liberal education, and was distinguished as an orator. In 248, he was elected bishop of Carthage. His first efforts were to re tore the long neglected discipline of the church. Very soon the flames of persecution burst forth in Carthage; from which he repaired to a retreat provided by his friends, where he remained two years. From this place he continued to send forth epistles to his distressed and persecuted brethren. During his exile, an unhappy schism took place in the churches of Alexandria and Rome, called "the Novatian schism;" against which he successfully employed his pen. Being threatened with death, if he continued in his zeal and activity, he abated nothing; but continued in his boldness and zeal for the Christian cause, until he was banished by the proconsul of Carthage. In the year 259 he was permitted to return, but not to remain long in peace; for orders had been given by Valerian, that all ministers should be put to death. He was conducted to a spacious plain: on his arrival, he fell on his knees, and worshipped. He then laid aside his garments, a napkin was bound over his eyes, and a sword severed his head from his body.

10. *Ambrose* was born in Gaul, A. D. 333. He was appointed governor over several small provinces, and settled at Milan. In 374, the bishop dying, a great contest arose between the Catholics and Arians concerning his successor. He thought it his duty, as governor, to go to the church, in order to compose the tumult. On addressing the multitude, they with one voice exclaimed, "Let Ambrose be bishop." He yielded, and was ordained. He died at Milan, leaving behind him several choice works on religious subjects.

11. *Jerome* was born at Strido, near Pannonia. His father took care he should have all the advantages of learning, sacred and profane. After a while he retired

into a desert in Syria, scarcely inhabited by a human being. Here he applied himself to the study of the Scriptures (which he is said to have gotten by heart) and to the oriental languages. After four years' solitude, his reputation for piety and learning began to be spread abroad. He visited Rome, where he composed several works. He translated the Bible into Latin, which was afterwards exclusively adopted by the Romish church; and of all the Latin fathers, he was considered the most able in unfolding the Scriptures. He finished his days in a monastery, in Bethlehem, near to Jerusalem, A. D. 420, aged ninety years.

12. *Augustine* was born in Africa, A. D. 354. His father, designing him for some of the learned professions, placed him at school. But such was his vicious make, that he neglected study, and substituted gaming, and attendance at shows, &c. &c., and invented a thousand false stories, to escape the rod, with which he was often severely chastened. After a while, he acquired a taste for learning. While on his way to Rome, at a certain time, he stopped at Milan, and heard the preaching of Ambrose. He became a convert, and was elected bishop of Hippo. From this date, he set himself for the defence of the gospel, and became the admiration of the Christian world. From his writings was formed a body of theology, which for centuries after was the guide of those who desired the truth. He died A. D. 430, aged seventy-six years.

13. *John Chrysostom* was born at Antioch, A. D. 354. At an early age, he determined to adopt a monastic life, and accordingly spent six years in this way; until, worn out with watchings, fastings, and other severities, he was forced to return to Antioch. After he was elected bishop of Constantinople, he began to attempt a reformation in his diocese, which greatly enraged the clergy, and through their influence he was banished. But soon after, the emperor recalled him, and restored him to his bishopric. No sooner was he established in his office, than he began to display his customary zeal; whereupon, his ene-

mies again procured his banishment. But before he arrived at his port of exile, through fatigue and hard treatment from the soldiers, he expired. He was one of the most able preachers that have adorned the church.

---

10. The ten Persecutions.

Historians usually reckon ten general persecutions, the *first* of which was under the emperor Nero, thirty-one years after our Lord's ascension, when that emperor, after having set fire to the city of Rome, threw the odium of that execrable action on the Christians. First, those were apprehended who openly avowed themselves to be of that sect; and by them were discovered an immense multitude, all of whom were convicted. Their death and tortures were aggravated by cruel derision and sport; for they were either covered with the skins of wild beasts and torn in pieces by devouring dogs, or fastened to crosses, and wrapped up in combustible garments, that, when the daylight failed, they might, like torches, serve to dispel the darkness of night. For this tragical spectacle, Nero lent his own gardens, and exhibited at the same time the public diversions of the circus; sometimes driving a chariot in person, and sometimes standing as a spectator, while the shrieks of women, burning to ashes, supplied music to his ears.

The *Second* general persecution was under Domitian, in the year 95, when 40,000 were supposed to have suffered martyrdom.

The *Third* began in the third year of Trajan, in the year 100, and was carried on with violence for several years.

The *Fourth* was under Antoninus, when the Christians were banished from their houses, forbidden to show their heads, reproached, beaten, hurried from place to place, plundered, imprisoned, and stoned.

The *Fifth* began in the year 127, under Severus, when great cruelties were committed. In this reign happened the martyrdom of Perpetua and Felicitas, and their companions. These two beautiful and amiable young women, mothers of infant children, after suffering much in prison, were exposed before an insulting multitude, to a wild cow, who mangled their bodies in a horrid manner; after which they were carried to a conspicuous place, and put to death by the sword.

The *Sixth* began with the reign of the emperor Maximinus, 235.

The *Seventh*, which was the most dreadful ever known, began in 250, under the emperor Decius, when the Christians were in all places driven from their habitations, stripped of their estates, tormented with racks, &c.

The *Eighth* began under Valerian. Both men and women suffered death, some by scourging, some by the sword, and some by fire.

The *Ninth* was under Aurelian, in 274; but this was inconsiderable, compared with others before mentioned.

The *Tenth* began in the nineteenth year of Dioclesian, 303. In this dreadful persecution, which lasted ten years, houses which were filled with Christians were set on fire, and whole droves were tied together with ropes, and thrown into the sea. It is related that 17,000 were slain in one month's time; and that during the continuance of this persecution, in the province of Egypt alone, no less than 144,000 Christians died by the violence of their persecutors; besides 700,000 that died through the fatigues of banishment, or the public works to which they were condemned.—***Buck's Theological Dictionary.***

---

11. Martyrdom of the Theban Legion.

During the reign of the emperor Maximian, A. D. 286, a legion of soldiers, consisting of 6666 men, contained none but Christians. This legion was called the Theban legion, because the men had been raised in

Thebais; they were quartered in the east, till the emperor Maximian ordered them to march for Gaul, to assist him against the rebels in Burgundy; when passing the Alps into Gaul, under the command of Mauritius Candiaso and Experuis, their commanders, they at length joined the emperor. About this time, Maximian ordered a general sacrifice, at which the whole army were to assist; and he commanded, that they should take the oaths of allegiance, and swear, at the same time, to assist him in the extirpation of Christianity in Gaul.

Terrified at these orders, each individual of the Theban legion absolutely refused either to sacrifice, or to take the oath prescribed. This so enraged Maximian, that he ordered the legion to be decimated; that is, every tenth man to be selected from the rest and put to the sword. This cruel order having been put into execution, those who remained alive were still inflexible, when a second decimation took place, and every tenth man of those living were again put to the sword. But this second severity made no more impression than the first had done; the soldiers preserved their fortitude and principles; but, by the advice of their officers, drew up a remonstrance to the emperor, in which they told him "that they were his subjects and his soldiers, but could not at the same time forget the Almighty; that they received their pay from him, and their existence from God.

"While your commands (say they) are not contradictory to those of our common Master, we shall always be ready to obey, as we have been hitherto; but when the orders of our prince and the Almighty differ, we must always obey the latter. Our arms are devoted to the emperor's use, and shall be directed against his enemies; but we cannot submit to stain our hands with the effusion of Christian blood; and how, indeed, could you, O emperor, be sure of our allegiance and fidelity, should we violate our obligations to our God, in whose service we were solemnly engaged before we entered into the army? You command us to search out and destroy the Christians; it is not necessary to look any further for persons of that denomination; we ourselves are such, and we glory in the name. We saw our companions fall without the least opposition or murmuring, and thought them happy in dying for the sake of Christ. Nothing shall make us lift up our hands against our sovereign; we had rather die wrongfully, and by that means preserve our innocence, than live under a load of guilt; whatever you command we are ready to suffer; we confess ourselves to be Christians, and therefore cannot persecute Christians, nor sacrifice to idols."

Such a declaration, it might be presumed, would have affected the emperor, but it had a contrary effect; for, enraged at their perseverance and unanimity, he commanded that the whole legion should be put to death, which was accordingly executed by the other troops, who cut them to pieces with their swords.—*Milner's History of Christian Martyrdom.*

---

12. Willingness of the ancient Christians to suffer for Christ's sake.

The ancient Christians counted it an honour to suffer for their religion, and oftentimes gave up their lives with joy, for the sake of their Lord.

In the fourth century, the emperor Valens ordered the Christians in Edessa to be slain, on a certain day, while they were at their devotions, in their churches. The officers, however, being more compassionate than the emperor, privately gave notice to the Christians not to assemble on the day appointed, so that they might escape death. The Christians thanked the officers for their advice, but disregarded both that and the emperor's menaces, rather than neglect their duty. They accordingly repaired to the church, and the troops were put in motion to destroy them. As they marched along, a woman, with a child in her arms, broke through their ranks, when the officer ordered her to be brought before him, and asked her where she was going? She replied, to the church, whither others were making all the haste they could. "Have you not heard," says the officer, "of the emperor's order, to put to death all who are found there?"—"I have," says she, "and for that cause I make the more haste." —"And whither," said the officer, "do you lead that child?"—"I take him," replied she, "with me, that he also may be reckoned in the number of the martyrs." Upon this, the humane officer returned to the emperor, and told him that all the Christians were prepared to die in defence of their faith, represented to him the rashness of murdering so great a multitude, and entreated the emperor to drop the design, at least for the present; with which he at length complied.—*Milner's History of Christian Martyrdom.*

---

13. Letter of Pliny to Trajan, relative to the first Christians.

In the conduct and writings of ancient pagans, a great variety of important testimonies to the truth and spread of the Christian religion, and the purity of Christian principles, may be found. But perhaps in no instance is this testimony so clear, and yet so undesignedly given, as in the epistle of Caius Plinius, or "the younger Pliny" (so called), addressed to the Roman emperor Trajan.

Pliny was born A. D. 61, or 62, and about 107 was sent to the provinces of Pontus and Bithynia, by Trajan, to exercise the office of governor. The persecutions of Christians, under Trajan, had commenced about 100; and in these provinces, there were prodigious numbers of them, against whom Pliny, by the emperor's edict, was obliged to use all manner of severity. But being a person of good sense and moderation, he judged it prudent, before he proceeded to the extreme rigour of the law, to represent the case to Trajan, and receive further orders concerning it. He therefore wrote the following letter:—"Pliny, to the emperor Trajan, wisheth health and happiness:—It is my constant custom, sir, to refer myself to you, in all matters concerning which I have any doubt. For who can better direct me when I hesitate, or instruct me where I am ignorant? I have never been present at any trials of Christians; so that I know not well what is the subject-matter of punishment, or of inquiry, or what strictness ought to be used in either. Nor have I been a little perplexed to determine whether any difference ought to be made on account of age, or whether the young and tender, and the full-grown, and robust, ought to be treated all alike; whether repentance should entitle to pardon; or whether all who have once been Christians ought to be punished, though they are now no longer so; whether the name itself, although no crimes be detected, or crimes only belonging to the name, ought to be punished. Concerning all these things I am in doubt.

"In the mean time, I have taken this course with all who have been brought before me, and have been accused as Christians. I have put the question to them, whether they were Christians? Upon their confessing to me that they were, I repeated the question a second time, threatening to punish them with death. Such as still persisted, I ordered away to be punished; for it was no doubt with me that contumacy, and inflexible obstinacy, whatever might be their opinion, ought to be punished. There were others of the same infatuation, whom, because they are Romans, I have noted down to be sent to the city.

"In a short time, the crime spreading itself, even whilst under persecution, as is usual in such cases, divers sorts of people came in my way. An information was presented to me, without mentioning the author, containing the names of many persons, who, upon examination, denied that they were Christians, or had ever been so; who repeated after me an invocation of the gods, and with wine and frankincense made supplication to your image, which, for that purpose, I had caused to be brought and set before them, together with the statues of the deities. Moreover, they reviled the name of Christ, none of which things, as is said, they who are really Christians can by any means be compelled to do. These, therefore, I thought proper to discharge.

"Others were named by an informer, who at first confessed themselves Christians, and afterwards denied it; the rest said they had been Christians, but had left them—some three years ago, some longer, and one, or more, above twenty years. They all worshipped your image, and the statues of the gods; these also reviled Christ. They affirmed that the whole of their fault, or error, lay in this, that they were wont to meet together, on a stated day, before it was light, and sing among themselves alternately, a hymn to Christ as God; and bind themselves by an oath, not to the commission of any wickedness, but not to be guilty of theft, robbery, or adultery, never to falsify their word, nor to deny a pledge committed to them, when called upon to return it. When these things were performed, it was their custom to separate, and then to come together at a meal, which they ate in common without any disorder; but this they had forborne since the publication of my edict, by which, according to your commands, I prohibited assemblies.

"After receiving this account, I judged it the more necessary to examine, and that by torture, two maid-servants, which were called ministers. But I have discovered nothing beside an evil and excessive superstition. Suspending, therefore, all judicial proceedings, I have recourse to you for advice; for it has appeared to me a matter highly deserving consideration; especially upon account of the great number of persons who are in danger of suffering; for many, of all ages, and every rank, of both sexes likewise, are accused, and will be accused. Nor has the contagion of this superstition seized cities only, but the lesser towns also, and the open country. Nevertheless, it seems to me, that it may be restrained and corrected. It is certain that the temples, which were almost forsaken, begin to be more frequented; and the sacred solemnities, after a long intermission, are revived. Victims likewise are every where bought up, whereas for some time, there were few purchasers. Whence it is easy to imagine what numbers of men might be reclaimed, if pardon were granted to those who shall repent."

To this epistle, the emperor sent the following reply:—"Trajan to Pliny, wisheth health and happiness:—You have taken the right method, my Pliny, in your proceedings with those who have been brought before you as Christians; for it is impossible to establish any one rule that shall hold universally. They are not to be sought for. If any are brought before you, and are convicted, they ought to be punished. However, he that denies his being a Christian, and makes it evident in fact, that is, by supplicating to our gods, though he be suspected to have been so formerly, let him be pardoned upon repentance. But in no case, of any crime whatever, may a bill of information be received, without being signed by him who presents it; for that would be a dangerous precedent, and unworthy of my government."*

By this epistle it will appear that Christianity had rapidly been spread almost over the then known world; that the Christians bore all their sufferings with noble fortitude, peculiar to none but Christians; that their purity and innocence is fully attested; and against whom, after the strictest examination, their enemies could find nothing of which they were guilty, save that they professed and maintained the character of Christians.

---

14. Introduction of Christianity into Britain.

The tradition which has been most generally received by our ancient historians, and by the nations at large, says Dr. A. Clarke, is that which attributes the introduction of the Christian religion into Britain, to

---

* Pliny's Epist. Lib. X

Joseph of Arimathea. The substance of this history is as follows:—About sixty-three years after the incarnation of our Lord, and thirty after his ascension, Joseph of Arimathea, who had buried our Lord's body in his own tomb, was furnished by Philip the evangelist with eleven disciples, and sent into Britain to introduce the gospel of Christ in place of the barbarous rites of the Druids. With these rites, as well as with the character of the people, the Roman empire had become well acquainted, through the writings of Julius Cæsar.

These holy men, on their landing, applied to Arviragus, a British king, for permission to settle in a rude and uncultivated spot, called *Yuswytryn* by the British, *Avaloai* by the Romans, and *Glaestingbyrig* by the Saxons, and is still known by the name of *Glastonbury*. Their petition was granted, and twelve hides of land were assigned for their support; and the place to this day is denominated the *twelve hides of Glastonbury*. Here, according to this tradition, the standard of the cross was first erected; and a chapel made of wicker work was the first church, or oratory of God in Britain. The walls of this church, according to Malmsbury, were made of twigs twisted together. The length of it was sixty feet, and the breadth of it twenty-six feet. The roof, according to the custom of the Britons, was of straw, hay, or rushes. The extent of the yard was so large as to contain, according to Melkinus, who lived in the year A. D. 550, a thousand graves.

That this nation was converted to the faith of Christ by those who had been disciples of our Lord, was the early and constant belief of our forefathers. This runs through all our histories, and even through some of our regal acts. In the charter granted by Henry II., in the year of our Lord 1185, for the rebuilding of Glastonbury church, which had been burnt, it is styled "the mother and burying place of the saints, founded by the very disciples of our Lord," and adds, "it has the venerable authority of the ancients;" and elsewhere the same charter continues, "which is incontrovertibly acknowledged to be the fountain and origin of the whole religion of England." This church was the head of all ecclesiastical authority in those nations, till the year 1154, when Pope Adrian IV. transferred that honour to St. Alban's.

It is stated by several authorities, that when the church built by Joseph of Arimathea was decayed by time, Deni, a Welsh or British bishop, erected a new one in the same place; that this also, in time, falling away in decay, twelve men came from north Britain, and put it in good repair. And, lastly, king Ina, donor of the Peterpence, pulled down the old one, and built a stately church, to the honour of Christ. St. Peter and St. Paul were filletted under the highest coping, with heroic verses in Latin, celebrating the memory of the founder, and the saints to whom it was dedicated. But afterwards, this church was, by the renowned Dunstan, converted to a monastery of Benedictine monks, himself being sometimes abbot there; and so it continued till the reign of Henry VIII., when it shared in the downfall of monastic establishments.

The story of Lucius, king of Britain, who, in A. D. 156, is said, by the venerable Bede, to have embraced the Christian faith, and who is called the first Christian king, is generally known. Historians say, that this king sent Elwan and Medwin to Eleutherus, the twelfth bishop of Rome, praying that he might be instructed in the Christian faith; which was accordingly done.

Lucius, when convinced of the truth himself, and being confirmed therein, by the preaching of some persons well versed in the doctrines of Christianity, took on him the profession of that religion, and used his influence for the promotion of it among the people, with whom his example must have had considerable weight. Idolatry hitherto prevailed among the Silurian Britons; but now the religion of Christ was publicly sanctioned, and the idolaters became ashamed of their practices. The ministers of the true religion were poor and obscure men, and they had no regular places set apart for divine worship, and their adherents were in a forlorn and unprotected state. This generous prince raised the Christians from their low condition, erected suitable places for the celebration of religious services, and thus became a nursing-father to the church.

During the tenth general persecution, under the emperor Dioclesian, the Christians in Britain were for a short time great sufferers. It is said that at this time the Christian religion was nearly rooted out of the country, and they who suffered martyrdom were almost without number. Gildas says, "that their churches were thrown down, and all the books of the Holy Scriptures that could be found were burnt in the streets, and the chosen priests of the flock of our Lord, together with the innocent sheep, murdered; so that in some parts of the province, no footsteps of the Christian religion appeared. How many did then flee, how many were destroyed, how many different kinds of sufferings some did endure, how great was the ruin of apostates, how glorious the crown of martyrdom!" Bede adds, "It made Britain to be honoured with many holy martyrs, who firmly stood and died in the confession of their faith."

---

15. An Account of the Druids.

Druidism prevailed chiefly in Britain and in Gaul; though it may be found among other Celtic nations; and owing to a peculiarity of national character, which perhaps may be said to remain to the present day, the Britons were more famous for the observance of their religion than the Gauls. For this circumstance we have the authority of Cæsar, who says that "such of the Gauls as were desirous of being thoroughly instructed in the principles of their religion (which was the same with that of the Britons), usually took a journey into Britain for that purpose."

The religion obtained its name from the Druids, who were its principal priests, and held in very high estimation. Cæsar affirms, that the nobles and the Druids were the only two privileged orders among the Britons. So greatly were they honoured, that the people, supposing them peculiar favourites of the gods, were perfectly obedient to their commands; and even when two hostile armies met, and were on the point of engaging in battle, they sheathed their swords on the mediation of the Druids. The persons of these priests were esteemed sacred and inviolable; they were even exempted from all taxes and military services; and, in fact, they enjoyed so many immunities and distinctions, that princes were ambitious of being admitted among them. The dignity of Arch-druid, or the supreme head of the order, was attended with so many honours, and so much power and riches, that the election of a person to fill it sometimes even occasioned a civil war.

The generality of the Druids seem to have lived a kind of monastic life. The services of every temple required the attendance of a considerable number of them; and these lived in community in the neighbourhood of the temple. The Arch-druid had his residence in the isle of Anglesea, and he there maintained an ecclesiastical court in all the magnificence of the times. Vestiges of his palaces are still remaining. It is also very probable, that some of these ancient priests lived in seclusion as hermits; and the small circular houses in the western islands of Scotland, which are called by the people "Druids' houses," were most likely inhabited by such persons. All of them are supposed to have lived in celibacy; but this is not absolutely certain. They were at any rate attended and associated with a number of female devotees, called Druidesses, who assisted in the duties, and shared the honours and emoluments of the priesthood. The Roman soldiers were much terrified at seeing a number of these consecrated females, who ran up and down among the ranks of the British army, with flaming torches in their hands and imprecated the wrath of heaven on the invaders of their country.

With respect to the doctrines of the Druids, they had two sets of opinions—the one for the initiated, and the other for the vulgar. The former was considered to contain only genuine truth, in its simple form; the other admitted a variety of fables, which were thought better adapted for popular comprehension. The Druids were exceedingly jealous of their secret doctrines, and took a variety of precautions to prevent them from transpiring. They never committed them to writing, and they taught their disciples in caves, or the deepest recesses of forests, that they might not be heard by the uninitiated. In consequence of this strict concealment, we have at the present time but a very imperfect knowledge of these doctrines.

It is tolerably certain that the unity of the Godhead, and that there is one God, the creator and governor of the universe, was one of the doctrines of the Druids. There is also abundant evidence that the Druids taught the immortality of the souls of men; and Mela tells us, that this was one of their secret doctrines, which they were permitted to publish for political rather than religious reasons.

But though such might be the secret doctrines of the Druids, their public ones were far less agreeable to truth and reason. They taught the people that there were a great number of gods; and they partly invented, and partly adopted, an infinity of fables respecting them. These fables were generally contained in sacred verses, and were delivered by the Druids from little eminences (many of which are still remaining) to the surrounding multitudes. With these narratives were, of course, mixed many moral precepts; and their orations are said to have made great impression on the people, inspiring them with veneration for their gods, "an ardent love to their country, an undaunted courage, and a sovereign contempt for death."

"Their Supreme Being was originally worshipped under the name of *Heses*: the worship of the sun was joined with that of fire, which was held sacred as a symbol of the Divinity. Those celebrated circles of stones, which are still remaining at Stonehenge, and many other places, seem to have been temples of the sun, or of the moon, or probably of both. The Druids likewise adored a very considerable number of deified mortals, who substantially corresponded with the Greek and Roman gods; they also held certain plants sacred, especially the misletoe.

Their mode of worship consisted in sacrifices, prayers, and offerings. Their sacrifices were principally such animals as they used for food; but on some occasions human victims were offered. These occasions, too, were more frequent than we may be willing to suppose; for it was a part of the Druid's creed, that "nothing but the life of man could atone for the life of man." In times of particular emergency or national calamity, or for persons of very high rank, not merely a single victim, but a great number, were sacrificed at once. It is well known that huge colossal figures, made of osier, were filled with men, and then set on fire and reduced to ashes. But the avarice of the priests encouraged the people to present offerings as well as sacrifices. These generally consisted of the most costly and excellent things that could be procured, and of course contributed much to the luxury and splendour both of the temples and of the priesthood.

Like other heathen nations, also, the Druids had their acts of divination, their auguries, and omens. With respect to their times of worship, it is probable that they had daily sacrifices, and other acts of religion; and from the authority of Lucan, they seem to have chosen the hour of noon for the worship of the sun and the celestial gods; and midnight for that of the moon and the infernal gods. They certainly knew the division of time into weeks, although it is doubtful whether one of the seven days was consecrated to religion. The sixth day of every lunar month, which by them was reckoned as the first day, was a religious festival. The first day of May was a great annual festival in honor of Belinus, or the sun. There are some vestiges of this festival still remaining in Ireland, and in the highlands of Scotland. Midsummer day. and the first of November, were likewise annual festivals. All their gods and goddesses seem to have had similar festivals. The chief festival was, when the ceremony of cutting the misletoe from the oak was performed; the day was about the beginning of March. On these festivals, after the appointed sacrifices and acts of devotion were finished, the rest of their time was spent in feasting, singing, dancing, and other diversions.

The places in which the Druids performed their worship were always in the open air; for it was considered unlawful to build temples to the gods, or to worship them within walls or under roofs. Sacred groves, if possible of oak trees, were especially chosen. In the centre of the grove was a circular area, enclosed with one or two rows of large stones, placed perpendicularly on the earth. This was the temple; and within it stood the altar upon which the sacrifices were offered. It does not appear, though the Druids admitted a great number of gods, that they had any images. All the Celtic nations worshipped their principal deity under the symbol of an oak; and this seems to be the nearest approach to the worship of images.

The period at which the religion of the Druids took its rise cannot be well ascertained; but it seems to have been at its zenith at the time of the invasion of the Romans; after this it declined. The Druids both possessed and exerted a political as well as a religious influence upon the minds of the people; and the Romans, finding it inimical and dangerous to their authority, soon manifested a great animosity against the persons and the religion of these priests. They used every means to deprive them of their power, and showed them no mercy when they were found engaged in a revolt. At last, they pursued them into their sacred island of Anglesea; and Suetonius Paulinus, who was governor of Britain, having defeated the Britons who attempted to defend it, made a cruel use of his victory.

He cut down their sacred groves, demolished their temples and altars, and burnt many of the Druids in the fires they themselves kindled for sacrificing the Roman prisoners, had the Britons gained the victory. So great were the numbers who perished on this occasion, and in the unfortunate revolt of the Britons under Boadicea, which happened immediately after; that the Druids never after made any considerable figure. The Britons, however, clung long to their ancient superstitions; and so late as the eleventh century, Canute found it necessary to make the following law against them:—"We strictly charge and forbid all our subjects to worship the gods of the Gentiles; that is to say, the sun, moon, fires, rivers, fountains, hills or trees, or woods of any kinds."

---

16. Alban, the first British Martyr.

Alban, from whom St. Alban's, in Hertfordshire, received its name, was the first British martyr. He was originally a pagan, and being of a very humane dispotion, he sheltered a Christian ecclesiastic, named Amphibalus, who was pursued on account of his religion. The pious example, and edifying discourses of the refugee, made a great impression on the mind of Alban; he longed to become a professor of a religion which charmed him; the fugitive minister, happy in the opportunity, took great pains to instruct him; and, before his discovery, perfected Alban's conversion.

Alban now took a firm resolution to preserve the sentiments of a Christian, or to die the death of a martyr. The enemies of Amphibalus, having intelligence of the place where he was secreted, came to the house of Alban, in order to apprehend him. The noble host, desirous of protecting his guest, changed clothes with him, in order to facilitate his escape; and, when the soldiers came, offered himself up as the person whom they were seeking. Being accordingly carried before the governor, the deceit was immediately discovered; and Amphibalus being absent, that officer determined to wreak his vengeance upon Alban; with this view he commanded the prisoner to advance to the altar and sacrifice to the pagan deities. The brave Alban, however, refused to comply with the idolatrous injunction, and boldly professed himself to be a Christian. The governor, therefore, ordered him to be scourged, which punishment he bore with great fortitude, seeming to acquire new resolution from his sufferings; he was then beheaded.

The venerable Bede states, that upon this occasion the executioner suddenly became a convert to Christianity, and entreated permission either to die for Alban or with him. Obtaining the latter request, they were beheaded by a soldier, who voluntarily undertook the task. This happened on the 22d of June, A. D. 287, at Verulam, now St. Alban's, in Hertfordshire, where a magnificent church was erected to his memory, about the time of Constantine the Great. This edifice was destroyed in the Saxon wars, but was rebuilt by Offa, king of Mercia, and a monastery erected adjoining to it, some remains of which are still visible.

---

17. Martyrdom of Maximilian, in the fourth Century.

About the fourth century, many Christians, upon mature consideration, thought it unlawful to bear arms under a heathen emperor. Their reasons were:

1st. They thereby were frequently under the necessity of profaning the Christian Sabbath. 2d. That they were obliged, with the rest of the army, frequently to be present at idolatrous sacrifices, before the temples of idols. 3d. That they were compelled to follow the imperial standards, which were dedicated to heathen deities, and bore their representations. Such reasons induced many to refuse to enter into the imperial army, when called upon so to do; for the Roman constitution obliged all young men, of a certain stature, to make several campaigns.

Maximilian, the son of Fabius Victor, being pointed out as a proper person to bear arms, was ordered by Dion, the proconsul, to be measured, that he might be enlisted in the service. Maximilian, however, boldly declared himself a Christian, and refused to do military duty. Being found of the proper height, Dion gave directions that he should be marked as a soldier, according to the usual custom. He, however, strenuously opposed this order, and told Dion that he could not possibly engage in the service. The proconsul instantly replied, that he should serve either as a soldier, or die for disobedience. "Do as you please with me," replied Maximilian; "behead me if you think proper; I am already a soldier of Christ, and cannot serve any other power."

Dion wishing, however, to save the young man, commanded his father to use his authority over him, in order to persuade him to comply; but Victor coolly replied, "My son knoweth best what he has to do." Dion again demanded of Maximilian, with some acrimony, if he was yet disposed to receive the mark? To which the young man replied, he had already received the mark of Christ. "Have you!" exclaimed the proconsul in a rage, "then I shall quickly send you to Christ."—"As soon as you please," answered Maximilian; "that is all I wish or desire." The proconsul then pronounced this sentence upon him:—"That for disobedience in refusing to bear arms, and for professing the Christian faith, he should lose his head." This sentence he heard with great intrepidity, and exclaimed, with apparent rapture, "God be praised."

At the place of execution, he exhorted those who were Christians to remain so, and such as were not, to embrace a faith which led to eternal salvation. Then, addressing his father with a cheerful countenance, he desired that the military habit intended for him might be given to the executioner; and after taking leave of him, said, he hoped they should meet again in the other world, and be happy to all eternity. He then received the fatal stroke, which separated his head from his body. The father beheld the execution with amazing fortitude, and saw the head of his son severed from his body, without any emotions but such as seemed to proceed from a conscious pleasure, in being the parent of one whose piety and courage rendered him so great an example for Christians to imitate.

---

18. Noble Fortitude and Martyrdom of three Christian Friends.

While Maximus, governor of Cilicia, was at Tarsus, three Christians were brought before him by Demetrius, a military officer. Tarachus, the eldest, and first in rank, was addressed by Maximus, who asked him what he was. The prisoner replied, "a Christian." This reply offending the governor, he again made the same demand, and was answered in a similar manner. Hereupon the governor told him, that he ought to sacrifice to the gods, as that was the only way to promotion, riches, and honours; and that the emperors themselves did what he recommended to him to perform. But Tarachus replied, that avarice was a sin, and gold itself an idol as abominable as any other; for it promoted frauds, treacheries, robberies, and murders; it induced men to deceive each other, by which in time they deceived themselves; and it bribed the weak to their own eternal destruction. As for promotion, he desired it not, as he could not in conscience accept of any place which would subject him to pay adoration to idols; and with regard to honours, he desired none greater than the honourable title of Christian. As to the emperors themselves being pagans, he added, with the same undaunted and determined spirit, that they were superstitiously deceived in adoring senseless idols, and evidently misled by the machinations of the devil himself. For the boldness of this speech, his jaws were ordered to be broken. He was then stripped, scourged, loaded with chains, and thrown into a dismal dungeon, to remain there till after the trials of the other two prisoners. Probus was then brought before Maximus, who as usual asked him his name. Undauntedly he replied, the most valuable name he could boast of was that of a Christian. To this Maximus replied in the following words:—"Your name of a Christian will be of little service to you; be therefore guided by me; sacrifice to the gods, engage my friendship, and the friendship of the emperor." Probus nobly answered, "that as he had relinquished a considerable fortune to become a soldier of Christ, it might appear evident that he neither cared for his friendship, nor the favour of the emperor." Probus was then scourged; and Demetrius, the officer, reminding him how his blood flowed, advised him to comply; but his only answer was, that those severities were agreeable to him. "What!" cried Maximus, "does he still persist in his madness?" To which Probus rejoined, "That character is badly bestowed on one who refuses to worship idols, or what is worse, devils." After being scourged on the back, he was scourged on the belly, which he suffered with as much intrepidity as before; still repeating, "the more my body suffers and loses blood, the more my soul will grow vigorous, and be a gainer." He was then committed to jail, loaded with irons, and his hands and feet stretched upon the stocks. Andronicus was next brought up, when, being asked the usual question, he said, "I am a Christian, a native of Ephesus, and descended from one of the first families in that city." He was ordered to undergo punishments similar to those of Tarachus and Probus, and then to be remanded to prison.

Having been confined some days, the three prisoners were again brought before Maximus, who began first to reason with Tarachus, saying that as old age was honoured from the supposition of its being accompanied by wisdom, he was in hopes what had already passed must, upon deliberation, have caused a change in his sentiments. Finding himself, however, mistaken, he ordered him to be tortured by various means; particularly, fire was placed in the hollow of his hands; he was hung up by his feet, and smoked with wet straw; and a mixture of salt and vinegar was poured into his nostrils; and he was then again remanded to his dungeon. Probus being again called, and asked if he would sacrifice, replied, "I come better prepared than before; for what I have already suffered has only confirmed and strengthened me in my resolution. Employ your whole power upon me, and you will find, that neither you, nor your masters, the emperors, nor the gods whom you serve, nor the devil who is your father, shall oblige me to adore the gods whom I know not." The governor, however, attempting to reason with him, paid the most extravagant praises to the pagan deities, and pressed him to sacrifice to Jupiter; but Probus turned his casuistry into ridicule, and said, "Shall I pay divine honours to Jupiter; to one who married his own sister; to an infamous debauchee; as he is acknowledged to have been by your own priests and poets?" Provoked at this speech, the governor ordered him to be struck upon the mouth, for uttering what he called blasphemy; his body was then seared with hot irons, he was put to the rack, and afterwards scourged; his head was then shaved, and red-hot coals placed upon the crown; and after all these tortures he was again sent to prison. When Andronicus was again brought before Maximus, the latter attempted to deceive him, by pretending that Tarachus and Probus had repented of their obstinacy, and owned the gods of the empire. To this the prisoner answered, "Lay not, O governor, such a weakness to the charge of those, who have appeared here before me in this cause, nor imagine it to be in your power to shake my fixed resolution with artful speeches. I cannot believe that they have disobeyed the laws of their fathers, renounced their hopes in our God, and consented to your extravagant orders; nor will I ever fall short of them in faith and dependence upon our common Saviour; thus armed, I neither know your gods nor fear your authority; fulfil your threats, execute your most sanguinary inventions, and employ every cruel art in your power on me; I am prepared to bear it for the sake of

Christ." For this answer he was cruelly scourged, and his wounds were afterwards rubbed with salt; but being well again in a short time, the governor reproached the jailer for having suffered some physician to attend him. The jailer declared that no person whatever had been near him or any of the other prisoners, and that he would willingly forfeit his head if any allegation of the kind could be proved against him. Andronicus corroborated the testimony of the jailer, and added, that God, whom he served, was the most powerful of physicians. These three Christians were finally brought to a third examination, when they retained their constancy, were again tortured, and at length ordered for execution. Being brought to the amphitheatre, several beasts were let loose upon them; but none of the animals, though hungry, would touch them. Maximus became so surprised and incensed at this circumstance that he severely reprehended the keeper, and ordered him to produce a beast that would execute the business for which he was wanted. The keeper then brought out a large bear that had that day destroyed three men; but this creature and a fierce lioness also refused to touch the Christians. Finding the design of destroying them by means of wild beasts ineffectual, Maximus ordered them to be slain by means of the sword, which was accordingly executed on the 11th of October, A. D. 303. They all declared, previous to their martyrdom, that as death was the common lot of all men, they wished to meet it for the sake of Christ; and to resign that life to faith which must otherwise be the prey of disease.

---

19. Vision of Constantine.

The reign of Constantine the Great, the first Christian emperor, is an important era in the history of the Christian church.

The miraculous circumstances attending his conversion, though doubted by some, are fully credited by others. According to Eusebius (who received the account from the emperor's own mouth, and who also confirmed it by his solemn oath) these extraordinary circumstances are as follows:

"As the emperor was marching at the head of his army, from France into Italy, against Maxentius, on an expedition which he was fully aware involved in it his future destiny; oppressed with extreme anxiety, and reflecting that he needed a force superior to arms, for subduing the sorceries and magic of his adversary, he anxiously looked out for the aid of some deity, as that alone could secure him success. About 3 o'clock in the afternoon, when the sun began to decline, whilst praying for supernatural aid, a luminous cross* was seen by the emperor and his army, in the air, above the sun, inscribed with the words, "BY THIS CONQUER;" at the sight of which amazement overpowered both himself and the soldiery on the expedition with him. He continued to ponder on the event till night, when, in a dream, the Author of Christianity appeared to him to confirm the vision, directing him, at the same time, to make the symbol of the cross his military ensign."†

Constantine, having vanquished his adversary, now built places for Christian worship, and showed great beneficence to the poor. He removed the seat of the empire from Rome to Byzantium, which he afterwards honoured by the name of Constantinople, and prohibited, by a severe edict, the performance of pagan rites and ceremonies.

He died on the 22d of May, in the year 337, at the age of sixty-four, after a reign of thirty-three years, having fully established the Christian religion in the Roman empire.

---

* Historians are much divided in their judgment respecting this miraculous appearance. It is in vain for us to attempt to ascertain a doubtful matter, at a period so remote from the event; it is certain, however, that such a device was upon the standards and shields of Constantine's army, and also upon several coins in existence at this day.

† Milner's Church History.

20. Origin of the Monastic Life.

St. Anthony, of Egypt, in the fourth century, first instituted the monastic life. He was an illiterate youth of Alexandria, and happening one day to enter a church, he heard the words of our Lord to the young ruler, "Sell all that thou hast, and give to the poor." Considering this as a special call to him, he distributed his patrimony, deserted his family and house, took up his residence among the tombs, and in a ruined tower. After remaining there a long time he at length advanced three days' journey into the desert, to the eastward of the river Nile, where, discovering a lonely spot which possessed the advantages of shade and water, he fixed his last abode. His example and his lessons infected others, whose curiosity pursued him to the desert; and before he quitted life, which was prolonged to the term of a hundred and five years, he beheld a numerous progeny imitating his original. Anthony formed his followers into a regular body, engaged them to live in society with each other, and prescribed to them fixed rules for their conduct. From this time monks multiplied incredibly, on the sands of Lybia, upon the rocks of Thebais, and the cities of the Nile. Travellers, even to this day, may explore the remains of fifty monasteries, which were planted directly south of Alexandria, by the disciples of Anthony.

These regulations, which were made in Egypt, were soon introduced into Palestine, Syria, Mesopotamia, and the adjacent countries; and their example was followed with such rapid success, that in a short time the whole east was filled with a set of indolent mortals, who, abandoning all human connexions, advantages, pleasures, and concerns, wore out a languishing and miserable existence, amidst the hardships of want, and various kinds of suffering, in order to arrive at a more close and rapturous communication with God and angels.

From the east this gloomy disposition passed into the west, and Martin of Tours founded a monastery at

Poictiers, and thus introduced the monastic institutions into France. So rapid was the increase of his disciples, that two thousand monks followed in his funeral procession; very soon all Christendom became infected with this superstition, and various orders of monks were founded, such as Franciscans, Dominicans, Benedictines, &c. This kind of life was not confined to males. Females also began to retire from the world and dedicate themselves to solitude and devotion. *Nunneries* were founded, and such as entered were henceforth secluded from all worldly intercourse. They were not allowed to go out, nor was any one permitted to go in to see them.

---

21. Julian, the Apostate.

Julian, the Roman emperor, began his reign about the year 360. He is commonly called *Julian, the apostate*, from his casting off the profession of Christianity and restoring the ancient pagan worship. In order to give the lie to our Saviour's prophecy, he attempted to rebuild the temple and the city of Jerusalem. He knew the Christians were firmly persuaded that by the advent of Christ the typical dispensation had come to an end; and could he succeed in restoring the Jews to their city and the ritual of their worship, he might convert it into an argument against the faith of prophecy and the truth of revelation.

He therefore resolved to erect on Mount Moriah a stately temple; and gave instructions to his minister Alypius, to commence without delay the vast undertaking. At the call of their supposed great deliverer, the Jews, from all the provinces of the empire, repaired to Jerusalem. Every purse was now opened in liberal contributions, every hand claimed a share in the labour, and the commands of the emperor were executed with enthusiasm by the whole people. But they entirely failed in attaining their object. Ammianus Marcellinus (a heathen writer who lived during this transaction) says, "whilst Alypius, assisted by the governor of the

DRUID SACRIFICE.

The Druids in time of national calamity made colossal figures of osier, filled them with men, then set them on fire and reduced them to ashes.

ST. ANTHONY

of Egypt in the Fourth Century, retired to a desert eastward of the Nile. He is considerd the first that instituted the Monastic life.

province, urged with vigour and diligence the execution of the work, horrible balls of fire, breaking out near the foundations with frequent and reiterated attacks, rendered the place from time to time inaccessible to the scorched and blasted workmen; and the victorious element continuing in this manner obstinately and resolutely bent, as it were, to drive them to a distance, the undertaking was abandoned." This remarkable event is fully attested by various historians of that age.*

During Julian's reign open persecution was prohibited; but by every other means were the followers of Christ humbled and oppressed. The Saviour he always distinguished by the name of *Galilean.* Being engaged in a war with the Persians, he was mortally wounded by a lance. As he was expiring he filled his hand with blood, and indignantly casting it up into the air, exclaimed, "*O Galilean! thou hast conquered!*"

It is mentioned that about this time one *Libanius,* an admirer of Julian, meeting a Christian schoolmaster at Antioch, asked him in derision, What the carpenter's son was now doing? "*The carpenter's son,*" replied the schoolmaster, "*is making a coffin for your hero.*" The event proved the truth of this prediction.

---

22. Arian Controversy.

About the year 315 lived one Arius, who was a presbyter of the church of Alexandria. He maintained that the Son of God was totally and essentially distinct from the Father; that he was the first and noblest of those beings whom God had created—the instrument by whose subordinate operations he formed the universe; and therefore inferior to the Father both in nature and dignity; also, that the Holy Ghost was not God, but created by the power of the Son. He owned the Son

* Jones's History of the Christian Church.

was the Word, but denied that Word to have been eternal. He gained many followers, who were called *Arians*. They were first condemned and anathematized by a council held at Alexandria in 320, under Alexander, bishop of that city; who accused Arius of impiety, and caused him to be expelled from the church. In 325 they were again condemned by the council of Nice, composed of 380 fathers, assembled by Constantine. Their *doctrines*, however, were not extinguished; but soon became the reigning religion in the east. In two or three years Arius was recalled by the emperor, and the laws which had been enacted against him were repealed. Athanasius, then bishop of Alexandria, refused to admit him or his followers to communion; whereupon the Arians became so enraged, that by their interest at court they procured him to be deposed and banished. But the church at Alexandria still refused to admit Arius to their communion; upon which the emperor sent for him to Constantinople, where he delivered a fresh confession in terms less offensive. The emperor then commanded him to be admitted to their communion. But that very night he suddenly expired as his friends were conducting him in triumph to the great church at Constantinople.

The Arians found a protector in Constantius, who succeeded his father. In 349 he was influenced to recall Athanasius, and to restore him to his office. But no measure could be so repulsive to his enemies, who rose up against him in the most bitter accusations. Athanasius was obliged to flee before the storm and take shelter in a desert. The blast fell upon his friends, whom he had left behind. Some were banished, some loaded with chains and imprisoned; while others were scourged to death.

The Arians underwent various revolutions and persecutions under succeeding emperors. Theodosius the Great put forth a mighty effort to suppress them; but to no avail. Their doctrines were carried into Africa in the fifth century, under the Vandals; and into Asia under the Goths; and also into Italy, Gaul, and

Spain. In the commencement of the sixth century, Arianism was triumphant in many parts of Asia, Europe, and Africa. But when the Vandals were driven out of Africa, and the Goths out of Italy, by the arms of Justinian, it sunk almost at once.

The state of the church, during these scenes, was deplorable. The Scriptures were disregarded, and what was error, and what was truth, was to be determined by fathers and councils. Ministers had departed from the simplicity of Christian doctrine and manners; avarice and ambition ruled; and as either party, at any time, gained the advantage, it treated the other with marked severity. As the Arians, however, were generally in power, the orthodox party experienced almost uninterrupted oppression. But when they possessed the power, they were not much less violent than the Arians. Even Athanasius, who was at the head of the orthodox party, was a man of a restless disposition, and of ambitious and aspiring views; and cannot be exempted from the charge of oppressing his opponents, whenever he had the means in his possession.

At length, the Arians became divided among themselves, and a great variety of sects sprang up from among them. Arianism has made its appearance, in a great variety of forms, down to the present time.

23. Councils.

These councils were an assemblage of deputies, or commissioners, representing the body of the Christian church; and were generally held to decide upon some controversial points, in religious sentiments. Of these, there have been quite a number held since the days of Constantine; of which the following may be considered as the most important.

The "*Council of Nice*," assembled by Constantine in 325, was the first general council. Its object was to scan the doctrine of Arius. In this council, which was composed of three hundred and eighteen bishops, besides presbyters, deacons, and others, the emperor presided. It resulted in the deposition and banishment of Arius, and the adoption of the "*Nicene Creed*;" to which all were commanded to subscribe, upon pain of banishment. During its session, the different bishops began to complain to the emperor of each other, and to vindicate themselves. He listened for a while to their mutual recriminations, which were reduced to writing. At length, growing impatient, he threw all their billets into the fire; saying, it did not belong to him to decide the differences of Christian bishops; which must be deferred till the day of judgment. The council determined, that Easter should be kept at the same time throughout the church; that celibacy was a virtue; that new converts should not be introduced to orders; and that a certain course of penitence should be enjoined on the lapsed, &c.

The "*Council of Constantinople*" was summoned, in the year 383, by Theodosius the Great; which decreed that the "*Nicene Creed*" should be the standard of orthodoxy, and all heresies condemned. Two edicts were issued against these; the one, prohibiting holding any assemblies; the other, by the emperor, prohibiting the worshipping any inanimate idol, by the sacrifice of any animal, upon pain of death. This was a deathblow to paganism; for it soon began to fall, and, in twenty-eight years after the death of Theodosius, not a vestige of it could be found.

In 787, the question concerning the worship of images greatly agitated the Catholic church; and a council was assembled at Nice, under the empress Irene, and her son. This council established the worship of images, and anathematized all who should refuse. The language employed in this anathema was as follows:—"*Long live Constantine, and his mother;—damnation to all heretics;—damnation on the council that roared against venerable images;—the Holy Trinity hath deposed them.*"

The "*Council of Clermont*" was held in 1095. Here, the first crusade was determined upon; also the name of *pope* was first given to the head of the church.

exclusive of the bishops, who had occasionally assumed that title.

The "*Council of Constance*" convened in 1414; and was composed of several European princes, or their deputies, with the emperor of Germany at their head; twenty archbishops; one hundred and fifty bishops; one hundred and fifty other dignitaries; and two hundred doctors; with the pope at *their* head. At this time, there were three persons who claimed the papal chair; between whom a violent contest was carried on. But the council deposed them all, and placed one Martin in the chair, as the legal head of the church.

The object of this council was, to put an end to the papal schism; which was finally effected, after it had existed about forty years. Before this body, Huss and Jerome of Prague were cited to appear, condemned, and afterwards burnt alive. The writings of John Wickliffe, also, were here condemned.

The "*Council of Trent*" was assembled in 1545, by Paul III., and was continued by twenty-five sessions, for eighteen years, under Julius III. and Pius IV., whose object was, to correct, illustrate, and fix, with perspicuity, the doctrines of the church, to restore the vigour of its discipline, and to reform the lives of its ministers. The decrees of this council, together with the creed of Pope Pius IV., contain a summary of the doctrines of the Romish church.

---

24. Conversion of Justin Martyr.

This great man was born at Neapolis, in Samaria, anciently called Sichem. His father was a Gentile (probably one of the Greeks belonging to the colony transplanted thither), who gave his son a philosophical education. In his youth he travelled for the improvement of his understanding; and Alexandria afforded him all the entertainment which an inquisitive mind could derive from the fashionable studies. The Stoics appeared to him, at first, the masters of happiness. He gave himself up to one of this sect, till he found he could learn nothing from him of the nature of God. It is remarkable (as he tells us himself), that his tutor told him that this was a knowledge by no means necessary; which much illustrates the views of Dr. *Warburton* concerning these ancient philosophers— that they were atheists in reality. He next betook himself to a Peripatetic, whose anxious desire of settling the price of instruction convinced Justin that truth did not dwell with him. A Pythagorean next engaged his attention, who, requiring of him the previous knowledge of music, astronomy, and geometry, dismissed him for the present, when he understood he was unfurnished with those studies. In much solicitude, he applied himself to a Platonic philosopher, with a more plausible appearance of success than from any of the foregoing. He now gave himself to retirement. As he was walking near the sea, he was met by an aged person, of a venerable appearance, whom he beheld with much attention. "Do you know me?" says he: when he answered in the negative, he asked why he surveyed him with so much attention? "I wondered," says he, "to find any person here." The stranger observed, that he was waiting for some domestics. "But what brought you here?" says he. Justin professed his love of private meditation; the other hinted at the absurdity of mere speculation abstracted from practice; which gave occasion to Justin to express his ardent desire of knowing God, and to expatiate on the praise of philosophy. The stranger, by degrees, endeavoured to cure him of his ignorant admiration of Plato and Pythagoras, and to point out to him the writings of the Hebrew prophets, as being much more ancient than any of those called philosophers; and led him to some view of Christianity in its nature and its evidences, adding, "Above all things, pray that the gates of light may be opened unto thee; for they are not discernible, nor to be understood by all, except God and his Christ give to a man to understand." The man having spoken these things, and much more, "left me (says Justin), directing me to pursue these things, and I saw him no more. Immediately a fire was kindled in my soul, and I had a strong affection for the prophets, and those men who are the friends of Christ; and weighing within myself his words, I found this to be the only sure philosophy." We have no more particulars of the exercises of his soul in religion. His conversion took place from hence, sometime in the reign of Adrian. But he has shown us enough to make it evident, that conversion was then looked on as an inward spiritual work upon the soul, and that he had the substance of the same work of grace which the Spirit operates at this day on real Christians.—*Milner's Church History.*

---

25. Pelagians.

About the end of the fourth century, there appeared a sect called Pelagians. They maintained the following doctrines:—1. That Adam was by nature mortal, and, whether he had sinned or not, would have died; 2. That the consequences of Adam's sin were confined to his own person; 3. That newborn infants are in the same situation with Adam before the fall; 4. That the law qualified men for the kingdom of heaven, and was founded upon equal promises with the gospel; 5. That the general resurrection of the dead does not follow in virtue of our Saviour's resurrection; 6. That the grace of God is given accordingto our merits; 7. That this grace is not granted for the performance of every moral act, the liberty of the will and information in points of duty being sufficient.

The founder of this sect was one Pelagius, a native of Great Britain. He was educated in the monastery of Banchor, in Wales, of which he became a monk, and afterwards an abbot. In the early part of his life he went over to France, and thence to Rome, where he and his friend Celestius propagated their opinions, though in a private manner. Upon the approach of the Goths, A. D. 410, they retired from Rome, and went thence into Sicily, and afterwards into Africa, where they published their doctrines with more freedom. From Africa, Pelagius passed into Palestine, while Celestius remained at Carthage, with a view to preferment, desiring to be admitted among the presbyters of that city. But the discovery of his opinions having blasted all his hopes, and his errors being condemned in a council held at Carthage, A. D. 412, he departed from that city, and went into the east. It was from this time that Augustine, the famous bishop of Hippo, began to attack the tenets of Pelagius and Celestius, in his learned and elegant writings; and to him, indeed, is principally due the glory of having suppressed this sect in its very birth.

Things went more smoothly with Pelagius in the east, where he enjoyed the protection and favour of John, bishop of Jerusalem, whose attachment to the sentiments of Origen led him naturally to countenance those of Pelagius, on account of the conformity that there seemed to be between these two systems. Under the shadow of this powerful protection, Pelagius made a public profession of his opinions, and formed disciples in several places; and though, in the year 415, he was accused by Orosius, a Spanish presbyter (whom Augustine had sent into Palestine for that purpose), before an assembly of bishops met at Jerusalem, yet he was dismissed without the least censure; and not only so, but soon after fully acquitted of all errors by the council of Diospolis.

This controversy was brought to Rome, and referred to the decision of Zosimus, who was raised to the pontificate, A. D. 417. The new pontiff, gained over by the ambiguous and seemingly orthodox confession of faith that Celestius, who was now at Rome, had artfully drawn up, and also by the letters and protestations of Pelagius, pronounced in favour of these monks; declared them sound in the faith, and unjustly persecuted by their adversaries. The African bishops, with Augustine at their head, little affected at this declaration, continued obstinately to maintain the judgment they had pronounced in this matter, and to strengthen it by their exhortations, their letters, and their writings.

Zosimus yielded to the perseverance of the Africans, changed his mind, and condemned with the utmost severity Pelagius and Celestius, whom he had honoured with his approbation, and covered with his protection. This was followed by a train of evils, which pursued these two monks without interruption. They were condemned, says Mosheim, by that same Ephesian council which had launched its thunder at the head of Nestorius. In short, the Gauls, Britons, and Africans, by their councils—and emperors, by their edicts and penal laws—demolished this sect in its infancy, and suppressed it entirely, before it had acquired any tolerable degree of vigour or consistence.—*Buck's Theological Dictionary*.

---

26. Religion of the Goths, or Scandinavians.

Goths is the name generally given to those nations in the northern part of Europe who directed their arms against the Roman empire, and finally, under Alaric, one of their most celebrated kings, plundered Rome, A. D. 401, and introduced disorders, anarchy, and revolutions, in the west of Europe. The Goths came from Scandinavia, a name generally given by the ancients to the tract of territory which contains the modern kingdoms of Norway, Sweden, Denmark, &c.

The theology of the Scandinavians or Goths was most intimately connected with their manners. They held three great principles, or fundamental doctrines of religion:—"To serve the Supreme Being with prayer and sacrifice; to do no wrong or unjust action; and to be intrepid in fight." These principles are the key to the *Edda*, or sacred book of the Scandinavians, which, though it contains the substance of a very ancient religion, is not itself a work of high antiquity, being compiled in the thirteenth century by Snorro Sturlson, supreme judge of Iceland. *Odin*, characterized as the terrible and severe God, the Father of carnage, the avenger, was the principal deity of the Scandinavians; from whose union with Frea, the heavenly mother, sprung various subordinate divinities; as, *Thor*, who perpetually wars against Loke and his evil giants, who envy the power of Odin, and seek to destroy his works. Among the inferior deities were the virgins of the Valhalli, whose office was to administer to the heroes in paradise. The timid wretch who allowed himself to perish by disease or age, was unworthy the joys of paradise. These joys were fighting, ceaseless slaughter, and drinking beer out of the skulls of their enemies, with a renovation of life to furnish a perpetuity of the same pleasures. The favourites of Odin were all who die in battle, or, what was equally meritorious, by their own hand.

As the Scandinavians believed this world to be the work of some superior intelligences, so they held all nature to be constantly under the regulation of an Almighty will and power, and subject to a fixed and unalterable destiny. These notions had a wonderful effect on the national manners, and on the conduct of individuals. The Scandinavian placed his sole delight in war; he entertained an absolute contempt of danger and of death, and his glory was estimated by the number he had slain in battle.* The death-song of *Regner Lodbrok*, king of Denmark, who fell into the hands of his enemies, was thrown into prison, and by them condemned to be destroyed by serpents, is a faithful picture of the Scandinavian character. The following is an exact translation of a part of his song:—

"We have fought with our swords. I was young, when, towards the east, in the bay of Oreon, we made torrents of blood flow, to gorge the ravenous beast of prey, and the yellow footed bird. There resounded the bared steel upon the lofty helmets of men. The whole ocean was one wound. The crow waded in the blood of the slain. When we had numbered twenty years, we lifted our spears on high, and every where spread our renown. Eight barons we overcame in the east, before the port of Diminum; and plentifully we feasted the eagle in that slaughter. The warm stream of wounds ran into the ocean. The army fell before us. When we steered our ships into the mouth of the Vistula, we

* Tytler's History.

sent the Helsingians to the hall of *Odin.* Then did the sword bite. The waters were all one wound. The earth was dyed red with the warm stream. The swords rung upon the coats of mail, and clove the bucklers in twain. None fled on that day, till among his ships Herandus fell. Than him no braver baron cleaves the sea with ships; a cheerful heart did he ever bring to the combat. Then the host threw away their shields, when the uplifted spear flew at the breasts of heroes. The sword bit the Scarfian rocks; bloody was the shield in battle, until Rafuo the king was slain. From the heads of warriors the warm sweat streamed down their armour. The crows around the Indirian islands had an ample prey. It were difficult to single out one among so many deaths. At the rising of the sun I beheld the spears piercing the bodies of foes, and the bows throwing forth their steel-pointed arrows. Loud roared the swords in the plains of Lano. The virgin long bewailed the slaughter of that morning."

He thus laments the death of one of his sons in battle:—

"When Rogvaldus was slain, for him mourned all the hawks of heaven," as lamenting a benefactor who had so liberally supplied them with prey; "for boldly," as he adds, "in the strife of swords, did the breaker of helmets throw the spear of blood."

The poem concludes with sentiments of the highest bravery and contempt of death.

"What is more certain to the brave man than death, though amidst the storm of swords, he stands always ready to oppose it? He, only, regrets this life, who hath never known distress. The timorous man allures the devouring eagle to the field of battle. The coward, whenever he comes, is useless to himself. This I esteem honourable, that the youth should advance to the combat fairly matched one against another; nor man retreat from man. Long was this the warrior's highest glory. He who aspires to the love of virgins ought always to be foremost in the war of arms. It appears to me of truth, that we are led by the Fates. Seldom can any overcome the appointment of destiny. Little did I foresee that Ella* was to have my life in his hands, in that day when, fainting, I concealed my blood, and pushed forth my ships into the waves, after we had spread a repast for the beasts of prey throughout the Scottish bays. But this makes me always rejoice, that in the halls of our father Balder (or Odin) I know there are seats prepared, where in a short time, we shall be drinking ale out of the hollow skulls of our enemies. In the house of the

* This was the name of his enemy who had condemned him to death.

mighty Odin, no brave man laments death. I come not with the voice of despair to Odin's hall. How eagerly would all the sons of Aslauga now rush to war, did they know the distress of their father, whom a multitude of venomous serpents tear! I have given to my children a mother who hath filled their hearts with valour. I am fast approaching to my end. A cruel death awaits me from the viper's bite. A snake dwells in the midst of my heart. I hope that the sword of some of my sons shall yet be stained with the blood of Ella. The valiant youths will wax red with anger, and will not sit in peace. Fifty and one times have I reared the standard in battle. In my youth, I learned to dye the sword in blood; my hope was then, that no king among men would be more renowned than me. The goddesses of death will now soon call me; I must not mourn my death. Now I end my song. The goddesses invite me away; they whom Odin has sent to me from his hall. I will sit upon a lofty seat, and drink ale joyfully with the goddesses of death. The hours of my life are run out. I will smile when I die."

---

27. Taking of Rome by Alaric, King of the Goths.

In the year 401, the imperial city of Rome was besieged and taken by Alaric, king of the Goths, who delivered it over to the licentious fury of his army. A scene of horror ensued, scarcely paralleled in the history of war. The plunder of the city was accomplished in six days; the streets were deluged with the blood of murdered citizens, and some of the noblest edifices were razed to their foundation.

The city of Rome was at this time an object of admiration. Its inhabitants were estimated at twelve hundred thousand. Its houses were but little short of fifty thousand; seventeen hundred and eighty of which were similar in grandeur and extent to the palaces of princes. Every thing bespoke wealth and luxury. The market, the race-courses, the temples, the fountains, the porticos, the shady groves, unitedly combined to add surpassing splendour to the spot.

Two years before the surrender of the city, Alaric had laid siege to it, and had received from the proud and insolent Romans, as a price of his retreat from the walls, five thousand pounds of gold, thirty thousand

ERUPTION OF FIRE
defeating the attempt of Julian the Apostate, to rebuild the City and Temple of Jerusalem, in order to disprove the prophecy of Christ.

JUSTIN MARTYR
the Gentile philosopher, conversing with an aged Christian, previous to his conversion to the Christian faith.

pounds of silver, and an incredible quantity of other valuable articles.

In the following year, he again appeared before the city; and now took possession of the port of Ostia, one of the boldest and most stupendous works of Roman magnificence. He had demanded the surrender of the city, and was only prevented from razing it to its foundation by the consent of the senate to remove the unworthy Honorius from the throne of the Cæsars, and to place Attalus, the tool of the Gothic conqueror, in his place.

But the doom of the city was not far distant. In 410, Alaric again appeared under the walls of the capital. Through the treachery of the Roman guard, one of the gates was silently opened, and the inhabitants were awakened, at midnight, by the tremendous sound of the Gothic trumpet. Alaric and his bands entered in triumph, and spread desolation through the streets. Thus this proud city, which had subdued a great part of the world; which, during a period of 619 years, had never been violated by the presence of a foreign enemy; was itself called to surrender to the arms of a rude and revengeful Goth, who was well entitled the *Destroyer of Nations*, and the *Scourge of God!*

From this period, the barbarians continued their ravages until 476, which is commonly assigned as making the total extinction of the western part of the Roman empire.

Although the barbarians were idolaters, yet upon the conquest of the Roman empire, they generally, though at different periods, conformed themselves to the religious institutions of the nations among whom they settled. They unanimously agreed to support the hierarchy of the church of Rome, and to defend and maintain it as the established religion of their respective states. They generally adopted the Arian system, and hence the advocates of the Nicene creed met with bitter persecution.—*Goodrich's Ecclesiastical History.*

28. Augustine's City of God.

The following summary account of St. Augustine's celebrated production, *The City of God*, is extracted from Milner's Church History.

"The capture of Rome, by Alaric the Goth, and the subsequent plunder and miseries of the imperial city, had opened the mouths of the pagans, and the true God was blasphemed on the account. Christianity was looked on as the cause of the declension of the empire; and however trifling such an argument may appear at this day, at that time it had so great weight, that it gave occasion to Augustine, *in his zeal for the house of God*, to write this treatise.

"The work itself consists of twenty-two books. The first states the objections made by the pagans, and answers them in form. It was a remarkable fact, that all who fled to the church called the *Basilicæ* of the Apostles, whether Christians or not, were preserved from military fury. The author takes notice of this singular circumstance, as a proof of the great authority of the name and doctrine of Christ, even among pagans, and shows that no instance can be found in their history, where many vanquished people were spared out of respect to their religious worship. He justly observes, therefore, that the evils accompanying the late disaster ought to be ascribed to the usual events of war—the benefits to the power of the name of Christ. His thoughts on the promiscuous distribution of good and evil in this life are uncommonly excellent. "If all sin," he observes, "were now punished, nothing might seem to be reserved to the last judgment. If the Divinity punished no sin openly now, his providence might be denied. In like manner, in prosperous things, if some petitions for temporal things were not abundantly answered, it might be said that they were not at God's disposal. If all petitions were granted, it might be thought that we should serve God only for the sake of worldly things." And in a number of elegant allusions, he goes on to show the benefit of afflictions to the righteous, and the curse which accompanies them to the wicked. He mentions also the propriety of punishing the godly often in this life, because they are not sufficiently weaned from the world, and because they do not rebuke the sins of the world as they ought, but conform too much to the tastes of ungodly men. He answers the objections drawn from their sufferings in the late disaster. "Many Christians," say they, "are led captive. It would be very miserable," he owns, "if they could be led to any place where they could not find their God." In the same book he excellently handles the subject of suicide, demonstrates its cowardice, and exposes the pusillanimity of Cato. He mentions the prayer of Paulinus, bishop of Nola, who had reduced himself to poverty for the sake of Christ, when the barbarians laid waste his city,—"Lord, suffer me not to be tormented on account of gold and silver; for where all my wealth is, thou knowest." For there he had his all where the Lord hath directed us to lay up our treasure, and he strongly insists, as the fullest answer to objections, that the saint loses nothing by all his afflictions.

"Having sufficiently spoken to the particular occasion, he proceeds, in the second book, to wage *offensive war with the pagans*, and shows that while their religion prevailed, it never promoted the real benefit of men. In this book he proves his point with respect to moral evils. Immoral practices were not discouraged or prohibited in the least by the popular idolatry; but, on the contrary, vice and flagitiousness were encouraged. He triumphs in the peculiar excellence of Christian institutes, because by them instruction was constantly diffused among the body of the people, of which the whole system of pagan worship was void. His observations on stage-plays, and on the vicious manners of the Romans, even in the best times of their republic, as confessed by Sallust, or at least deduced by fair inference from his writings, are extremely worthy of attention. In the same book will be found some valuable remains of Cicero de Republica, a most profound and ingenious treatise, of which a few fragments are introduced by him, to show that, by Cicero's confession, the Roman state was completely ruined before the times of Christianity. The book concludes with a pathetic exhortation to unbelievers.

"In the third book, he demonstrates that the pagans had no more help from their religion against natural evils, than they had against moral. He recounts the numberless miseries endured by the Romans long before the coming of Christ, such as would by malice have been imputed to the Christian religion had it then existed, some of which were more calamitous than any thing which they had lately sustained from the Goths.

"In the fourth book, he demonstrates that the Roman felicity, such as it was, was not caused by their religion. Here he weighs the nature of that glory and extent of empire with which the carnal heart is so much captivated, and shows the futility of all the then popular religions. In the conclusion he gives a short view of the dispensation of Providence toward the Jews, and shows, while they continued obedient, the superiority of their felicity to that of the Romans.

"In the fifth book, he describes the virtue of the old Romans, and what reward was given to it here on earth—shadowy reward for shadowy virtue. He gives an excellent account of the vice of vain glory, and contrasts it with the humility of Christians. He demonstrates that it was the true God who dispensed his mercies and judgments towards the Romans. In the same book he argues against Cicero, and shows the consistency of the prescience of God with the free agency of man.

"Having shown in the five first books, that paganism could do nothing for men in temporal things, in the five following books he proves that it was as totally insignificant with respect to the next life. Here we meet with some valuable fragments of the very learned Varro, who divides religion into three kinds; the

fabulous, the philosophical, and the political. Here, too, we have a clear and historical detail of the opinions of the ancient philosophers."

Of the remaining books, the first four describe the beginning, the middle four the progress, and the last four the issues of the two states, namely, the city of God, and the world; the history of both, and the different genius and spirit of each, are, throughout, conceived with great energy by the author, and are illustrated with copiousness and perspicuity.

"The eleventh book begins with a just and solid view of the knowledge of God by the Mediator, and the authority of the Scriptures. A number of questions which respect the beginning of things, rather curious than important, follow.

"In the twelfth book, the question concerning the origin of evil is still more explicitly stated; and the opinions of those who pretend to account for the origin of the world in a manner different from the Scriptures, and to give it an antiquity much superior to that which is assigned to it in them, are refuted.

"The thirteenth book describes the fall of man; but questions of little or no moment are interspersed.

"The fourteenth book contains matter more interesting than the foregoing three; though it is not without unimportant speculations. A just idea of the magnitude of the first sin is given, and the justice of God is excellently vindicated.

"In the fifteenth book, he enters upon the second part of the history of the two states, namely, their progress. He describes very justly the two types, Sarah and Agar, and illustrates the spirit and genius of the two sects by the cases of Cain and Abel. He confutes those who would make the lives of the antediluvians of shorter duration than that assigned them in Scripture.

"The sixteenth book carries on the history of the city of God from Noah to David, and contains important instruction throughout, especially to those who have not read the same things in modern authors.

"The seventeenth book may be called the prophetic history.

"In the eighteenth he displays much learning in describing the times of the world coeval with those of the church of God, to the birth of Christ. He proves the superior antiquity of prophetic authority to that of any philosophers. The remarkable harmony of the sacred writers in the promotion of one system, and the endless discordances of philosophers, are ably contrasted. Yet, he proves, from the earliest times, that the citizens of the new Jerusalem were not confined absolutely to Jewry.

"The last four books describe the issues of the two states. The twentieth undertakes to describe the last judgment. In the last two books, he gives his ideas of the punishment of the wicked and of the happiness of the righteous, in a future state. In the last book, which describes the eternal rest of the city of God, he dwells a little on the external evidences of Christianity; and in speaking on miracles, he describes some which were wrought in his own time; one of them, the healing of a disorder, seems peculiarly striking, because it was in answer to prayer. He closes his work with a delightful view of the eternal felicity of the church of God."

---

29. Mahomet, the Arabian Impostor.

Mahomet was born at Mecca, a city in Arabia, near the Red Sea, A. D. 569. Possessing but a scanty education, but of great natural talents, he sought to raise himself to celebrity by feigning a divine mission, to propagate a new religion for the salvation of mankind. Early in life he was instructed in the business of a merchant, and employed by a rich widow of the name of Hadijah, as a factor. Into her favour he so effectually insinuated himself, as to obtain her in marriage. By this event, he became possessed of considerable wealth and power, and continued in the mercantile occupation for several years. About the thirty-eighth year of his

age he retired to the desert, and pretended to hold conferences with the angel Gabriel, who delivered to him, from time to time, portions of the *Koran* (the sacred book of the Mahometans), containing revelations from God, with the doctrines which he required his prophet (Mahomet) to communicate to the world.

His first converts were his wife, his servant, his pupil, and his friend. In process of time some of the citizens of Mecca were introduced to the private lessons of the prophet; they yielded to the voice of enthusiasm, and repeated the fundamental creed, "*There is but one God, and Mahomet is his prophet.*"

Being opposed in propagating his doctrines, he was obliged to flee. His flight, called the *Hegira* (A. D. 622), is the era of his glory. He betook himself to Medina, was joined by the brave Omar, and thence commenced propagating his religion by the sword. He divided his spoil among his followers, and from all sides the roving Arabs were allured to the standard of *religion* and *plunder;* the prophet sanctioned the license of embracing the female captives as their wives or concubines, and the enjoyment of wealth and beauty was the type of Paradise. "The sword," says Mahomet, "is the key of heaven and hell; a drop of blood shed in the cause of God, a night spent in arms, is of more avail than two months of fasting and prayer; whoever falls in battle, his sins are forgiven; at the day of judgment his wounds shall be resplendent as vermilion, and odoriferous as musk; and the loss of his limbs shall be supplied by the wings of angels and cherubim."

In a few years, Mahomet subdued all Arabia and a part of Syria. In the midst of his victories, he died at the age of 63, A. D. 632, being poisoned, as it was supposed, by a Jewish female. He was buried on the spot where he expired, but his remains were afterwards removed to Medina, whither innumerable pilgrims to Mecca often turn aside to bow in devotion before the humble tomb of their prophet. His successors extended their conquests and religion till their empire was widely extended in many countries of the east; and in the eighth century threatened the conquest of Europe, and the extermination of Christianity.

---

30. An Account of the Koran.

The *Koran* or *Alcoran*, the sacred book of the Mahometans, contains the revelations and doctrines of their pretended prophet.

The great doctrine of the Koran is the unity of God; to restore which, Mahomet pretended was the chief end of his mission; it being laid down by him as a fundamental truth, that there never was, nor ever can be, more than one true orthodox religion; that, though the particular laws or ceremonies are only temporary, and subject to alteration according to the divine direction, yet the substance of it, being eternal truth, is not liable to change, but continues immutably the same; and that, whenever this religion became neglected or corrupted in essential, God had the goodness to reinform and readmonish mankind thereof, by several prophets, of whom Moses and Jesus were the most distinguished, till the appearance of Mahomet, who is their seal, and no other to be expected after him. The more effectually to engage people to hearken to him, a great part of the Koran is employed in relating examples of dreadful punishments, formerly inflicted by God on those who rejected and abused his messengers; several of which stories, or some circumstances of them, are taken from the Old and New Testaments, but many more from the apocryphal books and traditions of the Jews and Christians of those ages, set up in their Koran as truths, in opposition to the Scriptures, which the Jews and Christians are charged with having altered; and, indeed, few or none of the relations of circumstances in the Koran were invented by Mahomet, as is generally supposed; it being easy to trace the greatest part of them much higher, as the rest might be, were more of these books extant, and were it worth while to make the inquiry. The rest of the

Alcoran is taken up in prescribing necessary laws and directions, frequent admonitions to moral and divine virtues, the worship and reverence of the Supreme Being, and resignation to his will. There are also a great number of occasional passages in the Alcoran, relating only to particular emergencies. For, by his piecemeal method of receiving and delivering his revelations, Mahomet had this advantage—that, whenever he happened to be perplexed with any thing, he had a certain resource in some new morsel of revelation. It was an admirable contrivance to bring down the whole Alcoran only to the lowest heaven, not to earth; since, had the whole been published at once, innumerable objections would have been made, which it would have been impossible for him to have solved; but as he received it by parcels, as God saw fit they should be published for the conversion and instruction of the people, he had a sure way to answer all emergencies, and extricate himself with honour from any difficulty which might occur.

It is the common opinion, that Mahomet, assisted by one Sergius, a monk, composed this book; but the Mussulmans believe, as an article of their faith, that the prophet, who, they say, was an illiterate man, had no concern in inditing it; but that it was given him by God, who to that end made use of the ministry of the angel Gabriel; that, however, it was communicated to him by little and little, a verse at a time, and in different places, during the course of twenty-three years. "And hence," say they, "proceed that disorder and confusion visible in the work;" which, in truth, are so great, that all their doctors have never been able to adjust them; for Mahomet, or rather his copyist, having put all the loose verses promiscuously in a book together, it was impossible ever to retrieve the order wherein they were delivered. These twenty-three years which the angel employed in conveying the Alcoran to Mahomet, are of wonderful service to his followers; inasmuch as they furnish them with an answer to such as charge them with those glaring contradictions of which the book is full, and which they piously father upon God himself; alleging that, in the course of so long a time, he repealed and altered several doctrines and precepts which the prophet had before received of him.

The Alcoran, while Mahomet lived, was kept only in loose sheets. His successor, Abubeker, first collected them into a volume, and committed the keeping of it to Haphsa, the widow of Mahomet, in order to be consulted as an original; and there being a good deal of diversity between the several copies already dispersed throughout the provinces, Ottoman, successor of Abubeker, procured a great number of copies to be taken from that of Haphsa, at the same time suppressing all the others not conformable to the original.

The Mahometans have a positive theology built on the Alcoran and tradition, as well as a scholastical one built on reason. They have likewise their casuists, and a kind of canon law, wherein they distinguish between what is of divine and what of positive right. They have their beneficiaries, too; chaplains, almoners, and canons, who read a chapter every day, out of the Alcoran, in their mosques, and have prebends annexed to their office. The *hatif* of the mosque is what we call the parson of the parish; and the *scheiks* are the preachers, who take their texts out of the Alcoran.

It is of general belief among the Mahometans, that the Koran is of divine origin; nay, that it is eternal and uncreated; remaining, as some express it, in the very essence of God; and the first transcript has been from everlasting, near God's throne, written on a table of vast bigness, called the *preserved table*, in which are also recorded the divine decrees, past and future; that a copy from this table, in one volume upon paper, was, by the ministry of the angel Gabriel, sent down to the lowest heaven, in the month of Ramadan, on the night of *power*, from whence Gabriel revealed it to Mahomet in parcels, some at Mecca, and some at Medina, at different times, during the space of twenty-three years, as the exigency of affairs required; giving him, however, the consolation to show him the whole (which they tell us was bound in silk, and adorned with gold and precious stones of paradise) once a year; but in the last year of his life he had the favour to see it twice. They say, that only ten chapters were delivered entire, the rest being revealed piecemeal, and written down from time to time by the prophet's amanuensis, in such a part of such and such a chapter, till they were completed, according to the directions of the angel. The first parcel that was revealed is generally agreed to have been the first five verses of the ninety-sixth chapter. In fine, the book of the Alcoran is held in the highest esteem and reverence among the Mussulmans. They dare not so much as touch the Alcoran without being first washed, or legally purified; to insure which, an inscription is put on the cover or label—*Let none touch but they who are clean.* It is read with great care and respect, being never held below the girdle. They swear by it; take omens from it on all weighty occasions; carry it with them to war; write sentences of it on their banners; adorn it with precious stones; and will not knowingly suffer it to be in the possession of any of a different religion.

The following is the Mahometans' belief respecting the destination of the righteous and wicked after death. They hold that both these characters must first pass the bridge called in Arabic *Al Sirat*, which, they say, is laid over the midst of hell, and described to be finer than a hair, and sharper than the edge of a sword; so that it seems very difficult to conceive how any one shall be able to stand upon it. For this reason, most of the sect of the Motazalites reject it as a fable; though the orthodox think it a sufficient proof of the truth of this article, that it was seriously affirmed by him who never asserted a falsehood, meaning their prophet; who, to add to the difficulty of the passage, has likewise declared, that this bridge is beset on each side with briers and hooked thorns, which will, however, be no impediment to the good; for they shall pass with wonderful ease and swiftness, like lightning, or the wind, Mahomet and his

Moslems leading the way; whereas the wicked, in consequence of the slipperiness and extreme narrowness of the path, the entangling of the thorns, and the extinction of the light which directed the former to paradise, will soon miss their footing, and fall down headlong into hell, which is gaping beneath them.—*Extracted from Buck's Dict.*

---

31. Venerable Bede, the English Presbyter.

Bede was born in England about the year 672, and was so distinguished for his piety and humility, that he acquired the surname of "Venerable." Losing both his parents at the age of seven years, he was, by the care of relations, placed in the monastery of Wiremouth, was there educated with much strictness, and appears to have been devoted to the service of God from his youth. He was afterwards removed to the neighbouring monastery of Jerrow, where he ended his days. He was looked on as the most learned man of his time. Prayer, writing, and teaching were his familiar employments during his whole life. He was ordained deacon in the nineteenth, and presbyter in the thirtieth year of his age. He gave himself wholly to the study of the Scriptures, the instruction of disciples, the offices of public worship, and the composition of religious and literary works.

His character was celebrated through the western world; the bishop of Rome invited him warmly to the metropolis of the church; but in the eyes of Bede the great world had no charms. It does not appear that he ever left England; and, however infected with the fashionable devotion to the Roman see, he was evidently sincere and disinterested.

The catalogue of Bede's works exhibits the proofs of his amazing industry. Genuine godliness, rather than taste and genius, appear on the face of his writings. His labours in the sciences show a love of learning, however inconsiderable his acquisitions must appear, in comparison with the attainments of the present age.

FLIGHT OF MAHOMET

Being opposed in propagating his doctrines, Mahomet fled from Mecca to Medina A.D. 632. from this period Mahometism rapidly progressed.

PETER THE HERMIT

Encouraged by Pope Urban 2d. succeeded in rousing all classes of men in Christendom to engage in a Crusade to recover the Holy Land.

In his last sickness, he was afflicted with a difficulty of breathing for two weeks. His mind, however, was serene and cheerful; his affections were heavenly; and amidst these infirmities, he daily taught his disciples. A great part of the night was employed in prayer and thanksgiving; and the first employment of the morning was to ruminate on the Scriptures, and to address his God in prayer; "God scourgeth every son whom he receiveth," was frequently in his mouth. Even amidst his bodily weakness, he was employed in writing two little treatises. Perceiving his end to draw near, he said, "If my Maker please, I will go to him from the flesh, who, when I was not, formed me out of nothing. My soul desires to see Christ, my king, in his beauty." He sang glory to the Father, the Son, and the Holy Ghost, and expired with a sedateness, composure, and devotion, that amazed all who saw and heard.

A year before our presbyter's death, he wrote a letter to Egbert, archbishop of York, which deserves to be immortalized for the solid sense it exhibits, a quality with which Bede was very eminently endowed.

"Above all things," says he, "avoid useless discourse, and apply yourself to the Holy Scriptures, especially the epistles to Timothy and Titus; to Gregory's pastoral care, and his homilies on the gospel. It is indecent for him who is dedicated to the service of the church, to give way to actions or discourse unsuitable to his character. Have always those about you who may assist you in temptation; be not like some bishops, who love to have those about them who love good cheer, and divert them with trifling and facetious conversation.

"Your diocese is too large to allow you to go through the whole in a year; therefore appoint presbyters in each village, to instruct and administer the sacraments; and let them be studious, that every one of them may learn by heart the creed and the Lord's prayer; and that if they do not understand Latin, they may repeat them in their own tongue. I have translated them into

English, for the benefit of English presbyters. I am told that there are many villages in our nation, in the mountainous parts, the inhabitants of which have never seen a bishop or pastor; and yet they are obliged to pay their dues to the bishop.

"The best means to reform our church, is to increase the number of bishops. Who sees not how much more reasonable it is for numbers to share this burden? Gregory, therefore, directed Augustine to appoint twelve bishops, to be under the archbishop of York, as their metropolitan. I wish you would fill up this number, with the assistance of the king of Northumberland.

"I know it is not easy to find an empty place for the erection of a bishopric. You may choose some monastery for the purpose. In truth, there are many places which have the name of monasteries without deserving it."

He goes on to show how, for thirty years past, the scandalous abuse of monasteries had prevailed, and how useless many of them were to church and state, as they preserved neither piety nor decency. He directs Egbert to see that his flock be instructed in Christian faith and practice, and that they frequently attend on the communion. He finds fault with the excessive multiplication of monks, and expresses his fears, lest, in process of time, the state should be destitute of soldiers to repel an invasion.

---

32. The dark Ages.

From the seventh to the tenth century of the Christian era was a time of universal darkness, ignorance, and superstition, among all classes of people. Pure Christianity was but little known, amidst a multitude of idle ceremonies, external show, and pomp; all ranks of the clergy were characterized by ambition, voluptuousness, and ignorance. The want of an acquaintance with the first rudiments of literature, even among the higher clergy, was so general, that it was scarcely deemed disgraceful to acknowledge it, and many bishops who attended councils, &c. could not even write their names to the acts that were passed, but were obliged to have others sign for them. This time is emphatically called the *Dark Ages*, especially the tenth century, which all historians, civil and ecclesiastical, agree in describing as the darkest epoch in the annals of mankind. "Every thing sacred in religion," says a celebrated historian, "was disfigured by customs the most ridiculous and extravagant. In several churches in France a festival was celebrated in commemoration of the Virgin Mary's flight into Egypt: it was called the Feast of the Ass. A young girl, richly dressed, with a child in her arms, was placed on an ass, superbly decorated with trappings. The ass was led to the altar in solemn procession—high mass was said with great pomp—the ass was taught to kneel at a proper place—a hymn no less childish than impious was sung in his praise; and when the ceremony was ended, the priest, instead of the usual words with which he dismissed the people, brayed three times like an ass; and the people, instead of the usual response, brayed three times in return."*

"The history of the Roman pontiffs that lived in this century," says Mosheim, "is a history of so many monsters, and not of men; and exhibits a horrible series of the most flagitious, tremendous, and complicated crimes, as all writers, even those of the Roman community, unanimously confess. Nor was the state of things much better in the Greek church at this period; Theophylact, patriarch of Constantinople, sold every ecclesiastical benefice as soon as it became vacant, and had in his stables above two thousand hunting horses, which he fed with pignuts, pistachois, dates, dried grapes, figs, steeped in the most exquisite wines, to all of which he added the richest perfumes."

The method of propagating Christianity during this

* History of Charles V., vol. i.

period partook of the character of the age. Whole nations were compelled, under pain of death, to receive baptism, and the most cruel methods were used to compel them to receive the Christian faith.

33. Massacre by the Saracens.

Forty-two persons of Armorian, in Upper Phrygia, were martyred in the year 845, by the Saracens; the circumstances of which are thus related:

"In the reign of Theophilus the Saracens ravaged many parts of the eastern empire, gained considerable advantages over the Christians, and at length laid siege to the city of Armorian. The garrison bravely defended the place for a considerable time, and would have obliged their enemies to raise the siege, but the place was betrayed by a renegado. Many were put to the sword; and two general officers with some persons of distinction were carried prisoners to Bagdat, where they were loaded with chains and thrown into a dungeon. They continued in prison for some time without seeing any persons but their jailers, having scarcely food enough for their subsistence. At length they were informed that nothing could preserve their lives but renouncing their religion and embracing Mahometanism. To induce them to comply, the caliph pretended zeal for their welfare, and declared he looked upon converts in a more glorious light than conquests. Agreeably to these maxims, he sent some of the most artful of the Mahometans, with money and clothes, and the promise of other advantages that they might secure to themselves by an abjuration of Christianity; which, according to the casuistry of the infidels, might be made without quitting their faith; but the martyrs rejected the proposal with contempt. After this they were attacked with that fallacious and delusive argument which the Mahometans still use in favour of themselves, and were desired to judge of the merits of the cause by the success of those engaged in it, and choose that religion which they saw flourished most, and was best rewarded with the good things of this life, which they called the blessings of heaven. Yet the noble prisoners were proof against all these temptations, and argued strenuously against the authority of the false prophets. This incensed the Mahometans, and drew greater hardships upon the Christians during their confinement, which lasted seven years. Boidizius, the renegado who had betrayed Armorian, then brought them the welcome news that their sufferings would conclude in martyrdom next day. When taken from their dungeon they were again solicited to embrace the tenets of Mahomet; but neither threats nor promises could induce them to espouse the doctrines of an impostor. Perceiving that their faith could not by any means be shaken, the caliph ordered them to be executed. Theodore, one of the number, had formerly received priest's orders, and officiated as a clergyman; but afterwards quitting the church, he had followed a military life, and raised himself by the sword to some considerable posts, which he enjoyed at the time he was taken prisoner. The officer who attended the execution being apprized of these circumstances, said to Theodore, "You might, indeed, pretend to be ranked amongst the Christians while you served in their church as a priest; but the profession you have taken up, which engages you in bloodshed, is so contrary to your former employment, that you should not now think of passing upon us for one of that religion. When you quitted the altar for the camp you renounced Jesus Christ. Why then will you dissemble any longer? Would you not act more conformably to your own principles, and make your conduct all of a piece, if you came to a resolution of saving your life by owning our prophet?" Theodore, covered with religious confusion at this reproach, but still unshaken in his faith, made the following answer: "It is true," said he, "I did in some measure abandon my God when I engaged in the army, and scarce deserve the name of a Christian. But the Almighty has given me grace to see myself in a true light, and made me sensible of my fault; and I hope he will be pleased to accept my life as the only sacrifice I can now offer to expiate my guilt." This pious answer confounded the officer, who only replied that he should presently have an opportunity of giving that proof of his fidelity to his master. Upon which Theodore and the rest, forty-two in number, were beheaded."—*Fox's Martyrs.*

---

34. Greek Church.

This church was so called in contradistinction from the Latin, or Romish church. About the middle of the ninth century a controversy, which began in the sixth century, was carried on with great spirit between these two churches, concerning the "*procession of the Holy Ghost.*" The Romish church maintained that the Spirit proceeded from the Father *and* the Son; while the Greek Christians maintained that he proceeded from the Father *by* or *through* the Son. In 1054 the heat engendered by this controversy resulted in the final separation of the *eastern* and *western*, or, as they are termed, the Greek and Latin churches; from which date the Greek church took its rise.

Until 1453 the state of this church was deplorable. On the one hand, the Mahometan power was making rapid inroads upon her dominions, converting her churches into mosques, and by bribes and terrors alluring or compelling her friends to adopt the religion of the impostor. On the other hand, the fanatic crusaders poured in from the west, avowedly to recover her lost territory, but in reality to spread a deeper moral corruption than existed before.

In 1453 the empire of the Greeks was overthrown by Mahomet II., since which period the Greek church has been under Turkish bondage, until their religion has become but little better than a succession of idle ceremonies.

In 1589 the Russian church separated from the *government*, though not from the communion of the Greek church; by which separation the latter became considerably limited in extent. Her people are now scattered over a considerable part of Greece, the Ionian Isles, Wallachia, Moldavia, Egypt, Abyssinia, Nubia, Lybia, Arabia, Syria, Cilicia, and Palestine.

Repeated, yet unavailing efforts have been made by the Romish church to restore the Greek church to their faith and fellowship. But the latter has ever been unyielding. It denies the authority of the pope; that the former is the true church; abhors the doctrines of purgatory by fire—graven images—and the celibacy of the clergy.

The Greek church receives the doctrines of the Trinity, and most of the articles of the Nicene and Athanasian creeds; rests much on the "procession of the Holy Ghost;" uses pictures in its worship; invokes saints; has seven sacraments; has a fast or festival almost every day in the year; knows of no regeneration but baptism; and believes in transubstantiation.

The head of this church is the patriarch of Constantinople; who is elected by twelve bishops and confirmed by the Grand Vizier. The other patriarchs are those of Damascus, Cairo, and Jerusalem. The secular clergy are subject to no rules, and never rise higher than high priests. This church has a few nunneries and a great many convents of monks, who are all priests, and obliged to follow some handicraft employment, and generally lead a very austere life.

---

35. Empire of the Assassins.

This singular sect (from which the familiar term *assassin* is derived) was formed in the eleventh century, the object of which was to expel the Mahometan religion and government by establishing an empire of their own.

The founder of this society, that for more than a century and a half filled Asia with terror and dismay, was the celebrated Hassan Ben Sahab, who was one of those characters that appear from time to time in the world, as if sent to operate some great change in the destinies of mankind.

Having strengthened himself by a large number of followers, Hassan looked about for some strong position as a centre from which he might gradually extend his possessions; and he fixed his eye upon the hill-fort of Alamoot, in Persia, situated in the district of Roodbar, to the north of Kasveen. Alamoot was gained partly by force and partly by stratagem: he first sent thither one of his most trusty missionaries, who converted a great number of the inhabitants, and with their aid expelled the governor.

In possession of a strong fortress, Hassan turned his mind to the organization of that band of followers whose daggers were to spread the dread and the terror of his power throughout Asia. Experience and reflection had shown him that the many could never be governed by the few without the salutary curb of religion and morality; that a system of impiety, though it might serve to overturn, was not calculated to maintain and support a throne; and his object was now to establish a fixed and lasting dominion. Though he had been long satisfied of the nothingness of religion, he determined to maintain among his followers the religion of Islam in all its rigour. The most exact and minute observances of even its most trivial ordinances was to be required from those who, generally unknown to themselves, were banded for its destruction; and the veil of mystery, within which few were permitted to enter, shrouded the secret doctrine from the eyes of the major part of the society. The claims of Ismail (a Mahometan devotee), the purity of religion were ostensibly advanced; but the rise of Hassan Sahab, and the downfall of all religion, were the real objects of those who directed the machinery.

The Ismailite doctrine had hitherto been disseminated by missionaries and companions alone. Heads without hands were of no avail in the eyes of Hassan; it was necessary to have a third class, which, ignorant of the secret doctrine, would be the blind and willing instruments of the designs of their superiors. This class were named the Fedavee or Devoted, were clothed in white, with red bonnets or girdles, and armed with daggers. These were the men who, reckless of their lives, executed the bloody mandates of the Sheikhel Jebel, the title assumed by Hassan. As a proof of the fanaticism that Hassan contrived to instil into his followers, we give the following instance.

In the year 1126, Kasim-ed-devlet Absoncor, the brave prince of Mosul, was, as he entered the mosque, attacked by eight assassins disguised as dervises; he killed three, and the rest, with the exception of one young man, were massacred by the people; but the prince had received his death wound. When the news spread that Kasim-ed-devlet had fallen by the hand of the assassins, the mother of the young man who had escaped painted and adorned herself, rejoicing that her son had been found worthy to offer up his life in support of the good cause; but when he came back the only survivor, she cut off her hair and blackened her face, through grief that he had not shared the death of glory.

A display of the means by which the chief of the assassins succeeded in infusing this spirit of strong faith and devotion into his followers, forms an interesting chapter in the history of man.

Of those who fell in executing the orders of their superiors, it was said that the gates of paradise were unfolded, and that they entered into the enjoyment of the ivory palace, the silken robe, and the black-eyed houries; and to increase their longing after the joys of paradise, and a disregard of earthly existence, Hassan made use of the following means:—There was at Alamoot, and also at Masiat, in Syria, a delicious garden, encompassed with lofty walls, adorned with trees and flowers of every kind—with murmuring brooks and translucent lakes—with bowers of roses and trellices of vines—airy halls and splendid kiosks, furnished with the carpets of Persia, and the silks of Byzantium. Beautiful maidens and blooming boys were the inhabitants of this delicious spot, which ever resounded with the melody of birds, the murmur of streams, and the ravishing tones of voices and instruments; all respired contentment and pleasure. When the chief had noticed any youth to be distinguished for strength and resolution, he invited him to a banquet, where he placed him beside himself, conversed with him on the happiness reserved for the faithful, and contrived to administer an intoxicating draught prepared from the hyoscyamus. While insensible, he was conveyed into the garden of delight, and there awakened by the application of vinegar. On opening his eyes, all paradise met his view; the black-eyed and green-robed houries surrounded him, obedient to his wishes; sweet music filled his ears; the richest viands were served up in the most costly vessels; and the choicest wines sparkled in the golden cups. The fortunate youth believed himself really in the paradise of the prophet, and the language of his attendants confirmed the delusion. When he had had his fill of enjoyment, and nature was yielding to exhaustion, the opiate was again administered, and the sleeper transported back to the side of the chief, to whom he communicated what had passed, who assured him of the truth and reality of all he had experienced, telling him such was the bliss reserved for the obedient servants of the Imaum, and enjoining at the same time the strictest secrecy. Ever after, the rapturous vision possessed the imagination of the deluded enthusiast, and he panted for the hour when death, received in obeying the commands of his superiors, should dismiss him to the bowers of paradise.

The power of Hassan soon began to display itself. By force or by treachery, the castles or hill-forts of Persia fell one after another into his hands. A bloody period ensued; the doctors of the Mahometan law excommunicated the adherents of Hassan, and the sultan, Melek Shah, directed his generals to reduce their fortresses; the daggers of the assassins were displayed against the swords of the orthodox Mahometans, and the first victim to Hassan's revenge was the great and good Nizam-ul-mulk, who fell by the dagger of a

Fedavee. His death was followed by that of his master, not without strong suspicion of poison. "The governments were arrayed in open enmity against the order, and heads fell like an abundant harvest, beneath the two-fold sickle of assassination and the sword of justice."*

After a reign of thirty-five years, Hassan Sahab saw his power extended over a great portion of the Mahometan world, which continued under his successors till they were overthrown by the Tartars.

---

36. Crusades, or Holy Wars.

The crusades were religious wars, waged by Christian Europe, chiefly against the Turks or Mahometans, with a view to recover Palestine out of their hands These expeditions commenced, A. D. 1095. The foundation of them was a superstitious veneration for those places where our Saviour performed his miracles, and accomplished the work of man's redemption.

Palestine having been conquered by the Turks, Jerusalem was now in their hands, which rendered it unsafe and vexatious to the pilgrims, who flocked from all parts, to visit the tomb of our Saviour.

Peter the hermit, a native of France, on his return from his pilgrimage, complained in loud terms of the grievances the Christians suffered from the Turks. He conceived the project of leading all the forces of Christendom against the infidels, and driving them out of the Holy Land. Being encouraged in his project by pope Urban II.,† Peter went from province to province, and

---

* Von Hammer's Hist. of the Assassins.

† As the popes were the great promoters of these holy wars, so to them accrued the chief advantages which resulted from them. By means of them, they greatly increased their temporal authority; they being in fact the military commanders in these extravagant enterprises, while emperors and kings were only subordinate officers. The crusades were sources, also, of incalculable wealth to the popes, to the churches and monasteries; for to them the pious crusaders bequeathed their lands, houses, and money; and as few of them ever returned, they became their lawful possessions.—*Goodrich's Eccl. Hist.*

succeeded in arousing princes and people to undertake this holy warfare. All ranks of men, now deeming the crusades the only road to heaven, were impatient to open the way with their swords to the holy city. Nobles, artizans, peasants, and even priests enrolled their names; and to decline this service was branded with the reproach of impiety or cowardice. The infirm and aged contributed by presents and money, and many attended it in person; being determined, if possible, to breathe their last in the sight of the holy city. Even women, concealing their sex under the disguise of armour, attended the camp; and the greatest criminals were forward in a service which they considered as an expiation for all crimes.

In the first crusade, an army of 80,000 men, a disorderly multitude, led on by Peter, were destroyed; but the army which followed, consisting of 700,000 men, under Godfrey, conquered Syria and Palestine, and took possession of Jerusalem, which they held for several years. The crusaders, however, weakened their power by dividing their conquests into four separate states.

In this situation they found it necessary to solicit aid from Europe, and accordingly, in 1146, an army of 200,000 men, under Hugh, brother to the French king, set out upon another crusade. But these met with the same fate as the army of Peter. Another army of 300,000 soon followed, and were soon destroyed or dispersed.

Palestine having fallen into the hands of the infidels, under the great Saladin, Europe felt the indignity, and France, England, Germany, each sent forth an army headed by its own sovereign. Richard I. of England bore the weight of the contest, and defeated Saladin, on the plains of Ascalon.

The fourth crusade took place in 1202, and was directed against the Greek empire. The fifth was against Egypt, in revenge for an attack on Palestine by its sultan. But this expedition, like the rest, was ruinous in the end.

It is computed that, in the whole of the crusades to

Palestine, two millions of Europeans were buried in the east.

When Jerusalem was taken, the crusaders were guilty of the most shocking barbarities; the numerous garrisons were put to the sword, and the inhabitants were massacred without mercy, and without distinction. No age nor sex were spared, not even sucking children. What shows the blind enthusiasm which animated those ferocious conquerors is, their behaviour after this terrible slaughter. They marched over heaps of dead bodies towards the Holy Sepulchre; and while their hands were polluted with the blood of so many innocent persons, sung anthems to the common Saviour of mankind!

---

37. Chivalry, or Knighthood.

Chivalry, or knighthood, was an institution common to Europe during the middle ages, having principally for its objects the correction of those evils that were peculiar to the state of society which then existed. It sought to support the weak, to protect the oppressed, to restrain the lawless, to refine the rude, to avenge wrongs, and especially to maintain the rights and defend the purity of the female sex. In its elements, it combined bravery, honour, courtesy, love and religion.

Knighthood was certainly a distinction of society before the days of Charlemagne. But it wanted religion. When it began to be marked by religious rites, it formed a religious institution. Its union with religion took place somewhere between the ninth and eleventh centuries. Its character was raised and perfected by the crusades.

Knighthood was always, and essentially, a personal distinction, and in this respect, different from nobility. The nobility of Europe were the lords of particular districts of country, and although originally they held their dignities only for life, yet their title soon became hereditary.

Every person of noble birth was required, when twelve years old, to take a solemn oath, before the bishop of his diocese, to defend the oppressed, &c. This was ordained at the council of Clermont, in the eleventh century; thus giving a public and sacred sanction to the humanities of chivalry. But besides the nobility, others might be promoted to the order, by meritorious valour. Almost the whole of Europe was affected with the chivalric spirit. It flourished most, however, in France, Spain, and Germany, and more early developed itself, as a fixed principle of action, in these countries than in others. England, at length, was not undistinguished for its chivalry.

There were three degrees in the chivalry of Europe: knights bannerets, knights, and esquires. The full dignity of knighthood was seldom conferred on a squire before the age of twenty-one. The ceremonies of inauguration were solemn. The preparation consisted in prayer, confession, and fasting; was accompanied by clothing him with a white dress, which was considered symbolical of the purity of his new character; and by throwing over him a red garment, which was to mark his resolution to shed his blood in the cause of heaven. These and other rites were a necessary preliminary.

A church, or hall of a castle, was generally the place of inauguration. The candidate first offered his sword to the priest, who blessed it. Before it was returned to him he took his oaths of chivalry. He solemnly swore to defend the church, to attack the wicked, to respect the priesthood, to protect woman and the poor, to preserve the country in tranquillity, and to shed his blood, even to the last drop, in behalf of his brethren.

The young warrior having kneeled with clasped hands before the supreme lord in the assembly (a purely feudal ceremony), and having declared his only object, to maintain religion and chivalry, was now invested with all the exterior marks of the order. The knights and ladies of the court attended on him, and delivered to him the various pieces of his harness. The armour varied at different periods and in different countries, but some matters were of permanent usage. The spurs were always put on first, and the sword was belted on last. The concluding sign of being dubbed or adopted into the order of knighthood, was a slight blow given by the lord to the cavalier, and called the acolade, from the part of the body, the neck, whereon it was struck. The lord then proclaimed him a knight, in the name of God and the saints.

In the character of a true knight were combined many virtues and noble endowments. It necessarily included, also, some prominent defects. *Companionship in arms* was a sacred principle, and a knight would fly to the relief of his companion in arms, even were his services demanded by a female at the time. His valour was connected with modesty, and both were, in the highest degree, conspicuous. In chivalric war, much humanity was displayed; though in contentions of a different kind, it was unhappily suppressed. As a knight fought for the church, he was intolerant, and towards infidels and heretics he ceased to exhibit his wonted forbearance. His sense of honour was keen, and his independence was consistent with discipline and submission. His whole course was dictated by a regard to religion. His devotions were frequent. Religion entered into all the observances of chivalry; but it was only the religion of the times—a form rather than spirit—too corrupt to be a safe guide. The knight, finally, was characterized by a very remarkable fidelity to obligations, by generosity, and by courtesy.

The latter principle, like every other blessing of modern times, had its origin in the Christian religion. The world thought that courtesy and chivalry accorded together, and that villanous and foul words were contrary to an order which was founded in piety.

Chivalry had its various orders or associations of cavaliers, formed for specific purposes, generally of a benevolent character. Ten of them remain to the present time. Most of the present orders are otherwise than of a chivalric origin. The orders of chivalry were of two general descriptions, viz. religious and military. They extended over various countries, particularly the Holy Land, England, Spain, France, and Italy. Some of the religious orders were those of the Templars, St. James, Calatrava, Alcantrava, the Lady of Mercy, and St. Michael. In the religious orders, the cavaliers were bound by three great monastic vows, of chastity, poverty, and obedience.

The military orders were imitations of the religious. Those of the Garter, the Golden Fleece, and St. Michael, in France, were clearly of chivalric origin. Many others that now exist cannot boast of such a descent. All these institutions had particular rules by which they professed to be governed, but they varied with the spirit of the times.

It is difficult to define the precise period of the duration of chivalry. It was a light which was kindled in a dark age, and it went out when that age was beginning to be brightened with superior luminaries. Viewing the subject in its great and leading bearings, chivalry may be said to be coeval with the middle ages of Europe, and all its power ceased when new systems of warfare were matured, when the revival of letters was complete and general, and the reformation of religion gave a new subject for the feelings and thoughts of men.—*Robbins' Ancient and Modern History.*

---

38. Dramatic Mysteries, or Scriptural Plays.

These mysteries or miracle plays, as they were indifferently called, were dramatic illustrations of various scenes taken from the Bible; and in the middle centuries were common in every country in Europe.

How, or at what time, precisely, these plays were first introduced into England, cannot be ascertained, although there is good evidence of such exhibitions having taken place as far back as the eleventh century. As Coventry and Chester became particularly famous for these exhibitions during the middle ages, a description of the performances described as having there taken place may not be uninteresting.

The *Pageant*, or moving exhibition of the Chester and Coventry games, was a modern building of two stories, on wheels, which was drawn by men from street to street. It was also customary to have scaffolds or stages in the streets, for the accommodation of the spectators, probably those of better quality; and these scaffolds were also on wheels and moved with the pageant. In the lower room of the pageant, which contained also the machinery for raising storms, representing the infernal regions, &c. the players "apparalled themselves," says old archdeacon Rogers, "and in the higher room they played, beinge all open at the tope, that all behoulders might hear and see them. The places where they played them was in every streete. They begane first at the Abay-gates (at Chester), and when the first pagiante was played, it was wheeled to the High Crosse before the mayor, and soe to every streete, and soe every streete had a pagiante playinge before them at one time, till all the pagiantes for the daye appoynted were played; and when one pagiante was neare ended, word was broughte from streete to streete, that soe they mighte come in place thereof, exceedinge orderlye, and all the streetes have their pagiantes afore them all at one time, playeinge togeather; to se wich playes was great resorte, and also scafoldes and stages made in the streetes in those places where they determined to playe theire pagiantes."

Whatever we most reverence, and all that we adore, was debased and travestied in these wretched, and as they must appear to us, most impious performances. Not only the first parents of mankind, patriarchs, apostles, and angels, were perpetually introduced on the stage, but even the personification of God the Father, of Christ, and of the Holy Ghost, was equally common. Nor were heavenly personages alone introduced. The great one of evil, and his attendant demons, figured in the pageant of doomsday; and Satan was indeed usually a particular favourite with the spectators. In the ancient religious plays, says Malone, the devil was very frequently introduced. He was usually represented with horns, a very wide mouth (by means of a mask), staring eyes, a large nose, a red beard, cloven feet and a tail. His constant attendant was the Vice (the buffoon of the piece), whose principal employment was to belabour the devil with his wooden dagger, and to make him roar for the entertainment of the populace.

The following passage from the MS. life of John Shaw, vicar of Rotherham, curiously illustrates the state of religious knowledge in Lancashire, even late in the sixteenth century.

"I found," says he, "a very large spacious church, with scarce any seats in it; a people very ignorant, and yet willing to learn; so I had frequently some thousands of hearers. I catechised in season and out of season. The churches were so thronged at nine in the morning, that I had much ado to get to the pulpit. One day, an old man of sixty, sensible enough in other things, and living in the parish of Cartmel, coming to me on some business, I told him that he belonged to my care and charge, and I desired to be informed in his knowledge of religion. I asked him how many Gods there were? He said, he knew not. I, informing him, asked again how he thought to be saved. He answered, he could not tell; yet thought that was a harder question than the other. I told him that the way to salvation was by Jesus Christ, God-man, who, as he was a man, shed his blood for us on the cross, &c. 'Oh sir,' said he, 'I think I heard of that man you speak of, once, in a play at Kendall, called Corpus Christi's play, where there was a man on a tree, and blood ran down,' &c. And afterwards, he professed he could not remember that he ever heard of salvation by Jesus, but in that play."

The entries of payments to the players are almost always made in the name of the character and not of the performer. In the pageant of the Crucifixion, Pilate was evidently considered the most important character; for we find his representative constantly receiving 3*s*. 4*d*., and sometimes 4*s*., the highest sum paid to any player in the same pageant. Herod was also a prominent character, receiving usually 3*s*. 4*d*. The "Devil and Judas" are paired, with 1*s*. 6*d*. between them; and "Peter and Malchus" are similarly coupled for a less sum. At another time, the performer of this last character was rewarded only with 4*d*. Once we have a payment of 4*d*. also, to "Fawston, for hanging Judas," and again to the same accomplished person, "Itm, to Fawston for coc crowing, iiijd." Angels and demons, "savyd and dampnyd sowles," "pattryarkys," and "wormes of conscyence," are variously paid.

If such were the wages of the actors, it is amusing to learn the rates at which the playwrights were rewarded. "Robert Croo for ij leaves of ore pley-boke," that is, for adding two leaves of dialogue, receives eight-pence. Again, some one who had written a new part for a character is permitted to rejoice in the receipt of *one penny*. Far otherwise was it that the learned Master Smyth was treated, touching his play of the Destruction of Jerusalem. "For his paynes for writting of the tragedye," he is set down for 13*l*. 6*s*. 8*d*., "a proper round bonus!—a goodly reward! and a mint of money for a poor scholar of those days."

Among a variety of items for dresses, charges for mitres for Annas and Caiaphas are frequent; for by a strange anachronism, these Jewish high-priests seem always to have been arrayed in the habiliments of Christian prelates, and are constantly termed "byshoppis." A quart of wine is charged for the hiring of a gown for Pilate's wife; and "Itm to a reward to Maisturres Grymsby for lending off heir geir ffor Pylatt's wife, xijd." Items for wine and meat, for drinking, breakfasts, dinners, and suppers of the players, are of perpetual recurrence; and once there appears, "Paid Pilate, the bishops, and knights, to drink between the stages." Thus, too, there are charges for wings for the angels, and sundry expenses for washing their albs or white surplices. So also we have charges for mending the devil's hide (vizor); to a chevril gyld for Peter; to 3*lb.* of hair for the devil's coat and hose; and "for velves of canvas for shirts and hose for the blakke sowles, and for colorying the same."

With the spectators, the most favourite part of the machinery of the mysteries, was the exhibition of the infernal regions. Here, accordingly, we have numerous items of charges formaterials; such as "the baryll for the yerthequake." Also, "paid to Crowe for making of iijworldys," 3*s.* 4*d.* (to be set on fire at successive exhibitions), and "payd for setting the world on fyer," 5*d.*; and farther, "Itm, payd for keeping of fire at hell-mothe, 4*d.*," &c. &c.

Such was the passion of our forefathers for all kinds of pompous processions and pageants, and for religious plays in particular, that these arrangements and shows became matters of municipal regulation; and the archives, not only of Coventry, but of Chester, York, and many other places, are full of evidence that the celebration of a series of mysteries was assigned in succession to the different guilds of trade. Each company, or sometimes two or three minor fraternities, had its subject; and the series, which lasted throughout a whole day, or sometimes occupied two or even several entire days, not uncommonly embraced the story of both the Old and New Testament, from the creation to the day of judgment.

---

39. Popish Miracles, Relics, &c.

The following will give some idea of the manner of performing miracles in the Romish church.

"St. Anthony is thought to have had a great command over fire, and a power of destroying, by flashes of that element, those who incurred his displeasure. A certain monk of St. Anthony one day assembled his congregation under a tree where a magpie had built her nest, into which he found means to convey a small box filled with gunpowder, and out of the box hung a long thin match that was to burn slowly, and was hidden among the leaves of the tree. As soon as the monk, or his assistant, had touched the match with a lighted coal, he began his sermon. In the mean time the magpie returned to her nest, and finding in it a strange body which she could not remove, she fell into a passion, and began to scratch with her feet and chatter most unmercifully. The friar affected to hear her without emotion, and continued his sermon with great composure; only he would now and then lift up his eyes towards the top of the tree, as if he wanted to see what was the matter. At last, when he judged that the match was near reaching the gunpowder, he pretended to be quite out of patience; he cursed the magpie, wished St. Anthony's fire might consume her, and went on again with his sermon. But he had scarcely pronounced two or three periods, when the match, all of a sudden, produced its effect, and blew up the magpie with its nest; which miracle wonderfully raised the character of the friar, and proved afterwards very beneficial to him and to his convent.

Galbert, monk of Marchiennes, informs us of a strange act of devotion in his time, and which, indeed, is attested by several cotemporary writers. When the saints did not readily comply with the prayers of their votarists, they flogged their relics with rods, in a spirit of impatience, which they conceived was proper to make them bend into compliance.

When the reformation was spread in Lithuania, Prince Radzivil was so affected, that he went in person to visit the pope, and pay him all possible honours. His holiness on this occasion presented him with a box of precious relics. Having returned home, the report of this invaluable possession was spread: and, at length, some monks entreated permission to try the effects of these relics on a demoniac who had hitherto resisted every kind of exorcism. They were brought into church with solemn pomp, deposited on the altar, and an innumerable crowd attended. After the usual conjurations, which were unsuccessful, they applied to the relics. The demoniac instantly became well. The people cried out "*A miracle!*" and the prince, lifting his hands and eyes to heaven, felt his faith confirmed. In this transport of pious joy, he observed that a young gentleman, who was keeper of this rich treasure of relics, smiled, and appeared by his motions to ridicule the miracle. The prince, with violent indignation, took our young keeper of the relics to task; who, on a promise of pardon, gave the following secret intelligence concerning them:—He assured him that, in travelling from Rome, he had lost the box of relics, and that, not daring to mention it, he had procured a similar one, which he had filled with small bones of cats, and dogs, and other trifles, similar to what was lost. He hoped he might be forgiven for smiling, when he found that such a collection of rubbish was idolized with such pomp, and had even the virtue of expelling demons. It was by the assistance of this box that the prince discovered the gross impositions of the monks and the demoniacs, and he afterwards became a zealous Lutheran.

The following account of the liquefaction of the blood of St. Januarius is related by a respectable eyewitness:—"The grand procession on this occasion was composed of a numerous body of clergy, and an immense number of people of all ranks, headed by the archbishop of Naples himself, who carried the phial containing the blood of the saint. A magnificent robe of velvet, richly embroidered, was thrown over the shoulders of the bust; a mitre, refulgent with jewels, was placed on its head. The archbishop, with a solemn pace, and a look full of awe and veneration, approached, holding forth the sacred phial which contained the precious lump of blood; he addressed the saint in the humblest manner, fervently praying that he would graciously condescend to manifest his regard to his faithful votaries, the people of Naples, by the usual token of ordering that lump of his sacred blood to assume its natural and original form; in these prayers he was joined by the multitude around, particularly by the women. My curiosity prompted me to mingle with the multitude. I got, by degrees, very near the bust. Twenty miuutes had already elapsed since the archbishop had been praying with all possible earnestness, and turning the phial round and round without any effect. An old monk stood near the archbishop, and was at the utmost pains to instruct him how to handle, chafe, and rub the phial; he frequently took it into his own hand, but his manœuvres were as ineffectual as those of the archbishop. By this time the people had become noisy; the women were quite hoarse with praying; the monk continued his operations with increased zeal, and the archbishop was all over in a profuse sweat with vexation. An acquaintance whispered it might be prudent to retire. I directly took the hint, and joined the company I had left. An universal gloom overspread all their countenances. One very beautiful young lady cried and sobbed as if her heart had been ready to break. The passions of some of the rabble without doors took a different turn; instead of sorrow, they were filled with rage and indignation at the saint's obduracy—and some went so far as to call him an *old ungrateful yellow-faced rascal.* It was now almost dark, and, when least expected, the signal was given that the miracle was performed. The populace filled the air with repeated shouts of joy; a band of music began to play; *Te Deum* was sung; couriers were despatched to the royal family (then at Portici) with the glad tidings; the young lady dried up her tears; the countenances of our company brightened in an instant; and they sat down to cards, without further dread of eruptions, earthquakes, or pestilence."

The mysteries, as they were called, or representations of the Divine Being, the crucifixion, &c. were formerly very common in the church of Rome. They served for the amusement and instruction of the people; and so attractive were these gross exhibitions in the dark ages, that they formed one of the principal ornaments of the reception which was given to princes when they entered towns.

In the year 1437, when Conrad Bayer, bishop of Metz, caused the mystery of the Passion to be represented on the plain of Veximiel, near that city, *Christ* was personated by *an old gentleman* named Nicholas Neufchatel, of Tourain, curate of Saint Victory, of Metz, and who was very near expiring on the cross, had he not been timely assisted. He was so enfeebled, that it was agreed another priest should be placed on the cross the next day, to finish the representation of the person crucified, which was done; at the same time, the said Nicholas undertook to perform the resurrection, which being a less difficult task, he did it, it is said, admirably well. Another priest, whose name was John De Nicey, curate of Metrange, personated Judas; and he had liked to have been stifled while he hung upon the tree, for his neck was dislocated; this being at length luckily perceived, he was quickly cut down, and recovered.

Addison, in his travels through Italy, makes mention of a wonderful sermon having been preached to the fishes by the famous St. Anthony, who lived about six hundred years ago, and is the favourite saint of Padua, where a magnificent monument has been erected by the Catholics to his memory.

It seems that when the heretics would not regard his preaching, he betook himself to the sea-shore, where the river Maxechin disembogues itself into the Adriatic. He here called the fish together, in the name of God, that they might hear his holy word. The fish came swimming towards him in such vast shoals, both from the sea and from the river, that the surface of the water was quite covered with their multitudes. They quickly ranged themselves, according to their several species, into a very beautiful congregation, and like so many rational creatures, presented themselves before him to hear the word of God.

After addressing them for a length of time, he concluded in the following words:—"And since for all

HENRY IV. OF GERMANY,

Having displeased Pope Gregory 7th. was compelled by that Pontiff to do penance three days before his residence in the depth of winter.

TORTURE BY THE INQUISITION

This bloody Tribunal in order to extort a confession from its victims often put them to extreme tortures—one method is seen in the engraving

this you cannot employ your tongues in the praises of your benefactor, and are not provided with words to express your gratitude, make at least some sign of reverence; bow yourselves at his name; give some show of gratitude, according to the best of your capacities; express your thanks in the most becoming manner that you are able; and be not unmindful of all the benefits which have been bestowed upon you."

He had no sooner done speaking, but—behold a miracle! the fish, as though they had been endued with reason, bowed down their heads with all the marks of a profound humility and devotion; moving their bodies up and down with a kind of fondness, as approving what had been spoken by the blessed father St. Anthony. The legend adds, that after many heretics, who were present at the miracle, had been converted by it, the saint gave his benediction to the fish, and dismissed them.

---

40. Supremacy of the Pope of Rome.

The Roman Catholics believe the pope of Rome is, under Christ, supreme pastor of the whole church, and has a power and jurisdiction over all Christians. He is called the successor of St. Peter, and is believed to be infallible, that is, he cannot err, when he addresses himself to the faithful on matters of doctrine, &c. The pope is believed by the protestants to be the *Antichrist*, the *Man of Sin*, mentioned in 2 Thess. ii. and Rev. xiii.

"In ages of ignorance and credulity," says a celebrated writer, "the ministers of religion are the objects of superstitious veneration. When the barbarians who overran the Roman empire first embraced the Christian faith, they found the clergy in possession of considerable power; and they naturally transferred to those new guides the profound submission and reverence which they were accustomed to give to the priests of the pagan religion which they had forsaken.

It was about the year 606 that pope Boniface III., by flattering Phocas, the emperor of Constantinople, one of the worst of tyrants, procured for himself the title of *Universal Bishop.* From this time he was raised above all others, and his supremacy was by imperial authority: it was now also that the most profound ignorance, debauchery, and superstition reigned. From this time, the popes exerted all their power in promoting the idolatrous worship of images, saints, relics, and angels. They now took the most blasphemous titles, such as *Christ's Vicegerent, His Holiness, Prince over all Nations and Kingdoms, King of Kings and Lord of Lords, The Lord God the Pope, &c.*

About the year 751, the pope began to establish himself as a *temporal prince,* and to dethrone kings, and put others in their places. Henry IV., emperor of Germany, having displeased pope Gregory VII., the Roman pontiff summoned a council, and passed the following sentence upon him:—"In the name of Almighty God, and by your authority," said Gregory, addressing the members of the council, "I prohibit Henry from governing the Teutonic kingdom of Italy; I release all Christians from their allegiance to him; and I strictly forbid all persons to serve or attend him as king."

When this sentence became known, the greater part of Henry's subjects cast off their allegiance, and appeared against him. Henry was humbled; he came to the resolution of throwing himself at the feet of Gregory, in order to implore his absolution. The pontiff was at that time on a visit to the countess or dutchess Matilda, at Canosa, a fortress on the Appenines. At the gate of this mansion the emperor presented himself as a humble penitent. He alone was admitted within the outer court, where being stripped of his robes, and wrapped in sackcloth, he was compelled to remain three days, in the month of January, A. D. 1077, barefoot and fasting, before he was permitted to kiss the feet of his holiness.

The indulgence was, however, granted him; he was

permitted to throw himself at the feet of the haughty pontiff, who condescended to grant him absolution, after he had sworn obedience in all things, and promised to submit to his solemn decision. The pontiff, elate with triumph, now considered himself as the lord and master of all the crowned heads in Christendom, and said in several of his letters, that "it was his duty to pull down the pride of kings."*

The following is said to be one form of excommunication in the church of Rome. It is called *the pope's dreadful curse.**

"By the authority of God Almighty, the Father, Son, and Holy Ghost, and of the holy canons, and of the undefiled Virgin Mary, the mother and patroness of our Saviour, and of all the celestial virtues, angels, archangels, thrones, dominions, powers, cherubims, and seraphims, and of the holy patriarchs, prophets, and of all the apostles, evangelists, and of the holy innocents, who, in the sight of the holy lamb, are found worthy to sing the new song, and of the holy martyrs and holy confessors, and of the holy virgins, and of all the saints, and together with all the holy and elect of God; we excommunicate and anathematize him or them, malefactor or malefactors, and from the threshold of the holy church of God Almighty we sequester them.

"May the holy choir of the holy virgins, who for the honour of Christ have despised the things of the world, curse him or them; may all the saints who, from the beginning of the world to everlasting ages, are found to be the beloved of God, curse him or them; may the heavens and the earth, and all the holy things remaining therein, curse him or them. May he or they be cursed wherever he or they be; whether in their house or in the field, or in the highway, or in the path, or in the wood, on the water, or in the church; may he or they be cursed in living, in dying, in eating, in drinking, in being hungry, in being thirsty, in fasting, in

* Jones' History of the Christian Church.

* Similar forms of excommunication are used in the Greek church.

lying, in working, in resting, * * * * * *, and in blood-letting; may he or they be cursed inwardly and outwardly; may he or they be cursed in the hair of his or their head; may he or they be cursed in his or their brain; may he or they be cursed in the top of his or their head, in their temples, in their forehead, in their ears, in their eyebrows, in their cheeks, in their jawbones, in their nostrils, in their foreteeth or grinders, in their lips, in their throat, in their shoulders, in their wrists, in their arms, in their hands, in their fingers, in their breast, in their heart, and in all the interior parts, to the very stomach; in their reins, in their groin, in their thighs, * * * * * *, in the hips, in the knees, in the legs, in the feet, in the joints, and in the nails; may he or they be cursed in all their joints, from the top of the head to the sole of the feet; may there not be a soundness in him or them.

"May the Son of the living God, with all the glory of his majesty, curse him or them; and may heaven, with all the powers that move therein, rise against him or them, to damn him or them, unless it shall repent him or them, or that he or they shall make satisfaction. Amen, so be it. Amen."

---

41. Inquisition.

The inquisition is a tribunal in Roman Catholic countries, erected by the popes for the examination and punishment of heretics. This court was founded in the twelfth century, under the patronage of pope Innocent, who issued orders to excite Catholic princes and people to extirpate heretics, to search into their number and quality, and to transmit a faithful account thereof to Rome. Hence, they were called *Inquisitors*, and gave birth to the formidable tribunal called the *Inquisition*.

One of the most celebrated inquisitors was one *Dominic*, who was canonized by the pope, in order to render his authority the more respectable. He and the other inquisitors spread themselves into various countries, and treated the protestants with the utmost severity;

at length the pope, not finding these inquisitors so useful as he had imagined, resolved upon the establishment of fixed and regular courts of inquisition; the first office of which was established in Toulouse, and Dominic became the first regular inquisitor.

Courts of inquisition were also established in several countries; but the Spanish inquisition became the most powerful and dreadful of any. Even the kings of Spain, themselves, though arbitrary in all other respects, were taught to dread the power of the lords of the in-inquisition.

This diabolical tribunal takes cognizance of heresy, Judaism, Mahometanism, sodomy, polygamy, witchcraft, &c. Heresy in their view comprises many subdivisions; and upon the suspicion of any of these, the party is immediately apprehended. Advancing an offensive proposition; failing to impeach others who may advance such; contemning church ceremonies; defacing images; reading books condemned by the *inquisition;* lending such books to others to read; deviating from the ordinary practices of the Roman church; letting a year pass without going to confession; eating meat on fast days; neglecting mass; being present at a sermon preached by a heretic; contracting a friendship with, or making a present to, or assisting a heretic, &c., are all matters of suspicion, and prosecuted accordingly.

In the countries where this dreadful tribunal is established, the people stand in so much fear of it, that parents deliver up their children, husbands their wives and friends, masters their servants, to its officers; without daring in the least to murmer or make resistance. The prisoners are kept a long time, till they themselves turn their own accusers, and declare the cause of their imprisonment, for which they are neither told their crime nor confronted with witnesses. As soon as they are imprisoned, their friends go into mourning, and speak of them as dead, not daring to solicit their pardon, lest they should be brought in as accomplices. When there is no shadow of proof against the pretended criminal, he is discharged, after suffering the most cruel tortures, a tedious and dreadful imprisonment, and the loss of the greater part of his effects. Those who are condemned to death are delivered over to secular power, and perish in the flames.

"Senor Llorente, who was secretary to the inquisition of Madrid about the year 1790, makes the following calculation of the number of victims whom the inquisition has sacrificed;—that during the three hundred years from 1481 to 1781, 31,912 heretics perished in the flames; and adding to this period the years up to the present time, 17,639 effigies have been burned, representing such criminals as the inquisition could not catch for more substantial vengeance—and 291,456 have been condemned to severe penances."*

---

42. Grosseteste, Bishop of Lincoln.

Robert Grosseteste was born about the year 1175, and was a divine of principal note in the university of Oxford. He associated with both the Mendicant orders, and was the first lecturer in the Franciscan school of that seminary. He seems to have been always serious in religion, according to the degree of light which he had.

In the year 1234, he was elected, by the dean and chapter, bishop of Lincoln; and king Henry III. confirmed their choice. He continued to patronize the friars. These were his most intimate companions, with whom he used to hold conferences on the Scriptures; and at one time he had thoughts of entering into the Franciscan order himself. Events, however, occurred, which in some measure unfolded to the eyes of the bishop the real character of the friars. In 1247 two English Franciscans were sent into England to extort money for the pope. They applied to the prelates and abbots, but seem, at this time at least, to have met with little success. Grosseteste was amazed at the insolence

* British Critic.

and pompous appearance of the friars, who assured him that they had the pope's bull, and who earnestly demanded six thousand marks for the contribution of the diocese of Lincoln. "Friars," answered he, "with all reverence be it spoken, the demand is as dishonorable as it is impracticable. The whole body of the clergy and people are concerned in it equally with me. For me, then, to give a definite answer in an instant, to such a demand, before the sense of the kingdom is taken upon it, would be rash and absurd." The native good sense of the bishop suggested this answer; but the true antichristian character of the pope was as yet unknown to Grosseteste. The blood of our Saviour was about the same time pretended to be brought into England, and he had the weakness to vindicate the delusion. In 1248 he obtained at a great expense, from Innocent IV., letters to empower him to reform the religious orders. If he had understood at that time the real character of antichrist, he would have foreseen the vanity of all attempts to reform the churches, which were grounded on papal authority. The rectitude, however, of his own mind, was strikingly apparent in the transaction. He saw with grief the waste of large revenues made by the monastic orders; and being supported by the pope, as he thought, he determined to take into his own hand the rents of the religious houses, most probably with a design to institute and ordain vicarages in his diocese, and to provide for the more general instruction of the people. But the monks appealed to the pope; and Grosseteste, in his old age, was obliged to travel to Lyons, where Innocent resided. Roman venality was now at its height, and the pope determined the cause against the bishop. Grieved and astonished at so unexpected a decision, Grosseteste said to Innocent, "I relied on your letters and promises, but am entirely disappointed."—"What is that to you?" answered the pope; "you have done your part, and we are disposed to favour them. Is your eye evil, because I am good?" With such shameless effrontery can wicked men trifle with scriptural passages. The bishop, in a low tone, but so as to be heard, said with indignation, "O, money, how great is thy power, especially at the court of Rome!" The remark was bold and indignant, but perfectly just. It behooved Innocent to give some answer; and he used the common method of wicked men in such cases, namely, to retort the accusation. "You English," said he, "are always grinding and impoverishing one another. How many religious men, persons of prayer and hospitality, are you striving to depress, that you may sacrifice to your own tyranny and avarice?" So spake the most unprincipled of robbers to a bishop, whose unspotted integrity was admitted by all the world.

The bishop often preached to the people in the course of his perambulation through his diocese; and he required the neighbouring clergy to attend the sermons. He earnestly exhorted them to be laborious in ministering to their flocks; and the lazy Italians, who by virtue of the pope's letters had been intruded into opulent benefices, and who neither understood the language of the people, nor wished to instruct them, were the objects of his detestation. He would often with indignation cast the papal bulls out of his hands, and absolutely refuse to comply with them, saying that he should be the friend of Satan if he committed the care of souls to foreigners. Innocent, however, persisting in his plan, peremptorily ordered him to admit an Italian, perfectly ignorant of the English language, to a very rich benefice in the diocese of Lincoln; which Grosseteste absolutely refused to obey. Innocent, on receiving this positive denial, was incensed beyond measure; and "Who," said he, "is this old dotard, who dares to judge my actions? By Peter and Paul, if I were not restrained by my generosity, I would make him an example and a spectacle to all mankind. Is not the king of England my vassal and my slave? and, if I gave the word, would he not throw him into prison, and load him with infamy and disgrace?"

In the latter end of the summer of 1253, Grosseteste was seized with a mortal disease, at his palace of Buckden; and he sent for friar John de St. Giles, to converse with him on the state of the church. He blamed Giles, and his brethren the Dominicans, and also the Franciscans, because, though their orders were founded in voluntary poverty, they did not rebuke the vices of the great. "I am convinced," said he, "that both the pope, unless he amend his errors, and the friars, except they endeavour to restrain him, will be deservedly exposed to everlasting death." He breathed his last at Buckden, October 9th, 1253. Innocent heard of his death with pleasure; and said, with exultation, "I rejoice, and let every true son of the Roman church rejoice with me, that my great enemy is removed." He ordered a letter to be written to king Henry, requiring him to take up the bishop's body, to cast it out of the church, and to burn it. The cardinals, however, opposed the tyrant, and the letter was never sent, probably on account of the decline of Innocent's health, for he died the succeeding year.

---

43. Peter Celestine, the Roman Pontiff.

In the thirteenth century there was one pope who, as Milner, in his Church History, remarks, deserves to be commemorated in the annals of the church of Christ. Peter Celestine was born in Apulia about the year 1221, and lived as a hermit in a little cell. He was admitted into holy orders; but after that he lived five years in a cave on Mount Moroni, near Sulmona. He was molested with internal temptations, which his confessor told him were a stratagem of the enemy that would not hurt him if he despised it. He founded a monastery at Mount Moroni, in 1274. The see of Rome having been vacant two years and three months, Celestine was unanimously chosen pope, on account of the fame of his sanctity. The archbishop of Lyons, presenting him with the instrument of his election, conjured him to submit to the vocation. Peter, in astonishment, prostrated himself on the ground; and after he had continued in prayer some time, he rose up, and fearing to oppose the will of God, he consented to his election, and took the name of Celestine V.

Since the days of the first Gregory, no pope had ever assumed the pontifical dignity with more purity of intention. But he had not Gregory's talents for business and government; and the Roman see was immensely more corrupt in the thirteenth than it was in the sixth century. Celestine soon became sensible of his incapacity; he was lost as in a wilderness. He attempted to reform abuses, to retrench the luxury of the clergy—to do, in short, what he found totally impracticable. He committed mistakes, and exposed himself to the ridicule of the scornful. His conscience was kept on the rack through a variety of scruples, from which he could not extricate himself; and from his ignorance of the world, and of canon law, he began to think he had done wrong in accepting the office. He spent much of his time in retirement; nor was he easy there, because his conscience told him that he ought to be discharging the pastoral office. Overcome with anxiety, he asked Cardinal Cajetan whether he might not abdicate? It was answered, yes. Celestine gladly embraced the opportunity of assuming again the character of brother Peter, after he had been distressed with the phantom of dignity for four or five months. He abdicated in 1294. The last act of his pontificate was worthy of the sincerity of his character. He made a constitution, that the pontiff might be allowed to abdicate, if he pleased. It is remarkable that no pope has, since that time, taken the benefit of this constitution.

That same Cajetan who had encouraged his resignation contrived to be elected his successor, and took the name of Boniface VIII. Though Peter had given the most undoubted proofs of his love of obscurity, and desired nothing more than that he might spend the rest of his days in private devotion; yet Boniface, who measured other men by himself, apprehended and imprisoned him, lest he should revoke his resignation.

Peter gave such proofs of his sincerity as convinced all persons, except Boniface himself, that nothing was to be dreaded from his ambition. The tyrant sent him into the castle of Fumone, under a guard of soldiers; the old hermit was shut up in a hideous dungeon, and his rest was interrupted by the jailers, who nightly disturbed his sleep. These insults and hardships he seems to have borne with Christian patience and meekness. He sent this message to Boniface; "I am content; I desired a cell, and a cell you have given me." But ambition is made of sterner stuff than to yield to the suggestions of conscience or humanity. In the year 1296, after an imprisonment of ten months, Celestine died of a fever, most probably contracted by the unworthy treatment which he received.

---

44. The Albigenses.

Albi, an inconsiderable town in Languedoc, has had the honour of giving the name of Albigeois, or Albigenses, to the protestants of France, who were distinguished in the thirteenth century by their determined opposition to the usurpations of the pope; but whose entire history occupies little more than half a century.

It was at this place that a *celebrated public conference* was held between the opponents and the adherents of the church of Rome. This conference was held in the year 1176, which gave the name of Albigenses to all such as avowed the principles then and there publicly advanced against the superstition and abuses of the Romanists. The conference at Albi was the prelude to the bloody drama which commenced at the beginning of the thirteenth century. The popish bishops, priests, and monks, who took part in that conference, finding that they could not persuade their adversaries to join in communion with themselves, tried to compel them, and began by ascribing false sentiments to the advocates of the cause against which they could not prevail in fair argument. They branded them with the name of Arians and Manichees; they preached against them in the cities and villages, and charged them with atrocities of which they never were guilty.

Raymond, Count of Thoulouse (and sovereign of the provinces where the doctrines propounded at Albi, and from thenceforward styled Albigensian, had long taken deep root), was solemnly invoked by the pope to exterminate the heretics by an armed force. But Raymond was too well convinced of the value which his state derived from the enterprising and industrious spirit of his nonconforming subjects, to comply with this demand. His refusal drew down fresh denunciations from the pope, and renewed charges of scandalous proceedings against the protestants. To refute these slanders the protestants consented to hold another meeting with the Romanists, at Montreal, in the year 1206. The same opinions were freely expressed as before at Albi, and soon afterwards a general crusade was preached, not only against the impugners of the papal authority, but against all who should protect or refuse to destroy them. Count Raymond himself was involved in the edict of excommunication; and the term Albigenses was indiscriminately applied to all such of the natives of the south of France as had incurred the resentment of the Roman pontiff, either by questioning his infallibility, or refusing to persecute those who questioned it.

The Romanists record, as meritorious deeds, instances of carnage and spoliation committed by their own people, and do not disguise that the forces opposed to the Albigenses massacred the inhabitants of whole towns and villages; that they *twice* put "sixty thousand" to the sword; burnt "three hundred" in one castle, "and eighty in another."

At the siege of Marmande, Prince Louis induced the inhabitants to deliver up the town upon his sacred promise that their lives should be spared. But all the men, women, and children, five thousand in number, were massacred, in order that this human holocaust might bring God's blessing upon the arms of the crusaders. The slaughter was in direct opposition to the will of

Louis; but the council of the bishop of Saintes prevailed. "My advice," said that prelate, "is that you immediately kill and burn all these people as heretics and apostates, and that none of them be left alive." Romish authors record this fact.

The only enemy the Albigenses had was the Roman church, and when their legitimate prince, the count of Thoulouse, after being reproached for indulging pity for the heretics, and saving them from punishment, was solicited by the popish clergy to carry the sentence of the church into effect against them, he pleaded that "he *could not* and *dare not* undertake any thing against them." And why? "Because," said he, "the majority of the lords, and the greatest part of the common people, have drunk the poison of their infidelity." The count was writing to the abbot of Cisteaux, and therefore he spoke in language which that churchman would understand.

In the celebrated conference at Albi, which gave name to the Albigenses, where the leaders of protestants were met face to face by their accusers, the burden of the lay which was echoed in full chorus against them, was "heresy" and "infidelity." No insurrection, no act of iniquity, was so much as mentioned in the impeachment. The Albigenses were condemned as heretics, excommunicated, and anathematized; and all Christian powers, whether civil or ecclesiastical, were exhorted and commanded by the pope to exterminate a race of people whose principles (as the bull of extermination set forth) were subversive of all religion, natural and revealed, and of every moral tie.

When Innocent III. found it was not enough to excommunicate Raymond of Thoulouse, and to lay his territories under an interdict, he resorted to a measure which bigotry has ever found to be much more effectual than preaching or persuasion. He determined to hasten the work of conversion by fire and sword. For this purpose he first instituted the inquisition, and commissioned the members of that execrable tribunal with full powers to search out and denounce as infidels deserving of death, all such as should dispute the authority of the Roman see. He then enlisted the very worst passions of men in his service; promised the pardon of sins, the property of the heretics, and the same privileges which had been granted to those who fought against the Saracens in Palestine, to all who would "take the cross against the Albigenses."

The prospect of absolution, of booty, of freedom from restraint, and the barbarous superstition of the times brought hordes of relentless savages upon the devoted Albigenses; and Simon de Montfort, by general consent, was put at the head of the crusaders.

Chassineuil was one of the first places that fell before the invaders. It capitulated. The garrison was permitted to march out, but the inhabitants were left to the sentence of the *pope's legate.* He pronounced them to be heretics, and all were committed to the flames. Beziers was attacked next. It relied upon the strength of its walls and the courage of its defenders; but the multitude of assailants was such that "it appeared as if the whole world was encamped before it." The city was taken at the first assault, and some of the crusaders, thirsting after heretic blood only, desired the legate to take care and have a distinction made between the faithful and the unbelievers. "*Kill all,*" said the pope's representative; "*the Lord will afterwards select those that are his.*" The sentence of death was fulfilled to the very letter, and all were slain. Of men, women, and children, not one was left alive, and the town was reduced to ashes.

The forces of de Montfort marched on in triumph to invest Carcassone. Strong intercession was made to the legate in favour of the young viscount, who was shut up with the citizens of Carcassone; and the terms of mercy offered to him were, that he might quit the city with twelve others, upon condition of surrendering up the rest of the townsmen and soldiers to the pleasure of the besiegers. "Rather than comply with the demand of the legate," replied the heroic youth, "I would give myself to be flayed alive." The people of the city afterwards escaped by a secret passage. The legate took possession of Carcassone "in the name of the church," and in malignant resentment at the thought of so many victims having escaped his fury, burnt or hanged three hundred knights who had previously capitulated upon the guaranty of his solemn oath that they should not be put to death!

Levaur was one of the cities which made the most memorable defence. By their frequent sorties, their perseverance in repairing the breaches, and intrepid exposure of life upon the walls, the Albigenses showed upon this and all other occasions, a generous courage, which would have insured success to the cause if the ranks of their enemies had not been filled up by hosts of new levies, as fast as they were thinned by the casualties of the war. In the year 1212 the army of the crusaders was four times renewed; and so universally was it understood to be the quarrel of the church that ecclesiastical dignitaries came from all quarters to give a colour to the proceedings. A practicable breach was soon made in the walls, and a monkish historian relates that the bishops, the abbot of Courdieu, who exercised the functions of vice-legate, with all the priests, clothed in their sacred vestments, gave themselves up to thanksgiving when they saw the carnage beginning, and sung the hymn, *Veni Creator.* He mentions, also, that when the castle of Amery fell, eighty knights were taken and condemned to be hanged; but as this process was too slow, an order was given to destroy them *en masse*; that the order "was received by the pilgrims with avidity, and that they burnt the heretics alive, *with great joy.*"

At length this horrible war ended as it began, by command of the sovereign pontiff, because all open resistance to his will was put down, and popish ascendancy was finally established in a quarter where the right of liberty of conscience had hitherto been claimed from the first introduction of the gospel. The church had gained her object by the total destruction of all who dared to oppose her. There remained no Albigenses in the south of France bold enough to preach their doctrines, or administer their forms of worship. Some of the more fortunate had fled to other countries, where they preserved and kept alive the lamp of truth amidst the surrounding darkness. The extirpation was so complete that in less than thirty-three years from the beginning of the crusade, the Albigenses were no more; and when protestantism reared its head again in Provence and Languedoc, after an interval of three centuries, it was recognised under another name.

---

45. Persecution of the Waldenses.

In the darkest period in the history of the Christian church, there have ever been some who have borne their testimony in support of the pure doctrines of Christianity, and raised their voices against the general corruption of the church.

The most distinguished of these reformers were the Waldenses, who made their appearance about the year 1160. They were the most numerous about the valley of Piedmont.

Peter Waldo, an opulent merchant of Lyons, in France, being extremely zealous for the advancement of true piety and Christian knowledge, caused a translation of the four gospels, and other parts of the Holy Scriptures, to be made into the French language. Perusing these books with deep attention, he perceived that the religion which was taught by the church of Rome was totally different from that which was taught by Christ and his apostles. Being animated with zeal for the truths of the gospel, he abandoned his mercantile vocation, distributed his riches among the poor, and forming an association with other pious men who had adopted his sentiments, he began in 1180, as a public teacher, to instruct the multitude in the doctrines and precepts of Christianity.

The attempts of Peter Waldo and his followers were crowned with great success; they formed religious assemblies, first in France, then in Lombardy, from whence they propagated their sect thorughout the other provinces of Europe with great rapidity, and with such invincible fortitude that neither fire nor sword, nor the most cruel inventions of merciless persecution, could damp their zeal, or entirely ruin their cause.

The Roman pontiff and his ministers often instigated the civil rulers to exterminate or drive the Waldenses from their dominions. For this purpose, troops were sent against them many times, who plundered and destroyed their villages, and murdered many of the inoffensive inhabitants.

The persecution in 1655, 1656, and 1686 was carried on with peculiar rage and violence, and seemed to threaten nothing less than the total extinction of this unhappy people. They were hunted like wild beasts upon the rocks and mountains, where they fled for safety. The banditti and soldiers of Piedmont massacred all sorts of persons, of every age, sex, and condition; they were dismembered, and hung up; females violated, and numerous other horrid atrocities committed.

The few Waldenses that survived were indebted for their existence and support to the intercession made for them by the English and Dutch governments, and also by the Swiss cantons, who solicited the clemency of the duke of Savoy on their behalf.

Milton, the poet, who lived at this time, touched with sympathy for the suffering of the Waldenses, penned the following exquisite sonnet:

On the late Massacre in Piedmont.

Avenge, O Lord, thy slaughter'd saints, whose bones
Lie scatter'd on the Alpine mountains cold;
E'en them who kept thy truth so pure of old,
When all our fathers worshipp'd stocks and stones,
Forget not; in thy book record their groans
Who were thy sheep, and in their ancient fold
Slain by the bloody Piedmontese, that roll'd
Mother with infant down the rocks. Their moans
The vales redoubled to hills, and they
To heav'n, their martyr'd blood and ashes sow

O'er all th' Italian fields, where still doth sway
The tripled tyrant; that from these may grow
A hundred fold, who, having learned thy way,
Early may fly the Babylonian wo.

---

46. Mendicants, or begging Friars.

This sort of society began in the thirteenth century, and the members of it, by the tenor of their institution, were to remain entirely destitute of all fixed revenues and possessions; though in process of time their number became a heavy tax upon the people. Innocent III. was the first of the popes who perceived the necessity of instituting such an order; and accordingly, he gave such monastic societies as made a profession of poverty the most distinguishing marks of his protection and favour. They were also encouraged and patronized by the succeeding pontiffs, when experience had demonstrated their public and extensive usefulness. But when it became generally known that they had such a peculiar place in the esteem and protection of the rulers of the church, their number grew to such an enormous and unwieldly multitude, and swarmed so prodigiously in all the European provinces, that they became a burden, not only to the people, but to the church itself. The great inconvenience that arose from the excessive multiplication of the Mendicant orders was remedied by Gregory X., in a general council, which he assembled at Lyons in 1272; for here all the religious orders that had sprung up after the council held at Rome in 1215, under the pontificate of Innocent III., were suppressed; and the extravagant multitude of Mendicants, as Gregory called them, were reduced to a smaller number, and confined to the four following societies or denominations, viz. the Dominicans, the Franciscans, the Carmelites, and the Augustins, or hermits of St. Augustine.

As the pontiffs allowed these four Mendicant orders the liberty of travelling wherever they thought proper, of conversing with persons of every rank, of instructing the youth and multitude wherever they went; and as those monks exhibited, in their outward appearance and manner of life, more striking marks of gravity and holiness than were observable in the other monastic societies, they rose all at once to the very summit of fame, and were regarded with the utmost esteem and veneration through all the countries of Europe. The enthusiastic attachment to these sanctimonious beggars went so far, that, as we learn from the most authentic records, several cities were divided or cantoned out into four parts, with a view to these four orders: the first part being assigned to the Dominicans, the second to the Franciscans, the third to the Carmelites, and the fourth to the Augustins. The people were unwilling to receive the sacraments from any other hands than those of the Mendicants, to whose churches they crowded to perform their devotions while living, and were extremely desirous there to deposite, also, their remains after death. Nor did the influence and credit of the Mendicants end here; for we find in the history of this and of the succeeding ages, that they were employed not only in spiritual matters, but also in temporal and political affairs of the greatest consequence; in composing the differences of princes, concluding treaties of peace, concerting alliances, presiding in cabinet councils, governing courts, levying taxes, and other occupations, not only remote from, but absolutely inconsistent with, the monastic character and profession. However, the power of the Dominicans and Franciscans greatly surpassed that of the other two orders, insomuch that these two orders were, before the reformation, what the Jesuits have been since that happy and glorious period—the very soul of the hierarchy, the engines of the state, the secret springs of all the motions of the one and the other, and the authors and directors of every great and important event, both in the religious and political world. By very quick progression their pride and confidence arrived at such a pitch, that they had the presumption to declare publicly, that they had a divine impulse and commission to illustrate and maintain the religion of Jesus. They treated with the utmost insolence and contempt all the different orders of the priesthood; they affirmed, without a blush, that the true method of obtaining salvation was revealed to them alone; proclaimed with ostentation the superior efficacy and virtue of their indulgences; and vaunted beyond measure their interest at the court of heaven, and their familiar connexions with the Supreme Being, the Virgin Mary, and the saints in glory. By these impious wiles they so deluded and captivated the miserable, and blinded the multitude, that they would not intrust any other but the Mendicants with the care of their souls. They retained their credit and influence to such a degree towards the close of the fourteenth century, that great numbers of both sexes, some in health, others in a state of infirmity, others at the point of death, earnestly desired to be admitted into the Mendicant order, which they looked upon as a sure and infallible method of rendering heaven propitious. Many made it an essential part of their last wills, that their bodies after death should be wrapped in old ragged Dominican or Franciscan habits, and interred among the Mendicants. For such was the barbarous superstition and wretched ignorance of this age, that people universally believed they should readily obtain mercy from Christ at the day of judgment, if they appeared before his tribunal associated with the Mendicant friars.

About this time, however, they fell under an universal odium; but being resolutely protected against all opposition, whether open or secret, by the popes, who regarded them as their best friends and most effectual supports, they suffered little or nothing from the efforts of their numerous adversaries. In the fifteenth century, besides their arrogance, which was excessive, a quarrelsome and litigious spirit prevailed among them, and drew upon them justly the displeasure and indignation of many. By affording refuge at this time to the Beguins in their order, they became offensive to the bishops, and were hereby involved in difficulties and perplexities of various kinds. They lost their credit in the sixteenth century by their rustic impudence, their ridiculous superstitions, their ignorance, cruelty, and brutish manners. They discovered the most barbarous aversion to the arts and sciences, and expressed a like abhorrence of certain eminent and learned men, who endeavoured to open the paths of science to the pursuits of the studious youth, recommended the culture of the mind, and attacked the barbarism of the age in their writings and discourses. Their general character, together with other circumstances, concurred to render a reformation desirable, and to accomplish this happy event.

Among the number of Mendicants are also ranked the Capuchins, Recollects, Minims, and others, who are branches or derivations from the former.

Buchanan tells us, the Mendicants in Scotland, under an appearance of beggary, lived a very luxurious life; whence one wittily called them, not *Mendicant*, but *Manducant* friars.—*Buck's Theological Dictionary*.

---

47. JOHN WICKLIFFE, THE FIRST ENGLISH REFORMER.

THIS famous man was born in Yorkshire, in 1324. He was professor of divinity at Oxford for many years. England, at this time, was completely under the papal dominion. The pure gospel of Christ was almost wholly buried beneath the load of errors and deceits which the corruption, pride, and ignorance of the pope and Romish clergy had introduced. The country swarmed with the Mendicant orders; who, invading the universities, attempted to persuade the students to join their fraternity. This state of things at length aroused the indignation of Wickliffe, who had for a long time been much concerned on its account; and he commenced writing against the Mendicant orders, and even against the tyranny of the pope; denying his power to be beyond that of any bishop, and asserting that the bread and wine used in the sacrament was not turned into the real body and blood of

Christ. He declared the gospel to be a sufficient rule of life, without any other; that if a man was truly penitent towards God, it was sufficient, without making a confession to the priests; that friars (an order in the Romish church, who supported themselves by begging) should *labour* for their support; and that Christ never meant his word to be locked up in a learned language, which the poor could not understand; but that it was to be read and understood by all classes of men. He therefore translated the whole Bible into the English language, and circulated it abroad; which was read, and by it very many were made wise unto salvation.

These new doctrines greatly enraged the bishops, monks, and priests; who summoned him to appear before them in St. Paul's church, London, to answer for his conduct. On the appointed day, he went, accompanied by the duke of Lancaster, and others; and it was with great difficulty they could gain an entrance, on account of the vast crowds that had assembled to hear the trial. Just as the trial commenced, a violent quarrel arose between the duke and bishop of London, as to whether Wickliffe should be permitted to sit down. One angry word led to another, till at length both parties became so furious, that a riot ensued, and the assembly broke up. By this means he escaped the malicious intentions of his enemies. In the mean time his followers increased greatly. Again he was apprehended; but so many persons interested themselves in his favour, that he was released, with a charge to preach no more. This charge did not quench his zeal, or daunt him in the least.

Some time after this, his enemies succeeded in having a law passed, the object of which was to imprison him and his followers; this was the beginning of a violent persecution, which was carried on against him without mercy.

His latter days were spent in peace. He died at Lutterworth, 1385. So great was the malice of his enemies, that forty years after his death, they dug up his bones, burned them, and threw the ashes into the river.

His *doctrines*, however, were not to be destroyed; and all the combined efforts of his enemies could not crush his followers; and although some were burnt, and others barbarously tortured and imprisoned, still others arose who bore decided testimony to the truth.

He was the author of a great number of books, tracts, &c., some of which were dispersed into Germany and Bohemia, thus preparing the way for that glorious reformation of religion afterwards effected by Martin Luther; in consequence of which, Wickliffe is often called "*the morning star of the Reformation*."

---

48. Translation of the Bible into the English Language.

The first English Bible we read of was that translated by *J. Wickliffe*, about the year 1360, but never printed; though there are manuscript copies of it in several public libraries. The first printed Bible in our language was that translated by *W. Tindal*, assisted by *Miles Coverdale*, printed abroad in 1526; but most of the copies were bought up and burnt by bishop Tunstal and sir Thomas Moore. It contained only the New Testament, and was revised and republished by the same persons in 1530.

After this, several translations were made—such as Mathews' Bible, in 1537, being published by John Rogers, under the borrowed name of John Mathews; Cranmer's Bible, in 1540, having been examined and prefaced by archbishop Cranmer; Geneva Bible, so called from having been printed in Geneva, which was the first English Bible where any distinction of verses was made; and the bishops' Bible, so termed from several bishops having been employed in the translation of it. After the translations of the Bible by the bishops, two other private versions had been made of the New Testament: the first by Lawrence Thompson, from

Beza's Latin edition, with the notes of Beza, published in 1582, in quarto, and afterwards in 1589, varying very little from the Geneva Bible; the second, by the papists at Rheims, in 1584, called the Rhemish Bible, or Rhemish translation.

In consequence of dissatisfaction with those translations, king James I. selected fifty-four persons, eminent in learning, and particularly well acquainted with the original languages in which the Old and New Testaments were written, to make a new translation of the whole Bible. In the year 1607, forty-seven of those persons (the other seven having probably died) assembled together and arranged themselves into committees, to each of which a portion was given to translate. They were favoured not only with the best translations, but with the most accurate copies, and the various readings of the original text. After about three years' assiduous labour, they severally completed the parts assigned them. They then met together, and while one read the translation newly formed, the rest had each a copy of the original text in his hand, or some one of the ancient versions; and when any difficulty occurred they stopped, till, by common consultation, it was determined what was most agreeable to the inspired original. This translation was first published A. D. 1613, and is the one that has been, ever since that time, printed by public authority, and the same now in common use.

The following is a specimen of Wickliffe's New Testament, in the old English of his time:—

"Matth. x. 25, 26. In thilke tyme Jhesus answeride & seid, I knowleche to thee, Fadir, Lord of Hevene & of earthe, for thou hast hid these thingis fro wise men and redy, & hast schewid hem to littl children. So, Fadir; for so it was plesynge to fore thee.

"John x. 26–30. Ye beleven not, for ye ben not of my scheep. My scheep heren my vois, and I knowe hem, and thei suen me. And I gyve to hem everlastynge life, & thei schulen not perische, withouten

MASSACRE OF THE WALDENSES.
About the year 1656 the Waldenses in the vallies of Piedmont refusing to embrace the Catholic Faith suffered the vengeance of the Papal power

BURNING OF THE BONES OF WICKLIFFE.
Wickliffe the English Reformer died in 1385 His enemies forty years after his death, burnt his bones, and threw the ashes into the river.

end; & noon schal rauysche hem fro myn hond. That thing that my Fadir gaf to me, is more than alle thingis: & no man may rauysche from my Fadirs hond. I & the Fadir ben onn.

"Rom. ix. 12. It was seid to hem, that the more schulde serve the lesse: as it is written, Iouyde Jacob, but I hatide Esau. What therfore schulen we scie? wher wickidnesse be enentis God? God forbede. For he seith to Moises, I schal have mercy on whom I have mercy. Therefore, it is not neither of man willynge, neither rennynge; but of God hauynge mercy. And the Scripture seith to Farao, For to this thinge have I styrrid thee, that I schewe in the my vertu, and that my name be teeld in all erthe. Therefore of whom God wole, he hath mercy; & whom he wole he endurith. Thanne seith thou to me, what is sought ghit, for who withstondith his will? Oo man what art thou that answerist to God? Wher a maad thing seith to him that maad it, What hast thou made me so? Wher a pottere of cley hath not power to make, of the same gobet, oo vessel unto onour, a nothir into dispyt!"

The following is (according to Dr. Clarke), the first translation of the 13th chapter of 1st Corinthians, which is known to exist in the English language. The peculiar *orthography* and *points* are preserved as in the manuscript. The words printed in italics may be considered the translator's marginal readings; for though incorporated with the text, they are distinguished from it by having lines drawn underneath.

"Gyf I speke with tungis of men an aungels sotheli I have not charite: I am maad as brasse sounynge or a symbale tynking. And gif I schal have prophecie and have knowen alle mysteries and alle kunnynge *or science*, and gif I schal have al feith so that I overbere hillis fro oo place to an other. forsothe gif I schal not have charite: I am nougt. And gif I schal deperte al my goodis into metis of pore men. And gif I schal bitake my body so that I brenne forsothe gif I schal not have charite it profitith to me no thing.

Charite is pacient *or suffringe.* It is denynge *or of good wille.* Charite envyeth not. It doth not gyle it is not inblowen with pride it is not ambyciouse or covetouse of wirschippis. It seekyth not the thingis that ben her owne. It is not stirrid to wrath, it thinkith not yvel, it joyeth not on wickidnesse; forsythe it joyeth to gydre to treuthe. It suffreth alle thingis, it bileeveth alle thingis. It hopith alle thingis; it susteeneth alle thingis. Charite fallith not doun. Whether prophecies schuln be voide eyther langagis schuln ceese: eyther science shal be destruyed. Forsothe of party we han knowen: and of partye propecien. Forsothe whenne that schal cum to that is perfit: that thing that is of partye schal be avoydid. When I was a litil chiilde: I spake as a litil chiilde: I understode as a litil chiilde: I thougte as a littil chiilde. Forsothe whenn I was maad a man: I avoydid the thingis that weren of a litil childe. Forsothe we seen now bi a mirror in derenesse: thanne forsothe face to face. Nowe I know of partye: thanne forsothe I schal know as I am known. Nowe forsothe dwellen feith, hoope, charite. These three: forsothe the more of hem is charite."

---

49. Lollards.

The term Lollards is given to a religious sect, differing in many points from the church of Rome, which arose in Germany about the beginning of the fourteenth century; and some writers have imagined that this term is so applied from Walter Lollard, who began to dogmatize in 1315, and was burnt at Cologne; though others think Lollard was no surname, but merely a term of reproach applied to all heretics who concealed the poison of error under the appearance of piety.

The monk of Canterbury derives the origin of the word lollard among us from *lolium*, "a tare," as if the Lollards were the tares sown in Christ's vineyard. Abelly says that the word signifies "praising God," from the German *loben*, "to praise;" and *heu*, "lord," because the Lollards employed themselves in travelling about from place to place, singing psalms and hymns. Others, much to the same purpose, derive *lollhard*, *lullhard*, or *lollert*, *lüllert*, as it was written by the ancient Germans, from the old German word, *lullen*, *loilen*, or *lallen*, and the termination *hard*, with which many of the high Dutch words end. *Lollen* signifies "to sing with a low voice," and therefore lollard is a singer, or one who frequently sings; and in the vulgar tongue of the Germans it denotes a person who is continually praising God with a song, or singing hymns to his honour.

The Alexians or Cellites were called *Lollards* because they were public singers, who made it their business to inter the bodies of those who died of the plague, and sang a dirge over them, in a mournful and indistinct tone, as they carried them to the grave. The name was afterwards assumed by persons that dishonoured it; for we find among those Lollards who made extraordinary pretences to religion, and spent the greatest part of their time in meditation, prayer, and such acts of piety, there were many abominable hypocrites, who entertained the most ridiculous opinions, and concealed the most enormous vices under the specious mark of this extraordinary profession. Many injurious aspersions were therefore propagated by the priests and monks, against those who assumed this name; so that, by degrees, any person who covered heresies or crimes under the appearance of piety, was called a *Lollard*. Thus the name was not used to denote any one particular sect, but was formerly common to all persons or sects who were supposed to be guilty of impiety towards God, or the church, under an external profession of great piety. However, many societies, consisting both of men and women, under the name of Lollards, were formed in most parts of Germany and Flanders, and were supported partly by their labours, and partly by the charitable donations of pious persons. The magistrates and inhabitants of the towns where these brethren and sisters resided, gave them particular marks of favour and protection, on account of their great usefulness to the sick and needy. They were thus supported against their malignant rivals, and obtained many papal constitutions, by which their institute was confirmed, their persons exempted from the cognizance of the inquisitor, and subjected entirely to the jurisdiction of the bishops; but as these measures were insufficient to secure them from molestation, Charles, duke of Burgundy, in the year 1472, obtained a solemn bull from Sextus IV., ordering that the Cellites or Lollards should be ranked among the religious orders, and delivered from the jurisdiction of the bishops. And pope Julius II., granted them still greater privileges, in the year 1506. Mosheim informs us that many societies of this kind are still subsisting at Cologne, and in the cities of Flanders, though they have evidently departed from their ancient rules.

Lollard and his followers rejected the sacrifice of the mass, extreme unction, and penances for sin; arguing that Christ's sufferings were sufficient. He is said, likewise, to have set aside baptism, as a thing of no effect; and repentance as not absolutely necessary, &c. In England, the followers of Wickliffe were called, by way of reproach, *Lollards*, from the supposition that there was some affinity between some of their tenets; though others are of opinion that the English Lollards came from Germany.—*Buck's Theological Dictionary.*

---

50. John Oldcastle, or Lord Cobham.

About 1413, during the reign of Henry V., a universal synod of all the bishops and clergy of England was collected by archbishop Arundel, in St. Paul's church, London. The principal object of this assembly was to repress the growing sect of reformers, and as sir John Oldcastle (lord Cobham) had on all occasions discovered a partiality for this sect, the resentment of the archbishop, and of the whole body of the clergy, was particularly levelled at this nobleman. Certainly, at that time, no man in England was more obnoxious to the ecclesiastics; for he made no secret of his opinions. He had very much distinguished himself in opposing the abuses of popery. At a great expense he had collected, transcribed, and dispersed the works of Wickliffe among the common people, without reserve; and it is well known that he maintained a great number of itinerant preachers in many parts of the country. This nobleman was arrested by the king's order, and lodged in the tower of London. On the day appointed for his trial, Thomas Arundel, the archbishop, "sitting in Caiaphas' room, in the chapter-house at St. Paul's," with the bishops of London and Winchester, sir Robert Morley brought personally before him lord Cobham, and left him there for the time. "Sir," said the primate, "you stand here both detected of heresies and also excommunicated for contumacy. Notwithstanding we have, as yet, neither shown ourselves unwilling to give you absolution, nor yet do at this hour, provided you would meekly ask for it."

Lord Cobham took no notice of this offer, but desired permission to read an account of his faith, which had long been settled, and which he intended to stand to. He then took out of his bosom a certain writing respecting the articles whereof he was accused, and when he had read it, he delivered the same to the archbishop.

"I never trespassed against you," said this intrepid servant of God: "and therefore I do not feel the want of your absolution." He then kneeled down on the pavement, and lifting up his hands to heaven, he said, "I confess myself here unto thee, my eternal living God, that I have been a grievous sinner. How often in my past youth have I offended thee by ungoverned passions, pride, concupiscence, intemperance! How often have I been drawn into horrible sin by anger, and how many of my fellow subjects have I injured from this cause! Good Lord, I humbly ask thy mercy; here I need absolution."

With tears in his eyes, he then stood up, and with a loud voice cried out, "Lo! these are your guides, good people. Take notice; for the violation of God's holy laws and his great commandments they never cursed me; but for their own arbitrary appointments and traditions they most cruelly beat me and other men. Let them, however, remember, that Christ's denunciations against the Pharisees shall all be fulfilled."

The dignity of his manner, and the vehemence of his expression, threw the court into some confusion. After the primate had recovered himself, he proceeded to examine the prisoner respecting the doctrine of transubstantiation. "Do you believe that after the words of consecration there remains any material bread?"—"The Scriptures," said Cobham, "make no mention of material bread; I believe that Christ's body remains in the form of bread. In the sacrament there is both Christ's body and the bread; the bread is the thing that we see with our eyes; but the body of Christ is hid, and only to be seen by faith." Upon this, with one voice, they cried "Heresy! heresy!" One of the bishops in particular said, "That it was foul heresy to call it bread." Cobham answered smartly, "St. Paul, the apostle, was as wise a man as you, and perhaps as good a Christian; and yet he calls it bread. The bread, saith he, that we break, is it not the communion of the body of Christ? To be short with you, I believe the Scriptures most cordially, but I have no belief in your lordly laws and idle determinations; ye are no part of Christ's holy church, as your deeds do plainly show." Doctor Walden, the prior of the Carmelites, and Wickliffe's great enemy, now lost all patience, and exclaimed, "What rash and desperate people are these followers of Wickliffe!"—"Before God and man," replied Cobham, "I solemnly here profess, that till I knew Wickliffe, whose judgment ye so highly disdain, I never abstained from sin; but after I became acquainted with that virtuous man, and his despised doctrines, it hath been otherwise with me; so much grace could I never find in all your pompous instructions."—"It were hard," said Walden, "that in an age of so many learned instructors you should have had no grace to amend your life till you heard the devil preach."—"Your fathers," said Cobham, "the old Pharisees, ascribed Christ's miracles to Beelzebub, and his doctrines to the devil. Go on; and, like them, ascribe every good thing to the devil; go on, and pronounce every man a heretic who rebukes your vicious lives. Pray what warrant have you from Scripture for this very act you are now about? Where is it written in all God's laws, that you may thus sit in judgment upon the life of man? Hold—perhaps you will quote Annas and Caiaphas, who sat upon Christ and his apostles?"—"Yes, sir," said one of the doctors of law, "and Christ, too, for he judged Judas."—"I never heard that he did," said lord Cobham. "Judas judged himself, and thereupon went out and hanged himself. Indeed, Christ pronounced a wo against him for his covetousness, as he does still against you, who follow Judas's steps."

Some of the last questions which were put to him respected the worship of the cross; and his answers prove that neither the acuteness of his genius was blunted, nor the solidity of his judgment impaired.

One of the friars asked him whether he was ready to worship the cross upon which Christ died. "Where is it?" said lord Cobham. "But suppose it was here at this moment?" said the friar. "A wise man, indeed, to put me such a question," said Cobham; "and yet he himself does not know where the thing is! But, tell me, I pray, what sort of worship do I owe to it?" One of the conclave answered, "Such worship as St. Paul speaks of, when he says, 'God forbid that I should glory, save in the cross of our Lord Jesus Christ.'"—"Right," replied Cobham, and stretched out his arms—"that is the true and the very cross—far better than your cross of wood."—"Sir," said the bishop of London, "you know very well that Christ died upon a material cross."—"True," said Cobham;

"and I know also that our salvation did not come by that material cross, but by him who died thereupon. Further, I know well, that St. Paul rejoiced in no other cross, but in Christ's passion and death only, and in his own sufferings and persecutions, for the same truth which Christ had died for before."

He was then sent back to the tower, where he remained for some weeks, and then made his escape; but in the year 1417 was again apprehended, and brought to London.

His fate was soon determined. He was dragged into St. Giles's fields with all the insult and barbarity of enraged superstition; and there, both as a traitor and a heretic, he was suspended alive in chains upon a gallows, and burnt to death.

This exemplary knight appears to have possessed the humility of a Christian, as well as the spirit of a soldier; for he not only protested faithfully against the idolatry of the times, the fictitious absolutions, and various corruptions of popery, by which the creatures of the pope extorted the greatest part of the wealth of the kingdom; but he also openly made such penitential declarations and affecting acknowledgments of having personally broken God's commandments, as imply much salutary self-knowledge and self-abasement, strong convictions of sin, and bitter sorrow for the same, together with a firm reliance on the mercy of God, through the mediation of Jesus Christ.

---

51. John Huss and Jerome of Prague.

John Huss was born about the year 1380, in a village in Bohemia, called Hussenits, and lived at Prague in the highest reputation, both on account of the sanctity of his manners and the purity of his doctrines. He performed in that city, at the same time, both the offices of professor of divinity in the university, and of a pastor in the church of that city.

He adopted the sentiments of Wickliffe and the Waldenses; and, in the year 1407, began openly to oppose and preach against the doctrines and corruptions then in the Romish church. This inflamed the resentment of the clergy against him, and he was summoned to appear before the council of Constance. Secured, as he thought, from the rage of his enemies, by the safe conduct granted him by the emperor Sigismund for his journey to Constance, his residence in that place, and his return to his own country, Huss obeyed the order of the council, and appeared before it to demonstrate his innocence, and to prove that the charge of his having deserted the church of Rome was entirely groundless. However, his enemies so far prevailed, that, by the most scandalous breach of public faith, he was cast into prison, declared a heretic, because he refused to plead guilty against the dictates of his conscience, and burnt alive in 1415; a punishment which he endured with unparalleled magnanimity and resolution. When he came to the place of execution he fell on his knees, sang portions of psalms, looked steadfastly towards heaven, and repeated these words:—"Into thy hands, O Lord, do I commit my spirit; thou hast redeemed me, O most good and faithful God. Lord Jesus Christ, assist and help me, that with a firm and present mind, by thy most powerful grace, I may undergo this most cruel and ignominious death, to which I am condemned for preaching the truth of thy most holy gospel." When the chains were put upon him at the stake, he said, with a smiling countenance, "My Lord Jesus Christ was bound with a harder chain than this for my sake, and why should I be ashamed of this old and rusty one!" When the fagots were piled up to his very neck, the duke of Bavaria was officious enough to desire him to abjure. "No," says Huss, "I never preached any doctrine of an evil tendency; and what I taught with my lips I seal with my blood." He said to the executioner, "Are you going to burn a goose?* In one century you will have a *swan* you can neither roast nor boil." If he were prophetic he must have meant Lu-

* *Huss*, in the language of his country, signifies *goose*

ther, who had a swan for his arms. The fire was then applied to the fagots; when the martyr sang a hymn. At last his voice was cut short, after he had uttered, "Jesus Christ, thou son of the living God, have mercy upon me;" and he was consumed in a most miserable manner. The duke of Bavaria ordered the executioner to throw all the martyr's clothes into the flames; after which his ashes were carefully collected and cast into the Rhine.

Jerome of Prague, the intimate friend and companion of Huss, was born at Prague, and suffered martyrdom one year after Huss. He was educated at the university of Prague, had travelled into many countries in Europe, and was greatly celebrated for his learning, virtues, and uncommon eloquence.

Being of the sentiments of Huss, he was summoned before the council of Constance. It is said that it was amazing to hear with what force of expression, fluency of speech, and excellent reasoning, he answered his adversaries. It was impossible to hear him without emotion. Every ear was captivated and every heart touched. But wishes in his favour were in vain; he threw himself beyond a possibility of mercy. He launched out into a high encomium of Huss, calling him a holy man, and lamenting his cruel and unjust death. He had armed himself, he said, with a full resolution to follow the steps of that blessed martyr, and to suffer with constancy whatever the malice of his enemies could inflict. Firm and intrepid, he stood before the council, collected in himself; not only contemning, but seeming even desirous of death. Two days were allowed him for reflection, and many persons of consequence endeavoured to make him recant his opinions; but all was in vain, and he was condemed as a heretic.

With a cheerful countenance he came to the place of execution, pulled off his upper garment, and made a short prayer at the stake, to which he was soon bound with wet cords, and an iron chain, and enclosed with fagots as high as his breast.

Observing the executioner about setting fire to the

wood behind his back, he cried out, "Bring thy torch hither. Perform thy office before my face. Had I feared death I might have avoided it."

As the wood began to blaze he sang a hymn, which the violence of the flame scarce interrupted; and the last words he was heard to say, were,

"This soul in flames I offer, Christ, to thee!"

---

52. Martin Luther.

Martin Luther, the great reformer of the church, was born at Eisleben, in Saxony, in 1483. Though his parents were poor, they endeavoured to give their son an education; but, young Luther, with other poor students, was obliged to earn his bread by singing before the doors of houses. In this occupation he often met with hard language and bitter reproaches at many doors. One day being much dejected, the worthy wife of a citizen, penetrated with pity for him, called the hungry youth into the house and refreshed him with food. This worthy woman, with her husband, were so well pleased with young Luther, that they determined to provide him food and clothing, that he might, without interruption and care for his support, the more zealously pursue his studies, in which he gave many indications of future worth. As his mind was naturally susceptible of serious impressions, and tinctured with that religious melancholy which delights in the solitude of a monastic life, he retired into a convent of Augustinian friars; where he acquired great reputation, not only for piety, but for love of knowledge and unwearied application to study.

Happening to find a Bible in the monastery, he applied himself to the study of it with so much eagerness and assiduity as to astonish the monks, and increased his reputation for sanctity so much that he was chosen professor of theology in the university of Wittemburg.

While Luther was thus employed, Tetzel, a Dominican friar, came to Wittemburg in order to publish indulgences. This appeared so contrary to the gospel that Luther published his sentiments respecting them, which spread over Germany with great rapidity, and were read with the greatest eagerness.

Luther, having thus begun to oppose one practice of the Romish church, was also led to examine other practices and tenets of the same church; the result of which entirely convinced him that the popish religion was not the religion of the Bible, and he boldly declared the pope to be the antichrist, or man of sin, whose appearance is foretold in the New Testament.

The court of Rome being alarmed at the progress of Luther's sentiments among all classes of people, excommunicated him as a heretic, and would probably have put him to death had he not been befriended by some of the princes of Germany, who were friendly to the new doctrines he set forth. Being at Augsburg in 1518, whither he had been summoned to answer for his opinions, Luther declared he could not renounce opinions founded in reason, and derived from Scripture, and at the same time delivering a formal protest, the cardinal asked, "What do you mean? Do you rely on the force of arms? When the just punishment and the thunder of the pope's indignation break in upon you, where do you think to remain?" His answer was, "*Either in heaven or under heaven.*"

Luther was at length summoned to appear before the diet at Worms, to answer for his heresy. The emperor Charles V. having granted him a safe conduct, he yielded obedience and set out for Worms. While on his journey, many of his friends (whom the fate of Huss under similar circumstances, and notwithstanding the same security of an imperial safe conduct, filled with solicitude) advised and entreated him not to rush wantonly into the midst of danger. But Luther, superior to such terrors, silenced them with this reply:—"*I am lawfully called,*" said he, "*to appear in that city:*

MARTIN LUTHER

Before the Diet of Worms, when urged to recant his opinions, firmly refused, unawed by the multitude and power of his enemies.

DEATH OF ZUINGLIUS.

Zuinglius mortally wounded on the field of battle refusing to comply with Popish ceremonies, fell a martyr of the Reformation in Switzerland.

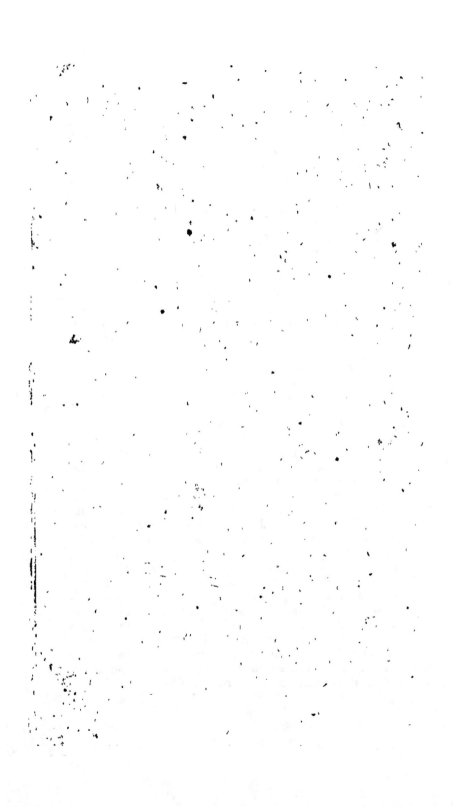

and thither I will go in the name of the Lord, though as many devils as there are tiles on the houses were there combined against me."

When Luther arrived at Worms, greater crowds than had appeared at the emperor's public entry assembled to behold him. At his appearance before the diet he behaved with great decency and firmness. When called upon to recant his opinions, Luther replied, in a truly exalted manner, "Except I can be convinced by clear reasoning, or by proofs taken from the Holy Scriptures, I neither can nor will recant, because it is neither safe nor advisable to do any thing which is against my conscience. Here I stand; I cannot do otherwise; so help me God! Amen!" Luther persisting in this answer, he was dismissed from the assembly under a strong escort, and was permitted by the emperor to return from Worms.

Luther, after this, in 1534, translated the Bible into the German language, wrote many works, and laboured with unwearied zeal in propagating the doctrines of the reformation. He had during his life the pleasure of seeing vast numbers of the people adopting his sentiments, and the reformed religion firmly established in many parts of Europe.

"Luther died February the 18th, A. D. 1546, at Eisleben, where he was born. The Almighty, who had protected him against so many dangers, saved him by a seasonable death from the tempest which was gathering, and ready to break forth against his followers. When he felt his strength declining, he made his last will, which is preserved in its original state at Wittemburg, and concludes as follows:—'I had my reason to omit in my last will the usual legal formalities, and I hope I shall be credited more than a notary; for I am well known in the world, since God, the Father of all mercy, has intrusted me, an unworthy sinner, with the gospel of his Son, and enabled me to this day to preach it with truth, faithfulness, and perseverance; and many persons in the world have been converted by my ministry, and think me a doctor of truth, notwithstanding the ban of the pope, the emperor, and the wrath of many kings, princes, parsons, yea, and of all the devils. Why then should I not be credited in a matter so insignificant; particularly since my handwriting is well known, and sufficient, if it can be said, this is written by Dr. Martin Luther, the notary of God, and witness of his gospel?'

"Though he felt great pain during his last illness, his native intrepidity did not forsake him; he conversed with his friends to the last about the happiness of the future world, and of meeting again hereafter. When the pain began to increase, and death approached, he called for Justus Jonas, who had accompanied him from Halle to Eisleben, who heard him repeat three times these words: 'Father, into thy hand I give my spirit' —and say the following prayer:—'O, my heavenly Father, who art the God and Father of our Lord Jesus Christ, thou God of all comfort, I thank thee for having revealed to me thy dear Son Jesus Christ, on whom I believe, whom I have preached and professed, loved and praised, but who is despised and persecuted by the pope and all the wicked. I pray to thee, Lord Jesus Christ, let my soul be recommended to thee. O my heavenly Father, though I must leave this body of clay, and depart this life, I know for certain that I shall remain for ever with thee, and that no one shall pluck me out of thy hand.' When marks of approaching death appeared in his face, Jonas asked him, 'Reverend father, do you die in Christ, and upon the doctrine which you have preached?' Having answered with a loud voice, 'Yes!' he fell into a soft sleep, and expired."

---

53. Zuinglius, the Swiss Reformer.

Ulric Zuinglius was the son of a peasant of the Swiss valley of Tockenburgh, and was born January 1st, 1483. He was destined for the church, and was sent successively to Basil, Bern, and Vienna, where he acquired the meagre literature usual in the fifteenth century. After four years' residence at Basil, he was ordained by the bishop of Constance, on being chosen by the burghers of Glaris as their pastor. From this epoch commenced his religious knowledge. It occurred to him, still in the darkness of popery, that to be master of the true doctrines of Christianity, he should look for them in the first instance, not in the writings of the doctors, nor in the decrees of councils, but in the Scriptures themselves.

With the force of his clear and sincere mind turned to the great subjects of Christianity, he must have been in a constant advance to a more vigorous conviction of the errors of the popish system ; and the time must arrive when that conviction would declare itself. But the piety of Zuinglius was the direct reverse of the desire of exciting popular passion. The first appeal of the Swiss reformer was to his ecclesiastical superiors. His addresses to the bishop of Constance and the cardinal of Sion pointed out, for their correction, the errors which it was in their power safely to extinguish ; but which could not, without public danger, be left to be extinguished by the people.

The period had arrived when profound study, continued interchange of opinion with the leading philosophers and divines of his country, and holy convictions, matured during many years, had fitted Zuinglius for the solemn and public commencement of his work of immortality.

For this perilous effort, which required the heroism of the age of the martyrs, the great reformer chose a prominent occasion. The history of the convent of Einsiedlen was a striking compound of the wild legend and fantastic miracle of the dark ages. In the ninth century a monk of noble family, probably disturbed by some memory of the furious excesses of the time, determined to hide himself from human eyes in the most lonely depths of Switzerland.

The spot which he chose was even then called " The Gloomy Forest." Here he built a chapel and a hermitage, and after a solitude of twenty-six years, closed his career under the daggers of a banditti. A miracle sanctified his death. Two crows, his only associates in the wilderness, flew on the track of the murderers, screaming round them, until, in the market-place of Zurich, the popular suspicion was fixed on the robbers, and the crime was finally confessed and avenged.

Once every seven years the consecration of this chapel was solemnized with great pomp. The event itself had been fixed in the papal history, by a bull of Leo VIII., and the details had been preserved for posterity in a volume entitled "*De Secretis Secretorum.*"

On the festival of this "Consecration of the Angels," Zuinglius ascended the pulpit. The concourse was immense, from the whole range of Switzerland, and every ear was turned to catch the panegyric of the "Mighty Mother" and the "Host of Glory" that had descended to pour the oil of holiness on that selected spot of the world. But a mightier strength, that was to break the power of the idol, was there. With the sincerity and the zeal of a new apostle to the Gentiles, Zuinglius thundered on them.

"Blind are ye," exclaimed he, "in seeking thus to please the God of earth and heaven. Believe not that the Eternal, He whom the heaven and the heaven of heavens cannot contain, dwells especially here. Whatever region of the world you may inhabit, there he is beside you; he surrounds you, he grants your prayers if they deserve to be granted. It is not by useless vows, by long pilgrimages, by offerings to senseless images, that you can obtain the favour of God—that you can resist temptation—repress guilty desires—shun injustice—relieve the unfortunate—or console the afflicted. Those alone are the works that please the Lord.

"Alas, alas! I know our own crime. It is we, the ministers of the altar—we who ought to be the salt of the earth—who have plunged the ignorant and credulous multitude into error. To accumulate treasures for our avarice, we raised vain and worthless practices to the rank of good works, until the people neglect the laws of God, and only think of offering compensation for their crimes instead of renouncing them. What is their language?—let us indulge our desires—let us enrich ourselves with the plunder of our neighbour—let us not fear to stain our hands with blood and murder. When all is done we shall find easy expiation in the favour of the church.

"Madmen! can they think to obtain remission of their lies, their impurities, their adulteries, their murders, their treacheries, by a litany to the Queen of Heaven? Is she to be the protectress of all evildoers? Be deceived no longer, people of error! The God of justice disdains to be moved by words which, in the very utterance, the heart disowns. The Eternal Sovereign of truth and mercy forgives no man his trespasses who does not forgive the trespasses against himself. You worship the saints. Did those sons of God, at whose feet you who fling yourself, enter into heaven by relying on the merits of others? No; it was by walking in the path of the law of God, by fulfilling the will of the Most High, by facing death rather than deny their Lord and Saviour.

"What is the honour that you ought to pay those saints? Imitate the holiness of their lives—walk in their footsteps—suffer yourselves to be turned aside by neither seduction nor terrors.

"But in the day of trouble put your trust in none but God, who created the heaven and earth with a word. At the coming of death, invoke no name but that of Christ Jesus, who bought you with his blood, and who is the ONE and ONLY MEDIATOR between God and man!"

This discourse struck at all the pillars of popery at once. Absolution for money—pilgrimages—the worship of the Virgin—and the intercession of the saints. It was listened to in mingled astonishment, wrath, and admiration. Its effect upon the multitude was to inflame, in some instances, the jealousy which no prudence of the pastor could have stifled; of the monks, some were indignant, yet many heard in it only the doctrines that had been the subject of long meditation among themselves. In some instances the conviction was immediate and complete, and pilgrims, who had brought offerings to the shrine, now refused to join in what they had learned to be an act of impiety, and took their offerings home. The great majority were awakened to a sense of their condition, and, from that hour, were prepared to abjure the crimes and superstitions of Rome.

But, like the light that fell on St. Paul in his journey, the fullest illumination descended on the preacher himself.

Others heard and acknowledged the voice of heaven; but it was to the preacher that the words of God came with living power. From that day forth, he was no longer the same man. His energy, intrepidity, and defiance of the common obstacles of Christianity, in the popular prejudices and the tyranny of the popedom, raised him to the highest rank of the champions of the gospel.

The mind of this great man, deeply imbued with scriptural knowledge by his ten years' residence in his pastorship of Glaris, and further matured by his three years' enjóyment of the literature of the intelligent members of Einsiedlen, was now prepared for the sterner duties of a leader of the reformation. Through the advice of Myconius, a Greek professor in the school of Zurich, whom he had known in the convent, Zuinglius was chosen preacher in the cathedral of Zurich, Dec. 4th, 1518.

The tenets of Luther, which were now spreading abroad in Germany, encouraged Zuinglius to oppose the sale of indulgences in Zurich, where he was seconded by the public authorities and the people. In 1527, some districts of Bern, the most powerful of the cantons, petitioned its senate for the introduction of the system established at Zurich, and for the suppression of the mass. The senate was divided, but the proposal was finally referred to a council of the clergy of Bern and the other states of the league. Some of the cantons objected to the meeting, but it was at length held, and attended by names still memorable in the history of protestantism:—Œcolampadius, Pellican, Collinus, Bullinger, Capito, and Bucer. On Zuinglius's arrival, the sittings commenced. The protestant doctrines were proposed in the shape of ten theses, and they were so powerfully sustained by the learning and talent of the reformers, that, after eighteen debates, the great majority of the Bernese clergy signed their adherence to them, as the true doctrines of the gospel.

The "Grand Council" of Bern then proceeded to act upon the decision. It declared the bishops of Lausanne, Basil, Sion, and Constance to be divested of all rights in its territory; ordered the priests to teach nothing contradictory to the theses, permitted priests to marry, and monks and nuns to leave their convents, and appropriated the religious revenues to lawful purposes. Within four months, protestantism was the religion of the whole canton; but this triumph was finally purchased by the death of the great leader and light of Switzerland. The accession of so powerful a state as Bern threw the Catholic cantons into general alarm. A league, prohibiting the preaching of the reformation, was made between the five cantons of Lucerne, Uri, Schweitz, Underwalden, and Zug. Protestant ministers were persecuted, and in some instances put to death, and all alliances were formed with the German princes hostile to protestantism. Their persecutions awakened the resentment and fears of the reformed cantons, and to enforce the treaty by which they were to be protected, the cantons of Zurich and Bern determined to blockade the five cantons. The blockade was contrary to the advice of Zuinglius, who deprecated it as involving the innocent with the guilty. At length the five cantons collected their troops, and advanced towards Cappel, a point where they might prevent the junction of the Zurichers and Bernese. Zurich was thrown into consternation; and when four thousand men were ordered to march, seven hundred only were equipped in a state to meet the enemy. News came that the division already posted at Cappel was attacked by a superior force. The officer in command of the Zurichers instantly marched to sustain the post. It was the custom of the Swiss, that their clergy should follow their troops to the field, to administer the last consolations to the dying. Zuinglius attended this detachment, but with a full consciousness of the hazard. "Our cause is good," said he to the friends who crowded anxiously round him, as the troops marched out, "but it is ill defended. It will cost my life, and that of a number of excellent men who would wish to restore religion to its primitive simplicity. No matter; God will not abandon his servants; he will come to their assistance when you think all lost. My confidence rests on him alone, and not upon men. I submit myself to his will."

Cappel is three leagues from Zurich. On the road the roaring of the cannon, attacking the position of the Zurichers, was heard. The march of the troops was slow, from the height of Mount Albis and the weight of their armour. Zuinglius, agitated for the fate of the post, urged the officers to push forward at speed. "Hasten," he cried, "or we shall be too late. As for me, I will go and join my brethren. I will help to save them, or we will die together." The little army, animated by his exhortation, rushed forward, and at three in the afternoon came in sight of the battle. The troops of the five cantons were eight thousand; an overwhelming superiority. After some discharges of cannon, they advanced to surround the Zurichers, who amounted to but fifteen hundred. The enemy were boldly repulsed for a while, but their numbers enabled them to outflank the protestants, and all was flight or slaughter.

Zuinglius fell by almost the first fire. He had advanced in front of his countrymen, and was exhorting them to fight for the cause of freedom and holiness, when a ball struck him. He sunk on the ground mortally wounded, and in the charge of the enemy was trampled over without being distinguished. When the tumult of the battle was passed, his senses returned, and raising himself from the ground, he crossed his arms upon his breast, and remained with his eyes fixed on heaven. Some of the enemy, who had lingered behind, came up, and asked whether he would have a confessor. His speech was gone, but he shook his head in refusal. They then exhorted him to commend his soul to the Virgin. He refused again. They were enraged by his repeated determination. "Die, then, obstinate heretic!" exclaimed one of them, and drove his sword through his bosom.

His body was recognised by the Catholics the next day, who held a mock trial over it, burned it, and scattered the ashes to the winds. He fell at the age of forty-seven; but he had gone through his course well; for he had sowed the seeds of virtue in a land barren before; he had let in light on a land of darkness, and his immortal legacy to his country was strength, wisdom, freedom, and religion!

---

54. Jesuits.

Jesuits, *or the Society of Jesus*, are a religious order of the Romish church, founded in the sixteenth century, by Ignatius Loyola, a Spanish knight. The plan which this fanatic formed of its constitution and laws was suggested, as he gave out, by the immediate inspiration of heaven.

Loyola proposed that besides the three vows of poverty, chastity, and of monastic obedience (which are common to all orders of regulars), the members of this society should take a fourth vow of obedience to the pope, binding themselves to go whithersoever he should command them, and without requiring aid from the holy see for their support.

At this time the papal authority received such a shock from the progress of the Reformation, and the revolt of nations from the Romish church, that the acquisition of a body of men thus devoted to that church was of much consequence.* Pope Paul therefore confirmed

* The following are the words of Damianus, a Jesuit historian: "In the same year (1521) that Luther, with consummate wicked-

the institution of Jesuits by his bull, and granted the most ample privileges to the members of the order.

The order of the Jesuits are peculiar in the operations. The primary object of almost all their monastic orders is to separate men from the world, and from any concern in its affairs. They can be of no benefit to mankind but by their example and prayers. On the contrary, the Jesuits consider themselves as formed for action. They are required to attend to all the transactions of the world, on account of the influence which these may have upon religion; they are directed to study the disposition of persons in high rank, and to cultivate their friendship, and, by the very constitution and genius of their order, a spirit of action and intrigue is infused into all its members.

From their first institution, the Jesuits considered the education of youth as their peculiar province; they aimed at being spiritual guides and confessors; they preached frequently, in order to instruct the people; they set out as missionaries to convert unbelieving nations.

Before the close of the sixteenth century they had obtained the chief direction of the education of youth in every Catholic country in Europe. They had become the confessors of all its monarchs, a function of no small importance. They were the spiritual guides of almost every person eminent for rank or power; possessed the highest degree of confidence and interest with the papal court; and, at different periods, the direction of the most considerable courts in Europe; they mingled in all affairs, and took part in every intrigue and revo-

ness, had openly declared war against the church, Ignatius raised the standard in the defence of religion."—"The sacrifice of the mass, the eucharist, the virgin mother of God, the guardian angels, and, the indulgences of the popes, which Luther attacks with so much fury, are the objects which Ignatius and his companions exert themselves continually to celebrate by new inventions and indefatigable industry."—"To Luther, that *disgrace of Germany*, that *epicurean swine*, that *curse of Europe*, that *monster* destructive of the whole earth, hateful to God and man, &c. God by his eternal decree hath opposed his son Ignatius."

lution. Under the pretext of promoting the success of their missions, and of supporting their missionaries, they engaged in an extensive and lucrative commerce, both in the East and West Indies; and had their warehouses in different parts of Europe. Not satisfied with trade alone, they imitated the example of other commercial societies, and aimed at obtaining settlements.

They acquired possession of the large and fertile province of Paraguay, which then stretched across South America, from the bottom of the mountains of Potosi to the confines of the Spanish and Portuguese settlements, on the banks of the river De la Plata.

In this country it must be confessed that the Jesuits were of some service; they found the inhabitants in a savage state, subsisting by hunting and fishing; and hardly acquainted with the first principles of subordination and government. The Jesuits set themselves to instruct and civilize these savages; they taught them to cultivate the ground, build houses, and brought them to live together in villages, &c. They trained them to arts and manufactures, and such was their power over them, that a few Jesuits presided over some hundred thousand Indians.

But at length the power and influence of the Jesuits became so formidable, that the nations of Europe found it expedient to check their progress. They were expelled from England in 1604; Venice in 1606; Portugal in 1759; France in 1764; Spain and Sicily in 1767; and finally were suppressed by pope Clement XIV. in 1773.

In 1814, however, the pope issued a bull for re-establishing the order of the Jesuits, and it is believed that human society is fearfully menaced by the revival of this atrocious order, whose principles engender and promote private and public collision and disorder. When their order was abolished in France, in 1764, the arret of the parliament of Paris states, as the ground of the expulsion of the Jesuits, that "the consequences of their doctrines destroy the law of nature; break all the bonds of civil society, by authorizing theft, lying, perjury, the utmost uncleanness, murder, all criminal passions and all sins; root out all sentiments of humanity; overthrow all governments; excite rebellion; and extinguish the foundation and practice of religion, and substitute all sorts of superstition, blasphemy, irreligion, and idolatry." This will appear to have some foundation by the following quotations from their most celebrated authors; and it may be premised that these are the dogmas ever taught and practised by Jesuits, in all places, whenever they deem it expedient to forward their designs.

The passages relating to chastity, found in Jesuit authors, are purposely omitted, being too abominable for public perusal. The following passages are but few, among many others of the same import, which might be selected.

1. *Escobar,* Theolog. Moral. Vol. 4. Lib. 34. Sect. 2. Prob. 16. page 348. "A child who serves his father, may secretly purloin as much as his father would have given a stranger for his compensation."

2. *Cardenas,* Crisis Theolog. Diss. 23. Cap. 2. Art. 1. page 474. "Servants may secretly steal from their masters as much as they judge their labour is worth, more than the wages which they receive." To this agrees *Taberna.*

3. *Gordonus,* Theolog. Moral. Univ. Lib. 5. Quest. 3. Cap. 4. page 826. "A woman may take the property of her husband, to supply her spiritual wants, and to *act like other women.*" [In plain English, wives and daughters may steal from their husbands and fathers, to satisfy their confessor priest!]

4. *Emmanuel Sa,* Aphorism. verbo *Furtum,* page 161. "It is not mortal sin to steal that from a man which he would have given if asked for it. It is not theft to take any thing from a husband or father, if the value be not considerable."

5. *Francis Xavier Fegeli,* Pars. 3. Cap. 6. Quest. 11. Page 158. "After a son has secretly robbed his father as a compensation, the confessor need not enforce restitution, if he has taken no more than the just reward of his labour."

6. *Sanchez,* Op. Moral. Precept. Decal. Pars. 2. Lib. 3. Cap. 6. Num. 13. "It is lawful to use ambiguous terms, to give the impression a different sense from that which you understood yourself. A person may take an oath that he has not done such a thing, though in fact he has, by saying to himself it was not done on a certain specified day, or before he was born, or by concealing

any other similar circumstance, which gives another meaning to it. This is extremely convenient, and is always *very just*, when necessary to your health, honour, or prosperity. A man who makes, whether sincerely or in dissimulation, a contract of marriage, is dispensed, by *any motive*, from accomplishing his promise."

7. *Filiucius*, Quest. Moral. vol. 2. Tract. 25. Cap. 11. Num. 328. "With what precaution may we equivocate? By intending to use only material words. A person may begin to say, *I swear*, he can add this mental restriction, *to-day*, or in a whisper he may repeat, I say, and then resume his former tone—*I did not do it*."

8. *Charli*, Prop. 6. page 8. "He who is not bound to state the truth before swearing, is not bound by his oath, provided he makes the internal restriction that excludes the present case."

9. *Taberna*, Vol. 2. Pars. 2. Tract. 2. Cap. 31. page 288. "Is a witness bound to declare the truth before a lawful judge? No—if his deposition will injure himself or his posterity; or *if he be a priest; for a priest cannot be forced to testify before* a secular judge."

10. *Laymann*, Lib. 4. Tract. 3. Cap. 1. page 73. "It is not sufficient for an oath that we use the formal words, if *we have not the* intention and will to swear, and do not sincerely invoke God as a witness."

11. *Tamburinus*, Lib. 3. Cap. 4. Sect. 2. page 27. "If any man conceals another's property, for the support of himself and his family, when asked, he may say that he has concealed nothing. For example—a *priest* may equivocate before a secular judge, that he is no delinquent, by understanding that *the judge is not a competent lawful authority to receive the testimony of ecclesiastics*."

12. *Emmanuel Sa*, Aphor. page 41. "*The rebellion of* Roman priests is not treason, because they are not subject to the civil government."

13. *Bellarmin*, Controvers. Lib. 5. Cap. 6. page 1090. "The spiritual power must rule the temporal by all sorts of means and expedients when necessary. Christians should not tolerate a heretic king."

14. *Salmeron*, Comment. Evan. Hist. Vol. 4. Pars. 3. Tract 4. page 411. "*The pope hath supreme* power over the whole earth, over all kings and governments, to command and enforce them to employ their power to promulge popery; which mandate of the pope they are bound to obey, and if they resist he must punish them as contumacious."

15. *Sanctarel*, Tract. de Hæres. Cap. 30. page 296. "The pope can depose negligent rulers, and deprive them of their authority."

16. *Lessius*, Lib. 2. Cap. 42. Dub. 12. page 632. "*The pope can annul and cancel every possible obligation arising from an oath.*"

17. *La Croix,* Vol. 1. page 294. "*A man condemned by the pope may be killed wherever he is found.*"

18. *Emmanuel Sa,* Aphor. page 178. "It is lawful to kill in defence of ourselves or another, or in defence of our property or honour. You may kill beforehand any person who may put you to death, *not* excepting *the judge and witnesses,* because it is self-defence."

19. *Henriquez,* Sum. Theol. Moral. Vol. 1. Lib. 14. Cap. 10. page 869. "If an adulterous priest, even aware of his danger, having visited an adulteress, is assailed by her husband, kills the man in his own defence, it is not criminal."

20. *Fagundez,* Precept. Decalog. Vol. 1. Lib. 4. Cap. 2. page 501, 655; and Vol. 2. Lib. 8. Cap. 32. page 390. "*Papist children may accuse their parents* for heresy, although they know that their parents will be burnt for it—not only they may deny them nourishment, but *they may justly kill them,* if the parents would turn their children from the popish faith."—"If a priest at the altar is attacked by any one, he may leave the ceremony and defend himself; and although he may kill the assailant, he may immediately return to the altar, and finish the mass."—"If a judge decides contrary to law, the injured person may defend himself by *killing the judge.*"

21. *Airault,* Cens. page 319. "If a person attempts to ruin my reputation by calumny, and I can avoid the injury only by secretly killing him, may I do it? Certainly. Although the facts are true; yet if the calumiator will not cease to publish them, *you may fitly kill him, not publicly, but in* secret, *to avoid scandal.*"

22. *Amicus,* Num. 131. "*A priest may kill those who hinder him from taking possession of any ecclesiastical office.*"

23. *Bauny,* Cap. 7. page 77. "We may wish every evil for our neighbour without sin, when we are impelled by a good motive—thus, a mother may desire the death of her daughters, when, from deformity or poverty, she cannot marry them to her satisfaction."

24. *Escobar,* Theolog. Moral. Vol. 4. Lib. 32. Sec. 2. Prob. 5. page 274. "*It is lawful to kill an accuser whose testimony may jeopard your life and honour.*"

Escobar, page 278. "*It is permitted to kill any person who is proscribed.*" Page 284. "It is lawful to kill those who injure our honour, or cover us with infamy before persons of distinction."

Escobar, Vol. 6. page 170. "Not only is it lawful to offer or accept a duel, but you may secretly kill a calumniator, if you have no other mode to avoid the danger, because *it is not murder,* but *self-defence.* You are obliged to refuse a duel, if *you can secretly kill your enemy;* because thereby you endanger not your own life, and you also hinder the commission of a new sin, in offering or accepting a duel."

25. *Molina*, Vol. 3. Disput. 16. page 1768. "Priests may *kill the laity, to preserve their goods.*"

26. *Francis Xavier Fegeli*, Quest. Prac. Pars. 4. Cap. 1. Quest. 7. Num. 8. page 285. "It is not mortal sin for parents to wish the death of their children—nor to desire the death of any one '*who troubles the church*, because considerable good is the direct and immediate object."

27. *Dicastillo*, Lib. 2. Tract. 1. Disput. 10. Dub. 1. Num, 15. page 290. "If a man becomes a nuisance to society, *the son may lawfully kill his father*."

28. *Escobar*, Theolog. Moral. Vol. 4. Lib. 31. Sec. 2. Precept 4. Prob. 5. page 239. "Children are obliged to denounce their parents or relations who are guilty of heresy, although they know that they will be burnt. They may refuse them all nourishment, and permit them to die with hunger—or may kill them as enemies, who violate the rights of humanity."

29 *Gobatus*, Op. Moral. Vol. 2. Pars. 2. Tract. 5. Cap. 9. Sec. 8. page 328. "A son who inherits great wealth by the death of his father may rejoice that when he was intoxicated he murdered his father."—"Persons may innocently desire to be drunk, if from their inebriation any great good will arise." [According to this doctrine, any man may innocently intoxicate himself, expressly to murder his father for his wealth!]

30. *Casnedi*, Cris. Theolog. Vol. 5. Disput. 13. Sec. 3. Num. 169. page 438. "I may rejoice in the death of my father, on account of the riches which I obtain by it." Num. 170. "We should become familiar with this doctrine, for it is useful to all who desire property, which can be obtained only by the death of another, especially secular offices and ecclesiastical dignities."

31. *Busembaum* et *Lacroix*, Theolog. Moral. Vol. 1. page 295. "In all the above cases, where a man has a right to kill any person, another may do it for him if affection moves the murderer." Page 163. "To avoid a great spiritual or temporal evil, a person may commit suicide."

---

55. Persecutions in China and Japan.

At the commencement of the sixteenth century, three Italian missionaries, namely, Roger the Neapolitan, Pasis of Bologna, and Matthew Ricci of Mazerata, entered China with a view of establishing Christianity there. In order to succeed in this important commission, they had previously made the Chinese language their constant study.

The zeal displayed by these missionaries in the discharge of their duty was very great; but Roger and Pasis in a few years returning to Europe, the whole labour devolved upon Ricci. The perseverance of Ricci was proportioned to the ardous task he had undertaken. Though disposed to indulge his converts as far as possible, he disliked many of their ceremonies, which seemed idolatrous. At length, after eighteen years' labour and reflection, he thought it most advisable to tolerate all those customs which were obtained by the laws of the empire, but strictly enjoined his converts to omit the rest; and thus, by not resisting too much the external ceremonies of the country, he succeeded in bringing over many to the truth. In 1630, however, this tranquillity was disturbed by the arrival of some new missionaries; who, being unacquainted with the Chinese customs, manners, and language, and with the principles of Ricci's toleration, were astonished when they saw Christian converts fall prostrate before Confucius and the tables of their ancestors, and loudly censured the proceedings as idolatrous. This occasioned a warm controversy; and, not coming to any agreement, the new missionaries wrote an account of the affair to the pope, and the society for the propagation of the Christian faith. The society soon pronounced that the ceremonies were idolatrous and intolerable, which sentence was confirmed by the pope. In this they were excusable, the matter having been misrepresented to them; for the enemies of Ricci had declared the halls in which the ceremonies were performed to be temples, and the ceremonies themselves the sacrifices to idols.

The sentence was sent over to China, where it was received with great contempt, and matters remained in the same state for some time. At length a true representation was sent over, explaining that the Chinese customs and ceremonies alluded to were entirely free from idolatry, but merely political, and tending only to the peace and welfare of the empire. The pope, finding that he had not weighed the affair with due consideration, sought to extricate himself from the difficulty in which he had been so precipitately entangled, and therefore referred the representation to the inquisition, which reversed the sentence immediately.

The Christian church, notwithstanding these divisions, flourished in China till the death of the first Tartar emperor, whose successor Cang-hi, was a minor. During his minority, the regents and nobles conspired to crush the Christian religion. The execution of this design was accordingly begun with expedition, and carried on with severity, so that every Christian teacher in China, as well as those who professed the faith, was surprised at the suddenness of the event. John Adam Schall, a German ecclesiastic, and one of the principals of the mission, was thrown into a dungeon, and narrowly escaped with his life, being then in the seventy-fourth year of his age.

In 1665, the ensuing year, the ministers of state published the following decree:—1st. That the Christian doctrines were false. 2d. That they were dangerous to the interests of the empire. 3d. That they should not be preached under pain of death. The result of this was a most furious persecution, in which some were put to death, many ruined, and all in some measure oppressed. Previous to this, the Christians had suffered partially; but the decree being general, the persecution now spread its ravages over the whole empire, wherever its objects were scattered.

Four years after, the young emperor was declared of age; and one of the first acts of his reign was to stop this persecution.

The first introduction of Christianity into the empire of Japan took place in 1552, when some Portuguese missionaries commenced their endeavours to make converts to the light of the gospel, and met with such success as amply compensated their labours. They continued to augment the number of their converts till 1616, when, being accused of having formed a plan to subvert the government and dethrone the emperor, great jealousies arose, and subsisted till 1622, when the court commenced a dreadful persecution against both foreign and native Christians. Such was the rage of this persecution, that during the first four years 20,570 Christians were massacred. Death was the consequence of a public avowal of their faith, and their churches were shut up by order of government. Many, on a discovery of their religion, by spies and informers, suffered martyrdom with great heroism. The persecution continued many years, when the remnant of the innumerable Christians with which Japan abounded, to the number of 37,000 souls, retired to the town and castle of Siniabara, in the island of Xinio, where they determined to make a stand, to continue in their faith, and to defend themselves to the very last extremity. To this place the Japanese army followed them, and laid siege to the place. The Christians defended themselves with great bravery, and held out against the besiegers three months, but were at length compelled to surrender, when men, women, and children, were indiscriminately murdered; and Christianity from that time ceased in Japan.

This event took place on the 12th of April, 1638, since which time no Christians but the Dutch have been allowed to land in the empire, and even they are obliged to conduct themselves with the greatest precaution, to submit to the most rigorous treatment, and to carry on their commerce with the utmost circumspection.

---

56. Attempt of the Mahometans to subdue Europe.

Constantinople, after having been for many ages an imperial Christian city, was invested, in 1453, by the Turks, under Mahomet II.,* whose army consisted of 300,000 men, and, after a siege of six weeks, it fell into the hands of the infidels; and the Turks have, to this day, retained possession of it.† They no sooner found

* He was the ninth of the Ottoman race, and subdued all Greece.

† About fifteen years before this fatal event took place, the city

themselves masters of it, than they began to exercise on the inhabitants the most unremitting barbarities, destroying them by every method of ingenious cruelty. Some they roasted alive on spits, others they starved, some they flayed alive, and left them in that horrid manner to perish; many were sawn asunder, and others torn to pieces by horses. Three days and nights was the city given to spoil, in which time the soldiers were licensed to commit every enormity. The body of the emperor being found among the slain, Mahomet commanded his head to be stuck on a spear, and carried round the town for the mockery of the soldiers.

About the year 1521, Solyman II. took Belgrade from the Christians. Two years after, he, with a fleet of 450 ships, and an army of 300,000 men, attacked Rhodes, then defended by the knights of Jerusalem. These heroes resisted the infidels till all their fortifications were levelled with the ground, their provisions exhausted, and their ammunition spent; when, finding no succours from the Christian princes, they surrendered, the siege having lasted about six months, in which the Turks suffered prodigiously, no less than 30,000 of them having died of the bloody flux. After this, Solyman retook Buda from the Christians, and treated those who were found there with great cruelty.

Mad with conquest, Solyman now proceeded westward to Vienna, glutting himself with slaughter on his march, and vainly hoping in a short time to lay all

---

had yielded the liberties of its church to the pope of Rome. A manifest want of patriotism was evidenced in the inhabitants, who, instead of bringing forth their treasures to the public service and defence of the place, buried them in vast heaps; insomuch, that when Mahomet, suspecting the case, commanded the earth to be dug up, and found immense hoards, he exclaimed, "How was it that this place lacked ammunition and fortification, amidst such abundance of riches?" The Turks found a crucifix in the great church of St. Sophia, on the head of which they wrote, "*This is the God of the Christians*," and then carried it with a trumpet around the city, and exposed it to the contempt of the soldiers, who were commanded to spit upon it. Thus did the superstition of Rome afford a triumph to the enemies of the cross.

Europe at his feet, and to banish Christianity from the earth.

Having pitched his tent before the walls of Vienna, he sent three Christian prisoners into the town, to terrify the citizens with an account of the strength of his army, while a great many more whom he had taken in his march were torn asunder by horses. Happily for the Germans, three days only before the arrival of the Turks, the earl palatine, Frederic, to whom was assigned the defence of Vienna, had entered the town with 14,000 chosen veterans, besides a body of horse. Solyman sent a summons for the city to surrender; but the Germans defying him, he instantly commenced the siege. It has before been observed, that the religion of Mahomet promises to all soldiers who die in battle, whatever be their crimes, admission into paradise. Hence arises that fury and temerity which they usually display in fighting. They began with a most tremendous cannonade, and made many attempts to take the city by assault. But the steady valour of the Germans was superior to the enthusiasm of their enemies. Solyman, filled with indignation at this unusual check to his fortune, determined to exert every power to carry his project. To this end he planted his ordinance before the king's gate, and battered it with such violence that a breach was soon made; whereupon the Turks, under cover of the smoke, poured in torrents into the city, and the soldiers began to give up all for lost. But the officers, with admirable presence of mind, causing a great shouting to be made in the city, as if fresh troops had just arrived, their own soldiers were inspired with fresh courage, while the Turks, being seized with a panic, fled precipitately, and overthrew each other; by which means the city was freed from destruction.

Grown more desperate by resistance, Solyman resolved upon another attempt, and this was by undermining the Corinthian gate. Accordingly, he set his Illyrians at work, who were expert at this kind of warfare. They succeeded in coming under ground to the foundations of the tower; but being discovered by the wary citizens, they, with amazing activity and diligence, countermined them; and having prepared a train of gunpowder, even to the trenches of the enemy, they set fire to it, and by that means rendered abortive their attempts, and blew up about 8000 of them. Foiled in every attempt, the courage of the Turkish chief degenerated into madness; he ordered his men to scale the walls, in which attempt they were destroyed by thousands, their very numbers serving to their own defeat; till, at length, the valour of his troops relaxed, and dreading the hardihood of their European adversaries, they began to refuse obedience. Sickness also seized their camp, and numbers perished from famine; for the Germans, by their vigilance, had found means to cut off their supplies. Frustrated in all his designs, Solyman, after having lost above 80,000 men, resolved to abandon his enterprise; and sending his baggage before him, proceeded homewards with the utmost expedition—thus freeing Europe from the impending terror of universal Mahometanism.

---

57. Doctrine of Romish Indulgences.

This doctrine of the Romish church proceeded upon the idea that all the good works of the saints, over and above those which were necessary towards their own justification, are deposited, together with the infinite merits of Christ, in one inexhaustible treasury; the keys of which were committed to St. Peter, and his successors, the popes, who may open it at pleasure; and by transferring a portion of this superabundant merit to any person, for a sum of money, may convey to him a pardon of all his sins, past, present, and future; or a release of any of his friends from purgatory, who might be suffering its pains.

Pope Leo X., in order to carry on the magnificent structure of St. Peter's, at Rome, published indulgences, and a plenary remission to all who should contribute money for this object. They were, in some parts, farmed out to the highest bidders; who, to make the best of their bargain, procured the most able preachers to cry up the value of their ware. The form of indulgences is as follows:—"May our Lord Jesus Christ have mercy upon thee, and absolve thee by the merits of his most holy passion. And I, by his authority, that of his blessed apostles, Peter and Paul, and of the most holy pope, granted and committed to me in these parts, do absolve thee, first, from all ecclesiastical censures, in whatever manner they have been incurred; then, from all thy sins, transgressions, and excesses, how enormous soever they may be, even from such as are reserved from the cognizance of the holy see, and as far as the keys of the holy church extend. I remit to you all punishment which you deserve in purgatory on their account; and I restore you to the holy sacraments of the church, to the unity of the faithful, and to that innocence and purity which you possessed at baptism; so that when you die, the gates of punishment shall be shut, and the gates of the paradise of delight shall be opened; and if you die not at present, this grace shall remain in full force when you are at the point of death; *in the name of the Father, the Son, and the Holy Ghost.*"

The prices of them were various, according to the character, ability, and crimes of the purchasers. For instance, if a man take a false oath, to be pardoned he must pay nine shillings; for robbing, twelve shillings; for murdering a layman, seven shillings and sixpence; for laying violent hands on a clergyman, ten shillings and sixpence, &c. &c.

In 1517, the sale of these indulgences was intrusted to one John Tetzel, who boasted that "he had saved more souls from hell, by his indulgences, than St. Peter had converted to Christianity by his preaching." He could assure a child who might fear his father was unhappy in another world; "that the moment the money tinkled in the chest his father's soul would mount up from purgatory!"

A certain nobleman, thinking there was some imposition in the case, put this question to him, "Can you grant absolution for a sin, which a man *shall intend to commit in future?*"—"Yes," replied he, "provided the proper sum of money be paid down." This being done, he received from Tetzel a certificate, absolving him from the crime he intended to commit; which he did not divulge at that time.

Not long after this, Tetzel left the place, with his chest of money. This nobleman concealed himself on the road, and when Tetzel appeared he rushed forth, attacked, robbed, and beat him soundly with a stick, and sent him back with an empty chest; at the same time producing the very certificate to him which he had a short time previous given him, and told him he had done only what he intended to when he purchased it, and presumed he was, by virtue of that, free from the crime.

Since the reformation, the popes have been more sparing in the exercise of their power; though indulgences are still sold in India for two rials apiece. A gentleman not long since being in Naples, to ascertain fully the fact respecting them, attended the sale; and, for two sequins, purchased a plenary remission of all his own sins, and for any two of his friends, whose names he was empowered to insert!

---

58. English Martyrs.

Queen Mary ascended the throne of England in 1553. She was strongly bigoted to the popish religion, and during her reign (which was of about five years' continuance) she carried on a most bloody persecution against the protestants. It was computed that during this persecution two hundred and seventy-seven persons were burnt, besides those punished by imprisonment, fines, and confiscations. Among those who suffered by fire, were five bishops, twenty-one clergymen, eight lay gentlemen, eighty-four tradesmen, one hundred husbandmen, fifty-five women, and four children.

Rogers, prebendary of St. Paul's, and Hooper, bishop

of Gloucester, were the first martyrs. Saunders and Taylor, two other clergymen, whose zeal had been distinguished in carrying on the reformation, were the next that suffered. "Bonner, bishop of London, bloated at once with rage and luxury, let loose his vengeance without restraint, and seemed to take a pleasure in the pains of the unhappy sufferers; while the queen, by her letters, exhorted him to pursue the pious work without pity or interruption. Soon after, in obedience to her commands, Ridley, bishop of London, and the venerable Latimer, bishop of Worcester, were condemned together. Ridley had been one of the ablest champions for the reformation; his piety, learning, and solidity of judgment, were admired by his friends, and dreaded by his enemies. The night before his execution he invited the mayor of Oxford and his wife to see him; and when he beheld them melted into tears, he himself appeared quite unmoved, inwardly supported and comforted in that hour of agony. When he was brought to the stake to be burnt, he found his old friend Latimer there before him. Of all the prelates of that age, Latimer was the most remarkable for his unaffected piety and the simplicity of his manners. He had never learned to flatter in courts; and his open rebuke was dreaded by all the great, who at that time too much deserved it. His sermons, which remain to this day, show that he had much learning and much wit; and there is an air of sincerity running through them, not to be found elsewhere. When Ridley began to comfort his ancient friend, Latimer on his part was as ready to return his kind office. "Be of good cheer, brother," cried he, "we shall this day kindle such a torch in England, as I trust in God shall never be extinguished." A furious bigot ascended to preach to them and the people while the fire was preparing; and Ridley gave a most serious attention to his discourse. No way distracted by the preparations about him, he heard him to the last; and then told him, that he was ready to answer to all that he had preached upon, if he were permitted a short indulgence, but this was refused him. At

FRENCH PROPHETS.

In 1688, five or six hundred persons in France professing to be divinely inspired, uttered many prophecies, accompanied with bodily contorsions.

SCOTCH COVENANTERS

assembled for divine worship, during the time of religious persecution which raged in Scotland.

length, fire being set to the pile, Latimer was soon out of pain; but Ridley continued to suffer much longer, his legs being consumed before the fire reached his vitals. Cranmer, archbishop of Canterbury, had less courage at first. His love of life, in an unguarded moment, induced him to sign a paper condemning the reformation. Of this act, he afterwards bitterly repented. Being led to the stake, and the fire beginning to be kindled round him, he stretched forth his right hand and held it in the flames till it was consumed; exclaiming several times, "This hand has offended! This wicked hand has offended!" When it dropped off, he discovered a serenity in his countenance, as if satisfied with sacrificing to divine justice the instrument of his crime. "When the fire attacked his body, he seemed to be insensible of his tortures; his mind was occupied wholly upon the hopes of a future reward. After his body was destroyed, his heart was found entire; an emblem of the constancy with which he suffered."*

---

59. Sufferings and Martyrdom of Anne Askew.

Anne Askew was the second daughter of sir William Askew, of Kelsey, in Lincolnshire. She had received a genteel education, which, with an agreeable person and good understanding, rendered her a very proper person to be at the head of a family. Her father, regardless of his daughter's inclination and happiness, obliged her to marry a gentleman who had nothing to recommend him but his fortune; and who was a most bigoted papist. No sooner was he convinced of his wife's regard for the doctrines of the reformation from popery, than, by the instigation of the priests, he violently drove her from his house, though she had borne him two children, and her conduct was unexceptionable. Abandoned by her husband, she came up to London in order to procure a divorce, and to make herself known to that part of the court who either professed or were favourers of protestantism; but as Henry VIII., with

* Goldsmith's History of England.

consent of parliament, had just enacted the law of the six articles, commonly called the Bloody Statute, she was cruelly betrayed by her own husband, taken into custody, upon his information, and examined concerning her faith. The act above mentioned denounced death against all those who should deny the doctrine of transubstantiation, or that bread and wine made use of in the sacrament were not converted, after consecration, into the *real* body and blood of Christ; or maintain the necessity of receiving the sacrament in both kinds; or affirm that it was lawful for priests to marry; that the vows of celibacy might be broken; that private masses were of no avail; and that auricular confession to a priest was not necessary to salvation. Upon these articles she was examined by the inquisitor, a priest, the lord mayor of London, and the bishop's chancellor, and to all their queries gave proper and pertinent answers; but not being such as they approved, she was sent back to prison, where she remained eleven days, to ruminate alone on her alarming situation, being even denied the small consolation of a friendly visit. The king's counsel being at Greenwich, she was once more examined by chancellor Wriothesley, Gardiner, bishop of Winchester, Dr. Cox and Dr. Robinson, but not being able to convince her of her supposed errors, she was sent to the tower. It was strongly suspected that Mrs. Askew was favoured by some ladies of high rank, and that she carried on a religious correspondence with the queen; so that chancellor Wriothesley, hoping that he might discover something that would afford matter of impeachment against that princess, the earl of Hertford, or his countess, who all favoured the reformation, ordered her to be put to the rack; but her fortitude in suffering, and her resolution not to betray her friends, were proof against that diabolical invention. Not a groan nor a word could be extorted from her. The chancellor, provoked with what he called her obstinacy, augmented her tortures with his own hands, and with unheard-of violence; but her courage and constancy were invincible, and these barbarians gained nothing by their cruelties but everlasting disgrace and infamy. As soon as she was taken from the rack, she fainted away; but, being recovered, she was condemned to the flames. Her bones were dislocated in such a manner that they were forced to carry her in a chair to the place of execution. While she was at the stake, letters were brought her from the lord chancellor, offering her the king's pardon if she would recant; but she refused to look at them, telling the messenger "that she came not thither to deny her lord and master." The same letters were also tendered to three other persons condemned to the same fate, and who, animated by her example, refused to accept them; whereupon the lord mayor commanded the fire to be kindled, and with savage ignorance, cried out, "*Fiat justitia*"—Let justice take its course. The fagots being lighted, she commended her soul, with the utmost composure, into the hands of her Maker, and, like the great founder of the religion she professed, expired praying for her murderers, July 16th, 1549, about the twenty-fifth year of her age.

"I do not know," observes a good English writer, "if all circumstances be considered, whether the history of this or any other nation can furnish a more illustrious example than this now related. To her father's will she sacrificed her own inclinations; to a husband unworthy her affections she behaved with prudence, respect and obedience; the secrets of her friends she preserved inviolable, even amidst the tortures of the rack. Her constancy in suffering, considering her age and sex, was equal, at least, if not superior, to any thing on record, and her piety was genuine and unaffected, of which she gave the most exalted proof in dying a martyr for the cause of her religion and liberty of conscience. But who can read this example, and not lament and detest that spirit of cruelty and inhumanity which are imbibed and cherished in the church of Rome? a spirit repugnant to the feelings of nature, and directly opposite to the conduct and disposition of the great Author of our religion, who came not to destroy men's lives, but to save them."

60. Massacre of St. Bartholomew's.

In the month of August, 1572, in the reign of Charles IX. of France, 30,000, or, as some affirm, 100,000 protestants were massacred in France by the Catholics. This bloody massacre commenced in Paris on the 24th of August, on St. Bartholomew's day.

In order the sooner to effect their purposes by cutting off the leaders of the protestants, many of the principal ones in the kingdom were invited to Paris under a solemn oath of safety, upon occasion of the marriage of the king of Navarre with the French king's sister. The queen-dowager of Navarre, a zealous protestant, however was poisoned by a pair of gloves before the marriage was solemnized. Upon a given signal the work of death began. Charles, the savage monarch, from the windows of his palace, encouraged the furious populace to massacre his protestant subjects, by crying out "Kill! kill!"

Cologni, admiral of France, was basely murdered in his own house, and then thrown out of the window, to gratify the malice of the duke of Guise; his head was afterwards cut off, and sent to the king and queen-mother; and his body, after many indignities offered to it, hung on a gibbet. After this, the murderers ravaged the whole city of Paris, and butchered in three days above ten thousand lords, gentlemen, presidents, and people of all ranks. "A horrible scene of things!" says a historian of the time; "the very streets and passages resounded with the noise of those who met together for murder and plunder; the groans of those who were dying, the shrieks of those who were just going to be butchered, were every where heard; the bodies of the slain were thrown out of the windows; the dead bodies of others were dragged through the streets; their blood running through the channels, in such plenty, that torrents seemed to empty themselves into the neighbouring river, in a word, an innumerable number of men, women, and children, were all involved in one common destruction, and the gates and entrances of the king's palace all besmeared with their blood."

From the city of Paris the massacre spread throughout the whole kingdom. In the city of Meaux they threw above two hundred into jail; and after they had ravished and killed a great number of women, and plundered the houses of the protestants, they exercised their fury on those they had imprisoned, and, calling them one by one, they were killed like sheep in a market. In Orleans they murdered above five hundred men, women, and children, and enriched themselves with the spoil. The same cruelties were practised at Angus, Troyes, Bouges, La Charite, and especially at Lyons, where they inhumanly destroyed above eight hundred protestants; children hanging on their parents' necks; parents embracing their children; putting ropes about the necks of some, dragging them through the streets, and throwing them, mangled, torn, and half-dead, into the river.

But what aggravates still more these scenes of wantonness and cruelty, was the manner in which the news was received at Rome. When the letters of the pope's legate were read in the assembly of the cardinals, by which he assured the pope that all was transacted by the express will and command of the king, it was immediately decreed that the pope should march with his cardinals to the church of St. Mark, and in the most solemn manner give thanks to God for so great a blessing conferred on the see of Rome and the Christian world; and on the Monday after, solemn mass should be celebrated in the church of Minerva, at which pope Gregory XIII. and his cardinals were present; and that a jubilee should be published throughout the whole Christian world, and the cause of it declared to be, to return thanks to God for the extirpation of the enemies of the truth and church in France.

In the evening the canon of St. Angelo were fired to testify the public joy; the whole city illuminated with bonfires; and no one sign of rejoicing omitted that was usually made for the greatest victories obtained in favour of the Roman church!!!

61. Auto de Fe, or Act of Faith.

"Act of faith" *(Auto de Fe)* in the Romish church is a solemn day held by the inquisition for the punishment of heretics and the absolution of the innocent accused. They usually contrive the auto to fall on some great festival, that the execution may pass with the more awe, and it is always on a Sunday. The *auto de fe* may be called the last act of the inquisitorial tragedy; it is a kind of jail-delivery, appointed as often as a competent number of prisoners in the inquisition are convicted of heresy, either by their own voluntary or extorted confession, or on the evidence of certain witnesses. The process is this:—In the morning they are brought into the great hall, where they have a peculiar habit put on, which they are to wear in the procession, and by which they know their doom. The procession is led up by the Dominican friars, after which come the penitents, being all in black coats without sleeves, and barefooted, with a wax candle in their hands. These are followed by the penitents who have narrowly escaped being burnt, who over their black coats have flames painted, with their points turned downwards. Next come the negative or relapsed, who are to be burnt, having flames painted on their habits, pointing upwards. After these come such as profess doctrines contrary to the faith of Rome, who, besides having flames painted upwards, have their picture painted on their breasts, with dogs, serpents, and devils, all open-mouthed, about it. Each prisoner is attended with a familiar of the inquisition, and those to be burnt have also a Jesuit on each hand, who is continually exhorting them to abjure. After the prisoners comes a troop of familiars on horseback; and after them the inquisitors, and other officers of the court, on mules: last of all, the inquisitor-general, on a white horse, led by two men.

A scaffold is erected, large enough for two or three thousand people; at one end of which are the prisoners. at the other the inquisitors. After a sermon, made up of encomiums of the inquisition, and invectives against heretics, a priest ascends a desk near the scaffold, and having taken the abjuration of the penitents, recites the final sentence of those who are to be put to death, and delivers them to the secular arm, earnestly beseeching, at the same time, the secular power *not to touch their blood, or put their lives in danger!!!* The prisoners, being thus in the hands of the civil magistrate, are presently loaded with chains, and carried first to the secular jail, and from thence in an hour or two, brought before the civil judge; who, after asking in what religion they intend to die, pronounces sentence on such as declare they die in the communion of the church of Rome, that they shall first be strangled, and then burnt to ashes; or such as die in any other faith, that they be burnt alive. Both are immediately carried to the Ribera, the place of execution, where there are as many stakes set up as there are prisoners to be burnt, with a quantity of dry furze about them. The stakes of the professed, that is, such as persist in their heresy, are about four yards high, having a small board towards the top for the prisoner to be seated on. The negative or relapsed being first strangled and burnt, the professed mount their stakes by a ladder, and the Jesuits, after several repeated exhortations to be reconciled to the church, part with them, telling them that they leave them to the devil, who is standing at their elbow to receive their souls, and carry them to the flames of hell. On this a great shout is raised, and the cry is, "*Let the dogs' beards be made!*" which is done by thrusting flaming furze, fastened to long poles, against their faces, till their faces are burnt to a coal, which is accompanied with the loudest acclamations of joy. At last, fire is set to the furze at the bottom of them, over which the professed are chained so high that the top of the flame seldom reaches higher than the seat they sit on; so that they are rather roasted than burnt. There cannot be a more lamentable spectacle. The sufferers continually cry out while they are able, "Pity, for the love of God!" Yet it is beheld by all sexes and ages with transports of joy and satisfaction.*

* **Buck's Theological Dictionary.**

62. The War of the Cevennes, in France.

The power of England being established by her great victory over the *Spanish Armada*, in the year 1588, made her the universal champion of protestantism. The popish kingdoms shrunk from provoking the resentment of a country which had thus shown the impotence of all external hostility. The church in France thenceforth continued undisturbed, except by the private jealousies and provocations of the monks. But the accession of Charles II., a popish hypocrite and a French slave to the English throne, degraded England, and stripped protestantism abroad of sword and shield.

The protestant church in France had increased rapidly under the reigns of Henry IV. and Louis XIII. At the beginning of the reign of Louis XIV. it amounted to two millions and a half, incomparably the most industrious, intelligent, and orderly portion of the people. Its clergy were distinguished for piety and learning. It had six hundred and twenty-seven places of worship, and six hundred and forty-seven ministers.

Protestantism is a safe religion in either master or subject; for the Christian honours the laws for conscience sake. The Huguenots were eminently loyal during the period from the edict of Nantes in 1598 to the beginning of the persecutions under Louis XIV. They have even the testimony of Louis to their unimpeachable allegiance. In a letter to Cromwell, who had desired that the duke of Savoy, in his cruelties to the Vaudois, should not be suffered to expect encouragement from France, the king stated "that it was not likely that he would co-operate in inflicting any punishment on the subjects of the duke of Savoy, on account of their attachment to the pretended reformed religion, seeing he conferred so many tokens of favour on his subjects of the same religious profession; for he had reason to *applaud their fidelity and zeal in his service*. They omitted no opportunity of giving him evidence of their loyalty, *even beyond all that could be imagined*, contributing in all things to the advantage of his affairs.

Laws against religion are justifiable only when that religion is made a political engine; where, under the pretence of pious zeal, treason lurks, and where a hatred to the recognized establishments of the state, and an alliance with its foreign enemies, are leading principles. The rebel must be restrained, let his pious pretence for rebellion be what it will. But the spirit of persecution waits for none of those things.

Within five years from this testimony to the pacific and obedient conduct of its protestant subjects, the government commenced a course of the most galling irritation. Every year some new drop of bitterness was instilled into the wound of the last, until the whole calamity was completed by the revocation of the edict of Nantes.

On the 22d of October, 1685, the decree of revocation announced—

1. A repeal of the whole edict of 1598, and of every concession in favour of the reformed, with a declaration that their churches should be demolished.

2. A prohibition of meeting for worship in any place or under any pretence.

3. An express interdict of every kind of religious exercise in the houses of those among the reformed of high rank or noble birth, under pain of *confiscation* and *death*.

4. The banishment of all their ministers from the kingdom within fifteen days, unless they become Roman Catholics.

5. An offer of a third more than their stipend to those ministers who would conform, with a continuation of it to their widows.

6. An offer of admission to the profession of the law three years sooner than the usual time.

7. The absolute shutting up of all their schools.

8. The baptism of their children by the popish priests, under a penalty of five hundred livres.

9. Permission given, by the king's clemency, for the refugees, if returned within four months, and converted to popery, to recover their property and privileges.

10. A prohibition of leaving the kingdom under the penalty of galleys or death.

11. The decrees against the relapsed were to be put in execution; but those who were not decided or prepared to declare themselves, might remain where they resided until it pleased God to enlighten them, continue their trade or arts, and enjoy their property without being disturbed, provided they refrained from all exercises of their religion, and from every kind of meeting, on that account.

The apparent lenity of the final article, which yet utterly prohibited the exercise of that religion in which was all the hope of the reformed, was soon found to be no defence. Hired informers were sent among the people. Soldiers hunted them down like wild beasts, and shot them. Their houses were burned, their property was plundered, their families were treated with the most cruel indignities; many were tortured, and numbers of the more important persons were sent for galley slaves. Above a million of people fled into the protestant countries, carrying with them their arts, industry, and manufactures. The loss to France in wealth was immense; but in character, honour, and religion, it was incalculable.

The difficulty of even this unhappy escape became at length so great, that the reformed in the south took up arms for the mere preservation of their lives. Success increased their numbers, and the war of the Caurisaries began. The whole mountain country of the Cevennes became the seat of a severe conflict. The king's troops were harassed and defeated, in a long series of encounters, by the undisciplined valour of a peasantry who fought the battle of despair. This war raged during four years. The Cevennes was the grave of a multitude of the persecutors. The shedding of the blood of the protestants was awfully repaid. The government finally found the necessity of gentler means; partial pacifications were offered; and it is probable that the comparative quiet of the remaining protestants, during the century, was largely due to the exploits of the men of the Cevennes.

But the persecution was to be retaliated by a deeper, though a more circuitous vengeance. Some links of the chain are traceable. It may be beyond human eyes to see how far they still extend. The first result was the encouragement of William III. to attempt the English throne. Holland had received with generous hospitality a vast number of the refugees. Many of them were military; they had among them distinguished officers, and William thus found himself in possession of a most valuable body of troops. He obtained an allowance for their pay from the states, and prepared for invasion!

Another striking result was its effect on the mind of England. The notorious connexion of James II. with Rome had already prepossessed the nation against the Stuarts. But this fearful development of the natural heart of popery; the cries that came on every wind across the channel; the spectacle of the unhappy emigrants flung on the British shore, worn out with flight and disease, terror and wounds; and those men, their fellow Christians; bound by the closest tie of faith, and those sufferings undergone for the purest cause of Christianity; put an end to all the insidious glosses and flatteries of priest or king. Within three years from the revocation, the Stuarts were driven into eternal exile; and William was placed on the throne, to be the champion of the church throughout Europe, and the leading enemy of France. Another, and still sterner result, was the national impurity; which at length, after undermining and consuming away the foundations of the public strength, flamed out in the French revolution.—*Croly's Sketch of the Hist. of the Church.*

63. The Spanish Armada.

Philip, king of Spain, husband to the deceased queen Mary of England, was no less inimical to the protestants than that princess. He had always disliked the English, and, after her death, determined if possible to crown that infamous cruelty which had disgraced the whole progress of her reign, by making a conquest of the island, and putting every protestant to death.

The great warlike preparations made by this monarch, though the purpose was unknown, gave an universal alarm to the English nation; as it appeared evident that he was taking measures to seize the crown of England, though he had not declared that intention. Pope Sixtus V., not less ambitious than himself, and equally desirous of persecuting the protestants, urged him to the enterprise. He excommunicated the queen of England, and published a crusade against her, with the usual indulgences. All the ports of Spain resounded with preparations for this alarming expedition; and the Spaniards seemed to threaten the English with a total annihilation.

Three years had been spent by Philip in making the necessary preparations for this mighty undertaking; and his fleet, which on account of its prodigious strength was called "*The Invincible Armada*," was now completed. A consecrated banner was procured from the pope, and the gold of Peru was lavished on the occasion. Several instruments of torture were also taken on board the Spanish fleet, designed for the tormenting of the English protestants, in case their scheme took effect.

Troops from Italy, Germany, Flanders, and Spain were embarked, or sent to the points from which they might be thrown on England. The Spanish nobles volunteered. Men of the highest rank in the popish realms solicited employment; the first sea officer of the age, the Marquis Santa Croce, whose very name seemed an omen, commanded the fleet; the first general of the age, the prince of Parma, marched the Spanish army, thirty-four thousand of the most celebrated troops in Europe, down to the Flemish shore, for invasion. The fleet numbered one hundred and thirty ships of war, carrying thirty thousand troops and seamen. But it had a darker freight of monks, papal bulls, and instruments of torture.

Elizabeth, finding that she must contend for her crown with the whole force of Spain, made preparations for resistance; and though her fleet (consisting of less than a hundred ships, and much inferior in point of size to her antagonist) seemed very inadequate to oppose so powerful an enemy, every place in the kingdom discovered the greatest readiness in defending their religion and liberty, by contributing ships, men, and money.

Men of reflection, however, entertained the greatest apprehensions, when they considered the force of the Spaniards, under the duke of Parma, the most consummate general of the age.

Elizabeth was sensible that, next to her popularity, the firmest support of her throne consisted in the zeal of the people for the protestant religion, and their abhorrence of popery. She reminded the English of their former danger from the tyranny of Spain; and of the bloody massacres in the Indies, and the unrelenting executions in the Low Countries; and a list was published of the several instruments of torture with which, it was said, the Spanish armada was loaded. The more to excite the martial spirit of the nation, the queen appeared on horseback in the camp at Tilbury; and riding through the lines, she exhorted the soldiers to remember their duty to their country and their God, declaring that she would rather perish in battle than survive the ruin and slavery of her people.

The armada, after sailing from Lisbon, suffered considerably from storms; but the damages being repaired, the Spaniards again put to sea. Effingham, admiral of the English fleet, who was stationed at Plymouth, had just time to get out of port, when he saw the armada advancing towards him, disposed in the form of a crescent, and stretching the distance of seven miles, from one extremity to the other. As the armada advanced up the channel, the English hung on its rear, and soon found that the great size of the Spanish ships was no advantage to them. Their bulk exposed them the more to the enemy's fire, while their cannon, placed too high, passed over the heads of the English.

The armada had now reached Calais, and cast anchor, in expectation that the duke of Parma would put to sea and join them. The English admiral, however, filling eight of his smaller ships with combustible materials, sent them one after another into the midst of the enemy. The Spaniards were so much alarmed, that they immediately cut their cables, and fled with the greatest precipitation. The English, whose fleet now amounted to one hundred and forty sail, fell upon them next morning, while in confusion; and besides doing great damage to other ships, they took or destroyed about twelve of the enemy.

The Spanish admiral, defeated in many rencounters, and perceiving the inevitable destruction of his fleet, prepared to return homewards; but conducting his shattered ships by the circuitous route of Scotland and Ireland, a violent tempest overtook them near the Orkneys. Many of the vessels were wrecked on the western isles of Scotland, and on the coast of Ireland; and not one half of this mighty armament returned to Spain.

---

64. Gunpowder Plot.

In order to crush popery in England, king James I., soon after his accession to the throne, took proper measures for eclipsing the power of the Roman catholics, by enforcing those laws which had been made against them by his predecessors. This enraged the papists to such a degree, that a conspiracy was formed by some of the principal leaders, the object of which was to blow up the king, the royal family, and both houses of parliament; and thus to involve the nation in utter and inevitable ruin.

The cabal who formed the resolution of putting in practice this scheme consisted of thirteen persons, most of whom were men both of birth and fortune.

Their consultations were held in the spring and summer of the year 1604, and it was towards the close of that year that they begun their operations. It was agreed that a few of the conspirators should run a mine below the hall in which the parliament was to assemble, and that they should choose the very moment when the king should deliver his speeches to both houses for springing the mine; and thus, by one blow, cut off the king, lords, commons, and all the other enemies of the Catholic religion, in that very spot where that religion had been most oppressed. For this purpose a house was hired adjoining the upper house of parliament, and the conspirators, expecting their victims would meet on the 17th of February following, began on the 11th of December to dig in the cellar, through the wall of partition, which was three yards thick. There were seven in number joined in this labour. They went in by night, and never after appeared in sight; for, having supplied themselves with powder, shot, and fire-arms, they had formed a resolution rather to die than be taken.

On Candlemas-day, 1605, they had dug as far through the wall as to be able to hear a noise on the other side; upon which unexpected event, fearing a discovery, Guido Fawkes (one of the principal actors in this conspiracy) was despatched to know the occasion, and returned with the favourable report, that the place from whence the noise came was a large cellar under the upper house of parliament, full of seacoal which was then on sale, and the cellar offered to be let.

On this information the cellar was hired, and the remainder of the coal was bought by one of the conspirators. He then sent for thirty barrels of gunpowder from Holland, and landing them at Lambeth, conveyed them gradually by night to this cellar, where they were covered with stones, iron bars, a thousand billets, and five hundred fagots; all which was done at their leisure, the parliament being prorogued to the 5th of November.

This being done, the conspirators next consulted how they should secure the duke of York (who was too young to be expected at the parliament-house) and his sister the princess Elizabeth. It was resolved that two persons should enter into the duke's chamber, and a dozen more, properly disposed at several doors, with two or three on horseback at the court-gate to receive him, should carry him safe away as soon as the parliament house was blown up; or if that could not be effected, that they should kill him, and declare the princess Elizabeth queen, having secured her under pretence of a hunting-match that day.

It was agreed, also, to apply to France, Spain, and other powers, for assistance after the plot had taken effect, and to proclaim the princess Elizabeth queen, spreading a report, after the blow was given, that the puritans were the perpetrators of this inhuman act.

All matters being now prepared by the conspirators, they waited with the utmost impatience the 5th of November. But all their counsels were blasted by a happy and providential circumstance. One of the conspirators having a desire to save William Parker, Lord Monteagle, sent him the following letter:

"My Lord,

"Out of the love I bear to some of your friends, I have a care for your preservation; therefore I advise you, as you tender your life, to devise you some excuse to shift off your attendance at this parliament; for God and man have concurred to punish the wickedness of this time; and think not slightly of this advertisement, but retire yourself into the country, where you may expect the event with safety; for though there be no appearance of any stir, yet I say they shall receive a terrible blow this parliament, and yet they shall not see who hurts them. This counsel is not to be contemned, because it may do you good, and can do you no harm; for the danger is past so soon (or as quickly) as you burn this letter; and I hope God will give you grace to make good use of it, to whose holy protection I commend you."

The lord Monteagle, was, for some time, at a loss what judgment to form of this letter, and unresolved whether he should slight the advertisement or not; and fancying it a trick of his enemies to frighten him into an absence from parliament, would have determined on the former, had his own safety only been in question; but apprehending the king's life might be in danger, he took the letter at midnight to the earl of Salisbury, who was equally puzzled about the meaning of it; and though he was inclined to think it merely a wild and waggish contrivance to alarm Monteagle, yet he thought proper to consult about it with the earl of Suffolk, lord chamberlain. The expression "that the blow should come without knowing who hurt them" made them imagine that no time would be more proper than the time of parliament, nor by any other way like to be attempted than by gunpowder, while the king was sitting in that assembly. The lord chamberlain thought this the more probable, because there was a great cellar under the parliament chamber not used for any thing but wood or coal, belonging to Wineyard, the keeper of the palace; and having communicated the letter to the earls Nottingham, Worcester, and Northampton, they proceeded no further till the king came from Royston on the 1st of November.

His majesty being shown the letter by the earls, who at the same time acquainted him with their suspicions, was of opinion that either nothing should be done or else enough to prevent the danger; and that a search should be made on the day preceding that designed for the execution of this plot.

Accordingly, on Monday the 4th of November, in the afternoon, the lord chamberlain, whose office it was to see all things put in readiness for the king's coming, accompanied by Monteagle, went to visit all places about the parliament-house, and taking a slight occasion to see the cellar, observed only piles of billets and fagots, but in greater number than he thought Wineyard could want for his own use. On his asking who owned the wood, and being told it belonged to one Mr. Percy, he began to have some suspicions, knowing him to be a rigid papist, and so seldom there, that he had no occasion for such a quantity of fuel; and Monteagle confirmed him therein by observing that Percy had made him great professions of friendship.

Though there were no other materials visible, yet Suffolk thought it was necessary to make a further search; and upon his return to the king, a resolution was taken that it should be made in such a way as should be effectual, without creating an alarm.

Sir Thomas Knevet, steward of Westminster, was accordingly ordered, under the pretext of searching for stolen tapestry hangings in that place, and other houses thereabouts, to remove the wood, and see if any thing was concealed underneath. This gentleman going at midnight, with several attendants, to the cellar, met Fawkes just coming out of it, booted and spurred, with a tinder box and three matches in his pockets; and seizing him without any ceremony, or asking him any questions, as soon as the removal of the wood discovered the barrels of gunpowder, he caused him to be bound and properly secured.

Fawkes, who was a hardened and intrepid villain, made no hesitation of avowing the design, and that it was to be executed on the morrow. He made the same acknowledgment at his examination before a committee of the council; and though he did not deny having some associates in this conspiracy, yet no threats of torture could make him discover any of them; he declaring that "he was ready to die, and had rather suffer ten thousand deaths than willingly accuse his master, or any other."

A number of the conspirators of this plot were apprehended and executed; several, however, succeeded in escaping from the country.

The lord Monteagle had a grant of two hundred pounds a year in land, and a pension of five hundred pounds for life, as a reward for discovering the letter which gave the first hint of the conspiracy; and the anniversary of this providential deliverance was ordered to be for ever commemorated by prayer and thanksgiving.

---

65. Irish Massacre of the Protestants, in 1641.

The gloom of popery had overshadowed Ireland, from its first establishment there till the reign of Henry VIII., when the rays of the gospel began to dispel the darkness, and afford that light which had till then been unknown in that island. The abject ignorance in which the people were held, with the absurd and superstitious notions they entertained, were sufficiently evident to many: and the artifices of their priests were so conspicuous, that several persons of distinction, who had hitherto been strenuous papists, would willingly have endeavoured to shake off the yoke, and embrace the protestant religion; but the natural ferocity of the people, and their strong attachment to the ridiculous doctrines which they had been taught, made the attempt dangerous. It was, however, at length undertaken, though attended with the most horrid and disastrous consequences.

Anxious to extirpate the protestant faith, the papists concerted and put in execution a most diabolical plot, the design of which was, that a general insurrection should take place at the same time throughout the kingdom; and that all the protestants, without exception, should be murdered. The day fixed for this massacre was the 23d of October, 1641, the feast of Ignatius Loyola, founder of the Jesuits: and the chief conspirators, in the principal parts of the kingdom, made the necessary preparations for the intended conflict.

In order that this detested scheme might the more infallibly succeed, the most distinguished artifices were practised by the papists; and their behaviour in their visits to the protestants, at this time, was with more seeming kindness than they had hitherto shown, which was done the more completely to effect the inhuman and treacherous designs then meditating against them.

The execution of this savage conspiracy was delayed till the approach of winter, that the sending of troops from England might be attended with greater difficulty. Cardinal Richlieu, the French minister, had promised the conspirators a considerable supply of men and money; and many Irish officers had given the strongest assurances that they would heartily concur with their Catholic brethren, as soon as the insurrection took place.

The day preceding that appointed for carrying this design into execution was now arrived, when, happily for the metropolis of the kingdom, the conspiracy was discovered by one Owen O'Connelly, an Irishman; for which most signal service the English parliament voted him five hundred pounds, and a pension of two hundred pounds during life.

So very seasonably was this plot discovered, even but a few hours before the city and castle of Dublin were to have been surprised, that the lords-justices had but just time to put themselves and the city in a proper posture of defence. The lord M'Guire, who was the principal leader here, with his accomplices, were seized the same evening in the city; and in their lodgings were found swords, hatchets, pole-axes, hammers, and such other instruments of death as had been prepared for the destruction and extirpation of the protestants in that part of the kingdom.

Thus was the metropolis happily preserved; but the bloody part of the intended tragedy was past prevention. The conspirators were in arms all over the kingdom early in the morning of the day appointed, and every protestant who fell in their way was immediately murdered. No age, sex, or condition was spared. The wife, weeping for her butchered husband, and embracing her helpless children, was pierced with them, and perished by the same stroke. The old, the young, the vigorous, and the infirm, underwent the same fate, and were blended in one common ruin. In vain did flight save from the first assault; destruction was every where let loose, and met the hunted victims at every turn. In vain was recourse had to relations, to companions, to friends; all connexions were dissolved, and death was dealt by that hand from which protection was implored and expected. Without provocation, without opposition, the astonished English, living in profound peace, and, as they thought, full of security, were massacred by their nearest neighbours, with whom they had long maintained a continued intercourse of kindness and good offices. Nay, even death was the slightest punishment inflicted by these monsters in human form! all the tortures which wanton cruelty could invent, all the lingering pains of body, all the anguish of mind, and agonies of despair, could not satiate revenge excited without injury, and cruelty derived from no just cause whatever. Depraved nature, or even perverted religion, though encouraged by the utmost license, cannot reach to a greater pitch of ferocity than appeared in these merciless barbarians. Even the weaker sex themselves, naturally tender to their own sufferings, and compassionate to those of others, here emulated their robust companions in the practice of every cruelty. The very children, taught by example, and encouraged by the exhortations of their parents, dealt their feeble blows on the dead carcasses of defenceless children of the English.

Nor was the avarice of the Irish sufficient to produce the least restraint on their cruelty. Such was their frenzy, that the cattle they had seized, and by rapine had made their own, were, because they bore the name of English, wantonly slaughtered, or, when covered with wounds, turned loose into the woods, there to perish by slow and lingering torments.

The commodious habitations of the planters were laid in ashes or levelled with the ground. And where the wretched owners had shut themselves up in the houses, and were preparing for defence, they perished in the flames; together with their wives and children. This massacre, in which many thousands perished, was retaliated upon the Irish, in 1649, by Oliver Cromwell; who was sent to Ireland to quell the rebellion in that country. This energetic man, having defeated the Irish army, took Drogheda by assault, and *put the whole garrison* to the sword. This struck such a terror, that the whole country soon after submitted to the authority of the English parliament.

---

66. Religious Rites, Opinions, &c. of the North American Indians.

The Indians of this country were generally polytheists, or believed in a plurality of gods. Some were considered as local deities; yet they believed that there was one supreme God, or *Great Spirit*, the creator of the rest, and of all creatures and things. Him the natives of New England called Kichtan. They believed that good men, at death, ascended to Kichtan, above the heavens, where they enjoyed their departed friends and all good things; that bad men also went and knocked at the gate of glory, but Kichtan bade them depart, for there was no place for such, whence they wandered in restless poverty. This Supreme Being they held to be good, and prayed to him when they desired any great favour, and paid a sort of acknowledgment to Him for plenty, victory, &c. The manner of worship in many of the Indian tribes was to sing and dance around a large fire.

There was another power which they called *Hobbamock;* in English, the devil—of whom they stood in greater awe, and worshipped him merely from a principle of fear, and it is said that they sometimes even sacrificed their own children to appease him.* They prayed to him to heal their wounds and diseases. When found curable, he was supposed to be the author of their

* Morse and Parish's History of New England.

complaints; when they were mortal, they were ascribed to Kichtan, whose diseases none are able to remove; therefore, they never prayed to him in sickness. Their priests, which were called *powaws*, and their chief warriors, pretended often to see Hobbamock in the shape of a man, fawn, or eagle, but generally of a *snake*. The duty and office of the powaws was to pray to Hobbamock for the removal of evils; the common people joined or said amen. In his prayer the powaw promised skins, kettles, hatchets, beads, &c., as sacrifices, if his request should be granted.

The apparent insensibility of the Indians under pains and wounds is well known; yet they had awful apprehensions of death.

When sick, and all hope of recovery was gone, their bursting sobs and sighs, their wringing hands, their flowing tears, and dismal cries and shrieks, were enough to excite sympathy from the hardest heart. Their affection was very strong for their children, who by indulgence were saucy and undutiful. A father would sometimes, through grief and rage for the loss of a child, stab himself. Some tribes of Indians would not allow of mentioning the name of a friend after death. When a person died they generally buried with him his bow and arrows, dogs, and whatever was valuable to him while living, supposing he would want them in another world, as their ideas of the happiness of heaven consisted in finding plenty of game, feasting, &c.

The Indians appeared to have distinct traditions of the creation and deluge, and some of their words, rites, and ceremonies bear a strong affinity to those of the ancient Hebrews. The following is from various authors.

"When the Indians determine on war or hunting, they have stated preparatory religious ceremonies for purification, particularly by fasting, as the Israelites had.

"Father Charlevoix gives an account of this custom

in his time. In case of an intention of going to war, he who is to command does not commence the raising of soldiers till he has fasted several days, during which he is smeared with black—has no conversation with any one—invokes by day and night his *tutelar* spirit, and above all, is very careful to observe his dreams. The fast being over, he assembles his friends, and with a string of wampum in his hands, he speaks to them after this manner: Brethren! the Great Spirit authorizes my sentiments, and inspires me with what I ought to do. The blood of —— is not wiped away; his body is not covered, and I will acquit myself of this duty towards him," &c.

Mr. M'Kenzie in some measure confirms this account, though among different nations. "If the tribes feel themselves called upon to go to war, the elders convene the people, in order to obtain the general opinion. If it be for war, the chief publishes his intention to smoke in the sacred stem (a pipe) at a certain time. To this solemnity meditation and fasting are required, as preparatory ceremonials. When the people are thus assembled, and the meeting sanctified by the custom of smoking (this may be in imitation of the smoke of the incense offered on the altar of the Jews), the chief enlarges on the causes which have called them together, and the necessity of the measures proposed on the occasion. He then invites those who are willing to follow him, to smoke out of the sacred stem, which is considered as a token of enrolment." A sacred feast then takes place, and after much ceremony, usual on such occasions, "the chief, turning to the east, makes a speech to explain more fully the design of their meeting, then concludes with an acknowledgment for past mercies received, and a prayer for the continuance of them, from the Master of Life. He then sits down, and the whole company declare their approbation and thanks by uttering the word *Ho!*" (in a very hoarse, guttural sound, being the third syllable of the beloved name), " with an emphatic promulgation of the last letter. The chief then takes up the pipe, and holds it to the mouth of the officiating person" (like a priest of the Jews with the incense), "who after smoking three whiffs, utters a short prayer, and then goes round with it from east to west, to every person present." The ceremony then being ended, "he returns the company thanks for their attendance, and wishes them, as well as the whole tribe, health and life."

"A writer (Adair) who has had the best opportunities to know the true idiom of their language, by a residence among them for forty years, has taken great pains to show the similarity of the Hebrew with the Indian languages, both in their roots and general construction; and insists that many of the Indian words, to this day, are purely Hebrew, notwithstanding their exposure to the loss of it to such a degree as to make the preservation of it, so far, little less than miraculous."

Mr. Boudinot, speaking of the Indian traditions as received by their nations, says, not having the assistance afforded by the means of writing and reading, they are obliged to have recourse to tradition, as Du Pratz, vol. ii. p. 169, has justly observed, "to preserve the remembrance of remarkable transactions or historical facts; and this tradition cannot be preserved but by frequent repetitions; consequently many of their young men are often employed in hearkening to the old beloved men narrating the history of their ancestors, which is thus transmitted from generation to generation." "In order to preserve them pure and incorrupt, they are careful not to deliver them indifferently to all their young people, but only to those young men of whom they have the best opinion. They hold it as a certain fact, delivered down from their ancestors, that their forefathers, in very remote ages, came from a far distant country, by the way of the west, where all the people were of one colour, and that in process of time they moved eastward to their present settlements."

This tradition is corroborated by a current report among them, related by the old Chickkasah Indians to our traders, that about one hundred years ago there came from Mexico some of the old Chickasah nation, or, as the Spaniards call them, Chichemicas, in quest of their brethren, as far north as the Aquahpah nation, above one hundred and thirty miles above the Natchez, on the south-east side of the Mississippi river; but through French policy, they were either killed or sent back, so as to prevent their opening a brotherly intercourse with them, as they had proposed. It is also said, that the Nauatalcas believe that they dwelt in another region before they settled in Mexico; that their forefathers wandered eighty years in search of it, through a strict obedience to the commands of the Great Spirit, who ordered them to go in quest of new lands, that had such particular marks as were made known to them, and they punctually obeyed the divine mandate, and that means found out and settled that fertile country of Mexico.

Our southern Indians have also a tradition among them, which they firmly believe, that of old time their ancestors lived beyond a great river; that nine parts of their nation out of ten passed over the river, but the remainder refused, and stayed behind; that they had a king when they lived far to the west, who left two sons; that one of them, with a number of his people, travelled a great way for many years, till they came to Delaware river, and settled there; that some years ago the king of the country from which they had emigrated, sent a party in search of them; this was at the time the French were in possession of the country on the river Alleghany; that after seeking six years, they found an Indian who led them to the Delaware towns, where they staid one year; that the French sent a white man with them on their return, to bring back an account of their country, but they have never been heard of since.

It is said among their principal, or beloved men, that they have it handed down from their ancestors, that the book which the white people have was once theirs; that while they had it they prospered exceedingly, but that the white people bought it of them, and learnt many things from it, while the Indians lost their credit, offended the Great Spirit, and suffered greatly from the neighbouring nations; that the Great Spirit took pity on them, and directed them to this country; that on their way they came to a great river which they could not pass, when God dried up the waters and they passed over dryshod. They also say that their forefathers were possessed of an extraordinary divine spirit, by which they foretold future events, and controlled the common course of nature, and this they transmitted to their offspring, on condition of their obeying the sacred laws; that they did by these means bring down showers of plenty on the beloved people; but that this power for a long time past had entirely ceased.

Mr. M'Kenzie, in his History of the Fur Trade, and his journey through North America, by the lakes, to the Pacific, in the year ——, says that "the Indians informed him, that they had a tradition among them that they originally came from another country, inhabited by wicked people, and had traversed a great lake, which was narrow, shallow, and full of islands, where they suffered great hardships and much misery, it being always winter, with ice and deep snows; at a place they called the Coppermine River, where they made the first land, the ground was covered with copper, over which a body of earth had since been collected, to the depth of a man's height. They believe also, that in ancient times their ancestors had lived till their feet were worn out with walking, and their throats with eating. They described a deluge, when the waters spread over the whole earth, except the highest mountain, on the top of which they were preserved. They also believe in a future judgment."—*M'Kenzie's History*, p. 113.

The Indians to the eastward say that previous to the white people coming into the country, their ancestors were in the habit of using circumcision, but latterly, not being able to assign any reason for so strange a practice, their young people insisted on its being abolished.

M'Kenzie says the same of the Indians he saw on his route, even at this day. (*History*, p. 34.) Speaking of the nations of the Slave and Dog-rib Indians, very far to the north-west, he says, "whether circumcision be practised among them, I cannot pretend to say; but the appearance of it was general among those I saw."

The Dog-rib Indians live about two or three hundred miles from the straits of Kamschatka. Dr. Beatty says, in his journal of a visit he paid to the Indians on the Ohio, about fifty years ago, that an old Christian Indian informed him, that an old uncle of his, who died about the year 1728, related to him several customs and traditions of former times; and among others, that circumcision was practised among the Indians long ago, but their young men making a mock of it, brought it into disrepute, and so it came to be disused. (*Journal*, p. 89.) The same Indian said, that one tradition they had was, that once the waters had overflowed all the land, and drowned all the people then living, except a few, who made a great canoe, and were saved in it. (Page 90.) And that a long time ago, the people went to build a high place; that while they were building of it, they lost their language, and could not understand one another; that while one perhaps called for a stick, another brought him a stone, &c. &c., and from that time the Indians began to speak different languages.

Father Charlevoix, the French historian, informs us that the Hurons and Iroquois, in that early day, had a tradition among them, that the first woman came from heaven, and had twins, and that the elder killed the younger.

In an account published in the year 1644 by a Dutch minister of the gospel in New-York, giving an account of the Mohawks, he says, "an old woman came to my house, and told the family that her forefathers had told her that the Great Spirit once went out walking with his brother, and that a dispute arose between them, and the Great Spirit killed his brother." This is plainly a confusion of the story of Cain and Abel. It is most likely from the ignorance of the minister in the idiom of the Indian language misconstruing; Cain being represented a great man, for the Great Spirit. Many mistakes of this kind are frequently made.

---

67. The Indian Mother.

The following account, taken from Mather's Magnalia, serves to show us that the Almighty has not left himself without a witness, even among pagan nations, and it ill becomes us to say that the Lord does not reveal himself at times to those who look to him for help, who never have heard of the way of life and salvation by Jesus Christ.

Pammehanuit, an Indian of prime quality, and his wife, on Martha's Vineyard, having buried their first five children successively, every one of them within ten days of their birth, notwithstanding all their use of *powaws* and of medicines to preserve them—they had a sixth child, a son, born about the year 1638, which was a few years before the English first settled on the Vineyard. The mother was greatly perplexed with fear that she should lose this child, like the former; and utterly despairing of any help from such means as had been formerly tried with so little success, as soon as she was able, with a sorrowful heart, she took up her child, and went out into the field, that she might weep out her sorrows. While she was musing on the insufficiency of all human help, she felt it powerfully suggested unto her mind, that *there is one Almighty God who is to be prayed unto;* that *this God had created all the things that we see;* and that *the God who had given being to herself, and all other people, and had given her child unto her, was easily able to continue the life of her child.*

Hereupon this poor pagan woman resolved that she would seek unto this God for that mercy, and she did accordingly. The issue was, that her child lived; and her faith in Him who thus answered her prayer, was wonderfully strengthened; the consideration whereof, caused her to *dedicate* this child unto the service of that God who had preserved his life; and educate him, as far as might be, to become the servant of God.

Not long after this, the English came to settle on Martha's Vineyard; and the Indians who had been present at some of the English devotions reported that they assembled frequently together, and that the man who spoke among them often looked upward. This woman, from this report, presently concluded that their assemblies were for prayers; and that their prayers were unto that very God whom she had addressed for the life of her child. She was confirmed in this, when the gospel was not long after preached by Mr. Mayhew to the Indians; which gospel she readily, cheerfully, and heartily embraced. And in the confession that she made publicly at her admission into the church, she gave a relation of the preparation for the *knowledge of Christ* wherewith God had in this remarkable way favoured her. Her child, whose name was *Japhet*, became afterwards an eminent minister of Christ. He was pastor to an Indian church on Martha's Vineyard; he also took much pains to carry the gospel unto other Indians on the main land, and his labours were attended with much success.

---

68. Plymouth Settlers.

The colony at Plymouth, Mass., the first European settlement in New-England, was planted principally for the sake of the free and undisturbed enjoyment of religious and civil liberty. The colonists were originally from the north of England; and were of that class of people in those days called *Puritans*, so named from their uncommon zeal in endeavouring to preserve the purity of divine worship.

Being persecuted by their enemies during the reign of James I., they fled with their pastor to Amsterdam, in Holland, in 1608. They afterwards removed to

Leyden, where they remained till they sailed for America.

Having resolved upon a removal, they procured two small ships and repaired to Plymouth, Eng., and from thence they proceeded about one hundred leagues on their voyage, when they were compelled to return, in consequence of one of the ships being leaky. This ship was condemned, and the other, called the *May Flower*, being crowded with passengers, again put to sea Sept. 6th. On the 9th of November, after a dangerous passage, they arrived at Cape Cod, and the next day anchored in the harbour which is formed by the hook of the cape.

Before they landed, having devoutly given thanks to God for their safe arrival, they formed themselves into a "body politic," and chose Mr. John Carver their governor for the first year.

Their next object was to fix on a convenient place for settlement. In doing this they encountered many difficulties—many of them were sick in consequence of the fatigues of a long voyage—their provisions were bad—the season was uncommonly cold—the Indians, though afterwards friendly, were now hostile—and they were unacquainted with the coast. These difficulties they surmounted; and on the 22d of December, 1620, they safely landed at a place which they named *Plymouth*. The anniversary of their landing is still celebrated by the descendants of the *Pilgrims* as a religious festival.

The whole company that landed consisted of but one hundred and one souls. Their situation and prospects were truly dismal and discouraging. The nearest European settlement was five hundred miles distant, and utterly incapable of affording them relief in a time of famine or danger. Wherever they turned their eyes, distress was before them. "Persecuted in their native land—grieved for profanation of the holy Sabbath, and other licentiousness in Holland—fatigued by their long and boisterous voyage—forced on a dangerous and unknown shore in the advance of a cold winter—surrounded with hostile barbarians, without any hope of human succour—denied the aid or favour of the court of England—without a patent—without a public promise of the peaceable enjoyment of their religious liberties—without convenient shelter from the rigours of the weather: such were the prospects and such the situation of these pious and solitary Christians. To add to their distresses, a very mortal sickness prevailed among them, which swept off forty-six of their number before the ensuing spring.

"To support them under these trials, they had need of all the aids and comforts which Christianity affords; and these were found sufficient. The free and unmolested enjoyment of their religion reconciled them to their lonely situation—they bore their hardships with unexampled patience, and persevered in their pilgrimage of almost unparalleled trials with such resignation and calmness, as gave proof of great piety and unconquerable virtue."

---

69. Friends, or Quakers.

The members of this society called themselves, at first, *Seekers*, from their seeking the truth; but afterwards assumed the appellation of *Friends*. The term *Quakers* was an epithet of reproach given them by their enemies. This sect, as a body, trace their origin to George Fox, who was born at Drayton, Leicestershire, in 1624. He was bred a shoemaker and glazier. In 1647 he became dissatisfied with the state of things in the church. He inveighed against the clergy and their vices; against the church, its modes of worship, and doctrines, and the manner in which it was supported. On account of his peculiar sentiments and conduct he was persecuted, and imprisoned at Nottingham, 1649. After his release he travelled into Ireland, Scotland, Holland, Germany, the West Indies, and the American colonies. During the whole of his laborious life he employed himself in persuading men to regard the "*divine light*" implanted in the human mind, as being sufficient to lead to salvation. He was imprisoned no less than eight different times. He is represented as having been a meek, devout, and inoffensive man, and died in London, 1690.

In 1656, the Friends first made their appearance in the colony of Massachusetts, where, on account of their singular views, they suffered some persecution. The legislature passed laws for their banishment, threatening all who should return with death. Under this law *four* were executed.

In practice, they do not hold to a regular gospel ministry, but admit any one, whether male or female, to exhort, as they are moved by the Spirit; nor do they strictly observe the Sabbath, or the ordinances of the gospel. Singing forms no part of their worship. They refuse to take an oath, but always practise affirmation. They also refuse to engage in war, or to pay outward homage to any man. In their dress they are neat and uniform. In their manners they are rather reserved; but distinguished for their love of order and sobriety.

A certain writer remarks of them, that their "benevolence, moral rectitude, and commercial punctuality, have excited, and long secured to them, very general esteem; and it has been observed, that in the multitudes that compose the legion of vagrants and street beggars, not a single Quaker can be found."

The principal residence of the Friends in America is in the state of Pennsylvania, so called after William Penn, an eminent Quaker, to whom this state was granted by Charles II., 1680. There are in this country about seven hundred congregations.

Within a few years a great division has been effected among the Friends in this country, by the preaching of Elias Hicks. His followers are called *Hicksites*, to distinguish them from other Friends, who are termed the *orthodox*.

70. JOHN BUNYAN.

THIS celebrated and valuable man was born A. D. 1628, at Elstow, a small village near Bedford, Eng. His father was by occupation a tinker, who bore a fair character, and brought up his son to the same business; and was anxious, also, that he should be taught to read, write, &c. But being a profligate youth, we are told, he soon forgot nearly all he had learned; yet, it is probable that he retained so much as enabled him to recover, in part, the rest, when his mind became better disposed; which was useful to him in the subsequent part of his life.

Notwithstanding he had been addicted to gross vice and impiety from his youth, still he was the subject of continual alarms and convictions, which at times were peculiarly overwhelming. But these produced no lasting good effect at the time. A copious narrative of these conflicts, temptations, and crimes, is contained in a treatise published by himself, under the title of "*Grace abounding to the Chief of Sinners.*"

During this part of his life he was twice preserved from the most imminent danger of drowning. He was a soldier in the parliament's army, at the siege of Leicester, in 1645. At one time he was drawn out to stand sentinel; but one of his comrades, by choice, took his place, and was shot through the head!

After this his mind was deeply exercised on the subject of religion; and he was enabled to believe to the saving of his soul; and was admitted, by baptism, a member of Mr. Gifford's church, at the age of twenty-seven, A. D. 1655. Soon after he was set apart, by fasting and prayer, to the ministerial office; after much reluctance on his part. At a certain time, previous to the restoration of Charles II.; he was expected to preach in a church, near Cambridge. A student of that university, not remarkable for sobriety, was induced by curiosity to hear "*the tinker prate;*" the discourse made a deep impression on his mind; he sought every opportunity to hear Mr. Bunyan, and at length became an eminent preacher in Cambridgeshire.

When the restoration took place, the laws were framed and executed with a severity evidently intended to exclude every man who scrupled the least tittle of the doctrine, liturgy, discipline, or government of the established church. Mr. Bunyan was one of the first who suffered by them; for being courageous and unreserved, he went on his ministry, without any disguise, until Nov. 12, 1660; when he, with sixty others, was apprehended and committed to the county jail! Security was offered for his appearance at the sessions; but it was refused, as his sureties would not consent that he should be restricted from preaching. He was accordingly confined till the quarter-sessions, when his indictment stated, "That John Bunyan, of the town of Bedford, labourer, had *devilishly* and *perniciously* abstained from coming to church, to hear divine service; and was a common upholder of several unlawful meetings and conventicles, to the great *disturbance* and *distraction* of the good subjects of this kingdom, contrary to the laws of our sovereign lord the king." The charges in this absurd indictment were never proved. He had confessed he was a dissenter, and had preached; this was considered equivalent to conviction, and recorded against him; and as he refused to conform, he was sentenced to perpetual banishment. This sentence, indeed, was not executed; but he was confined in Bedford jail more than twelve years.

During this tedious imprisonment, he had no books, save a Bible and Fox's Martyrology; yet, in this situation, he penned the "Pilgrim's Progress," which ranks high among the works of original genius, and which probably will be read with admiration and profit till the consummation of all things. He is the author of "The Holy War," "Solomon's Temple Spiritualized," Tracts, &c. &c., which are held in high estimation by the religious community.

In 1671 he was chosen pastor of the Baptist church at Bedford, and continued to exercise his ministry until his death, which took place August 31st, 1688, having arrived at the age of sixty years.

71. Piestical Controversy.

The commencement of Pietism was laudable and decent. It was set on foot by the pious and learned *Spener*, who, by the private societies he formed at *Frankfort*, with a design to promote vital religion, roused the lukewarm from their indifference, and excited a spirit of vigour in those who had been satisfied to lament, in silence, the progress of impiety. The remarkable effect of these religious meetings was increased by a book published by this well-meaning man, under the title of *Pious Desires*, in which he exhibited a striking view of the disorders of the church, and proposed the remedies that were proper to heal them. Many persons of good and upright intentions were highly pleased both with the proceedings and writings of Spener; and indeed the greatest part of those, who had the cause of virtue and practical religion truly at heart applauded his designs, though an apprehension of abuses retained numbers from encouraging them openly. These abuses actually happened. The remedies proposed by Spener to heal the disorders of the church fell into unskilful hands, were administered without sagacity or prudence, and thus, in many cases, proved to be worse than the disease itself. The religious meetings above mentioned (or the *Colleges of Piety*, as they were usually called by a phrase borrowed from the Dutch) tended in many places to kindle in the breasts of the multitude the flames of a blind and intemperate zeal, whose effects were impetuous and violent, instead of that pure and rational love of God whose fruits are benign and peaceful. Hence complaints arose against these institutions of *pietism*, as if under a striking appearance of piety they led people into false notions of religion, and fermented, in those who are of a turbulent and violent character, the seeds and principles of mutiny and sedition.

These first complaints would have been undoubtedly hushed, and the tumults they occasioned have subsided

DEPARTURE FROM HOLLAND
The Plymouth settlers being commended to God took affectionate leave of their friends and sailed for America to enjoy Religious freedom.

JOHN ELLIOT,
the "Apostle to the Indians" successfully preached the Gospel to the Indians in New England. He began his labors about the year 1646.

by degrees, had not the contest that arose at *Leipsic*, in the year 1689, added fuel to the flame.

This contest was by no means confined to *Leipsic*, but diffused its contagion, with incredible celerity, through all the Lutheran churches in the different states and kingdoms of Europe. For, from this time, in all the cities, towns, and villages where Lutheranism was professed, there started up, all of a sudden, persons of various ranks and professions, of both sexes, learned and illiterate, who declared that they were called, by *divine impulse*, to pull up iniquity by the root, to restore to its primitive lustre, and propagate through the world, the declining cause of piety and virtue, to govern the church of Christ by wiser rules than those by which it was at present directed, and who, partly in their writings, and partly in their private and public discourses, pointed out the means and measures that were necessary to bring about this important revolution. All those who were struck with this imaginary *impulse* unanimously agreed, that nothing could have a more powerful tendency to propagate among the multitude solid knowledge, pious feelings, and holy habits, than those private meetings that had been first contrived by Spener, and that afterwards were introduced into Leipsic. Several religious assemblies were accordingly formed in various places, which, though they differed in some circumstances, and were not all composed with equal wisdom, piety, and prudence, were however designed to promote the same general purpose. In the mean time these unusual, irregular, and tumultuous proceedings, filled with uneasy and alarming apprehensions both those who were intrusted with the government of the church and those who sat at the helm of the state. These apprehensions were justified by this important consideration, that the pious and well-meaning persons who composed these assemblies had indiscreetly admitted into their community a parcel of extravagant and hot-headed fanatics, who foretold the approaching destruction of *Babel* (by which they meant the Lutheran church), terrified the populace with fictitious visions, assumed the authority of prophets honoured with a divine commission, obscured the sublime truths of religion by a gloomy kind of jargon of their own invention, and revived doctrines that had long before been condemned by the church. These enthusiasts also asserted that the *millennium*, or thousand years reign of the saints on earth, mentioned by St. John, was near at hand. They endeavoured to overturn the wisest establishments, and to destroy the best institutions, and desired that the power of preaching and administering public instruction might be given promiscuously to all sorts of persons. Thus was the *Lutheran* church torn asunder in the most deplorable manner, while the votaries of *Rome* stood by, and beheld, with a secret satisfaction, these unhappy divisions. The most violent debates arose in all the Lutheran churches; and persons, whose differences were occasioned rather by mere words and questions of little consequence than by any doctrines or institutions of considerable importance, attacked one another with the bitterest animosity; and, in many countries, severe laws were at length enacted against the *Pietists*.

---

72. Emanuel Swedenborg.

Emanuel Swedenborg, a Swedish nobleman, was born at Stockholm in 1689. He appears to have had a good education, for his learning was extensive in almost every branch. He professed himself to be the founder of the New Jerusalem church, alluding to the New Jerusalem spoken of in the book of the Revelation. He asserts that in the year 1743 the Lord manifested himself to him by a personal appearance, and at the same time opened his spiritual eyes, so that he was enabled constantly to see and converse with spirits and angels. From that time he began to print and publish various wonderful things, which he says were revealed to him, relating to heaven and hell, the state of men after death, the worship of God, the spiritual sense of the Scriptures, the various earths in the universe, and their inhabitants; with many other strange particulars.

Swedenborg lived and died in the Lutheran communion, but always professed the highest respect for the church of England. He carried his respect for the person and divinity of Jesus Christ to the highest point of veneration, considering him altogether as "God manifested in the flesh, and as the fulness of the Godhead united to the man Christ Jesus." With respect, therefore, to the sacred Trinity, though he rejected the idea of three distinct persons, as destructive of the unity of the Godhead, he admitted three distinct essences, principles, or characters, as existing in it; namely, the divine essence or character, in virtue of which he is called the Father or Creator; the human essence, principle, or character, united to the divine, in the person of Jesus Christ, in virtue of which he is called the Son and Redeemer; and, lastly, the proceeding essence or principle, in virtue of which he is called the Holy Ghost. He further maintains, that the sacred Scripture contains three distinct senses, called celestial, spiritual, and natural, which are united by correspondences; and that in each sense it is divine truth accommodated respectively to the angels of the three heavens, and also to men on earth. This science of correspondences (it is said) has been lost for some thousands of years, viz. ever since the time of Job, but is now revived by Emanuel Swedenborg, who uses it as a key to the spiritual or internal sense of the sacred Scripture; every page of which, he says, is written by correspondence, that is by such things in the natural world as correspond unto and signify things in the spiritual world. He denies the doctrine of atonement, or vicarious sacrifice; together with the doctrines of predestination, unconditional election, justification by faith alone, the resurrection of the material body, &c.; and in opposition thereto, maintains that man is possessed of free will in spiritual things; that salvation is not attainable without repentance, that is, abstaining from evils, because they are sins against God, and living a life of charity and faith, according to the commandments; that man, immediately on his decease, rises again in a spiritual body, which was inclosed in his material body: and that in this spiritual body he lives as a man to eternity, either in heaven or in hell, according to the quality of his past life. That all those passages in the Scripture, generally supposed to signify the destruction of the world by fire, and commonly called the last judgment, must be understood according to the above-mentioned science of correspondences, which teaches that by the end of the world, or consummation of the age, is not signified the destruction of the world, but the destruction or end of the present Christian church, both among Roman catholics and protestants of every description or denomination; and that this last judgment actually took place in the spiritual world in the year 1757; from which era is dated the second advent of the Lord, and the commencement of a new Christian church, which they say is meant by the new heaven and new earth in the revelation and the New Jerusalem thence descending. They use a liturgy, and instrumental as well as vocal music, in their public worship.—*Buck's Theological Dictionary.*

---

73. Eliot, the Indian Missionary.

In 1650, the society in England instituted for propagating the gospel, began a correspondence with the commissioners of the colonies of New England, who were employed as agents of the society. In consequence, exertions were made to christianize the Indians. Mr. John Eliot, minister of Roxbury, distinguished himself in this pious work. He collected the Indian families and established towns; he taught them husbandry, the mechanic arts, and a prudent management of their affairs, and instructed them with unwearied attention in the principles of Christianity. For his uncommon zeal and success, he has been called the *apostle of New England.*

Mr. Eliot began his labours about the year 1646. His first labour was to learn the language, which was peculiarly difficult to acquire; for instance, the Indian word *Nummatchechodtantamoonganunnonash* signified no more in English than *our lusts*.* Eliot having finished a grammar of this tongue, at the close of it he wrote, "*prayers and pains through faith in Christ will do any thing!*" With very great labour, he translated the whole Bible into the Indian language. This Bible was printed in 1664, at Cambridge, and was the first Bible ever printed in America. He also translated the *Practice of Piety*, *Baxter's Call to the Unconverted*, besides some smaller works, into the Indian tongue.

In the course of his labours, Mr. Eliot passed through many scenes of danger, difficulty, and suffering. On one occasion, which may be taken as a specimen of the dangerous journeys which he made through the dreary wilderness to his scattered Indians, he says, "I was not dry, night nor day, from the third day to the sixth; but so travelled; and at night I pull off my boots, wring my stockings, and on with them again, and so continued; yet God helped. I considered that word, 2 Tim. ii. 3. *Endure hardness as a good soldier of Jesus Christ.*"

Many were the affronts that Mr. Elliot received while in his missionary work, when travelling through the wild parts of the country, unattended with any English friend. Sometimes the sachems would thrust him out from among them, telling him that he was impertinent to trouble himself with them or their religion, and that if he came again it was at his peril; but his usual reply was, "*I am about the work of the great God; and my God is with me; so that I fear neither you nor all the sachems in the country; I will go on, and do you touch me if you dare!*" The stoutest of them have, on these occasions, shrunk and fallen before him. Hav-

* Mather's Magnalia.

ing performed many wearisome journeys, and endured many hardships and privations, this indefatigable missionary closed his labours in 1690, aged eighty-six years.

The ardour and zeal of Eliot, Mayhew, and others were crowned with such success, that in 1669, there were ten towns of Indians in Massachusetts who were converted to the Christian religion. In 1665, there were not less than three thousand adult Indian converts in the islands of Nantucket and Martha's Vineyard.

74. The French Prophets.

We find in ecclesiastical history many accounts given of enthusiasts who have arisen, pretending to be under the immediate inspiration of God, and to have the gift of foretelling future events, the gift of tongues, discerning of spirits, &c., as in the apostles' time. Among those who have made the greatest figure in modern times were the *French prophets*, who first appeared in Dauphiny and Vivarais, in France. In the year 1688, five or six hundred protestants, of both sexes, gave themselves out to be prophets, and inspired of the Holy Ghost. They were people of all ages, without distinction, though the greatest part of them were boys and girls, from six or seven to twenty-five years of age. They had strange fits, which came upon them with tremblings and faintings as in a swoon, making them stretch out their arms and legs, and stagger several times before they dropped down. They struck themselves with their hands, fell on their backs, shut their eyes, and heaved with their breasts. They remained a while in trances, and, coming out of them with twitchings, uttered all which came into their mouths. They said they saw the heavens open, the angels, paradise, and hell. The least of their assemblies made up four or five hundred, and some of them amounted to even to three or four thousand persons. When the prophets had been for a while under agitations of body, they began to prophesy. The burden of their prophecies, was, "*Amend your lives; repent ye; the end of all things draws nigh!*"

In the year 1706, three or four of these prophets went over into England, and carried their prophetic spirit with them, which discovered itself in the same way and manner, by ecstasies, agitations, and inspirations, as it had done in France; and they propagated the like spirit to others, so that before the year was out, there were two or three hundred of these prophets in and about London, consisting of men, women, and children, who delivered four or five hundred warnings. The great thing pretended by their spirit was to give warning of the *near approach of the kingdom of God*, and the accomplishment of the Scriptures, concerning the *new heaven* and *new earth*, the *kingdom of the Messiah*, the *first resurrection*, the *new Jerusalem descending from above*, which they said was *now* even at the door; that this great operation was to be wrought on the part of man by spiritual arms only, proceeding from the mouths of those who should, by inspiration, or the mighty gift of the Spirit, be sent forth in great numbers to labour in the vineyard; that this mission of his servants should be attested by signs and wonders from heaven, by a deluge of judgments on the wicked throughout the world, as famine, pestilence, earthquakes, &c. They declared that all the great things they spoke of would be manifest over the whole earth within the term of three years.

These prophets also pretended to have the gift of languages, of discerning the secrets of the heart, the gift of ministration of the same spirit to others by the laying on of the hands, and the gift of healing.

---

75. Sabatai Sevi, the false Messiah.

Since the coming of our Saviour, there has arisen, according to his prediction, among the Jews (who still look for the Messiah to come) many false Messiahs. The most distinguished of these impostors, in modern times, was one *Sabatai Sevi*, who was born in Aleppo, and set himself up as the Messias in the year 1666.

Having visited various places in the Turkish empire, Sabatai began in Jerusalem to reform the Jewish constitution. He had one Nathan for his Elias, or forerunner, who prophesied that the Messiah should appear before the grand seignior in less than two years, and take from him his crown, and lead him in chains.

At Gaza, Sabatai preached repentance, together with faith in himself, so effectually, that the people gave themselves up to their devotion and alms. The noise of this Messias now began to fill all places. Sabatai resolved to go to Smyrna, and then to Constantinople. The Jews throughout Turkey were in great expectation of glorious times. They were now devout and penitent, that they might not obstruct the good they hoped for. Some fasted so long that they were famished to death; others buried themselves in the earth till their limbs grew stiff; with many other painful penances. Sabatai, having arrived at Smyrna, styled himself the only and first-born Son of God, the Messias, the Saviour of Israel. Here he met with some opposition, but prevailed at last to such a degree, that some of his followers prophesied, and fell into strange ecstasies; and four hundred men and women prophesied of his growing kingdom. The people were for a time possessed, and voices were heard from their bowels; some fell into trances, foamed at the mouth, recounted their future prosperity, their visions of the Lion of Judah, and the triumph of Sabatai: all which, says the narrator, were certainly true, being the effects of diabolical delusions, as the Jews themselves have since confessed. Sabatai, now feeling his importance, ordered that the Jews should no longer in their synagogues, pray for the grand seignior (as they were wont to do), for it was an indecent thing to pray for him who was so shortly to be his captive. He also elected princes, to govern the Jews in their march towards the Holy Land, and to minister justice to them when they should be possessed of it.

The people were now pressing to see some miracle, to confirm their faith, and to convince the Gentiles. Here the impostor was puzzled, though any juggling trick would have served their turn. But the credulous people supplied this defect. When Sabatai was before the cadi (or justice of the peace), some affirmed that they saw a *pillar of fire* between him and the cadi; and after some affirmed it, others were ready to swear it, and did swear it also; and this was presently believed by the Jews of that city. He that did not now believe him to be the Messias was to be shunned as an excommunicated person.

From Smyrna, the impostor embarked for Constantinople, where he said God had called him, and where he had much to do. He had a long and troublesome voyage, and upon his arrival, the grand vizier sent for him, and confined him in a loathsome dungeon. The Jews in this city paid him their visits, and appeared to be as infatuated as those of Smyrna. Sabatai, after remaining two months a prisoner in Constantinople, was sent by the grand vizier to the Dardanelli. The Jews here flocked in great numbers to the castle where he was confined, and treated him with great respect. They decked their synagogues with S. S. in letters of gold, and made a crown for him in the wall; they attributed the same titles and prophecies to him which we apply to our Saviour.

He was also, during this imprisonment, visited by pilgrims from all parts that heard his story. Among these was Nehemiah Cohen, from Poland, a man of great learning, who desired a conference with Sabatai, the result of which convinced him that he was an impostor.

Nehemiah accordingly informed the Turkish officers of state that Sabatai was a lewd and dangerous person, and that it was necessary to take him out of their way. The grand seignior being apprized of this, sent for Sabatai, who, much dejected, appears before him.

The grand seignior required a miracle, and chooses one himself. It was this: that Sabatai should be stripped naked, and set for a mark for his archers to shoot at; and if the arrows did not pierce his flesh, he would own him to be the Messiah. Sabatai had not faith enough to bear up under so great a trial. The grand seignior let him know that he would forthwith impale him, and that the stake was prepared for him, unless he would turn Turk. Upon this he consented to turn Mahometan, to the great confusion of the Jews.

---

76. Nonconformists.

Those who refused to conform to the church of England were called nonconformists. This word is generally used in reference to those ministers who were ejected from their living by an act of Uniformity, in 1662. The number of these were about two thousand. However some affect to treat these men with indifference, and suppose that their consciences were more tender than they need be, it must be remembered, that they were men of as extensive learning, great abilities, and pious conduct as ever appeared. Mr. Locke, if his opinion has any weight, calls them "worthy, learned, pious orthodox divines, who did not throw themselves out of service, but were forcibly ejected." Mr. Bogue thus draws their character: "*As to their public ministration,*" he says, "they were orthodox, experimental, serious, affectionate, regular, faithful, able, and popular preachers. *As to their moral qualities,* they were devout and holy; faithful to Christ and the souls of men; wise and prudent; of great liberality and kindness; and strenuous advocates for liberty, civil and religious. *As to their intellectual qualities,* they were learned, eminent, and laborious." These men were driven from their houses, from the society of their friends, and exposed to the greatest difficulties. Their burdens were greatly increased by the Conventicle act, whereby they were prohibited from meeting for any exercise of religion (above five in number) in any other manner than allowed by the liturgy or practice of the church of England. For the first offence the penalty was three months' imprisonment, or pay five pounds;

for the second offence, six months' imprisonment, or ten pounds; and for the third offence, to be banished to some of the American plantations for seven years, or pay one hundred pounds; and in case they returned, to suffer death without benefit of clergy. By virtue of this act, the jails were quickly filled with dissenting protestants, and the trade of an informer was very gainful. So great was the severity of these times, says Neal, that they were afraid to pray in their families, if above four of their acquaintance, who came only to visit them, were present; some families scrupled asking a blessing on their meat, if five strangers were at table.

But this was not all; to say nothing of the Test Act, in 1665, an act was brought into the House, to banish them from their friends (commonly called the Oxford Five Mile Act), by which all dissenting ministers, who would not take an oath, that it was not lawful, upon any *pretence whatever*, to take arms against the king, &c., were prohibited from coming within five miles of any city, town, corporate, or borough, or any place where they had exercised their ministry, and from teaching any school, on the penalty of forty pounds. Some few took the oath; others could not, and consequently suffered the penalty.

In 1663, "the mouths of the high church pulpiteers were encouraged to open as loud as possible. One, in his sermon before the House of Commons, told them, that the nonconformists ought not to tolerated, but to be cured by vengeance. He urged them to set fire to the fagot, and to teach them by scourges or scorpions, and to open their eyes with gall."

Such were the dreadful consequences of this intolerant spirit, that it is supposed near eight thousand died in prison in the reign of Charles II. It is said, that Mr. Jeremiah White had carefully collected a list of those who had suffered between Charles II. and the revolution, which amounted to sixty thousand. The same persecutions were carried on in Scotland; and there, as well as in England, many, to avoid persecution, fled from their country.

But, notwithstanding all these dreadful and furious attacks upon the dissenters, they were not extirpated. Their very persecution was in their favour. The infamous characters of their informers and persecutors; their piety, and zeal, and fortitude, no doubt, had influence on considerate minds; and, indeed, they had additions from the established church, which "several clergymen in this reign deserted as a persecuting church, and took their lot among them." In addition to this, king James suddenly altered his measures, granted a universal toleration, and preferred dissenters to places of trust and profit, though it was evidently with a view to restore popery.

King William coming to the throne, the famous Toleration Act passed, by which they were exempted from suffering the penalties above mentioned, and permission was given them to worship God according to the dictates of their own consciences. In the latter end of queen Anne's reign they began to be a little alarmed. An act of parliament passed, called the Occasional Conformity Bill, which prevented any person in office under the government from entering into a meeting-house. Another, called the Schism Bill, had actually obtained the royal assent, which suffered no dissenters to educate their own children, but required them to be put into the hands of conformists; and which forbade all tutors and schoolmasters being present at any conventicle, or dissenting place of worship; but the very day this iniquitous act was to have taken place, the queen died, (August 1, 1714.)

His majesty king George I. being fully satisfied that these hardships were brought upon the dissenters for their steady adherence to the protestant succession in his illustrious house, against a tory and jacobite ministry, who were paving the way for a popish pretender, procured the repeal of them in the fifth year of his reign; though a clause was left that forbade the mayor or other magistrate to go into any meeting for religious worship with the ensigns of his office.—*Buck's Theological Dictionary.*

FRENCH PROPHETS.

In 1688, five or six hundred persons in France professing to be divinely inspired, uttered many prophecies, accompanied with bodily contorsions.

SCOTCH COVENANTERS

assembled for divine worship, during the time of religious persecution which raged in Scotland.

77. Scotch Covenanters.

Scotland is among the last civilized countries where the horrors of religious persecution raged to any great extent.* In 1581 the general assembly of Scotland drew up a confession of faith, or national covenant, condemning the episcopal government under the name of *hierarchy*, which was signed by James I., and which he enjoined on all his subjects. It was again subscribed in 1590 and 1596. The subscription was renewed in 1638, and the subscribers engaged by oath to maintain religion in the same state as it was in 1580, reject all innovations introduced since that time. This oath, annexed to the confession of faith, received the name of *Covenant*, as those who subscribed it were called *Covenanters*.

During the storm of religious persecution which raged in Scotland, the Covenanters were hunted from crag to glen, throughout the highlands. "The story of their sufferings is almost incredible. Nothing can be more affecting than the measures they took to enjoy the privileges of religious worship. Watches were stationed from hill to hill—men so sunburnt and worn out, that they could be hardly distinguished from the heather of the mountains—who gave a note of alarm on the approach of danger, and the Covenanters had time to disperse, before the bloody swords gleamed in the retreats in which they worshipped. In the gloomy caverns and recesses, made by the awful hand that fashioned Scotland's mountain scenery, these martyrs, each one mourning some dear friend, who had been hunted down by the destroyers, met and heard the mysterious words of God, and sung such wild songs of devotion, that they might have been thought the chantings of the mountain spirits. As their sufferings increased, their sermons and devotional exercises approached nearer to the soul-chilling trumpetings of the ancient prophets, when they foresaw desolation coming out of the north like a whirlwind."

The meeting of an assembly of Covenanters to hear the preaching of the word of God is thus beautifully described by the Scottish poet, *Grahame.*

"But years more gloomy followed; and no more
The assembled people dared, in face of day,
To worship God, or even at the dead
Of night, save when the wintry storm raved fierce,
And thunder peals compell'd the men of blood
To couch within their dens; then dauntlessly
The scattered few would meet, in some deep dell,
By rocks o'er-canopied, to hear the voice,
Their faithful pastor's voice; he, by the gleam
Of sheeted lightnings, oped the sacred book,
And words of comfort spake: Over their souls
His soothing accents came—as to her young
The heath-fowl's plumes, when, at the close of eve,
She gathers in, mournful, her brood dispersed
By murderous sport, and o'er the remnant spreads
Fondly her wings; close nestling 'neath her breast
They, cherish'd, cower amid the purple blooms."

---

78. Moravian Missionaries.

The Moravians, or United Brethren, are a sect generally said to have arisen under count Zinzendorf, a German nobleman of the last century, who, when some of their brethren were driven by persecution from Bohemia, afforded them an asylum on his estates, built them a village called Hernnhut, or Watch-hill, and united himself with them.

According to the society's own account, however, they derive their origin from the Greek church in the ninth century.

The United Brethren are much distinguished for their missionary zeal; and it is said that there is no sect of Christians who have done so much, according to their number and means, for the cause of missions, as have the Moravians. "Their missionaries," as one observes, "are all volunteers; for it is an inviolable maxim with them to *persuade* no man to engage in missions. They are all of one mind as to the doctrines they teach, and seldom make an attempt where there are not half a dozen of them in the mission.

Their zeal is calm, steady, and persevering. They would reform the world, but are careful how they quarrel with it. They carry their point by address, and the insinuations of modesty and mildness, which commend them to all men, and give offence to none. Habits of silence, quietness, and decent reserve mark their character. If any of their missionaries are carried off by sickness, or casualty, men of the same stamp are ready to supply their place."

The following is from a respectable clergyman of their denomination:—"When brethren or sisters find themselves disposed to serve God among the heathen, they communicate their views and wishes to the committee appointed by the synods of the brethren to superintend the missions, in a confidential letter. If on particular inquiry into their circumstances and connexions, no objection is found, they are considered as candidates. As to mental qualifications, much erudition is not required by the brethren. To be well versed in the sacred Scriptures, and to have an experimental knowledge of the truths they contain, is judged indispensably necessary. And it has been found by experience, that a good understanding joined to a friendly disposition, and, above all, a heart filled with the love of God, are the best and the only essential qualifications of a missionary. Nor are the habits of a student in general so well calculated to form his body for a laborious life as those of a mechanic. Yet men of learning are not excluded, and their gifts have been made useful in various ways. When vacancies occur, or new missions are to be begun, the list of candidates is examined; and those who appear suitable are called upon, and accept or decline the call as they find themselves disposed."

The most flourishing missions of the brethren at present are those in Greenland, Antigua, St. Kitts, the Danish West India islands, the cape of Good Hope, and among the Esquimaux on the Labrador coast.

When we consider the hardships, the sufferings, and privations which a missionary must necessarily undergo while among the degraded Hottentots, amid the deserts of South Africa, the mountains of ice and snow in Greenland, or the barren coasts of Labrador, we must allow that the Moravian missionaries possess a large share of that zeal which distinguished the first apostles of Christianity.

At the close of the year 1827, the Moravians had thirty-eight missionary stations, and one hundred and eighty-seven missionaries, including females. The number of their converts in heathen countries, and remote settlements, far exceeds the number of the brethren in their home settlements.

---

79. Zeigenbalg and Swartz, the Danish Missionaries.

The first protestant mission in India was founded by Bartholomew Zeigenbalg, at Tranquebar, on the Coromandel coast, about the year 1707. Zeigenbalg was ordained by the bishop of Zealand, in the twenty-third year of his age, and sailed for India in 1705. In the second year of his ministry he founded a Christian church among the Hindoos, which has been extending its limits to the present time. He went on this mission under the direction of Frederic IV., king of Denmark; he was also patronized in Great Britain by "the Society for promoting Christian Knowledge." Principally through his great labours, a grammar and dictionary were formed, and the Bible was translated into the Tamul tongue, after his having devoted fourteen years to the work. Zeigenbalg died at the early age of thirty-six years. Perceiving that his last hour was at hand, he called his Hindoo congregation, and partook of the holy communion, "amidst ardent prayers and tears;" and afterwards, addressing them in a solemn manner, took an affectionate leave of them. Being reminded by them of the faith of the apostle of the Gentiles, at the prospect of death, who "desired to be with Christ, as far better," he said, "That is also my desire. Washed from my sins in his blood, and clothed with his righteousness, I shall enter into his heavenly kingdom. I pray that the things which I have spoken may be fruitful. Throughout this whole warfare I have entirely *endured* by Christ; and now I can say through him, 'I have fought the good fight; I have finished my course; I have kept the faith. Henceforth there is laid up for me a *crown* of righteousness;'" which words having spoken, he desired that the Hindoo children about his bed, and that the multitude about the house, might sing the hymn beginning "*Jesus, my Saviour Lord.*" When finished, he yielded up his spirit, amidst the rejoicings and lamentations of a great multitude; some rejoicing at his triumphant death and early entrance into glory, and others lamenting the early loss of their faithful apostle, who had first brought the light of the gospel to their dark region from the western world.

The Rev. *Christian F. Swartz* undertook a mission to India, under the government of Denmark, in 1750, and after labouring many years at Tranquebar, and in the neighbouring country, he finally removed to Tanjore, where he continued till his death, in 1798.

His unblameable conduct, and devotedness to the cause of his master, gave him a surprising influence over all classes, and secured the confidence of the bigoted Hindoo. Such was the respect that the Hindoos had for Mr. Swartz, that he could go through the country unarmed and unhurt in time of war, when parties of armed men and robbers infested the country. On seeing him they would say, "*Let him alone, he is a man of God.*" He twice saved the fort of Tanjore, when the credit of the English was lost, and the credit of the rajah also. On the view of an approaching enemy the people of the country refused to supply the fort with provisions; and the streets were covered with the dead. But upon the *bare word* of Mr. Swartz that they should be paid, they brought in a plentiful supply. He was appointed guardian to the family of the deceased king of Tanjore, and employed repeatedly as a mediator between the English government and the country powers. The last twenty years of his life were spent in the education and religious instruction of children, particularly those of poor parents, whom he maintained and instructed gratuitously, and at his death willed his property to the mission at Tanjore. His success was uncommon. It is said he reckoned two thousand persons savingly converted by his means.

After this apostolical and venerable man had laboured fifty years in evangelizing the Hindoos, so sensible were *they* of the blessing, that his death was considered as a public calamity. An innumerable multitude attended the funeral. The Hindoo rajah "shed a flood of tears over the body, and covered it with a gold cloth." His memory is still blessed among the people.*

The following beautiful anecdote is related by bishop Middleton, of this exemplary soldier of the cross. "When lying apparently lifeless, Gericke, a worthy fellow labourer in the service of the same society, who imagined the immortal spirit had actually taken its flight, began to chant over his remains a stanza of the favourite hymn which used to soothe and elevate him in his lifetime. The verses were finished without a sign of recognition or sympathy from the still form before him; but when the last clause was over, the voice which was supposed to be hushed in death took up the second stanza of the same hymn, completed it with distinct and articulate utterance, and then was heard no more!"

---

80. David Brainerd.

This pious and devoted missionary was born in Haddam, Connecticut, April 20th, 1718. From his earliest youth he was remarkably serious and thoughtful. "His natural constitution was tinctured with melancholy,

* Dr. Buchanan.

which, notwithstanding the power and influence of Christianity in his heart, often imbittered his life, and covered his mind with a veil of doubt and gloom. Against this natural infirmity he had to struggle till his dying day; and when this is considered, his abundant labours, indefatigable application, and ardent zeal were indeed surprising; they forcibly illustrated the truth of the Divine promise, 'My strength is made perfect in weakness.'"

At the age of twenty he commenced a course of study with a view of entering the sacred ministry. He became remarkably strict in all the outward duties of religion, but was soon convinced that all his outward acts of prayer, fasting, &c. would be of no avail while his heart remained unchanged and unreconciled to God. For the attainment of this divine change, he laboured and prayed incessantly, but it was with the secret hope of *recommending* himself to God by his religious duties. At length, however, this self-righteous foundation was swept away, he saw his entire helplessness and dependence on the mere mercy of God for salvation through Jesus Christ.

Mr. Brainerd, in the account which he gives of his conversion, says, "While I was endeavouring to pray, as I was walking in a dark, thick grove, *unspeakable glory* seemed to open to the view of my soul; it was a new inward apprehension I had of God, such as I never had before: my soul rejoiced with joy unspeakable, to see such a glorious, divine being. My soul was so captivated and delighted with the excellency, loveliness, greatness, and other perfections of God, that I was even swallowed up in Him, to that degree that, at first, I scarce reflected there was such a creature as myself."

In Sept. 1739, Brainerd entered himself as a student at Yale College, New Haven, Conn. While at this place he was distinguished for diligence and attention to his studies; likewise for his piety and ardent zeal for the promotion of religion.

After leaving college, his mind seemed deeply impressed with the spirit of a Christian missionary, and an ardent longing for the salvation of the heathen. He spent whole days in fasting and prayer, that God would prepare him for his great work; and indeed throughout his whole life he was truly a "man of prayer," lifting up his heart to God on all occasions, frequently spending whole days in prayer and meditation in the fields and woods, desiring holiness of heart far above every other object.

In 1743, Mr. Brainerd was sent by the "Society for the propagation of Christian Knowledge" to the Indians at Kaunaumeek, a place in the woods between Stockbridge and Albany. In this lonely place he continued about a year, and endured many hardships and privations; "yet," says he, "my spiritual conflicts and distresses so far exceed these that I scarcely think of them." The number of Indians being small at this place, and the field of his usefulness limited, Mr. Brainerd thought he could do more for the cause of Christ to labour among the Indians at the forks of the Delaware, in New Jersey. Here, at a place called Crosweeksung, was the scene of his great success. He laboured for a number of months with little apparent success, and became almost discouraged; but the love of Christ constrained him to go forward, and at length the power of God evidently attended the word, so that a number of these savages were brought under great concern for their souls. The work of grace now progressed. Mr. Brainerd, in his journal, gives an instance of the effects which followed the preaching of the word of God. "There was much concern," says he, "among them while I was discoursing publicly; but afterwards, when I spoke to one and another whom I perceived more particularly under concern, the power of God seemed to descend upon the assembly, 'like a mighty rushing wind,' and with an astonishing energy bore down all before it.

"I stood amazed at the influence that seized upon the audience almost universally. Almost all persons, of all ages, were bowed down together. Old men and women, who had been drunken wretches for many years, and some little children not more than six or seven years of age, appeared in distress for their souls, as well as persons of middle age. These were almost universally praying and crying for mercy in every part of the house, and many out of doors, and numbers could neither go nor stand; their concern was so great, each for himself, that none seemed to take any notice of those about them, but each prayed for himself. Methought this had a near resemblance to the day of God's power, mentioned Josh. x. 14; for I must say I never saw any day like it in all respects; it was a day wherein the Lord did much to destroy the kingdom of darkness among this people." A church was soon afterwards gathered among these poor pagans; and such was the change effected among them, that many exclaimed with astonishment, "What hath God wrought!"

Mr. Brainerd laboured excessively among the people of his charge; he frequently made long and tedious journeys to the English settlements, for assistance to forward the objects of his mission, and also among the surrounding tribes of Indians, to carry the gospel to the outcasts who were ready to perish. The hardships and dangers which he encountered and escaped in the wilderness are almost incredible. He continued among the Indians till March, 1747, when the ravages of disease, brought on by his hardships and exposures, forced him to leave the people of his charge. He died at Northampton, Mass., at the house of the Rev. Jonathan Edwards, Oct. 9th, 1747.

---

81. Anthony Benezet.

Anthony Benezet was born in France in the year 1713. His parents belonged to the society of Friends. The persecution on account of religious opinions, which then existed in that country, induced them to leave France. After a residence of many years in London, they and their son, the subject of this sketch, came to America, and settled in Philadelphia.

He was a man of sound understanding, great piety, humility, and self-denial, and of a very benevolent disposition. Being desirous of spending his life in a manner the most useful to his fellow-creatutres, he devoted himself to the education of youth. In this arduous but truly honourable employment he passed about forty years; and acquitted himself very much to the satisfaction of parents and children. His great object was, to imbue the minds of his pupils with reverence for religion, and to train them up in a course of virtue. Pecuniary advantages were of small moment in his estimation, of which he gave many striking proofs. A short time before his decease, he declared, in a letter to a friend, that though leisure and retirement would be very agreeable to him, he was well satisfied to remain in his occupation; and that he knew no other, whatever might be its advantages, for which he would exchange his employment, unless it were a commission to preach and propagate, as a minister, the gospel of Christ.

When the school established in Philadelphia "for the instruction of black people and their offspring" was suspended, on account of the indisposition of their teacher, he voluntarily surrendered his own school to other competent persons, and undertook the instruction of those people, though in a pecuniary respect he lost considerable by the change. His humility and his sympathy with that unhappy race of men disposed him to think no condescensions degrading by which he could be peculiarly useful to them; and he was greatly desirous that they might be so improved in their minds as to render the freedom which they had lately recovered a real blessing to themselves, and a benefit to the state.

He was a friend to the poor and the distressed of every description, and laboured most earnestly for their relief and welfare. It may indeed be said of him, that his whole life was spent in going about doing good unto men. He appeared to do every thing as if the words of his Saviour were continually sounding in his ears: 'Wist ye not that I must be about my father's business?" He was, as Dr. Rush observed, a man of a truly catholic spirit; one who loved piety and virtue in others, wherever he found them; and who respected all sincere worshippers of God, in whatever manner that worship was performed.

The miseries of the enslaved Africans, and the great injustice done to them, very deeply affected his compassionate heart. He published many tracts on the subject; supported an extensive correspondence with persons in Europe and America who were likely to aid his benevolent views; and exerted himself to the utmost to meliorate the condition of the blacks, and to procure the entire abolition of the trade. As he was one of the earliest advocates of these injured men, and indefatigably pursued his object, we may fairly attribute to his labours, with the divine blessing upon them, a great part of that spirit of inquiry into their situation, and sympathy with their distresses, which have spread over the world; and which, we trust, will ere long lead to the best results.

About a year before his decease, his health became much impaired; but being of a lively disposition, very temperate, and zealously concerned to occupy his talents to the last, he supported his school till he was quite disabled from performing the duties of it. But his charity and beneficence continued with life. The last time he walked across the room was to take from his desk six dollars, which he gave to a poor widow whom he had long assisted to maintain. Three hours before his death he delivered to his executors a number of tracts in sheets, on religious subjects, with directions for their being bound and dispersed. He devised nearly the whole of his estate, after the decease of his wife, to trustees, for the support and benefit of the African school, of which he had been the tutor. And thus, having lived a most useful and exemplary life, he was well prepared for the approach of death. He died in 1784. He endured his pains patiently; and, with Christian composure of mind, resigned this mortal life in the firm expectation of a happy immortality.

The loss of this benevolent man was deeply felt by his fellow-citizens; and his funeral was attended by a great number of persons of all ranks, and all religious professions; and many hundred of coloured persons joined the procession. It may justly be said that "the mourners went about the streets," and that his memory was embalmed with tears. An officer, who had served in the American army during the late war, in returning from the funeral, pronounced a striking eulogium upon him: "*I would rather*," said he, "*be Anthony Benezet, in that coffin, than the great Washington with all his honours.*"

82. Wesley and Whitefield.

Mr. John Wesley, the celebrated founder of Methodism, was the son of a clergyman of the church of England.

He was educated for the ministry, received episcopal ordination, and ever considered himself as a member of the church of England.

In the year 1729 Mr. Wesley, then a fellow of Lincoln College, Oxford, with some others at the college, began to spend some evenings in reading the Greek Testament. They began also to visit the sick in different parts of the town, and the prisoners in the castle. They continued in those laudable practices, and in 1735 they were joined by the celebrated George Whitefield, then in his eighteenth year. At this time their number in Oxford amounted to about fourteen. They obtained their name from the exact regularity of their lives, which gave occasion to a young gentleman of Christ's Church to say, "Here is a new sect of Methodists sprung up;" alluding to a sect of ancient physicians who were called Methodists, because they reduced the healing art to a few common principles, and brought it into some method and order.

At the time Mr. Wesley and Mr. Whitefield entered upon their public ministerial labours, it is said that the whole kingdom of England was tending fast to in-

MORAVIAN MISSIONARIES

Amid regions of ice and snow, the Moravian missionaries have with untiring zeal, successfully taught Christianity to the Esquimax Indians.

WHITEFIELD

the celebrated Preacher, addressing one of the numerous crowds that attended his ministry.

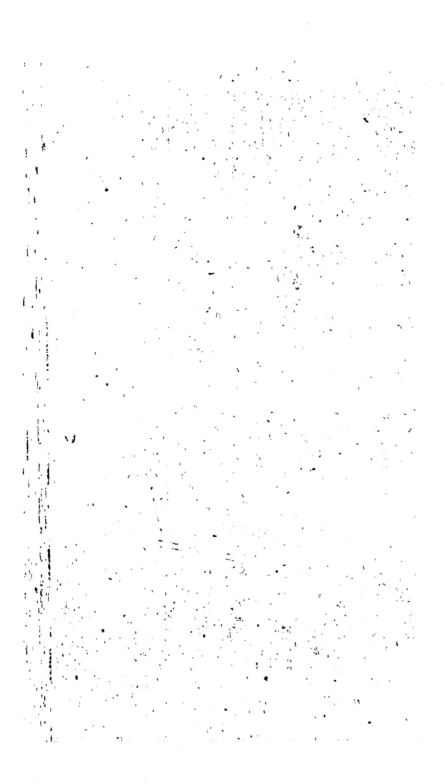

fidelity. These men of God, filled with love for the souls of their fellow-men, and fired with an ardent zeal for their salvation, went forth, preaching the gospel in many places, with uncommon energy and power. This brought upon them the opposition of the cold-hearted and formal professors of Christianity, and many refused to let them preach in their churches. In consequence of this, they were obliged to preach in the open air and in fields. They were oftentimes insulted, threatened, and hooted at by the mob, who in time of divine service cast at them stones, mud, dirt, &c., and in some instances they narrowly escaped with their lives.

But notwithstanding the opposition, their labours were crowned with success. By their preaching out of doors they drew together immense numbers, their congregations sometimes amounting to nearly twenty thousand persons. Thousands embraced the gospel, and many of the lower classes of society, who were degraded by vice and immorality of every kind, now changed their course of life, and became useful and respectable members of society.

Mr. Wesley is universally allowed to have been an extraordinary and highly distinguished character, and " whatever may be thought of his peculiar sentiments, no one can deny him the credit of truly apostolic zeal and perseverance in what he conceived to be the way of duty. His mode of address in public was chaste and solemn; there was a divine simplicity, a zeal, a venerableness in his manner, which commanded attention; and when at fourscore he still retained all the liveliness of vigorous old age. For upwards of fifty years he travelled eight thousand miles each year on an average, visiting his numerous societies, and presided at forty-seven annual conferences. For more than sixty years it was his constant practice to rise at four o'clock in the morning; and nearly the whole of that period to preach every morning at five. He generally preached near twenty times in a week, and frequently four times a day. Notwithstanding this, very few have written more than he; divinity, both controversial and practical; history, philosophy, medicine, politics, poetry, &c., were all, at different times, the subjects on which his pen was employed. Besides this, he found time for reading, correspondence, visiting the sick, and arranging the matters of his numerous societies; but such prodigies of labour and exertion would have been impossible, had it not been for his inflexible temperance, and unexampled economy of time." After passing through evil report and good report, during more than sixty years of incessant labour, he entered into his rest in the eighty-seventh year of his age.

Mr. Whitefield was remarkable for his uncommon eloquence and fervent zeal. His eloquence was indeed very great and of the truest kind. He was utterly devoid of all appearance of affectation. The importance of his subject, and the regard due to his hearers, engrossed all his concern. Every accent of his voice spoke to the ear; every feature of his face, every motion of his hands, and every gesture spoke to the eye; so that the most dissipated and thoughtless found their attention involuntarily fixed, and the dullest and most ignorant could not but understand.

Wherever he went, all ranks and sorts of people were attracted, prodigious numbers flocked to hear him, and thousands were brought into the kingdom of God through his instrumentality.

His zeal and labours were not confined to the British isles. He came over to our country several times, and preached in most of our principal cities; every where crowds attended his ministry, and his exertions were crowned with abundant success. It is said that he preached upwards of *eighteen thousand* sermons in the course of his ministry, which included thirty-four years. Mr. Whitefield died at Newburyport, Mass., on the 30th of Sept., 1770, in the fifty-sixth year of his age, on his seventh visit to America.

83. HOWARD, THE PHILANTHROPIST.

JOHN HOWARD, Esq., the celebrated philanthropist, was born at Hackney, in England, about the year 1727. His father died while he was young, and by his direction the son was apprenticed to a wholesale grocer; but this business neither suiting his health or disposition, and a handsome fortune falling into his hands, he bought out his time before its regular expiration, and commenced his first travels on the continent. After the death of his first wife, Mr. Howard, in 1756, made a voyage in order to view Lisbon after the earthquake at that place, but was taken by a French privateer, and suffered in his confinement. By this means his attention seems to have been first excited to compassionate those persons "who are sick, and in prison."

Upon his return from the continent, he married the second time, but his wife dying a short time after his marriage, he retired to an estate he purchased in Bedfordshire, where he very much gained the esteem and affection of the poor by building them cottages, employing the industrious, relieving the sick, and educating the children of the poor. In 1773 he served the office of sheriff for the county, which brought him further acquainted with the misery of prisons; and from this he commenced his career of benevolence and glory.

During the last seventeen years of his life he visited *every country* in Europe, exploring their prisons and dungeons, and relieving the miseries of the distressed. He also published a number of works on the state of prisons, hospitals, &c. In 1774 he received the thanks of the House of Commons for his inquiries and exertions. Mr. Howard's character is well drawn by the celebrated Mr. Burke, who, speaking of him, says, "I cannot name this gentleman without remarking that his labours and writings have done much to open the eyes and hearts of mankind. He has visited *all Europe*, not to survey the sumptuousness of palaces, nor the stateliness of temples; not to make accurate measurement of the remains of ancient grandeur, nor to form a scale of the curiosities of modern art; not to collect medals, nor to collate manuscripts; but to dive into the depths of dungeons, to plunge into the infections of hospitals; to survey the mansions of sorrow and pain; to take guage and dimensions of misery, depression, and contempt; to remember the forgotten; to attend to the neglected; to visit the forsaken; and to compare and collate the distresses of all men in all countries. His plan is original, and as full of genius as humanity. It is a *voyage of philanthropy—a circumnavigation of charity.*"

Mr. Howard commenced his last journey in July, 1789, in which he proposed to visit Turkey, Russia, and other parts of the east, and not to return under three years; withal apprehending that he, very probably, never might return, which proved to be the event; for while he was at Cherson, a Russian settlement, near the northern extremity of the Black Sea, he visited a young lady at some distance in a malignant fever, caught the fatal infection, and died January 20, 1790.

"And now, Benevolence! thy rays divine
Dart round the globe from Zembla to the line;
O'er each dark prison plays the cheering light,
Like northern lustres o'er the vault of night—
From realm to realm, with cross or crescent crown'd,
Where'er mankind and misery are found,
O'er burning sands, deep waves, or wilds of snow,
Thy Howard, journeying, seeks the house of wo."

---

84. Modern Infidelity.

Previous to the French revolution, *Voltaire* and some others formed a set design to destroy the Christian religion. For this purpose, they engaged, at different periods, a number of men of distinguished talents, power, and influence; all deadly enemies to the gospel; men of profligate principles, and profligate lives. These men distinguished themselves with diligence, courage, activity, and perseverance, in the propagation of their sentiments. Books were written and published in innumerable multitudes, in which infidelity was brought down to the level of peasants and even of children, and poured into the cottage and school. Others of a superior kind crept into the shop and the farm-house; and others, of a still higher class, found their way to the drawing-room, the university, and the palace. By these and other efforts, infidelity was spread with astonishing rapidity in many parts of Europe, particularly in France.

In the year 1776, Dr. Adam Weishaupt, professor of the canon law in the university of Ingoldstadt, in Bavaria, established the society of the *Illuminati*. This society was distinguished beyond all others for cunning, mischief, an absolute destitution of conscience, an absolute disregard of all the interests of man, and a torpid insensibility to all moral obligation. Their doctrines were, *that God is nothing; that government is a curse;* that the possession of *property is robbery; that chastity and natural affection are mere prejudices, and that adultery, assassination, poisoning, and other crimes of a similar nature, are lawful, and even virtuous.*

The disciples of Voltaire, finding this system one of more perfect corruption than their own, immediately united in its interests, and eagerly entered into all its plans and purposes. These legions of infidelity, united, went forward with astonishing success, till their abominable doctrines infected all classes of the French people. The bloody storm of the French revolution commenced. Then it was that infidelity obtained a complete triumph; the dagger of the assassin, the axe of the executioner, the infuriated mob, were now let loose, and thousands and tens of thousands perished; and the national assembly, in a public decree, declared that "*there is no God*, and that *death is an eternal sleep.*"

Voltaire laboured through a long life to diffuse the poison of infidelity. In life he was pre-eminent in guilt, and at death, in misery. He had for years been accustomed to call the adorable Saviour "the wretch," and to vow that he would crush him. He closed many of his letters to his infidel friend with these words—"Crush the wretch." This apostle of infidelity, being laid upon his death-bed, was in the utmost horror of mind. In the first days of his illness, he showed some signs of wishing to return to that God whom he had so often blasphemed. He made a declaration, he in fact renounced his infidelity, but in vain; despair and rage succeeded in such a manner, that the physicians who were called in to administer relief retired, declaring the death of the impious man too terrible to be witnessed.

In one of his last visits, the doctor found him in the greatest agonies, exclaiming, with the utmost horror, "I am abandoned by God and man." He then said, "Doctor, I will give you half of what I am worth, if you will give me six months' life." The doctor answered, "Sir, you cannot live six weeks." Voltaire replied, "Then I shall go to hell, and you will go with me!" and soon after expired.

The following account of the tenets of the principal English infidels is extracted from "*Dr. Dwight's Baccalaureate Sermon.*"

Lord Herbert, of Cherbury, the first considerable English deistical philosopher, and clearly one of the greatest and best, declares the following things, viz.

That Christianity is the best religion:

That his own universal religion of nature agrees wholly with Christianity, and contributes to its establishment:

That all revealed religion (viz. Christianity) is absolutely uncertain, and of little or no use:

That men are not hastily, or on small grounds, to be condemned, who are led to sin by bodily constitution:

That the indulgence of lust and of anger is no more to be blamed than the thirst occasioned by the dropsy, or the sleepiness produced by the lethargy:

That the soul is immortal; that there will be a future retribution, which will be according to the works and thoughts of mankind; and that he who denies these truths, is scarcely to be accounted a reasonable creature.

Mr. Hobbes declares,

That the Scriptures are the voice of God; and yet that they are of no authority, except as enjoined by the civil magistrate:

That inspiration is a supernatural gift, and the immediate hand of God; and that it is madness:

That the Scriptures are the foundation of all obligation; and yet that they are of no obligatory force, except as enjoined by the civil magistrate:

That every man has a right to all things, and may lawfully get them if he can:

That man is a mere machine; and that the soul is material and mortal.

Mr. Blount declares,

That there is one infinite and eternal God; and yet insinuates that there are two eternal, independent beings:

That God ought to be worshipped with prayer and praise; yet he objects to prayer as a duty:

That the soul is probably material, and of course mortal.

Lord Shaftsbury declares,

That the belief of future rewards and punishments is noxious to virtue, and takes away all motive to it:

That the hope of rewards, and the fear of punishments, make virtue mercenary:

That to be influenced by rewards is disingenuous and servile:

That the hope of reward cannot consist with virtue; and yet that the hope of rewards is not derogatory to virtue, but a proof that we love virtue.

He represents salvation as a ridiculous thing, and insinuates that Christ was influenced and directed by deep designs of ambition, and cherished a savage zeal and persecuting spirit; and

That the Scriptures were a mere artful invention to secure a profitable monopoly, i. e. of sinister advantages to the inventors:

That the magistrate is the sole judge of religious truth, and of revelation:

That miracles are ridiculous, and that if true, they would be no proof of the truth of revelation:

That ridicule is the test of truth; and yet that ridicule itself must be brought to the test of reason.

Mr. Collins, though chiefly a mere objector to revelation, declares,

That man is a mere machine:

That the soul is material and mortal:

That Christ and his apostles built on the predictions of fortune-tellers and diviners:

That the prophets were mere fortune-tellers and discoverers of lost goods:

That Christianity stands wholly on a false foundation (yet he speaks respectfully of Christianity; and also of the Epicureans, whom he at the same time considers as atheists).

Mr. Woolston, also a mere objector, declares,

That he is the farthest of any man from being engaged in the cause of infidelity:

That infidelity has no place in his heart:

That he writes for the honour of Jesus, and in defence of Christianity; and

That his design in writing is to advance the messiahship and truth of the holy Jesus; "to whom," he says, "be glory for ever, amen;" and yet,

That the gospels are full of incredibilities, impossibilities and absurdities:

That they resemble Gulliverian tales of persons and things, which, out of romance, never had a being:

That the miracles recorded in the gospels, taken literally, will not abide the test of reason and common sense; but must be rejected, and the authority of Jesus along with them.

At the same time he casts the most scurrilous reflections on Christ.

Dr. Tindal declares,

That Christianity, stripped of the additions which mistake, policy, and circumstances have made to it, is a most holy religion; and yet,

That the Scriptures are obscure, and fit only to perplex men, and that the two great parts of it are contradictory:

That all the doctrines of Christianity plainly speak themselves to be the will of an infinitely wise and holy God; and yet,

That the precepts of Christianity are loose, undetermined, incapable of being understood by mankind at large, giving wrong and unworthy apprehensions of God, and are generally false and pernicious:

That natural religion is so plain to all, even the most ignorant men, that God could not make it plainer; even if he were to convey, miraculously, the very same ideas to all men; and yet,

That almost all mankind have had very unworthy notions of God, and very wrong apprehensions of natural religion.

Mr. Chubb declares,

That he hopes to share with his friends the favour of God, in that peaceful and happy state which God hath prepared for the virtuous and faithful, in some other future world; and yet,

That God does not interpose in the affairs of this world at all, and has nothing to do with the good or evil done by men here:

That prayer may be useful as a positive institution, by introducing proper thoughts, affections, and actions; and yet he intimates,

That it must be displeasing to God, and directly improper:

That a state of rewards and punishments hereafter is one of the truths which are of the highest concern to men; and yet,

That the arguments for the immortality of the soul are wholly unsatisfactory; and that the soul is probably matter:

That Christ's mission is, at least in his view, probably divine; and yet,

That Christ, in his opinion, was of no higher character than the founder of the Christian sect, i. e. another Sadoc, Cerinthus, or Herbert:

That his birth and resurrection were ridiculous and incredible; and that his institutions and precepts were less excellent than those of other lawgivers and teachers:

That the apostles were impostors; and that the Gospels and Acts of the Apostles resemble Jewish fables, and popish legends, rather than accounts of facts:

That the belief of a future state is of no advantage to society:

That all religions are alike:

That it is of no consequence what religion a man embraces.

Mr. Hume declares,

That there is no perceptible connexion between cause and effect:

That the belief of such a connexion is merely a matter of custom:

That there is no reason to believe that the universe proceeded from a cause:

That there are no solid arguments to prove the existence of a God:

That voluntary actions are necessary, and determined by a fixed connexion between cause and effect:

That motives are causes operating necessarily on the will:

That man is a mere machine, i. e. an object operated on necessarily by external causes:

That there is no contingency, i. e. nothing happening without a settled cause in the universe; and

That matter and motion may be regarded as the cause of thought, i. e. the soul is a material cause, and thought its effect:

That no rewards or punishments can be rationally expected beyond what is already known by experience and observation:

That self-denial, self-mortification, and humility are not virtues, but are useless and mischievous; that they stupify the understanding, sour the temper, and harden the heart, and of course are gross crimes:

That pride and self-valuation, ingenuity, quickness of thought, easiness of expression, delicacy of taste, strength of body, health, cleanliness, taper legs, and broad shoulders are virtues;

That suicide, or self-murder, is lawful and commendable (and of course virtuous):

That adultery must be practised, if we would obtain all the advantages of life:

That female infidelity (or adultery), when known, is a small thing; when unknown, nothing; and

That skepticism is the true and only wisdom of man.

Lastly, as the soul of man, according to Mr. Hume, becomes every moment a different being, the consequence must be, that the crimes committed by him at one time cannot be imputable to him at another.

Lord Bolinbroke declares,

That God is just; and that justice requires that rewards and punishments be measured to particular cases, according to their circumstances, in proportion to the merit or demerit of every individual; and yet,

That God doth not so measure out rewards or punishments; and that, if he did, he would subvert human affairs; that he concerns not himself with the affairs of human beings at all; or if he does, that he regards only collective bodies of men, not individuals; that he punishes none except through the magistrate; and that there will be no state of future rewards and punishments;

That the religion of nature is clear and obvious to all mankind; and yet,

That it has been unknown to the greatest part of mankind:

That we know material substance, and are assured of it; and yet,

That we know nothing of either matter or spirit:

That there is undeniably something in our constitution, beyond the known properties of matter; and yet,

That the soul is material and mortal; and that to say the soul is immaterial is the same thing as to say that two and two are five. He also declares,

That there is no conscience in man, except artificially;

That it is more natural to believe many gods than to believe one. He teaches,

That ambition, the lust of power, avarice, and sensuality may be lawfully gratified, if they can be safely gratified:

That the sole foundation of modesty is vanity, or a wish to show ourselves superior to mere animals:

That man lives only in the present world:

That man is only a superior animal:

That man's chief end is to gratify the appetites and inclinations of the flesh:

That modesty is inspired by mere prejudice:

That polygamy is a part of the law, or religion of nature.

---

85. Thomas Paine.

Thomas Paine, a political and infidel writer, was born in England, in 1737, and bred a stay-maker. Coming to America, he published a number of pamphlets, which had a powerful effect in favour of the American cause; particularly that entitled, "Common Sense." He went to London in 1790, and published "The Rights of Man." To avoid prosecution, he fled to France, where he connected himself with the leaders of infidelity, and was chosen a member of the national assembly. Being sentenced to death by the revolutionary government, he was saved from the *guillotine* through the intercession of a number of American citizens then in Paris. During his imprisonment in that city he debased himself by writing a deistical book, called, "*The Age of Reason*," a work which has stamped his name with infamy.

"In this performance is found nothing new as to objections against Christianity. He takes the ground long occupied by infidels. In the manner of his writing there is a kind of novelty. In rashness, inconsistency, misrepresentation, ridicule, and false reasoning,

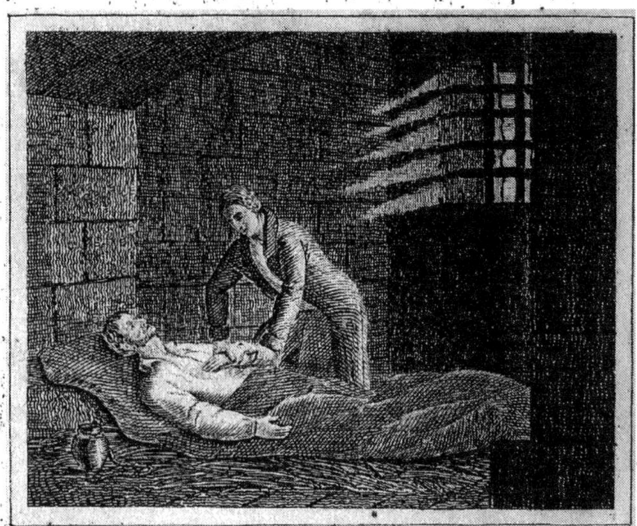

JOHN HOWARD

This philanthropist visited every country in Europe, exploring prisons and dungeons and relieved the miseries of the sick and distressed.

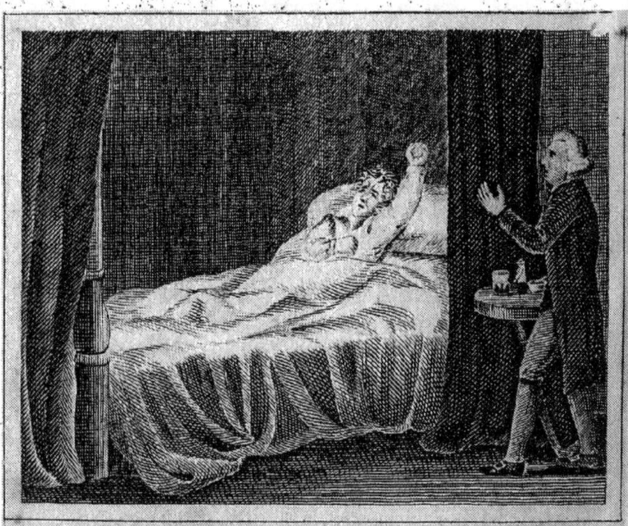

DEATH OF VOLTAIRE

This Apostle of Infidelity in life was pre eminent in guilt, and at death in horror and despair.

few men, perhaps, on any subject, have ever surpassed him." Mr. Paine speaks respectfully of Jesus Christ, but reprobates revealed religion as the origin of all human misery. His words are:—"The morality that he preached and practised was of the most benevolent kind. He preached most excellent morality." Again he says:—"The most detestable wickedness, the most horrid cruelties, and the greatest miseries that have afflicted the human race have had their origin in this thing called revelation, or revealed religion."

He tells us:—"The word of God cannot exist in any written or human language;" and in the same work he allows it possible for the Almighty to make a communication immediately to men. This is saying God can reveal truth to men; but such a revelation cannot exist among men—which, in effect, is saying nothing.

"Paine's method is, first, to misrepresent a fact, or assume a truth, and then cry out against a creature of his own imagination. None but a man of depraved morals, and a bad heart, can read his book without indignation. A bold, profane, and daring spirit runs through his whole work. He speaks of sacred things with indecency; he makes ridicule supply the place of solid argument; he is engaged with uncommon zeal to load men highly esteemed with abusive epithets; he calls Moses a chief assassin; Joshua, Samuel, and David monsters and impostors; the Jewish kings a parcel of rascals; the prophets liars, and St. Paul a fool."

Paine died in New York, in the year 1809. For some time previous to his death, he so degraded himself by his intemperate habits, that he was shunned by the respectable part of his associates. He lingered out a dark and gloomy period of several months, in a sullen, determined opposition to every religious thought or suggestion; he evinced a continued and marked hostility to the ministers of the gospel, and would not permit them, under any pretext, to visit him. The Rev. Mr. Ketchum, however, in the common garb of a citizen, succeeded in approaching him, and gained his attention in some desultory conversation; but he had no sooner indirectly mentioned the *name* of Jesus, than the enraged infidel, lost to all sense of decorum, actually drove him from his presence. But though he abhorred the sound of that name, yet Dr. Manly informs us, in his letter respecting Paine's death, that whenever he fell into paroxysms of pain, which were frequent before his death, he would cry out, without intermission, "O Lord, help me! O Jesus, help me! God help me! Jesus Christ help me!" &c. Dr. M. also states that he would not be left alone night or day; and would scream and halloo if left but for a minute.

The following is from good authority. A lady who resided in the neighbourhood of Paine, in his last illness occasionally administered to his necessities. One day he asked her if she had ever read his "Age of Reason." She answered in the affirmative; he then wished to know her opinion of that book; she said she thought it the most dangerous insinuating book she had ever seen; that the more she read, the more she wished to read, and the more she found her mind estranged from all that is good; and that, from a conviction of its evil tendency, she had burnt it. Paine replied to this, that he wished all who had read it had been as wise as she, and added, "If ever the devil had an agent on earth, I have been one."

All who saw him concur in describing him as exhibiting one of the most peculiarly awful *visages* that ever saddened the bed of death. It was an *unique* face, possessing an assemblage of every vicious and dismal passion; and so terrific as to deter many of his acquaintance from repeating their visit.

---

86. Worship of the Grand Lama.

The Grand Lama is a name given to the sovereign pontiff, or high-priest, of the Thibetian Tartars, who resides at a vast palace on a mountain, near the banks of the Burampooter, about seven miles from Lassa. The foot of the mountain is inhabited by twenty thousand lamas or priests, who have their separate apartments round about the mountain, and according to their quality are placed nearer or at a greater distance from the sovereign pontiff. He is not only worshipped by the natives of Thibet, but also by the various tribes of heathen Tartars, who roam through the greater part of Asia. The more remote Tartars are said absolutely to regard him as the Deity himself, and call him *God, the everlasting Father of Heaven.* They believe him to be immortal, and endowed with all knowledge and virtue. Every year they come from different parts to worship, and make rich offerings at his shrine; even the emperor of China, who is a Manchon Tartar, worships him, and entertains, at a great expense, in the palace at Pekin an inferior lama, deputed as his nuncio from Thibet.

The grand lama, it has been said, is never to be seen but in a secret place of his palace, amidst a great number of lamps, sitting cross-legged on a cushion, and decked all over with precious stones, where at a distance the people prostrate themselves before him, it not being lawful for any so much as to kiss his feet. He returns not the least sign of respect, nor even speaks to the greatest princes; but only lays his hand upon their heads, and they are fully persuaded they receive from thence a full forgiveness of all their sins.

It is the opinion of his worshippers that when the grand lama seems to die, either of old age or infirmity, his soul, in fact, only quits a crazy habitation to look for one younger or better; and is discovered again in the body of some child, by certain tokens known only to the lamas or priests, in which order he always appears.

Almost all nations of the east, except the Mahometans, believe the *metempsychosis* as the most important article of their faith; especially the inhabitants of Thibet and Ava, the Peguans, Siamese, the greatest part of the Chinese and Japanese, and the Moguls and

Kalmucks, who changed the religion of Shamanism for the worship of the grand lama. According to the doctrine of this *metempsychosis*, the soul is always in action, and never at rest; for no sooner does she leave her old habitation than she enters a new one. The dalai lama, being a divine person, can find no better lodging than the body of his successor; or the *Fo*, residing in the dalai lama, which passes to his successor; and this being a god, to whom all things are known, the dalai lama is therefore acquainted with every thing which happened during his residence in his former body.

This religion is said to have been of three thousand years standing; and neither time nor the influence of men has had the power of shaking the authority of the grand lama. This theocracy extends as fully to temporal as to spiritual concerns.

Though in the grand sovereignty of the lamas the temporal power has been occasionally separated from the spiritual by slight revolutions, they have always been united again after a time; so that in Thibet the whole constitution rests on the imperial pontificate in a manner elsewhere unknown. For as the Thibetians suppose that the grand lama is animated by the good Shaka, or Fo, who at the decease of one lama transmigrates into the next, and consecrates him an image of the divinity, the descending chain of lamas is continued down from him in fixed degrees of sanctity; so that a more firmly established sacerdotal government, in doctrine, customs, and institutions, than actually reigns over this country, cannot be conceived. The supreme manager of temporal affairs is no more than the viceroy of the sovereign priest, who, conformably to the dictates of his religion, dwells in divine tranquillity in a building that is both temple and palace. If some of his votaries in modern times have dispensed with the adoration of his person, still certain real modifications of the Shaka religion is the only faith they follow. The state of sanctity which that religion inculcates consists in monastic continence, absence of thought, and the perfect repose of nonentity

It has been observed that the religion of Thibet is the counterpart of the Roman Catholic, since the inhabitants of that country use holy water and a singing service; they also offer alms, prayers, and sacrifices for the dead. They have a vast number of convents filled with monks and friars, amounting to thirty thousand; who, besides the three vows of poverty, obedience, and chastity, make several others. They have their confessors, who are chosen by their superiors, and have licenses from their lamas, without which they cannot hear confessions or impose penances They make use of beads. They wear the mitre and cap like the bishops; and their dalai lama is nearly the same among them as the sovereign pontiff is among the Romanists.—*Buck's Theol. Dict.*

---

87. The Syrian Christians in India.

The Syrian Christians inhabit the interior of Travancore and Malabar, in the south of India; and have been settled there from the early ages of Christianity. The first notices of this ancient people in recent times are to be found in the Portuguese histories.

When the Portuguese arrived, they were agreeably surprised to find upwards of a hundred Christian churches on the coast of Malabar. But when they became acquainted with the purity and simplicity of their worship they were offended. "These churches," said the Portuguese, "belong to the pope."—"Who is the pope?" said the natives; "we never heard of him." The European priests were yet more alarmed when they found that these Hindoo Christians maintained the order and discipline of a regular church under episcopal jurisdiction; and that, for thirteen hundred years past, they had enjoyed a succession of bishops appointed by the patriarch of Antioch.

When the power of the Portuguese became sufficient for their purpose, they invaded these tranquil churches, seized some of the clergy, and devoted them to the death of heretics. They seized the Syrian bishop, Mar

Joseph, and sent him prisoner to Lisbon, and then convened a synod at one of the Syrian churches called Diamper, near Cochin, at which the Romish archbishop, Menezes, presided. At this compulsory synod one hundred and fifty of the Syrian clergy appeared. They were accused of the following practices and opinions:—"That they had married wives; that they owned but two sacraments, baptism and the Lord's supper; that they neither invoked saints nor worshipped images, nor believed in purgatory; and that they had no other orders or names of dignity in the church than bishop, priest, and deacon." These tenets they were called on to abjure, or to suffer suspension from all church benefices. It was also decreed that all the Syrian books on ecclesiastical subjects that could be found should be burned; "in order," said the inquisitors, "that no pretended apostolical monuments may remain."

The churches on the sea-coast were thus compelled to acknowledge the supremacy of the pope; but they refused to pray in Latin, and insisted on retaining their own language and liturgy. This point they said they would not give up with their lives. The pope compromised with them; Menezes purged their liturgy of its errors; and they retain their Syriac language, and have a Syriac college unto this day.

Two centuries had elapsed without any particular information concerning the Syrian Christians in the interior of India, but in the year 1806, Dr. Buchanan, in his tour through Hindoostan, paid the Syriac Christians a visit, after having obtained the consent of the rajah of Travancore, in whose dominions they resided. The following is extracted from his *Christian Researches in Asia:*

"The first Syrian church which I saw was at Mavelycar; but the Syrians here are in the vicinity of the Romish Christians, and are not so simple in their manners as those nearer the mountains. They at first suspected that I belonged to that communion. Soon, however, the gloom and suspicion subsided, and one of their number was deputed to accompany me to the churches in the interior.

"When we were approaching the church of Chingánoor, we met one of the *cassanars*, or Syrian clergy. He was dressed in a white loose vestment, with a cap of red silk hanging down behind. When we arrived at the village, I was received at the door of the church by three kasheeshas, that is, presbyters or priests, who were habited, in like manner, in white vestments. There were also present two *shumshanas*, or deacons. The elder priest was a very intelligent man, of reverend appearance, having a long white beard, and of an affable and engaging deportment. In looking around the village, I perceived symptoms of poverty and political depression. In the churches and in the people there was an air of fallen greatness. I said to the senior priest, 'You appear to me like a people who have known better days.'—'It is even so,' said he; 'we are in a degenerate state, compared with our forefathers. The learning of the Bible,' he added, 'is in a low state amongst us. Our copies are few in number, and that number is daily diminishing; and the writing out a whole copy of the sacred Scriptures is a great labour, where there is no profit and little piety. We have very few copies of the *prophetical* Scriptures in the church. Our church languishes for want of the Scriptures; but we generally expound them to the people in the Malayalim tongue, that being the vernacular language of the country.'

"The doctrines of the Syrian Christians are few in number, but pure, and agree in essential points with those of the church of England; so that although the body of the church appears to be ignorant, and formal, and dead, there are individuals who are alive to righteousness, and who are distinguished from the rest by their purity of life, and are sometimes censured for too rigid a piety. In every church, and in many of their houses, there are manuscripts in the Syriac language; and I have been successful in procuring some old and valuable copies of the Scriptures and other books, written in different ages and in different characters.

"The first view of the Christian churches in the sequestered region of Hindoostan, connected with the idea of their tranquil duration for so many ages, cannot fail to excite pleasing emotions in the mind of the beholder. The form of the oldest buildings is not unlike that of some of the old parish churches in England; the style of building in both being of Saracenic origin. They have sloping roofs, pointed arch windows, and buttresses supporting the walls. The beams of the roof, being exposed to view, are ornamented; and the ceiling of the choir and altar is circular and fretted. In the cathedral churches, the shrines of the deceased bishops are placed on each side of the altar. Most of the churches are built of a reddish stone, squared and polished at the quarry, and are of durable construction, the front wall of the largest edifices being six feet thick. The bells of the churches are cast in the foundries of the country; some of them are of large dimensions, and have inscriptions in Syriac and Malayalim. In approaching a town in the evening, I once heard the sound of the bells among the hills; a circumstance which made me forget for a moment that I was in Hindoostan, and reminded me of *another* country."

---

88. Abdallah, the Arabian Martyr.

Abdallah and Sabat were intimate friends, and being young men of family, in Arabia, they agreed to travel together, and to visit foreign countries. They were both zealous Mahometans; Sabat was the son of Ibraham Sabat, a noble family of the line of Beni Sabat, who trace their pedigree to Mahomet. The two friends left Arabia, after paying their adorations at the tomb of their prophet at Mecca, and travelled through Persia, and thence to Cabul. Abdallah was appointed to an office of state, under Zemaun Shah, king of Cabul; and Sabat left him there, and proceeded through Tartary.

While Abdallah remained at Cabul he was converted to the Christian faith by the perusal of a Bible (as is supposed) belonging to a Christian from Armenia, then residing at Cabul. In the Mahometan states it is death for a man of rank to become a Christian. Abdallah endeavoured for a time to conceal his conversion; but finding it no longer possible, he determined to flee to some of the Christian churches near the Caspian sea. He accordingly left Cabul in disguise, and had gained the great city of Bochara, in Tartary, when he was met in the streets of that city by his friend Sabat, who immediately recognised him. Sabat had heard of his conversion and flight, and was filled with indignation at his conduct. Abdallah knew his danger, and threw himself at the feet of Sabat. He confessed that he was a Christian, and implored him, by the sacred tie of their former friendship, to let him escape with his life. "But, sir," said Sabat, when relating the story himself, "I had no pity; I caused my servants to seize him, and I delivered him up to Morad Shah, king of Bochara.

"He was sentenced to die, and a herald went through the city of Bochara, announcing the time of his execution. An immense multitude attended, and the chief men of the city. I also went and stood near Abdallah. He was offered his life if he would abjure Christ, the executioner standing by him with his sword in his hand. 'No,' said he, as if the proposition were impossible to be complied with, 'I cannot abjure Christ.' Then one of his hands was cut off at the wrist. He stood firm, his arm hanging by his side with but little motion.

"A physician, by desire of the king, offered to heal the wound if he would recant. He made no answer, but looked up steadfastly towards heaven, like Stephen, the first martyr, his eyes streaming with tears. He did not look with anger towards me. He looked at me, but it was benignly, and with the countenance of forgiveness. His other hand was then cut off. But, sir," said Sabat, in his imperfect English, "he never *changed*, he never *changed*. And when he bowed his head to receive the blow of death, all Bochara seemed to say, 'What new thing is this?'."—*Dr. Buchanan.*

89. Worship of the Idol Juggernaut.

The idol Juggernaut is one of the deities worshipped by the Hindoos in India. The following account of this idol and its worship is extracted from the journal of Dr. Buchanan, who visited the temple of Juggernaut, in Orissa, in 1806.

"We know," says Dr. Buchanan, "that we are approaching Juggernaut (and yet we are more than fifty miles from it) by the human bones which we have seen for some days strewed by the way. We found large bodies of pilgrims coming from various parts of northern India; some had been two months on their march, travelling slowly in the hottest season of the year, with their wives and children. Some old persons were with them, who wished to die at Juggernaut. Many of the pilgrims die on the road; their bodies generally remain unburied; and their flesh is devoured by dogs, jackalls, and vultures.

"The temple of this idol is a stupendous building, and the walls and gates are covered with indecent emblems, sculptured upon them. The ground in many places about this temple is literally whitened by the bones of the pilgrims who have perished in this place.

"At the grand Hindoo festival of the *Rutt Jattra*, Juggernaut, the Moloch of Hindoostan, was brought out of his temple amidst the acclamations of hundreds of thousands of his worshippers. When the idol was placed on this throne, a tremendous shout was raised by the multitude, which gradually died away; after a short interval of silence, a body of men, having green branches or palms in their hands, approached with great celerity. The people opened a way for them; and when they came up to the throne they fell down before him that sat thereon, and worshipped. The multitude again sent forth a voice 'like the sound of a great thunder.'

"The throne of the idol was placed on a stupendous car or tower about sixty feet in height, resting on wheels which indented the ground deeply, as they slowly turned this ponderous machine. Attached to it were six cables, of the size and length of a ship's cable, by which the people drew it along. Upon the tower were the priests and satellites of the idol, surrounding his throne. The idol is a block of wood, having a frightful visage painted black, with a distended mouth of a bloody colour. His arms are of gold, and he is dressed in a gorgeous apparel.

"The car, as it was drawn along, would stop at intervals, at which time the priests would mount it, pronounce their obscene stanzas, and perform the most indecent actions, which would be responded by the people. After the tower had proceeded some way, a pilgrim offered himself as a sacrifice to the idol. He threw himself down in the road before the tower, as it was moving along, and was crushed to death by its wheels. A shout of joy was raised to the god. He is said to *smile* when the libation of blood is made.

"This festival continued a number of days, and numbers devoted themselves as sacrifices to the idol by falling down before the wheels of his car. As to the number of people who attend these festivals, no accurate calculation can be made. The natives themselves, when speaking of the numbers at particular festivals, usually say that a lack of people (100,000) would not be missed. It is said, however, of late years, such has been the influence of Christianity in India, that the number has been greatly lessened.

---

90. Henry Martyn.

This useful man was born in Truro, England, 1781. At the age of seven or eight years he was sent to a grammar school, where he made a great proficiency in his studies; and at length entered St. John's college, Cambridge. At this time he had a great dislike to religion; and he afterwards confessed that "the sound of the gospel, conveyed in the admonitions of a sister, was grating to his ears." While settled in college, his whole mind was wrapped up in the pursuits of knowledge, to the neglect of his spiritual concerns, until the death of a father; after which he became deeply impressed upon the subject of religion, and finally a devoted Christian.

He still continued to make rapid progress in literature; and in 1802 was chosen fellow of St. John's college, at the same time assuming the character of a minister of the gospel; and towards the last of this year was invested with the title of a "Christian missionary." He offered himself to the society of missions to Africa and the east, to go to any parts whither they deemed expedient to send him. He continued to exercise his pastoral office in Cornwall until July, 1805, when he sailed for Calcutta, where he safely arrived. But he soon left Calcutta for Dinapore, where his object was to establish schools to study the native languages, in order to preach to the people, and to prepare translations of the Scriptures, and tracts for distribution. In March, 1808, he completed "the version of the New Testament into Hindoostanee." In 1809 he removed to Cawnpore. Near the close of this year he began his public ministrations among the heathen, by appointing meetings and preaching to them. The following account of his first essay in his new labour is full of simplicity and meaning:—"I told them," says he, "that I gave with pleasure the alms I could afford, but that I wished to give them something better, namely, eternal riches; and then, producing a Hindoostanee translation of Genesis, read the first verse, and explained it word by word. In the beginning, when there was nothing, no heaven and no earth, but God only, he created without help, for his own pleasure. But who is God? One so great, so good, so wise, so mighty, that none can know him as he ought to know. But yet we must know that he knows us. When we rise up or sit down, or go out, he is always with us. He created heaven and earth; therefore every thing in heaven, sun, moon, and stars. How then can the sun be God? or moon be God? Every thing on earth; how then can Ganges be God? If a shoemaker make a pair of shoes, are the shoes like him? If a man make an image, it is not like

HENRY MARTYN

This devoted missionary having suffered much from fatigue and sickness, died at Tocat in Asia Minor, on his return from Persia, 1812.

BURNING OF IDOLS

by the natives of Otaheite in 1815.–The people assited by their Chiefs demolished their Morais and altars, and burnt their gods in the fire.

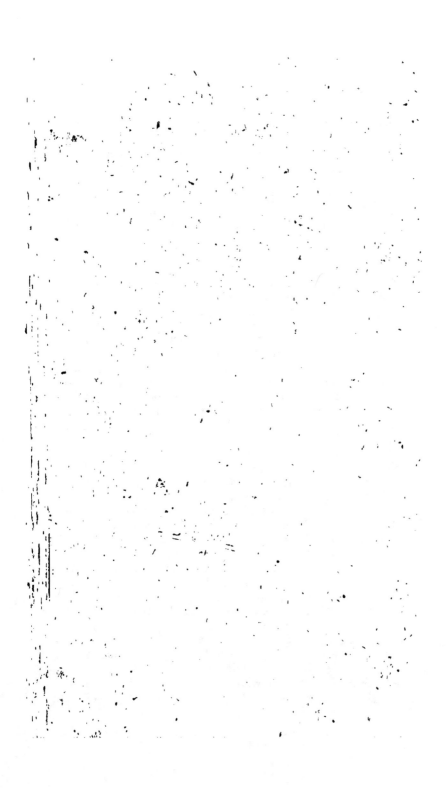

man, its maker. Infer, secondly, if God made the heaven and the earth for you, and made the meat also, will he not feed you? Know, also, that he that made heaven and earth can also destroy them, and will do it; therefore fear God, who is so great, and love God, who is so good." Having previously commenced a translation of the New Testament into the Persian language, he now made arrangements to visit Shiraz, the seat of Persian literature, for the purpose of collecting further materials for the work.

While at Shiraz he was visited by many vain philosophers, who endeavoured to entangle him by trying him with hard questions, or discoursing in unintelligible language of the mysticisms of Soofcism. The translation was completed by him in February, 1812; and the following May he left Shiraz, in order to visit and present a Persian testament to the king.

Upon his coming into the presence of the king, two Moolahs attacked him with their arguments against the law and gospel; and a violent controversy was kept up for an hour or two; when the vizier, joining in, said to Mr. Martyn, "You had better say, God is God, and Mahomet is the prophet of God." He replied, "God is God;" but added (instead of "Mahomet is the prophet of God"), "and Jesus is the Son of God." They no sooner heard this, than they all exclaimed in anger and contempt, "He is neither born nor begets," and rose up as if they would have torn him in pieces. One of them said, "What will you say when your tongue is burnt out for blasphemy?" They treated his book with contempt, and he went back to his tent.

At length he left Persia on his way homeward, but suffered much from fatigue and sickness on his way. At times he was pitied, again hated and persecuted. At Tocat, on the 16th October, 1812, he died. A short time previous to this event, he writes, "O, when shall time give place to eternity, and when shall appear that new heaven and earth wherein dwelleth righteousness? Then 'there shall in nowise enter in any thing that defileth;' none of that wickedness that has made men worse than wild beasts—none of those corruptions that add still more to the miseries of mortality—shall be seen or heard of any more." His memory is still, however, revered in Persia. A late traveller says:— "You little think how generally the English Moolah, Martyn of Shiraz, is known throughout Persia, and with what affection his memory is cherished."

The secretary to the embassy writes, "The Persians, who were struck with Martyn's humility, patience, and resignation, call him a *merdi Khodai*, or man of God." Another says that the Moolah who disputed with him says, "that Henry Martyn ought not to be named among mortals."

---

91. Joanna Southcot.

Joanna Southcot was a prophetess, who appeared in England about the beginning of the present century.

The book in which Joanna published her prophecies is dated London, April 25, 1804; and she begins by declaring she herself did not understand the communications given her by the Spirit till they were afterwards explained to her. In November, 1803, she was told to mark the weather during the twenty-four first days of the succeeding year, and then the Spirit informs her that the weather each day was typical of the events of each succeeding month: New-year's day to correspond with January, January 2 with February, &c.

After this she relates a dream she had in 1792, and declares she foretold the death of Bishop Buller, and appeals to a letter put into the hands of a clergyman whom she names.

One night she heard a noise as if a ball of iron was rolling down the stairs *three steps*; and the Spirit afterwards, she says, told her this was a sign of *three* great evils which were to fall upon this land, the *sword*, the *plague*, and the *famine*. She affirms that the late war, and that the extraordinary harvest of 1[illegible]7 and

1800 happened agreeably to the predictions which she had previously made known; and particularly appeals to the people of Exeter, where it seems she was brought up from her infancy.

In November, 1803, she says she was ordered to open her Bible, which she did at Eccles. i. 9; and then follows a long explanation of that chapter.

When she was at Stockton upon Tees, in the next month, she informs us, three Methodist preachers had the confidence to tell her she uttered *lies;* and she then refers them to four clergymen who could prove she and her friends were not *liars*.

After this she gives us a long communication on Gen. xlix., wherein Jacob warns his sons of what should befall them in the last days, and which she applies to our present times. She then favours her readers with a long ESSAY on the marriage of the Lamb, and as variety is always pleasing, it commences in sober prose, but ends in jingling rhyme.

The following is the conclusion of a communication which she had at Stockfort; "As wrong as they are, saying thou hast *children brought up* by the parish, and thou art Bonaparte's *brother*, and that thou hast been in prison; so false are their sayings, thy writings came from the devil or any spirit but the SPIRIT of the LIVING GOD; and that every soul in *this nation* shall know *before* the FIVE YEARS I mentioned to thee in 1802 are expired; and then I will turn as a DIADEM of beauty to the residence of my people, and they shall praise the GOD OF THEIR SALVATION."

In March, 1805, we find Joanna published a pamphlet in London, endeavouring to confute "FIVE CHARGES" against her, which had appeared in the Leeds Mercury, and *four* of which she says were absolutely false. The *first* charge was respecting the *sealing* of her disciples. The *second* on the *invasion.* The *third* on the *famine.* The *fourth* on her *mission.* The *fifth* on her *death.* *Sealing* is the grand peculiarity and ordinance of these people. Joanna gives those who profess belief in her mission, and will subscribe to the things revealed in her, "WARNING," a *sealed written paper*, with her signature, by which they are led to think they are *sealed against the day of redemption*, and that all those who are possessed of these *seals* will be signally honoured by the Messiah when he comes this spring. It is said they looked upon Joanna to be the bride, the Lamb's wife; and that as man fell by a woman, he will be restored by a woman. Some of her followers pretend also to have visions and revelations. At present it seems both warning and sealing have subsided; they are waiting, probably in awful suspense, for the commencement of the thousand years' reign on the earth, when peace will universally prevail. Yet it is said they do not mean that Christ will come in person, but in spirit, and that the *sealed* who are dead before this time will be raised from their graves to partake in this happy state.—*Buck's Theological Dictionary.*

---

92. MISSIONS AMONG THE HOTTENTOTS.

THE Hottentots in South Africa have been considered as the lowest and most degraded of any portion of the human race. In their religious views they are but little removed from the brute creation, having no idea of the Supreme Being, and are apparently destitute of any religious principle.* Their language is said to be a compound of discordant, inharmonious sounds, more resembling the jargon of the feathered tribes, than the musical sounds of the human voice. Through the influence of Christianity, the arts of civilized life have now been introduced among them, and the liberal support they give to religious and charitable institutions is a striking exhibition of the power of Christianity in raising men from ignorance and degradation to a rank among civilized and intelligent beings.

The United Brethren established a mission among

---

* Chapin's Missionary Gazetteer.

this people in 1737, which was renewed in 1792. Since this time the London Missionary Society has sent out many missionaries. Bethelsdorp, a settlement of Hottentots, is one of the principal stations of the London Society; it is situated about five hundred miles east of Cape Town, containing about twelve hundred inhabitants. Several missionaries have laboured here with great perseverance and success. Hundreds have been instructed in their schools, and from the lowest state of degradation have become civilized, adorned a Christian profession, and contributed liberally to the funds of the society and for the support of the poor. In the latter part of 1821, Rev. Dr. Philip, of Cape Town, the superintendent of the society's missions in the colony, visited this station, and made the following statement to the society. "I now can meet the calumniators of missions and the enemies of the Hottentots on their own ground, and challenge them to show me, in any part of the world, a people more capable of being improved than the abused Hottentots of South Africa, or attempts at civilization more complete in their success than what may now be seen at Bethelsdorp."

The following authentic and remarkable account of the progress and influence of the gospel among the Bechuans, an African people residing eight hundred miles north of Cape Town, was published originally in the South African Commerical Advertiser of December 15th, 1830. It is the substance of an address delivered by the Rev. Mr. Moffat, of Lattakoo, the principal of the town of the Bechuans, at a public meeting in Cape Town, after he had been fourteen years a missionary in South Africa.

Lattakoo was first visited by Mr. Campbell in 1813, when permission was obtained from the king of the country to send missionaries among his people. The first successful attempt to commence missionary operations among them was in 1816. The former condition and character of the inhabitants; the manner in which the missionaries sought to bring them under the purifying, civilizing, ennobling influence of the gospel; and the success of the self-denying and benevolent enterprise, are strikingly exhibited by Mr. Moffat.—*Missionary Herald.*

"It has frequently been said, by persons unfriendly to the great cause of missionary exertion, that psalm-singing was all that they taught the people; but he could appeal to the effects of their humble endeavours, to convince the prejudiced that the missionaries did more than sing psalms, for in many instances their exertions had the effect of turning almost devils into men.

"I speak from experience," continued Mr. M. "I appeal to the mission in which I am employed, and to the various stations which I have visited. I appeal to Lattakoo, where there is a church gathered from barbarians, who, a few years ago, were in an awful state of degradation, and on a level with the beasts that perish! I appeal to a well-filled chapel, marked with a decorum which would do honour to a British congregation. I appeal to the change which has been effected in the persons and habits of those residing on our station.

"It must be recollected that the Bechuans are altogether ignorant of a future state. They have no idea of an existence beyond the present. They suppose that all the pleasures, enjoyments, and honours of this world terminate in annihilation. When the spirit leaves the body they suppose that it has ceased to exist; and if a plebeian, the body is dragged away and left a prey to the beasts; and if that of one more honourable, the body is committed to the grave with many unmeaning ceremonies, while the females chant a dirge, deploring the eternal loss, and then return from the grave without one pleasing hope of immortality.

"The consequence of such deplorable ignorance is, that they participate in every species of sin, and think as little of plunging a spear into their neighbour's bosom as of killing a dog. A traveller among them, like a bird of passage, may be led to form a very favourable opinion of their humanity, their fidelity, and good sense; but far different will be the judgment of those who have half the acquaintance with the native tribes which the missionaries possess. There you will see man tyrannizing over the females; the weaker vessels doomed to bear infirmities and inflictions of which their husbands are comparatively ignorant. There you will see the men reclining under the shade of a spreading tree, while the females are most of the year employed in preparing the ground, sowing the grain, and gathering in the harvest. There you may see the mother of twins without compunction allow one to be strangled by the hands of her attendant, when it has just entered the world. If there be one of each sex, the female is the victim; if both of one sex, the weaker is cut off. They are 'earthly, sensual, devilish.' There might be seen a nation looking to a man called the 'rain maker,' to open the windows of heaven, and cause it to rain upon the earth; and while such deceivers maintained their influence over the people, the missionaries were made the butts of their indignation, and were treated as the supposed cause of every evil which befell them.

"In endeavouring to convey a knowledge of true religion to the natives, we taught them that they were men, fallen and sinful men; we exhibited to them the character of that God against whom they had sinned, and disclosed to them the doctrine of the eternal state. They were startled as if they had seen the Judge descend, the graves open, the dead arise, and the adjudication of the awful day. We unfolded to them the meaning of the gospel. In fulfilling the ministry committed to us, our faith was tried; and often have we hung our harps on the willows, and mourned over the condition of thousands, who were saying to us, 'Away, away,' and threatened to drive us back with the spear and with fire. While we were yet praying, the blessing descended; it ran from house to house, from heart to heart, and in a short time the whole station seemed to be filled with prayer and praises.

"That season was one I cannot easily forget. It was indeed a time of refreshing from the presence of the Lord. Many received the truth, and a church was formed. The natives have acquired a taste for reading and writing, and are taught in their own language. We trust we have also taught them to hold converse with heaven, and to meet the king of terrors with unshaken faith.

"They have been taught industrious habits, and to appreciate and be grateful for the boon which has been handed to them by British Christians. The station is increasing in size. Its capabilities are great: its prospects are encouraging.

"We have an extensive field of missionary labour. We have hundreds on the mission premises, and thousands in the neighbourhood."

---

93. Progress of Christianity in the South Sea Islands.

In the year 1796 the London Missionary Society sent out to Otaheite, and other islands of the South Seas, a number of missionaries, for the purpose of christianizing the natives. They were gladly received, as well as several others that were afterwards sent out in the year 1800. In consequence of disturbances in Otaheite in 1799, several of the missionaries were obliged to take refuge in New South Wales, some of whom afterwards returned to the islands. For fifteen years the missionaries laboured with little or no appearance of success, and were almost discouraged. The hopes and expectations of the friends of the mission, in respect to the success of their endeavours to establish Christianity in these islands, were nearly lost.

But in 1812 Pomare the king declared his full conviction of the truth of the gospel, his determination to worship the true God, and his desire to make a public profession of his faith by being baptized. About the same time several other natives embraced Christianity. In 1815 the missionaries estimated the professed worshippers of the true God at five hundred, among whom were several leading chiefs. In this year, the idolatrous chiefs in Otaheite formed a conspiracy, and resolved to massacre the praying people. They, being informed of their danger, fled to the neighbouring island of Eimeo. The pagans then quarrelled among themselves, and the chief instigators of the plot were slain. They were, however, still resolved on war, and for some time the issue was doubtful; but Pomare was finally restored to the government of Otaheite and its dependencies November, 1815. "This was the dawn of a most glorious day in this and the neighbouring islands." Pomare constituted as chiefs many of those who had made a public profession of their faith. The people, assisted by their chiefs, demolished their Morais, overthrew the altars, and burned their gods in the fire. Idolatry was at once abolished, the worship of Jehovah substituted in its place, numerous buildings were immediately erected for public worship and schools, in every district in the island. In June, 1816, one of the missionaries stated, "All accounts agree that a most wonderful change has been produced in all the Society islands; and the spread of the gospel seems to be almost universal." An auxiliary missionary society was formed in May, 1818, by the people of Otaheite and Eimeo, of which king Pomare was president. A missionary spirit is very prevalent. Eighteen natives have gone to distant islands to carry the knowledge of the gospel, some of whom went at the peril of their lives; and they have laboured with zeal, ability, and astonishing success. Several thousand have been taught to read, and two churches have been gathered by their means.

According to late accounts, the inhabitants of nineteen islands in the vicinity of Otaheite have renounced their idols, and those in many others are eager for Christian instruction, fulfilling the ancient prediction, "*The isles of the sea shall wait for thy law.*" Considerable portions of the Scriptures have been translated, printed, and widely diffused among a people eager to receive them. Elementary and devotional books have likewise been printed at their presses; and education, civilization, and the influence of Christianity are steadily advancing.

"These changes have been wrought by the blessing of God upon missionary exertions, among a people the most unlikely, on account of their savageness, sensuality, and every thing that degrades the human character. The chiefs were intriguing, perfidious, cruel, and prodigal of their people's lives, both in war and in furnishing sacrifices to demons; the people were universally thieves, lewd beyond description, enslaved to the grossest superstitions, and always ready to murder any one at the slightest intimations from their chiefs; the strangling of infants was also the crime of every day, perpetrated by almost every mother without shame or remorse. Now the Sabbath is most sacredly regarded, all worldly business is entirely suspended, and scarcely can an individual be found who does not attend some house of Christian worship, nor a family which neglects morning and evening prayers." The Rev. *D. Tyerman*, one of the deputation sent from England to visit these islands, states the following facts concerning the people here: "No public immorality or indecency is seen. All drunkenness and profane swearing are unknown here. All their former sports and amusements are completely put down. Never before did the gospel obtain so complete and so universal triumph in any country, over heathenism, cruelty, superstition, and ignorance."

The following is from a recent publication:

A writer in the London New Monthly Magazine, after candidly avowing his former hostility to missions, and stating that he now cheerfully yields to the convictions forced upon him by the evidence of facts, proceeds, in the following firm and unhesitating language, to contrast the past and the present state of the South-sea islands.

"Certainly, no parts of the habitable globe have

ever exhibited a more ignorant, barbarous, and demoralized race, than the Polynesian islands, while under the dominion of the idolatrous superstitions which governed them for ages. These dark places of the earth were full of the habitations of cruelty. Infancy and age were alike its victims. There was a perpetual warfare between all their institutions and the well-being of society. The latter maintained a constant struggle, even for existence, with the abominable customs which the former embodied and sanctioned. Population was rapidly diminishing, and the fairest portions of the world were becoming desolate. Man was the only contrast to the lovely scene around him, and it was perfect—a moral ruin made doubly hideous by the blooming Eden which exposed and reproached his deformity. But a change, as salutary as it is wonderful, was wrought by an agency which the philosophers and moralists of civilized Europe were accustomed to regard with derision and contempt. The fact can no longer be disguised. The principal islands of the Pacific have risen to a state of intellectual and social improvement which has scarcely a parallel in the history of nations; and all this has been accomplished, in the brief space of little more than thirty years, by the generous and self-denying labours of a few individuals who embarked from England, but slenderly endowed with general knowledge, ignorant of the languages, habits, and customs of the people they were destined to instruct, and unaccredited by the hierarchy of their native land. They were equally destitute of patronage, wealth, and power; but they were men of sound intellect, of patient industry, and, above all, sincerely and ardently devoted to the faith which had constrained them to become missionaries."

The following testimony to the truth of the above statement merits the attention of all who have been deceived by the studied attempts of the Quarterly Reviewers, and of some American writers, to misrepresent and undervalue the great moral change which has been wrought in these islands.

A French naval officer, in a despatch to his government, dated Matavai Bay, May 15, 1828, says:

"The state of the island of Tahiti is now very different from what it was in the days of Cook. The missionaries of the society of London have entirely changed the manners and customs of the inhabitants. Idolatry exists no longer; they profess generally the Christian religion; the women no longer come on board the vessels, and they are very reserved on all occasions. Their marriages are celebrated in the same manner as in Europe, and the king confines himself to one wife. The women are also admitted to the table with their husbands. The infamous society of the Arreoy exists no longer; the bloody wars in which the people engaged, and human sacrifices, have entirely ceased since 1816. All the natives can read and write, and have religious books translated into their language, printed either at Tahiti, Ulitea, or Eimeo. They have built considerable churches, where they repair twice in the week, and show the greatest attention to the discourse of the preacher. It is common to see numerous individuals take notes of the most interesting passages of the sermons they hear."

Another naval captain in the Russian service, in a letter dated as late as 1830, says,

"I was quite delighted with the pious people who have been converted from idolatry. They bear a *far larger proportion to the inhabitants than can be found in towns, and cities in Europe.* What I saw and heard of the Christian devotedness of many of the natives made me feel that my own religion was of a very low standard. I found, alas! that all the natives are not followers of Christ, but as it is in Europe, so it is there; many are still following 'divers lusts and pleasures,' particularly among the youthful part of the population. There were several ships lying near the island (one from London, and the rest from other nations) during my visit; but it appears to me that the generality of seafaring men *do not like the glorious change* which God has wrought among the natives, through the in-

A MISSIONARY PREACHING
to a native Congregation in Hawaii, one of the Sandwich Islands in 1823.

MURDER OF GEN. LA GARDE.
Gen. La Garde in attempting to stop the the violence of the Catholics against the Protestants in Nismes in 1815. was shot by one of the mob.

strumentality of the missionaries, and the *reason is obvious.*"

What the reason here spoken of was may probably be learned by the following extract from Mr. Ellis's journal.

"The traffic of prostitution carried on by the natives with foreigners on ship board, as well as on shore, is most public and shameless here. But this is a subject on which we must not, we dare not, record what we have seen and do know. The utter abolition of this infamy in the christianized islands of the southern Pacific is one of the most signal triumphs of the gospel in the history of human wickedness in any age or part of the world. It is painful to add (as we have intimated before) that for this very cause the gospel and its other triumphs are evil spoken of by many Christians (falsely so called) who visit these seas, and are filled with rage, disappointment, and malice, when they find that they cannot riot in licentiousness, as former voyagers did, on these once polluted shores; therefore do they abhor the change, and calumniate those who have been instrumental in its production."

We shall only add one testimony more, that of sir Thomas Brisbane, late governor of the colony of New South Wales, whose high official situation offered many opportunities for receiving correct information respecting the state of the islands, and the influence of Christianity on their inhabitants.

"You can declare my favourable opinion in the strongest terms of the value I attach to the missionary labours, and the inestimable benefits they have conferred on the vast extent of the population of the islands of the southern hemisphere.

"Captain Gambier, of the navy, stated to me, that he had touched at various of those islands, particularly at Owyhee, where he found the savages who had massacred Cook converted to peaceable Christians.

"Were it necessary, I could add various other testimonials in behalf of the inestimable blessing the missionaries have conferred on mankind."

94. Burman Mission.

The Burman empire is situated in that part of the continent of Asia lying between Hindoostan and China; and contains about eight millions of inhabitants. Rangoon is the principal sea-port town. In 1807 several missionaries from England visited this country, among whom was a son of Dr. Carey. All their attempts, however, to establish a mission at length failed.

In the mean time, a missionary spirit began to be felt in America. A society was formed, and the board appointed Messrs. Judson, Nott, Hall, Newell, and Rice as missionaries to the heathen; and in June, 1812, they arrived at Calcutta. While on their passage, Mr. Judson and wife and Mr. Rice changed their sentiments upon the subject of baptism, and adopted those held by the Baptist denomination. This circumstance eventually led to the establishment of the Burman mission, and in the formation of the Baptist General Convention in the United States.

In July, 1813, Mr. Judson and wife arrived at Rangoon. The Baptist board of foreign missions resolved to sustain this mission; and accordingly, in 1815, they sent Mr. Hough, a printer, and lady, to accompany the two solitary missionaries. For six years had the untiring Judson and his wife laboured before any fruits were produced. But on the 27th of June, 1819, their hearts were gladdened by the baptism of Moung Naw, the first that occurred in the Burman empire. Soon after, others embraced the Christian religion; which greatly enraged the king. In 1824, a war broke out between the Burmans and the British; upon which the missionaries were committed to prison, and when the English ships arrived, orders were given to have them executed the moment the first shot was fired upon the town. But after the English fired, the executioners, instead of performing the office, shrunk, terrified, into one corner of the prison. As the firing continued, they fled from the prison; when about fifty

Burmans rushed in, drew them out, and almost literally carried them on the points of their spears to the seat of judgment, where they were made to sit upon their knees, with their bodies leaning forward, for the convenience of the executioner, who at that moment was ordered to behead them; when, to their inexpressible joy, the English troops came up, and released them from the malice of the Burmans.

The sufferings of Mr. Judson were more intense. He was taken by the executioner, and hurled into the death-prison, loaded with three pair of iron fetters, and fastened to a long pole, to prevent his moving. After this, he was forced to go on foot, to Oung-pen-la, over burning sands, with blistered feet, while faint for the want of food. One of the company of prisoners, through fatigue and the intense heat of the sun, died. Being nearly exhausted, Mr. Judson was supported a little by leaning on the shoulder of a native, who kindly offered to assist him in this way. Had it not been for this, it is probable he must have been left on the road, a victim of the cruelty and barbarity of the enraged Burmese. After being imprisoned and subjected to the oppressive yoke of the natives for nearly two years, Mr. Judson was appointed to act as translator and interpreter to the Burmese army; and the missionaries felt that they were once more free. The affectionate courage of Mrs. Judson tended greatly to alleviate the sufferings of her husband; she, however, died soon after his release.

Since that time the mission has assumed a more interesting character. The number of converts has increased, and two or three of the natives are successfully preaching the gospel to their ignorant and idolatrous countrymen.

---

95. Sandwich Islands Mission.

The Sandwich islands are a group of eleven islands in the North Pacific Ocean, containing, according to the estimation of the missionaries, about one hundred and fifty thousand inhabitants. Of these islands, Owyhee, or (according to the orthography established by the missionaries) *Hawaii*, is the largest.

Till recently, the inhabitants of these islands were gross idolaters, their religion being similar to that of the natives of the Society islands before the introduction of Christianity.

In the year 1819 Tamehameha, king of the Sandwich islands, died, and was succeeded by his son Rihoriho. This young prince, in the early part of November, 1819, gave orders for the destruction of the monuments of idolatry in Owyhee, and a few days after sent the same orders to the other islands, which were promptly obeyed. In Atooi, the *Morais* and the consecrated buildings, with the idols, were set on fire the first evening after the order arrived. The same was done in all the islands. These events took place only a few days after the first missionaries sailed from Boston.

This change appears to have been effected by the reports of what had been done in the Society islands, the advice of foreigners, and some of the more intelligent chiefs. "The spell of diabolical enchantment was broken; the priests, having lost their proud and tyrannical pre-eminence, deserted their altars of abomination, the inveterate customs of three thousand years were abolished, and the people were left without the forms of any religion. Thus the Lord prepared the way for the introduction of the gospel into these islands."

One of the principal events which seems to have led to the establishment of this mission was the religious education of *Henry Obookiah*, a native of Owyhee, by the Rev. S. J. Mills, a zealous friend of missions. Obookiah was left an orphan in his native country, by one of those exterminating wars which often happened there, at the age of ten or twelve years. In a few years after he was taken by an American captain to the United States, and landed at New-Haven, Conn., in 1809. While at New-Haven, Mr. Mills, then a student of Yale

College, conceived the plan of educating Obookiah as missionary to his native island. Obookiah soon became hopefully pious, and strongly advocated a mission to his countrymen, in which he ardently longed to engage. He, however, died at the Foreign Mission School at Cornwall, Conn., Feb. 17th, 1818; but "his mantle fell" upon others, and three missionaries, an agriculturist, mechanic, printer, and physician, with their families, and four native youths who had been educated as teachers at Cornwall, were sent out by the American Board of Foreign Missions, and sailed from Boston Oct. 23d, 1819, and arrived off Owyhee March 30th, 1820. These missionaries were cordially received by the natives, and immediately engaged in the duties of the mission. They found the encouragement so great, that they sent to the board for more laborers. Accordingly, five missionaries, with their families, embarked at New-Haven, Nov. 19th, 1822, and arrived at the Sandwich islands, April 27th, 1823. In 1823 they were joined by the Rev. Mr. Ellis, with two pious Otaheitans from the Society islands. Mr. Ellis was patronized by the London Society, and has rendered important services to this mission.

An additional number of labourers were sent out by the Board in 1827, in 1830, and in 1831, so that the whole number of persons, male and female, who have left this country for the purpose of propagating Christianity in these islands, will be *fifty-seven*. According to the last accounts, there are about nine hundred schools, instructed by as many native teachers; the number of readers and learners is estimated at fifty thousand. The following is from the last report (1831) of the Board.

"The mission press at the Sandwich islands commenced its operations on the first Monday in January, 1822. From that time, when the language was just beginning to assume a written form, until March 20, 1830, scarcely ten years after the mission was commenced, twenty-two distinct books had been printed in the native language, averaging thirty-six small pages, and amounting to three hundred and eighty-seven thousand copies, and ten million two hundred and eighty-seven thousand and eight hundred pages. This printing was executed at Honolulu, where there are two presses. But besides this, three million three hundred and forty-five thousand pages in the Hawaiian language have been printed in the United States (viz. a large edition of the gospels of Matthew, Mark, and John), which swells the whole amount of printing in this time, for the use of the islanders, to thirteen millions six hundred and thirty-two thousand eight hundred pages. Reckoning the twenty-two distinct works in a continuous series, the number of pages in the series is eight hundred and thirty-two. Of these, forty are elementary, and the rest are portions of Scripture, or else strictly evangelical and most important matter, the best adapted to the condition and wants of the people that could be selected under existing circumstances.

"Perhaps never since the invention of printing was a printing press employed so extensively as that has been at the Sandwich islands; with so little expense, and so great a certainty that *every page* of its productions would be read with attention and profit.

"The language of the islands has been reduced to writing, and in a form so precise, that five vowels and seven consonants, or twelve letters in the whole, represent all the sounds which have yet been discovered in the native tongue. And as each of these letters has a fixed and certain sound, the art of reading, spelling, and writing the language is made far easier than it is with us. About one third part of the people in the islands have been brought into the schools, and one half of these have been taught to read. Many are able to write, and some are versed in the elementary principles of arithmetic. Nine hundred of the natives are employed as schoolmasters. The historical parts of the New Testament, and selections from the Old, and summaries of Christian doctrines and duties, have been printed in the native language, and placed in the hands of some thousands of the natives. The government of the islands has adopted the moral law of God, with a knowledge of its purport, as the basis of its own future administration; and the Christian religion is professedly the religion of the nation. Indeed most of the chief rulers are members of the visible church of Christ. Special laws have been enacted, and are enforced, against murder, theft, licentiousness, retailing ardent spirits, Sabbath-breaking and gambling. The Christian law of marriage is the law of the land. Commodious houses for public worship have been erected by the principal chiefs, with the cheerful aid of the people, in the places of their residence; and when there is preaching, these chiefs regularly and seriously attend, and their example is followed by great numbers of their subjects. Churches are gathered, as with us, wherever there are pastors to take the care of them, and accessions are made to them, from time to time, of such as we may reasonably hope will be saved. In one small district, which, but a few years since, rang through all the length and breadth of it with the cries of savage drunkenness, a thousand people have associated on the principle of entire abstinence from the use of intoxicating liquors. Moreover, in that same district and in two others, with a united population of perhaps forty thousand, where the morals were as degraded, a few years ago, as any where on earth, a fourth part of the inhabitants have formed themselves into societies for the better understanding and keeping of God's holy law, and require unimpeachable morals as a condition of membership in their several fraternities.

"All these are believed to be facts. And they are traceable wholly to the blessing of God on the establishment of a Christian mission on those islands a little more than eleven years ago."

The following hymn was composed by Mr. W. M. Tappan, on the occasion of the missionaries embarking at New Haven, Conn., for the Sandwich islands.

Wake, Isles of the South! your redemption is near,
No longer repose in the borders of gloom;
The strength of His chosen in love will appear,
And light shall arise on the verge of the tomb.
Alleluia to the Lamb who hath purchased our pardon:
We will praise him again when we pass over Jordan.
We will praise him, &c.

The billows that girt ye, the wild waves that roar,
The zephyrs that play where the ocean-storms cease,
Shall bear the rich freight to your desolate shore,
Shall waft the glad tidings of pardon and peace.
Alleluia, &c.

On the islands that sit in the regions of night,
The lands of despair, to oblivion a prey,
The morning will open with healing and light;
The young star of Bethlehem will ripen to day.
Alleluia, &c.

The altar and idol in dust overthrown,
The incense forbade that was hallowed in blood;
The Priest of Melchisedec there shall atone,
And the shrines of Atooi be sacred to God!
Alleluia, &c.

The heathen will hasten to welcome the time,
The day-spring the prophet in vision once saw—
When the beams of Messiah will 'lumine each clime,
And the Isles of the Ocean shall wait for his law.
Alleluia, &c.

And thou, OBOOKIAH! now sainted above,
Wilt rejoice, as the heralds their mission disclose;
And the prayer will be heard, that the land thou didst love
May blossom as Sharon, and bud as the rose!
Alleluia, &c.

---

96. Missions among the North American Indians.

The efforts which have been made by Christian benevolence to spread the gospel among the Indians in our country have been generally attended with much success. The success which attended the labours of Eliot, Mayhew, and others in New England, and of that devoted missionary *David Brainerd* (who went alone among the Indians in New Jersey about eighty years ago), will stand as a monument of the power of the gospel to change *savages* into mild, peaceable, and devoted Christians.

Of late years, the attention of the Christian public has been awakened on beholding the moral degradation of the Indians in our country, and efforts have been made to carry the light of Christianity and the arts of civilized life into various tribes. The commissioners of the American Board for Foreign Missions have established a number of missionary stations in various tribes, the principal of which are those of *Brainerd*, among the Cherokees; Eliot and Mayhew, among the Choctaws; and Dwight, among the Cherokees, in Arkansas territory. In these and other stations of the board churches have been organized, schools opened for the instruction of Indian children, and Christianity and civilization have progressed with pleasing success. Missionary operations, however, in our southern tribes of Indians, have been quite recently much retarded by the efforts which have been made to have them removed westward of the Mississippi. The effect which these proceedings will have upon the welfare of the Indians remains to be seen.

The Methodist Missionary Society, in the course of a few years, have established stations among a number of Indian tribes. Their mission among the Cherokees, the Wyandots in the state of Ohio, the mission among the Mohawks and Missisaugas in Upper Canada, have been highly prospered. According to the report of the society in 1827, the number of Indian converts belonging to the church was eleven hundred and sixty-four.*

A tribe of Indians consisting of one hundred and eighty souls, residing at the river Credit, Upper Canada, have, with the exception of a few families, embraced Christianity. "Here," says the Rev. Mr. Case, "are seen the effects of Christianity on the manners of a rude and barbarous people. Here are industry, civili-

* The whole number of Indians in the Methodist connexion in the United States, according to the *Minutes* of 1831, was four thousand five hundred and one.

zation, growing intelligence, peace, and grace; and those who have witnessed the change have expressed their persuasions that this new nation of Christians enjoys a sum of religious and earthly felicity which is not always found in civilized societies of longer standing and greater advantages. How great the change! A nation of wandering, idle drunkards, destitute of almost every comfort of life, have, in the course of twenty months, through the influence of Christianity, become a virtuous, industrious, and happy people! The conversion of the tribe in the vicinity of Bellville is as remarkable as that at the river Credit. Ten months ago these were the same unhappy, sottish drunkards. They are now, without an exception in the whole tribe, a reformed and religious community. They number about one hundred and thirty souls, and the society embraces every adult, of about ninety persons."

There are now supposed to be upwards of two hundred thousand Indians in the United States and their territories. When it is considered that we now inherit the land of their fathers; when we consider the success that has ever attended the efforts to introduce Christianity among them, we must consider that they have strong claims upon the sympathy and benevolence of the American people.

---

97. African Colonies at Sierra Leone and Liberia.

"Colonization in Africa, with reference to civilization, appears to have been contemplated in England as early as 1780. Several favourable circumstances soon after occurred, which excited the public attention to the subject, and gave rise to the *Society for the Abolition of the Slave trade*, and WILBERFORCE introduced the subject into the British parliament."*

The colony of Sierra Leone was commenced principally by the slaves who had served under the British

---

* Chapin's Gazetteer.

standard during the American revolutionary war. About four hundred of these slaves found their way to London, and were subject to every misery and vice. A committee was formed for their relief; they were embarked for Sierra Leone, and arrived May 9th, 1787. After struggling through many difficulties, the establishment was transferred to the British government in 1808. Since this time the colony has enjoyed a degree of prosperity, and large accessions have been made by the vigilance of the British cruisers in rescuing from slave-ships many an African who has been torn from his country and sold into bondage.

The *Wesleyan* and *Church missionaries* have laboured here with success, and a colony has been formed, "which, in order, decency, and sobriety, and in the knowledge and practice of Christian duty," says an English gentleman, "not only may rival, but, I firmly and from my heart believe, exceeds any equal population in the most favoured part of this highly favoured country."

In the year 1817 a few distinguished Christian philanthropists in our country, touched with commiseration for the degraded and unhappy condition of many of the free blacks, met at Washington, and laid the foundation of the *American Colonization Society.* The object of this society was to establish a colony to which the free coloured people of the United States might emigrate, and enjoy among themselves the blessings of free government, and be instructed in all the arts which pertain to a civilized and Christian community, which might also be an asylum for slaves recaptured from smuggling ships. The object that first claimed the attention of the society was the selection of a suitable place for the proposed colony. Accordingly, the Rev. *Samuel J. Mills* and Rev. *Ebenezer Burgess* were sent out as agents, on an embassy of inquiry to Africa, to survey the coast, and ascertain the most favourable situation. The result of their investigations and inquiries was such as to satisfy the managers that the establishment of a colony on the west coast of Africa might be attempted with every prospect of success Accordingly, after selecting two places, which were afterwards relinquished, *Dr. Ayres*, a distinguished member of the society, and Lieut. *Stockton*, of the United States' Navy, purchased another territory, which they called *Liberia*. To this place the colonists were removed from Sierra Leone, in April, 1821, and the foundation of a settlement laid at the town called *Monrovia*, in honour of the president of the United States (Mr. Monroe), for the services he rendered to the infant colony. In August, 1822, *Jehudi Ashmun*, with a company of emigrants, arrived as colonial agent for this colony. He found them feeble, houseless, disheartened, and defenceless; soon after his arrival the colony, which could muster only twenty-eight effective men, was attacked by more than eight hundred savages. By his energy and prowess they were driven back. Intent upon the destruction of this little band, the savages, with increased numbers and redoubled fury, in a few days renewed their attack, and were again repulsed. Under the management of Mr. Ashmun this feeble band became a nation in miniature. "From a chaos of heterogeneous materials he formed a well organized community of freemen. Like the patriarchs of old, he was their captain, their lawgiver, judge, priest, and governor."

It is said that a more prosperous community than the African colony can now scarcely be found. Some of the settlers, who began with nothing, are now in affluent circumstances. All the children in the colony are favoured with the privileges of a school education; a large library has been established, and houses of worship and other public buildings are erected. The whole population now consists of about seventeen hundred souls.

It is believed that the establishment of the African colony will afford rare facilities for the operations of Christian benevolence, among the benighted African tribes. It promises to be a blessed asylum for a degraded and wretched people. It is already, to the surrounding tribes, like "a city set upon a hill, which cannot be hid." It is also believed that the establishment of these colonies will have an important effect towards hastening on that time when "Ethiopia shall stretch forth her hands unto God."

The most recent important information from this colony is given in a letter from Capt. William Abels, who lately visited Liberia as master of the colonial schooner Margaret Mercer.

"On the 14th of Dec. (1831) I arrived, and on the 15th went on shore, and was received in the most polite and friendly manner by the governor, Mr. Mechlin, who introduced me to the minister and the principal inhabitants. All the colonists appeared in good health. All my expectations in regard to the aspect of things, the health, harmony, order, contentment, industry, and general prosperity of the settlers, were more than realized. There are about two hundred buildings in the town of Monrovia, extending along the cape Montserado not far from a mile and a quarter. Most of these are good substantial houses and stores (the first stories are made of stone), and some of them are handsome, spacious, painted, and with Venetian blinds. Nothing struck me as more remarkable than the great superiority, in intelligence, manners, conversation, dress, and general appearance, in every respect, of the people over their coloured brethren in America. So much was I pleased with what I saw, that I observed to the people, should I make a true report it would hardly be credited in the United States. Among all that I have conversed with I did not find one discontented person, or hear one desire to return to America. I saw no intemperance, nor did I hear a profane word uttered by any one. Being a minister of the gospel, on Christmas-day I preached both in the Methodist and Baptist church, to full and attentive congregations of from two to three hundred persons in each. Most of the settlers appear to be rapidly acquiring property, and I have no doubt are doing better for themselves and their children in Liberia than they could do in any other part of the world. Could the free people of colour in this country but see the real condition of their brethren who have settled in Africa, I am persuaded they would require no other motive to induce them to emigrate. This is my decided and deliberate judgment."

---

98. Modern Persecutions of the Protestants in the South of France.

The persecutions in this section of France had continued, with very little intermission, from the revocation of the famous edict of Nantes till a short period previous to the French revolution. Towards the close of the year 1790 these persecuted people were again freed from their alarms, and suffered to enjoy themselves in the exercise of their religion. This peaceful state continued through the reign of Napoleon Bonaparte till the accession of Louis XVIII. to the throne of France, in 1814, when the torch of persecution was again lit up, and great cruelties were committed by the papists upon those who professed the protestant faith. Many were plundered, and many were cruelly murdered, by infuriated popish mobs.

As soon as the news of the arrival of Louis at Paris became known at Nismes, a line of distinction was traced between men of different religious opinions; the spirit of the old catholic church was again to regulate each person's share of esteem and safety. The difference of religion was now to govern every thing else; and even catholic domestics, who had served protestants with zeal and affection, began to neglect their duties, or to perform them ungraciously and with reluctance. At the fetes and spectacles that were given at the public expense, the absence of the protestants was charged on them as a proof of their disloyalty; and in the midst of the cries of 'Vive le Roi,' the discordant sounds of 'A bas le maire' (down with the mayor) were heard. M. Castelnau was a protestant; he appeared in public with the prefect, M. Roland, a catholic, when potatoes were thrown at him, and the people declared that he ought to resign his office. The bigots of Nismes even succeeded in procuring an address to be presented to the king, stating that there ought to be in France but one God, one king, and one faith. In this they were imitated by the catholics of several towns.

Nismes soon exhibited a scene of most awful outrage and carnage, which was carried to such a length, that the protestant refugees in Paris presented the following petition to Louis, in behalf of their brethren at Nismes.

"We lay at your feet, sire, our acute sufferings. In your name our fellow citizens are slaughtered, and their property laid waste. Misled peasants, in pretended obedience to your orders, had assembled at the command of your commissioner, appointed by your august nephew. Although ready to attack us, they were received with the assurances of peace. On the 15th of July, 1815, we learnt your majesty's entrance into Paris, and the white flag immediately waved on our edifices. The public tranquillity had not been disturbed, when armed peasants introduced themselves. The garrison capitulated, but were assailed on their departure, and almost totally massacred. Our national guard was disarmed, the city filled with strangers, and the houses of the principal inhabitants, professing the reformed religion, were attacked and plundered. We subjoin the list. Terror has driven from our city the most respectable inhabitants.

"Your majesty has been deceived if there has not been placed before you the picture of the horrors which make a desert of your good city of Nismes. Arrests and proscriptions are continually taking place, and difference of religious opinions is the real and only cause. The calumniated protestants are the defenders of the throne. Your nephew has beheld our children under his banners; our fortunes have been placed in his hands. Attacked without reason, the protestants have not even by a just resistance afforded their enemies the fatal pretext for calumny. Save us, sire! extinguish the brand of civil war: a single act of your will would restore to political existence a city interesting for its population and its manufactures. Demand an account of their conduct from the chiefs who have brought our misfortunes upon us. We place before your eyes all the documents that have reached us. Fear paralyzes the hearts and stifles the complaints of our citizens. Placed in a more secure situation, we venture to raise our voice in their behalf," &c. &c.

At length the decree of Louis XVIII. was received, which annulled all the extraordinary powers confirmed either by the king, the princes, or subordinate agents at Nismes, and the laws were now to be administered by the regular organs, and a new prefect arrived to carry them into effect. But in spite of proclamations, the work of destruction, which stopped for a moment, was not abandoned; but soon renewed with fresh vigour and effect, and continued till the year 1820, since which time, owing to the interference of the English government in their behalf, no fresh complaints have issued from the south of France on the score of religion.

---

99. Bible Societies.

Before the art of printing was discovered, it is said that it would cost a poor man thirteen years of hard labour to obtain a copy of the Bible, so great was the expense of furnishing a manuscript copy. But now, through the providence of God, so great has been the change, that scarcely any person who lives in a Christian country, and sincerely desires the Bible, need remain a day without this precious gift of heaven.

The formation of the *British and Foreign Bible Society* is justly considered a new and important era in the Bible cause. This society was formed in London on the 7th of March, 1804, by an assembly consisting of about three hundred persons of different religious denominations.

"The primary occasion," says Dr. Owen, in his history of the Bible Society, "of all these measures, out of which this society grew, was the scarcity of *Welch Bibles* in the principalities, and the impracticability of obtaining adequate supplies from the only source existing at that period whence copies of the authorized version were to be derived—*the Society for the promotion of Christian knowledge.* A number of individuals associated for the purpose of satisfying this want; they found others disposed to co-operate in their views; they then extended those views to the whole country; and finally conceived the design of placing the gospel in the habitation of every Christian family, and of carrying the glad tidings of salvation and life by Jesus Christ to the people that are still walking in darkness and the shadow of death."

The British and Foreign Bible Society is the PARENT institution: its receipts during the last year (1831) amounted to upwards of 377,000 dollars; it has 2349 auxiliary and branch societies connected with it in Great Britain, including 1672 associations, 650 of which are conducted by females. The society has aided in printing or translating parts of the Bible in upwards of one hundred and forty languages or dialects. The number of Bibles circulated by the British and Foreign Bible Society during the last year (1831) was 343,727; making the total number circulated since the commencement of the society 7,424,727. The total amount of the expenditure of the society, since its establishment in 1804, has been nearly *eight millions of dollars.*

The *Russian Bible Society* was formed at St. Petersburg in 1813, and now consists of 196 auxiliaries and branches in almost all parts of the Russian empire. During the year 1823 the Russian society was engaged in printing editions of the Bibles and Testaments, in various languages, to the number of 85,000. The operations of the society, however, of late have been suspended by order of the Russian government.

The *American Bible Society* was instituted at New York in 1816. The receipts of the last year (1831) amounted to more than one hundred and twenty-five thousand dollars. The society issued from the depository during the last year 168,637 Bibles in English; 69,025 Testaments in English; 127 Bibles in Spanish;

164 Testaments in Spanish; 1884 Bibles in French; 933 Testaments in French; 1281 Bibles in German; 67 Testaments in German; 40 Bibles in Welch; 1 Bible in Dutch; 2 Gaelic Bibles; 3 Testaments in Irish; and 18 Indian Testaments:—making a total of 242,183 copies. The total number distributed since the formation of the society in 1816, is *one million, three hundred and twenty-six thousand, six hundred and ninety-eight.*

The *Paris Protestant Bible Society* was instituted in 1818; the operations of this society, however, are limited, in comparison with those either of the British and Foreign or the American Bible Societies.

The total number of Bible Societies in various parts of the world, at the present time, is said to be about four thousand, who have circulated, in 160 languages, about *nine millions of Bibles.*

---

100. Bethel Union Meetings.

Bethel Flag.

These meetings, which were instituted for the benefit of seamen, appear to have derived their origin from the prayer meetings of some pious colliers, who assembled on board of different ships in the river Thames, near London, in 1816. These meetings attracting some attention, a respectable number of gentlemen and ladies met in London, formed a society, and purchased a vessel, and fitted it up for public worship. This vessel, which is now called "THE ARK," is of four hundred tons, and capable of accommodating from seven to eight hundred hearers, and many thousands of seamen have had an opportunity of hearing the gospel on board this floating chapel.

Since this vessel was fitted up, "*The British and Foreign Seamen's-Friend Society and Bethel Union*" has been formed, *arks* fitted up in sea-ports, and the "*Bethel Flag*" now waves in various parts of the world.

On the 5th of June, 1818, the "Society for Promoting the Gospel among Seamen" was formed at New York, and in 1820 a mariner's church was erected in the same place (*being*, it is believed, *the first mariner's church ever erected*). "It is an interesting and novel feature in this institution, that sectarian views are discarded, and ministers of different denominations preach in its pulpit."

The New-York Bethel Union was established June 4th, 1821.* Since that time Bethel meetings have been regularly held, either on board of ships or in sailor

* On Friday, the 22d of June, 1821, for the first time in America, the Bethel Flag (a present from the London Bethel Union to the Port of New-York Society) was hoisted at the mast-head of the ship Cadmus, Capt. Whitlock, lying at the Pine-street wharf.

In the morning of the day the committee were apprehensive that they should have no hearers. The experiment here was novel —the issue was by many considered doubtful. They were told by several who are "wise in worldly matters", that a guard of constables would be necessary to preserve order. At first it was thought advisable to hold the meetings in the cabin, to prevent the possibility of disturbance. On arriving at the vessel, the deck was found cleared, an awning stretched, and all necessary preparations for holding the meeting there. At eight o'clock the president opened the meeting by stating the object and plans of the society, and inviting the co-operation of captains and their crews in promoting the benevolent designs of the society.

The mariners' (107) psalm was sung with great animation and feeling, and seamen were immediately seen pressing in from all quarters. After prayer by an aged sea captain, Dr. Spring addressed the seamen—other exercises followed. The vessel and wharf were crowded—order and solemnity prevailed throughout—every ear was open, every eye was fixed. Tracts were distributed among boarding-houses, and conducted by members of the Board of Managers, and appear to be attended with blessed effects. The engraving of the Bethel meeting in this work represents an evening prayer meeting, on the deck of a ship, during the warm season of the year.

When we consider the importance of seamen in a national or religious point of light; the low state of morals too generally prevalent among them; we must consider the efforts which are now making for their religious improvement in various parts of the world as an auspicious era in the efforts of Christian benevolence. Seamen, above every other class of people, have the opportunity to carry the light of the gospel to the remote and "dark places of the earth," and it is believed that their efforts will yet have an important effect in diffusing the light of Christianity throughout the world.

---

101. Sunday-schools.

Among the various institutions which have been established in modern times for the promotion of religious

---

the seamen, who received them with gratitude. Every circumstance was calculated to inspire the board with courage and confidence to go forward.

On the 21st of August a Bethel meeting was held on board the United States ship Franklin, 74, commodore Stewart, lying off the battery, about to depart on a long cruise. A congregation, consisting principally of seamen, about eight hundred in number, were present. Dr. Spring of New-York, Dr. Staughton and Rev. J. Eastburn of Philadelphia, conducted the exercises. The utmost decorum and solemnity prevailed. Several of the seamen came up to Mr. Eastburn, and thanked him for the many "good things he had told them." The crew were affectionately commended to the protection and mercy of that gracious Being who hath provided a Saviour for them, and who was inviting them, by the sweetest allurements of his love, to the everlasting enjoyment of his rest. The board, in behalf of themselves, the reverend clergy, and citizens who attended, embrace this opportunity of expressing their grateful feelings to commodore Stewart and his officers for their politeness and attention to them on this interesting occasion. —*Sailors' Magazine*, 1831.

instruction, and the benefit of mankind, that of Sunday-schools must stand in the foremost rank. The first Sunday-school was established by *Robert Raikes*, Esq., of Gloucester, England, in 1782.

"The beginning of this scheme," says Mr. Raikes, "was owing to accident. Some business leading me one morning into the suburbs of the city (Gloucester), where the lowest of the people chiefly reside, I was struck with concern at seeing a group of children, wretchedly ragged, at play in the street. I asked an inhabitant whether those children belonged to that part of the town, and lamented their misery and idleness. 'Ah! sir,' said the woman to whom I was speaking, 'could you take a view of this part of the town on a Sunday, you would be shocked indeed; for then the street is filled with a multitude of these wretches, who, released from employment, spend their time in noise and riot, playing at chuck, and cursing and swearing in a manner so horrid as to convey to any serious mind an idea of hell rather than any other place.'

"This conversation suggested to me that it would be at least a harmless attempt, if it were productive of no good, should some little plan be formed to check this deplorable profanation of the Lord's-day. I then inquired if there were any decent well disposed women in the neighbourhood who kept schools for teaching to read. I presently was directed to four. To these I applied, and made an agreement with them to receive as many children as I should send them upon Sunday, whom they were to instruct in reading and in the church catechism." This appears to have been the origin of Sunday-schools. Mr. Raikes soon found means to increase the number of schools; the Methodists were the first to unite with him in this undertaking, and in two years he saw a great change wrought in Gloucester. He laid his plan before the public; and before his death, which took place in 1811, he had the happiness to learn that the Sunday-schools in various parts of Britain comprehended three hundred thousand children.

These schools have now become numerous in England, Scotland, Ireland, and America; and it is believed that the influence they will exert on the rising generation will have an important effect towards hastening on that day when "all shall know the Lord, from the least unto the greatest," and "the earth shall be filled with the knowledge of the Lord as the waters cover the sea."

Several different modes have been adopted in conducting these schools, and improvements have been constantly made. In many places the instructors of Sunday-schools hold a weekly or monthly meeting by themselves, to report the progress of their respective classes, and to devise means for the religious improvement of the school. *Libraries*, for the use of the scholars and teachers, have produced very beneficial effects.

---

102. Temperance Societies.

In the early settlement of this country, great care was taken to prevent the sale and use of ardent spirits, unless in very moderate quantities; and for the first hundred years after its settlement the population of the country was peculiarly temperate, and, of course, free from the attending vices of drunkenness. The war of the revolution, however, was attended with disastrous results to the morals of a great portion of the army; and glorious as were their military achievements, they laid broad the foundation of a vice, which, if not speedily checked, will enslave the country to a tyranny worse, ten thousand times, than the stamp-act or Boston port-bill. From that period, intemperance, with all its train of deadly evils, marched through the length and breadth of the land, growing with the unparalleled increase of our population, and increasing in the same ratio with the cheapness of intoxicating material. During this period the only community who interposed their influence to stop the drunkenness of the nation was that of the Friends. But at length, between 1810 and 1820, the magnitude of the evil became so great and overwhelming, that, in various parts of our country, individuals, and some whole neighbourhoods, endeavoured to make a stand. Occasional sermons were preached and printed, and a few societies were formed to stop intemperance.

"The work went on at a tardy pace; those who were endeavouring to stop others were slowly making themselves drunkards, by drinking moderately; the true, *the grand principle* was not yet discovered In the spring of 1824 Charles C. P. Crosby laid a plan of a *national movement* before the Massachusetts Society for the suppression of Intemperance, at their annual meeting, in order to put a stop to this vice; but it was merely entered on file. This plan embraced nearly, if not fully, the *course of operations* now acted upon with so much vigour and applause by the American society for the promotion of temperance, formed in Boston, March, 1826.*

"In 1825, a meeting of a few individuals was called to consider the following question, viz.

"*What shall be done to banish intemperance from the United States?*" After prayer for divine guidance, and consultation on the subject, the result was a determination to attempt the formation of an American Temperance Society, whose grand principle should be *abstinence from strong drink;* and its object, by light and love, to change the habits of the nation, with regard to the use of intoxicating liquors. Some of the reasons of this determination were,

"1. Ardent spirit, which is one of the principal means of drunkenness, is not needful, and the use of it is, to men in health, always injurious.

"2. It is adapted to form intemperate appetites; and while it is continued the evils of intemperance can never be done away.

---

* United States Temperance Almanack, 1832.

"3. The use of this liquor is causing a general deterioration of body and mind; which, if the cause is continued, will continue to increase.

"4. To remove the evils, we must remove the cause; and to remove the cause, efforts must be commensurate with the evil, and be continued till it is eradicated.

"5. We never know what we can do by wise, united, and persevering efforts in a good cause, till we try.

"6. If we do not try to remove the evils of intemperance, we cannot free ourselves from the guilt of its effects."

A correspondence was therefore opened, and a meeting of men, of various Christian denominations, holden in Boston, January 10th, 1826.

The meeting was opened with prayer, and after consultation, the following resolutions were introduced by Jeremiah Evarts, Esq., corresponding secretary of the American Board of Commissioners for Foreign Missions, and adopted, viz.

"1. *Resolved,* That it is expedient that more systematic and more vigorous efforts be made by the Christian public, to restrain and prevent the intemperate use of intoxicating liquors.

"2. That an individual of acknowledged talents, piety, industry, and sound judgment, should be selected and employed as a permanent agent, to spend his time, and use his best exertions for the suppression and prevention of the intemperate use of intoxicating liquors."

A committee was then appointed to prepare a constitution, and the meeting was adjourned to February 13th, 1826.

At the adjourned meeting a constitution was presented and adopted, and the following persons were chosen by the members of the meeting, at the commencement, to compose the society, viz.

Rev. Leonard Woods, D. D.; Rev. William Jenks, D. D.; Rev. Justin Edwards; Rev. Warren Fay; Rev. Benjamin B. Wisner; Rev. Francis Wayland; Rev. Timothy Merritt; Hon. Marcus Morton; Hon. Samuel Hubbard; Hon. William Reed; Hon. George Odiorne; John Tappan, Esq.; William Ropes, Esq.; James P. Chaplin, M. D.; S. V. S. Wilder, Esq.; and Enoch Hale, M. D.

The Hon. Heman Lincoln, of the Baptist church, then offered the following resolution, which was unanimously adopted, viz.

"*Resolved*, That the gentlemen composing this meeting pledge themselves to the American Society for the Promotion of Temperance, that they will use all their exertions in carrying into effect the benevolent plans of the society."

The society then held its first meeting, and chose the following officers, viz.

Hon. Marcus Morton, president; Hon. Samuel Hubbard, vice president; William Ropes, Esq., treasurer, John Tappan, Esq., auditor.

Executive committee—Rev. Leonard Woods, D. D.; Rev. Justin Edwards; John Tappan, Esq.; Hon. George Odiorne, and S. V. S. Wilder, Esq.

On the 12th of March succeeding the society met, and chose eighty-four men from the northern and middle states, as additional members of the society.

In April, 1826, the National Philanthropist, a weekly paper devoted to the cause of temperance, was established in Boston by the Rev. William Collier. Its motto was, "*Temperate drinking is the downhill road to intemperance.*" This paper has been continued, and with some modifications is now published by Messrs. Goodell & Crandall, in New York. It is an able and efficient paper, and, under its successive editors. has been a valuable auxiliary to the cause. In November, 1827, the committee appointed the Rev. Nathaniel Hewit, of Fairfield, Conn., to an agency for three years. Mr. Hewit visited various places in the United States; preached powerfully on the subject, addressed public bodies, awakened public attention, and in various ways promoted successfully the great and good cause.

On the first of May, 1831, there were reported more than one hundred and forty societies in Maine, ninety-six in New Hampshire, one hundred and thirty-two in

Vermont, two hundred and nine in Massachusetts, twenty-one in Rhode Island, two hundred and two in Connecticut, seven hundred and twenty-seven in New York, sixty-one in New Jersey, one hundred and twenty-four in Pennsylvania, five in Delaware, thirty-eight in Maryland, ten in the district of Columbia, one hundred and thirteen in Virginia, thirty-one in North Carolina, sixteen in South Carolina, sixty in Georgia, one in Florida, ten in Alabama, nineteen in Mississippi, three in Louisiana, fifteen in Tennessee, twenty-three in Kentucky, one hundred and four in Ohio, twenty-five in Indiana, twelve in Illinois, four in Missouri, and thirteen in Michigan territory; making, in all, more than two thousand two hundred, and embracing more than one hundred and seventy thousand members. These members have been constantly increasing, and have, in many cases, been more than doubled since they were reported.*

"There are more than two hundred vessels sailing out of ports without ardent spirits for use among the crews. More than one thousand distilleries have been stopped. One hundred public houses have discontinued selling any kind of intoxicating liquors; and three thousand merchants have given up traffic in ardent spirits."

* Fourth Report of the American Temperance Society.

103. Religion and present State of the Jews.

A coin struck at Rome, after the destruction of Jerusalem by Titus, representing the conquered country —she that was full of people sitting a widow, solitary and weeping.

From the destruction of Jerusalem, by Titus, the Jews have been scattered, agreeably to the prediction of Moses, from one end of the earth to the other. Their preservation as a distinct people, through eighteen hundred years of awful suffering and disgrace, a "reproach and a by-word" among all nations, is a standing miracle, furnishing incontestable evidence of the truth of Divine revelation. The following account of the religion and present state of the Jews is extracted from Marsh's Ecclesiastical History.

"To their religion the Jews have adhered with an inflexible obstinacy. Such parts of their worship as were necessarily confined to Jerusalem, particularly sacrifices, have ceased; but as closely as they could, in their dispersed state, they have adhered to the Mosaic dispensation. They have continued to read the law of Moses; to venerate the Sabbath, which they have viewed as commencing an hour before sunset on Friday; to practise circumcision, and to observe the passover, feast of pentecost, of trumpets, of tabernacles, of Purim, and the great day of expiation. They have also had many festivals not appointed by the law of Moses. Since the destruction of Jerusalem they have had no high-priest. A rabbi, or priest, continues to preside in the synagogue worship, and occasionally preaches and marries. He is not confined to the tribe of Levi. The members of that tribe are now considered as laymen, yet they have some little deference paid them in the synagogue service.

The Jews, in their dispersion, have rigidly adhered to a few great articles of faith:—the unity of God; the inspiration and ever-binding power of the law of Moses; the future appearance of the Messiah; the resurrection of the dead; and future retribution. They have supposed that Christ will be a great temporal prince, will restore the Jews to their native land, and will subdue all nations before him and the house of Judah. As the prophets have predicted his mean appearance, and sufferings, they have supposed that there will be two Messiahs, Ban Ephraim, a person of low and mean condition, of the tribe of Ephraim, and Ban David, a prince of great power and glory, of the tribe of Judah.

Some new sects have from time to time appeared among the Jews; but the Pharisees have ever formed the bulk of the nation. A few Caraites, who reject the traditions, and are Jewish protestants, remain. A colony of these are on the Chimea. The Sadducees, as a sect, are nearly extinct. But there are many real Sadducees, that is, infidels, among the Jews; men who reject all belief in revelation and moral accountability, and any Saviour. A party has recently sprung up in Germany who despise both the Talmud and the Old Testament. They are little better than deists. The New Testament is read extensively.

The number of Jews in the world, and in various countries at different periods, is an interesting subject; but never can be estimated with much accuracy. At the time of the destruction of Jerusalem they probably numbered not far from three millions. This number has varied much in different ages and countries, according to the opportunity given them for increase.

For the first twelve hundred years they were far more numerous in the east than in the west. But in the tenth century their numbers were greatly diminished there by the invasion of the Tartars and persecution of the Persians. In Palestine their number has always been small. When they were banished from Spain in 1492, there were in that kingdom seventy thousand families. In 1619 there were in the province of Fez eighty thousand. In the ecclesiastical state they have numbered an hundred synagogues, nine of which were in Rome. Their present number is probably between three and four millions. In the Ottoman empire it is supposed that there are a million. At Constantinople eighty thousand, at Aleppo five thousand, Jerusalem three thousand. In China, India, and Persia, three hundred thousand. Of the white and black Jews at Cochin sixteen thousand. In Ethiopia one hundred thousand. In Morocco, Fez, and Algiers, four hundred thousand. In Poland three hundred thousand. England twenty thousand. Holland sixty thousand. France twenty thousand. The United States six thousand.

As the Jews were, at the destruction of Jerusalem, dispossessed of their lands and driven into foreign countries, they were compelled to resort to commerce for support. And having ever been in expectation of returning to Judea upon a sudden summons, they have never purchased to much extent any territory, nor engaged largely in agricultural employments; but have been the brokers and bankers of others. Their commercial pursuits were much promoted in the fifth century by the invasion of the northern nations, who had an abhorrence of commerce, and suffered it all to be transferred to a people whom they viewed with ignominy and contempt. In England they were for a long time the chief conductors of foreign trade, and wrought most of the gold and silver ornaments for the churches. In the Ottoman empire they obtained the privilege of selling wine, because it was supposed that they would strictly regard the Jewish law, which forbade their making any mixture. In Egypt and Morocco they have ever farmed the customs, coined the money, and conducted all foreign commerce. In most parts of the world, and in every age, they have accumulated great wealth. In Europe and America they are now generally brokers, dealers in clothes, watches, jewels, and a number of young people are teachers of children.

In Great Britain the Jews are not known in law, but they are connived at and valued for their enterprise. They have the free exercise of their worship, and the opportunity to acquire, and ability to hold, property to any extent. Their literature is respectable. They have five synagogues in London.

In Holland the Jews are numerous, wealthy, and respectable.

In Spain they are not known as Jews; but are numerous in every class of society, even among priests and inquisitors, as good catholics.

In Portugal they are in the same manner obliged to dissemble. The Spanish and Portuguese Jews claim their descent from a colony of the tribe of Judah, sent into Spain at the Babylonish captivity, and will have no intercourse with the German Jews. They are in every respect superior to the German Jews, and vie with other Europeans in refinement and intelligence. They have separate synagogues wherever they reside.

In Germany and Prussia most of the vexatious statutes of former ages have been repealed, and the Jews are living in quiet. At Frankfort, however, they are subject to many humiliating restrictions.

From Russia they were formerly excluded, but they have been united to it by the union of countries in which they resided, and favourable edicts have been passed by the emperor. A colony of Caraite, or protestant Jews, who adhere closely to the Scriptures, are on the Crimea. Poland has been their chief seat in modern ages. There are now in that country from 2 to 300,000, enjoying great privileges.

In Sweden and Denmark they have a good degree of liberty.

In France, from whence they were expelled in 1394, and where only a few for centuries were known at Metz and Bordeaux, their situation since the revolution has been very gratifying. In 1791, all who would take the civic oath were admitted to the rank of citizens. This act first gave them a country in Europe. The emperor Napoleon convened an assembly of them in Paris, May 30, 1806, that he might learn their principles, and the next year the grand Sanhedrim composed, according to the ancient custom, of seventy members, for the establishment of a civil and religious polity. A synagogue and a consistory were established in every department.

In Paris the Jews had, in 1812, a consistory and three grand rabbies, and are improving in literature and agriculture.

In the Ottoman empire the Jews are still numerous, but less affluent and more ignorant than in Europe. For a heavy tax to the porte they have the liberty of their own worship. They all wear beards, and are distinguished by their dress. Their priests are much respected. "In Jerusalem, their ancient city, they are, as a people, the objects of universal contempt; who suffer the most wanton outrages without a murmur; who endure wounds and blows without a sigh; who, when the sacrifice of their life is demanded, unhesitatingly stretch forth their necks to the sabre. If a member of the community, thus cruelly proscribed and abused, happens to die, his companions bury him clandestinely, during the night, in the valley of Jehoshaphat, within the purlieus of the temple of Solomon. Enter their habitation, and you find them in the most abject, squalid misery, and for the most part occupied in reading a mysterious book to their children, with whom again it becomes a manual for the instruction of future generations. The legitimate masters of Judea should be seen as they are in their own land, slaves and strangers—awaiting, under the most cruel and oppressive of all despotisms, a king who is to work their deliverance."

In China the Jews have existed for many centuries in considerable numbers. They have their synagogues, but so far conform to the Chinese customs and worship, and are so peaceable, as to meet with but little persecution.

In India the Jews are numerous. Dr. Buchanan, who visited that country in 1806 and 8, found their residence about a mile distant from Cochin, called Jewstown. They were divided into two classes, the Jerusalem or white Jews, and the ancient or black Jews. The former came into India soon after the destruction of Jerusalem. The latter have a tradition that their ancestors came thither soon after the Babylonish captivity. Their complexion differs much from the white Jews, and they are viewed by them as an inferior race. From these Dr. B. obtained a manuscript copy of the Pentateuch, handed down from their ancestors, which differs but little from the European copies.

---

104. Millennium.

This time is yet to come. Millennium is a term generally used to denote the time when, according to prophecy, a great moral change in our world will be effected by the universal prevalence of Christianity. "By this change the ruins of the fall, to a great extent, will be repaired: the power and influence of the Messiah's reign will be felt and acknowledged by all nations, producing universal peace and willing obedience to the law of the Creator; and the earth, with its inhabitants, in a manner and degree beyond our anticipations, will return to the happy state of perfection, innocence, and peace in which they were originally formed."*

We have many prophecies in the Bible respecting this time: the prophet declares that "The knowledge

*Dr. Morse.

of the Lord shall cover the earth as the waters cover the sea," and "all shall know the Lord, from the least unto the greatest."

This world, which has been the theatre of so much sin and misery, war and bloodshed, shall be changed, for in this time "swords shall be beat into ploughshares, and spears into pruning-hooks; nation shall not lift up sword against nation, neither shall they learn war any more." "There shall be nothing to hurt or offend in all the holy mountain," for "the wolf also shall dwell with the lamb, and the leopard shall lie down with the kid; and the calf and the young lion and the fatling together, and a little child shall lead them."

The following is from Buck's Theological Dictionary:—

"MILLENNIUM, 'a thousand years;' generally employed to denote the thousand years during which, according to an ancient tradition in the church, grounded on some doubtful texts in the Apocalypse and other Scriptures, our blessed Saviour shall reign with the faithful upon earth after the first resurrection, before the final completion of beatitude.

"Though there has been no age of the church in which the millennium was not admitted by individual divines of the first eminence, it is yet evident from the writings of Eusebius, Irenæus, Origen, and others among the ancients, as well as from the histories of Dupin, Mosheim, and all the moderns, that it was never adopted by the whole church or made an article of the established creed in any nation.

"About the middle of the fourth century the Millenarians held the following tenets:

"1st, That the city of Jerusalem should be rebuilt, and that the land of Judea should be the habitation of those who were to reign on the earth a thousand years.

"2dly, That the first resurrection was not to be confined to the martyrs, but that after the fall of Antichrist all the just were to rise, and all that were on the earth were to continue for that space of time.

"3dly. That Christ shall then come down from heaven, and be seen on earth, and reign there with his servants.

"4thly. That the saints, during this period, shall enjoy all the delights of a terrestrial paradise."

These opinions were founded upon several passages in Scripture, which the Millennarians among the fathers understood in no other than a literal sense; but which the moderns who hold that opinion consider as partly literal and partly metaphorical. Of these passages, that upon which the greatest stress has been laid we believe to be the following:—"And I saw an angel come down from heaven, having the key of the bottomless pit, and a great chain in his hand. And he laid hold on the dragon, that old serpent, which is the devil and Satan, and bound him a *thousand years,* and cast him into the bottomless pit, and shut him up, and set a seal upon him, that he should deceive the nations no more till *the thousand years* should be fulfilled; and after that he must be loosed a little season. And I saw thrones, and they sat upon them, and judgment was given unto them; and I saw the souls of them that were beheaded for the witness of Jesus and for the word of God, and which had not worshipped the beast, neither his image, neither had received his mark upon their foreheads, nor in their hands; and they lived and reigned with Christ a *thousand years.* But the rest of the dead lived not again till *the thousand years were finished.* This is the first resurrection." Rev. xx. 1–6. This passage all the ancient Millennarians took in a sense grossly literal, and taught that during the Millennium, the saints on earth were to enjoy every bodily delight. The moderns, on the other hand, consider the power and pleasures of this kingdom as wholly spiritual; and they represent them as not to commence till after the conflagration of the present earth. But that this last supposition is a mistake the very next verse but one assures us; for we are there told that "when the thousand years are expired, Satan shall be loosed out of his prison, and shall go out to deceive the nations which are in the four quarters of *the earth;*" and we have no reason to believe that he will have such power or such liberty in "the new heavens and the new earth, wherein dwelleth righteousness." We may observe, however, the following things respecting it: 1. That the Scriptures afford us ground to believe that the church will arrive to a state of prosperity which it never has yet enjoyed, Rev. xx. 4. 7. Psal. lxxii. 11. Is. ii. 2, 4; xi. 9; xlix. 23; lx. Dan. vii. 27. 2. That this will continue at least a thousand years, or a considerable space of time, in which the work of salvation may be fully accomplished in the utmost extent and glory of it. In this time, in which the world will soon be filled with real Christians, and continue full by constant propagation, to supply the place of those who leave the word; there will be many thousands born and live on the earth, to each one that has been born and lived in the preceding six thousand years: so that if they who shall be born in that thousand years shall be all, or most of them saved (as they will be), there will, on the whole, be many thousands of mankind saved to one that shall be lost. 3. This will be a state of great happiness and glory. Some think that Christ will reign personally on earth, and that there will be a literal resurrection of the saints, Rev. xx. 4, 7; but I rather suppose that the reign of Christ and resurrection of saints alluded to in that passage is only figurative; and that nothing more is meant than that before the general judgment, the Jews shall be converted, genuine Christianity be diffused through all nations, and that Christ shall reign by his spiritual presence in a glorious manner. It will, however, be a time of eminent holiness, clear light, and knowledge, love, peace, and friendship, agreement in doctrine and worship. Human life, perhaps, will rarely be endangered by the poisons of the mineral, vegetable, and animal kingdoms. Beasts of prey, perhaps, will be extirpated or tamed by the power of man. The inhabitants of every place will rest secure from fear of robbery and murder. War shall be entirely ended. Capital crimes and punishments be heard of no more. Governments placed on fair, just, and humane foundations. The torch of civil discord will be extinguished. Perhaps pagans, Turks, Deists, and Jews will be as few in number as Christians are now. Kings, nobles, magistrates, and rulers in churches shall act with principle, and be forward to promote the best interests of men; tyranny, oppression, persecution, bigotry, and cruelty shall cease. Business will be attended to without contention, dishonesty, and covetousness. Trades and manufactories will be carried on with a design to promote the general good of mankind, and not with selfish interests, as now. Merchandise between distant countries will be conducted without fear of an enemy; and works of ornament and beauty, perhaps, shall not be wanting in those days. Learning, which has always flourished in proportion as religion has spread, shall then greatly increase and be employed for the best of purposes. Astronomy, geography, natural history, metaphysics, and all the useful sciences will be better understood, and consecrated to the service of God; and I cannot help thinking that by the improvements which have been made, and are making, in ship-building, navigation, electricity, medicine, &c. that "the tempest will lose half its force, the lightning lose half its terrors," and the human frame not near so much exposed to danger. Above all, the Bible will be more highly appreciated, its harmony perceived, its superiority owned, and its energy felt by millions of human beings. In fact, the earth shall be filled with the knowledge of the Lord as the waters cover the sea. 4. The time when the Millennium will commence cannot be fully ascertained; but the common idea is, that it will be in the seven thousandth year of the world. It will, most probably, come on by degrees, and be in a manner introduced years before that time. And who knows but the present convulsions among different nations; the overthrow which popery has had in places where it has been so dominant for hundreds of years; the fulfilment of prophecy respecting infidels, and the falling away of many in the last times; and yet, in the midst of all, the

BETHEL MEETING AT NIGHT.

MILLENIUM.

The wolf also shall dwell with the lamb, and the leopard shall lie down with the kid; and the calf and the young lion and the fatling together; and a little child shall lead them. Isa. 11 Chap. 6 ver.

number of missionaries sent into different parts of the world, together with the increase of gospel ministers: the thousands of ignorant children that have been taught to read the Bible, and the vast number of different societies that have been lately instituted for the benevolent purpose of informing the minds and impressing the hearts of the ignorant; who knows, I say, but what these things are the forerunners of events of the most delightful nature, and which may usher in the happy morn of that bright and glorious day when the whole world shall be filled with his glory, and all the ends of the earth see the salvation of our God?"

For the coming of this blessed day Christians in all ages have prayed. Never, since the time of the first apostles, has there been such an universal effort to spread the gospel throughout the world as there is at the present time, and it is believed that we see the dawn of that glorious period when it will be said

> "One song employs all nations; and they cry
> Worthy the Lamb, for he was slain for us."
> "The dwellers in the vales, and on the rocks,
> Shout to each other; and the mountain tops,
> From distant mountains, catch the flying joy;
> Till nation after nation, taught the strain,
> Earth rolls the rapturous hosanna round."—*Cowper.*

A

BIOGRAPHICAL SKETCH

OF

PERSONS DISTINGUISHED IN RELIGIOUS HISTORY.

A.

Abbas, the uncle of Mahomet, opposed the ambitious views of the impostor; but when defeated in the battle of Bedr, was reconciled to his nephew, embraced his religion, and thanked heaven for the prosperity and grace he enjoyed as a mussulman. He died in the 32d year of the Hegira.

Abbot, George, archbishop of Canterbury, born 1562, at Guildford, in Surry. In 1604 that translation of the Bible now in use was begun by the direction of king James I., and Dr. Abbot was the second of eight divines of Oxford, to whom the care of translating the whole New Testament (excepting the epistles) was committed. He died at Croydon, Aug. 5th, 1633.

Abdias, a native of Babylon, who pretended to be one of the seventy-two disciples of our Saviour, wrote a legendary treatise, called Historia certaminis Apostolica, which was edited and translated into Latin by Wolgang Lazius, Basil, 1571.

Abelard, Peter, one of the most celebrated doctors of the twelfth century, was born in the village of Palais, in Brittany. "He thought it necessary to have a mis-

FOX
LUTHER
CALVIN
ARMINIUS
WESLEY

tress, and accordingly fixed his affections on *Heloise*, a niece of a canon at Paris. He boarded in his canon's house, whose name was Fulbert; where, pretending to teach the young lady the sciences, he soon made love to his scholar. Abelard now performed his public functions very coldly, and wrote nothing but amorous verses. Heloise, at length, being likely to become a mother, Abelard sent her to a sister of his in Brittany, where she was delivered of a son. To soften the canon's anger, he offered to marry Heloise privately; Fulbert, however, was better pleased with this proposal than his niece, who, from a strange singularity in her passion, chose rather to be the mistress than the wife of Abelard. At length, however, she consented to a private marriage; but even after this would, on some occasion, affirm with an oath, that she was still unmarried. Her husband thereupon sent her to the monastery of Argenteuil; where, at his desire, she put on a religious habit, but not the veil. Heloise's relations, looking upon this as a second piece of treachery in Abelard, were transported to such a degree of resentment, that they hired ruffians who forced into his chamber by night, and shamefully mutilated him. This infamous treatment forced Abelard to a cloister, to conceal his confusion, and he put on the habit in the abbey of St. Denis. He afterwards retired to a solitude in the diocess of Troyes, and there built an oratory, which he named the *Paraclete*, where great numbers of pupils resorted to him. Here again his success excited that envy by which he had through life been persecuted; and having been several times in danger of his life, by poison and other artifices, he was at length received by Peter the Venerable into his abbey of Clugni, in which sanctuary Abelard was treated with the utmost tenderness and humanity. At length, having become infirm from the prevalence of the scurvy and other disorders, he was removed to the priory of St. Marcellus, on the Saon, near Chalons, where he died, April 21st, 1142, in the 63d year of his age. His corpse was sent to Heloise, who deposited it in the Paraclete."

Abraham, Ben-choila, a Spanish rabbi, skilled in astrology, prophesied that the coming of the Messiah would be in 1358; died 1303.

Abucara, Theodore, the metropolitan of Caria, obtained a seat in the synod held at Constantinople, 869; he wrote treatises against the Jews and Mahometans, which have been published.

Abudhaher, the father of the Carmatians, in Arabia, opposed the religion of Mahomet, plundered the temple of Mecca, and died in possession of his extensive dominions, 953.

Acacius, a bishop of Amida, on the Tigris, sold the sacred vessels of his churches to ransom seven thousand Persian slaves; he lived in the reign of Theodosius the younger.

Acca, bishop of Hexham, author of treatises on the sufferings of the saints, died 1740.

Acesius, bishop of Constantinople, in the age of Constantine, maintained that those who committed any sin after being baptized ought not to be again admitted into the church, though they might repent.

Achards, Eleazer, Francis des, distinguished by his learning, piety, and humanity, was nominated bishop of Halicarnassus, and afterwards sent apostolic vicar to China; he died at Cochin, 1741.

Acontius, James, a famous philosopher, civilian, and divine, born at Trent, in the sixteenth century. He embraced the protestant religion, and, going over to England in the reign of Elizabeth, met with a very friendly reception from that princess, as he himself has testified in a work dedicated to her. This work is his celebrated "*Collection of the Stratagems of Satan,*" which has been often translated, and has gone through many different impressions.

Acuna, Christopher, a Jesuit of Burgos, employed as missionary in America, published an account of the Amazon river at Madrid, 1641.

Adalbert, archbishop of Prague, preached the gospel among the Bohemians, and afterwards to the Poles, by whom he was murdered, April 29, 997.

Adelgreiff, John Albretcht, natural son of a priest near Elbing, pretended to be the vicegerent of God on earth, was condemned to death at Konigsburg for blasphemy, 1636.

Adelphus, a philosopher of the third century, who mingled the doctrines of Plato with the tenets of the Gnostics.

Adhelme, William, nephew to Ina, king of the West Saxons, first bishop of Sherborne, and said to be the first Englishman who wrote Latin, died 709.

Adrian, a Greek author, in the fifth century, wrote an introduction to the Scriptures.

Adrian IV., pope, the only Englishman that ever had the honour of sitting in the papal chair. His name was Nicholas Bukespere; he was born at Langley, near St. Albans, in Hertfordshire, and after many vicissitudes of fortune, succeeded to the popedom in 1154. He died Sept. 1, 1159, leaving some letters and homilies which are still extant.

Adrichomia, Cornelia, a nun of Holland, of the Augustine order, published a poetical version of the psalms in the sixteenth century.

Æneas, Sylvius, or Pius II., born 1405 at Corsigny, in Sienna, where his father lived in exile. This pope was famous for his wise and witty sayings, some of which are as follows:—That common men should esteem learning as silver, noblemen prize it as gold, and princes as jewels: a citizen should look upon his family as subject to the city, the city to his country, the country to the world, and the world to God: that the chief place with kings was slippery: that the tongue of a sycophant was the king's greatest plague: that a prince who would trust nobody was good for nothing; and he who believed every body, no better: that those who went to law were the birds, the court the field, the judge the net, and the lawyers the fowlers: that men ought to be presented to dignities, not dignities to men: that a covetous man never pleases any body but by his death: that it was a slavish vice to tell lies: that lust sullies and stains every age of man, but quite extinguishes old age.

Agapius, a Greek monk of Mount Athos, in the seventeenth century, wrote a treatise in favour of transubstantiation, called the "salvation of sinners."

Agricola, Michael, a minister of Abo, in Finland, first translated the New Testament into the language of that country.

Alasco, John, a Roman catholic bishop, uncle to the king of Poland, became a convert to the protestant principles, and died 1560.

Alban, St., said to have been the first person who suffered martyrdom for Christianity in Britain, and therefore usually styled the proto-martyr of this island, was born at Verulam, and flourished towards the end of the third century. (See p. 75.)

Albert, Erasmus, a native of Frankfort, assisted Luther in the reformation.

Albert of Stade, author of a chronicle from the creation to 1286, a Benedictine of the thirteenth century.

Aleander, Jerome, archbishop under pope Leo X., and celebrated for his attack on the doctrines of Luther, died at Rome. 1542.

Alenio, Julius, a Jesuit, who went as a missionary to China, where he preached thirty-six years, and built several churches; he died 1698.

Alexander, bishop of Hierapolis, in the fifth century, who maintained that there were two natures in Christ; he died an exile.

Alexander I., bishop of Rome, 109. He was called a saint and martyr, and, according to Platina, was the first who introduced the use of holy water into the church.

Alexander IV., bishop of Ostia, was made pope in 1254. He bestowed the crown of Sicily on Edmund, son of the king of England; and tried to unite the Greek and Latin churches.

Alexander, a native of Asia Minor, was the founder of a sect called non-sleepers, because some of them always kept awake to sing; he died 430.

Alexander V., pope, was originally a beggar, but found means to cultivate his mind, so that he was distinguished both at Oxford and Paris. He was elected pope in 1409, but soon died by poison.

Ali Beg, a Pole, who was educated in the Mahometan faith, but employed himself in translating the Bible into Turkish. He also wrote on the religion of Mahomet, and died in 1675.

Allein, Joseph, a puritan of great learning and piety. His "Alarm" to sinners has been often published. He died at Taunton, England, 1668.

Allyn, Henry, preacher in Nova Scotia, author of several strange and absurd religious doctrines. He died in 1783. His followers were few. He published a volume of hymns and several sermons.

Allen, Ethan, a brigadier-general in the war of the American revolution. He sustained the character of an infidel, and in his writings ridiculed the Scriptures.

Ambrose, St., (see page 58.)

Anastasius II., was raised from a private station to the throne of Constantinople by the voice of the people. He abdicated the throne for a religious habit, and afterwards, in attempting to regain it, was put to death, 719.

Anastasius I., pope of Rome, succeeded Siricius; he reconciled the eastern and western churches, and died much respected for his sanctity and virtue, 402.

Andreas, John, a famous canonist of the fourteenth century, born at Mugello, near Florence. We are told, by good authors, strange things concerning the austerity of his life; as, that he macerated his body with prayer and fasting, and lay upon the bare ground for twenty years together, covered only with a bear skin. Andreas had a beautiful daughter, named Novella, whom he instructed so well in all parts of learning, that when any affair hindered him from reading lectures to his scholars he sent his daughter in his room; when, lest her beauty should prevent the attention of the hearers, she had a curtain drawn before her. To perpetuate the memory of his daughter, he entitled his commentary upon the Decretals of Gregory IX. "The Novellae." Andreas died of the plague at Bologna, in 1348, after he had been professor forty-five years, and was buried in the church of the Dominicans.

Andreas, John, was born a Mahometan, at Xativa, in the kingdom of Valencia, and in the year 1417 embraced the Christian religion. He afterwards wrote his famous work of "The Confusion of the Sect of Mahomet." This book was first published in Spanish, but has since been translated into several different languages, and is much quoted by those who write against Mahometanism.

Andrews, Lancelot, bishop of Winchester, was born in London, 1565. He died in 1626, having written many excellent religious tracts, particularly "A manual of private devotions and meditations for every day in the week;" and "A manual of directions for the visitation of the sick."

Anselm, archbishop of Canterbury, in the reigns of Rufus and Henry 1st, born 1033, at Aost, in Savoy, died at Canterbury, 1109. He was the first archbishop who restrained the English clergy from marrying, and was canonized in the reign of Henry VII.

Antes, John, a native of America, educated in Germany, a Moravian missionary to Abyssinia, died 1811.

Aquila, a mathematician of Pontus: he translated the Bible from Hebrew into Greek.

Aquinas, St. Thomas, a celebrated teacher of the school divinity in the universities of Italy, and commonly called the *angelical doctor*, was born in the castle of Aquino, in Italy, about the year 1224. In 1274 he was sent for to the second council of Lyons, by pope Gregory X., that he might read before them a book which he had written against the Greeks at the command of Urban IV.; but he fell sick on his journey and died at Fossanova, aged fifty years. Aquinas left a vast number of works, which have been repeatedly printed, in seventeen volumes folio.

Aretin, Guy, a Benedictine monk, who lived in the eleventh century. He rendered himself famous by discovering a new method of learning music; and was said to have been the inventor of the six notes in music, "Ut, Re, Mi," Fa, Sol, La.

Arius, (see page 85.)

Arminius, James, a professor of divinity at Leyden, and founder of the sect of Arminians; born in Holland 1560, and died in 1619. His sentiments are in opposition to those which are held by Calvinists.

Arnold, a famous heretic of the twelfth century, born at Brescia, in Italy, whence he went to France, where he studied under the celebrated Peter Abelard. Upon his return to Italy he put on the habit of a monk, and began to preach several new and uncommon doctrines, particularly that the pope ought not to enjoy any temporal estate; that those ecclesiastics who had any estates of their own, or held any lands, were entirely cut off from the least hope of salvation; that the clergy ought to subsist upon the alms and voluntary contributions of Christians: and that all other revenues belonged to princes and states, in order to be disposed of among the laity as they thought proper. He was hanged at Rome in the year 1155.

Asbury, Francis, the first bishop of the American methodist church. He died March 21st, 1816, in the seventy-first year of his age, having zealously devoted about fifty years of his life to the work of preaching the gospel.

Ascelin, an ecclesiastic of the eleventh century, defended transubstantiation against Berenger.

Ashmun, Jehudi, agent of the American colony at Liberia, Africa. This philanthropist was eminently qualified for the station appointed him. Upon his arrival in the colony he found it in a feeble and defenceless state, and only twenty-eight effective men could be mustered when the colony was attacked by more than eight hundred savages. By his uncommon energy and prowess, he saved the colony from destruction, and laid the foundation of a large and well-organized community of freemen. "Like the patriarchs of old, he was their captain, their lawgiver, judge, priest, and governor." By his hardships and exposure to the climate his health failed him, and he returned to the United States and, soon after his arrival, died, at the age of thirty-four, in New Haven, August 26th, 1828, deeply lamented by his Christian brethren.

Augustine, St. (see page 59.)

Augustine or Austin, St., the first archbishop of Canterbury, was originally a monk in the convent of St. Andrew, at Rome, and educated under St. Gregory, by whom he was despatched into Britain, with forty other monks of the same order, about the year 596, to convert the English Saxons to Christianity. He died at Canterbury, 604.

B.

Baba, a Turkish impostor. He announced himself in 1260, as the messenger of God; was opposed and overpowered by the Turks, and his sect dispersed.

Backus, Isaac, a distinguished Baptist minister of Massachusetts, and author of numerous publications. He was born at Norwich, Conn., in 1724, and died in 1806.

Bacon, Roger, a learned monk of the Franciscan order, descended of an ancient family, born near Ilchester, in Somersetshire, 1214. His discoveries were little understood by the generality of mankind; and because, by the help of mathematical knowledge, he performed things above common understanding, he was suspected of magic. He died 1294.

Barclay, Robert, an eminent writer of the society of Quakers, born at Edinburgh, 1648. In 1676 his famous "Apology for the Quakers" was published in Latin, at Amsterdam, and in 1678, translated into English. He did great service to his sect all over Europe by his writings, and died in 1690.

Barochebas, or *Barochab*, an impostor among the Jews; his followers were numerous, but afterwards destroyed by Julius Severus.

Barebone, Praise-God, a bigoted zealot of Cromwell's parliament, of such celebrity as a demagogue, that the parliament was ludicrously called after him. His two brothers adopted Scripture names, "Christ came into the world to save, Barebone," and "if Christ had not died, thou hadst been damned, Barebone," called by the wits of the day by the two last words

Barrow, Isaac, an eminent mathematician and divine, born in 1630 in London, and died in 1677. He is celebrated for his sermons, which are said to be richer in thought than any other in the English language.

Barton, Elizabeth, commonly called "The Holy Maid of Kent," was a religious impostor in the reign of Henry VIII., and executed at Tyburn, April 20th, 1534.

Baschi, Matthew, founder of a new order of Franciscans Capuchins, died 1552.

Baxter, Richard, an eminent non conformist divine, was born Nov. 12th, 1615, at Rowton in Shropshire, and died 1691. He wrote a vast number of books; and the author of a note in the Biographia Brittannica tells us that he had seen one hundred and forty-five distinct treatises of Mr. Baxter's: his practical works have been published in four vols. folio. He had a moving and pathetical way of writing; and was, his whole life, a man of great zeal and much simplicity.

Bellamy, Joseph, D. D., a divine of New England, settled in Bethlehem, Conn., in 1740, a teacher of candidates for the ministry, and distinguished for several religious works. He died in 1790, aged seventy-one.

Benedict, a celebrated abbot of the seventh century, of a noble Saxon family. He introduced many improvements in architecture into England from the continent. He founded two monasteries, and was canonized after his death.

Benedict IX. was elected pope when only twelve years old, by the intrigues of his father the duke of Tusculum, and compelled to abdicate by the Romans, on account of his debauchery; he died 1059.

Benezet, St., a shepherd of Vevarais, who pretended to be inspired to build the bridge of Avignon, four arches of which only remain, died in 1184.

Benezet, Anthony, (see page 249.)

Benson, Dr. George, a very distinguished pastor among the English dissenters, was born at Great Salkeld, in Cumberland, 1699, and died 1763. In 1740, he became colleague with Dr. Lardner at Crutched

Friars, and, on his death had the sole pastorship intrusted to him. Of his writings, the principal are, "Defence of the Reasonableness of Prayer;" an illustration of such of St. Paul's Epistles as Mr. Locke had not explained; "A History of the first planting of Christianity," 2 vols. 4to. "Tracts on Persecution;" and "A Life of Christ."

Bernard, of Menthon, an ecclesiastic of Savoy, founder of two monasteries in the passes of the Alps, for the relief of pilgrims and travellers, which still remain as monuments of his benevolence: born in 923.

Bernard, St., a Romish saint, who died in 1153.

Bernardine, an ecclesiastic, and very popular preacher, born at Massar. He was the founder of three hundred monasteries in Italy, and was canonized by pope Nicholas; he died in 1444.

Berkeley, George, bishop of Cloyne, in Ireland, a distinguished benefactor of Yale College (Conn.), was born March 12th, 1684, at Kilcrin, county of Kilkenny, Ireland. The excellence of his moral character is conspicuous in his writings. He was held by his acquaintance in the highest estimation. Bishop Atterbury, after being introduced to him, exclaimed: "So much understanding, so much knowledge, so much innocence, and so much humility, I did not think had been the portion of any but angels, till I saw this gentleman." He died January 14th, 1753.

Beveridge, William, a learned English divine, bishop of St. Asaph, born at Barrow, in Leicestershire, 1638, died in 1707, leaving behind him many learned and valuable works.

Blair, Dr. Hugh, a celebrated Scotch divine, was the son of a respectable merchant in Edinburgh, and born in that city April 7th, 1718. On the 15th June, 1758, he was made one of the ministers of the high church of Edinburgh, and for more than forty years amply evinced the propriety of the choice. Dr. Blair is well known by his "Lectures on Rhetoric and the Belles Lettres." His "Sermons," of which five volumes are before the public, have experienced a success unparalleled in the annals of pulpit eloquence, though justly merited by purity of sentiment, justness of reasoning, and grace of composition. They have circulated in numerous editions, and have been translated into almost all the languages of Europe. Doctor Blair died December 27, 1800.

Blair, James, M. A., a minister of the episcopal church in Scotland, was sent by the bishop of London as a missionary to Virginia, in 1685. He procured a patent for the erection of a college there, and was its first president for nearly fifty years; he was also president of the council of Virginia, and died in 1743.

Bogardus, Everardus, first minister of the reformed Dutch church in New York.

Bogoris, first Christian king of the Bulgarians; he embraced Christianity in 865.

Bois, Jean du, a Parisian ecclesiastic, became so conspicuous in the military service of Henry III., as to acquire the name of emperor of monks. On resuming his clerical character he became eminent as a preacher, but incurred the resentment of the church, he was confined at Rome, where he died in 1626.

Boleyn, Anne, wife of Henry VIII., king of England, and memorable for giving occasion to the reformation in that country, was born in 1507. Being accused (falsely, it is believed) of conjugal infidelity, she was beheaded, May 19th, 1536.

Bolsec, Jerome, a Carmelite, of Paris, forsook his order, and fled to Italy, and then to Geneva, where he lived as a physician. He there embraced the doctrines of Pelagius, and inveighed with so much bitterness and virulence against Calvin, that he was expelled from the city. He returned to France, where he died in 1584. His Lives of Calvin and Beza are a collection of falsehood and abuse.

Boniface VIII., Benedict Cajetan, a cardinal, and afterwards a pope in 1294. His ambition was unbounded. He hurled the thunder of the Vatican against the kings of Denmark and France, and declared that God had made him lord over king and kingdoms. Philip, despising his threats, had him seized by force, but escaping from his guards, he fled to Rome, where he died in 1303.

Bonner, Edmund, bishop of London, in the reign of Henry VIII., Edward VI., and queen Mary, was the son of an honest poor man, and born in Worcestershire. He was a most violent and cruel bigot, and was the occasion of several hundreds of innocent persons being put to death, for their firm adherence to the protestant faith. Upon queen Elizabeth's accession he refused to take the oath of allegiance and supremacy; for which he was deprived of his bishopric, and committed to the Marshalsea. After several years' confinement, he died in 1569.

Bore, Catharine Von, a nun, who, on the dissemination of Luther's principles, quitted the veil. Her heroic conduct attracted the notice of Luther, who afterwards married her. She was a woman of delicacy and virtue, and died in 1552.

Boudinot, Elias, LL.D., first president of the American Bible Society, died in 1821.

Bourg, Ann du, a learned counsellor of the parliament of Paris, was burnt by Henry II. for embracing the doctrines of Calvin, in 1559.

Bourignon, Antoniette, a famous female enthusiast, born in 1616, at Lisle, in Flanders. She came into the world so very deformed, that a consultation was held in the family for some days about stifling her as a monstrous birth. But her mind seems to have been raised far above the deformities of her person, for at four years of age she not only took notice that the people of Lisle did not live up to the principles of Christianity which they professed, but was so much disturbed as to desire a removal into some more Christian country. Her progress through life was suitable to this beginning. She died at Francher, in Holland, 1680. Her main principles of religion were nearly the same with those of the Quietists, excluding all external divine worship, and requiring a cessation of reason, wit, and understanding, that God might spread his divine light over them, or cause it to revive in them: without which the Deity is not sufficiently known.

Brady, Dr. Nicholas, an English divine of good parts and learning, born at Baudon, county of Cork, 1659, died in 1726. He translated the Ænead of Virgil; but he is best known by "A new version of the Psalms of David," written in conjunction with Mr. Tate.

Brandt, Gerard, a Protestant divine, and minister of Amsterdam, died at Rotterdam, in 1695. He was author of a "History of the Reformation of the Low Countries," in four volumes quarto. It is written in Flemish; and the grand pensioner Fagel said once to bishop Burnet, that it was worth learning Flemish merely to read Brandt's History.

Brandt, Col. Joseph, a famous Indian chief, was educated under the care of the Rev. Dr. Wheelock, first president of Dartmouth College. In the war of the American revolution, he attached himself to the British cause. He died in Upper Canada, in 1807. He translated into the Mohawk language the Gospel of St. Mark, and the liturgy of the English church, which was published for the benefit of the Indians.

Brainerd, David, (see page 246.)

Brown, Robert, a preacher, from whom the sect of *Brownists* derived their name. He died in 1630. His sect equally condemned episcopacy and presbytery.

Brown, John, professor of divinity in Scotland, born in 1722, and died in 1788; author of the "Self-interpreting Bible," and several other religious works.

Bucer, Martin, born in 1491, at Schelstadt, a town of Alsace. He is looked upon as one of the first authors of the reformation at Strasburgh, where he taught divinity for twenty years, and was one of the ministers of the town. In 1548, Cranmer invited him to England which invitation he accepted, and was appointed teacher of theology in the university of Cambridge. He died in 1551, and was buried in Cambridge.

Buchanan, Claudius, D. D., a Scotch divine; one of the chaplains of the East India Company, and provost of the college at Fort William. By his writings he excited a spirit of inquiry in reference to the moral condition of the heathen, and materially aided the cause of missions. He died in England in 1815.

Buell, Samuel, D. D., a presbyterian minister on Long Island, much distinguished for his piety. Died in 1798.

Bunyan, John. (See page 226.)

Burkitt, William, born at Hitcham, in Northamptonshire, 1650; died 1703. He was a pious and charitable man, who wrote several books, and among the rest a "Commentary upon the New Testament," in the same plain, practical, and affecting manner in which he preached.

Burnet, Gilbert, bishop of Salisbury, born at Edinburg in 1643. He was a very zealous promoter of the revolution which finally placed the present family on the English throne. As a writer he is distinguished by his "History of the Reformation," published between 1679 and 1681, and for which he had the thanks of both houses of parliament. In 1699 he published his "Exposition of the thirty-nine Articles of the Church of England;" and after his death, which happened in March, 1714–15, his "History of his own Times, with his Life annexed," was published by his son, Thomas Burnet, Esq., afterwards Sir Thomas.

Burnett, Dr. Thomas, a most ingenious and learned writer, born at Croft, Yorkshire, 1635. His most celebrated work, "The Sacred Theory of the Earth," was originally published in Latin, in two volumes quarto; the first two books, "concerning the Deluge and Paradise," in 1681: the last two, "concerning the burning of the World, and the New Heavens and New Earth," in 1689. This work met with uncommon approbation from various eminent authors. He died in 1715.

Butler, Joseph, bishop of Durham, a prelate of most distinguished piety, born at Wantage, Berks, 1692. His deep learning and comprehensive mind appear sufficiently in his writings, particularly in a work entitled "*The Analogy of Religion*, natural and revealed, to the constitution and course of Nature." He died in 1752.

C.

Caled, or *Khaled*, one of Mahomet's friends, called, from his courage, "*the sword of God*," died in 639.

Calef, Robert, a merchant of Boston, who published a work against witchcraft in 1700. He died in 1720.

Caligula, the Roman emperor and tyrant, began his reign A. D. 37, with every appearance of becoming the real, not the titular, father of his people; but at the end of eight months he was seized with a fever, which, it is supposed, left a frenzy upon his mind, for his disposition totally changed, and he committed the most atrocious acts of impiety, cruelty, and folly; such as proclaiming his horse consul, feeding it at his table, introducing it to the temple in the vestments of the priests of Jupiter, and causing sacrifices to be offered to himself, his wife, and his horse. After having murdered many of his subjects with his own hand, and caused others to be put to death without any offence, he was assassinated by a tribune of the people as he came out of the amphitheatre, A. D. 41, in the twenty-ninth year of his age.

Callixtus II., Guy, pope in 1119, held the first Lateran council, and died in 1124.

Calmet, Augustin, a Frenchman, born in 1672, died in 1757. He was a man of vast erudition, and a wonderfully voluminous writer. The most celebrated of his works are "A literal Commentary upon all the books of the Old and New Testament," and "A Historical, Critical, and Chronological Dictionary of the Bible."

Calvin, John, was born at Picardy, in France, July 10th, 1509. He received his early education at Paris, and being designed by his father for the church, at the age of twelve was presented to the chapel of la Gesine, in the church at Noyon.

Some time after, his father changed his resolution respecting his son, and put him to the study of law. In

1534 Calvin finally forsook the communion of the Roman church, and becoming interested in the doctrines of the reformation, espoused that cause, and began to forward it in the city of Paris.

The reformers being persecuted, Calvin deemed it expedient for his safety to retire to Basil, where, in 1535, he published his celebrated "*Institutions of the Christian Religion.*" In 1541 he settled at Geneva, where, by his preaching, his writings, and his correspondence, he wonderfully advanced the protestant cause, and was the author of that form of church government which is termed *presbyterian*. He became the head of a numerous sect of Christians, who adopted many of his religious sentiments, and from him were denominated *Calvinists.*

Calvin founded a seminary at Geneva, which obtained a legal charter, and continued to flourish under his presidency and direction until his death. In the literary pursuits of this college he was assisted by the celebrated Theodore Beza and other eminent men.

The character of Calvin stands pre-eminent among the reformers. Next to Luther he accomplished more for the reformation than any other individual. He died at Geneva in 1564.

Campbell, Dr. George, an eminent divine and theological writer of Scotland, was born in 1719, died April 6th, 1796, leaving several valuable works; the chief of which are "A Dissertation on Miracles," "Philosophy of Rhetoric," and "A new Translation of the four Gospels from the Greek, with Preliminary Dissertations and Notes," &c.

Capellus, Lewis, an eminent French protestant and learned divine, born about 1579. His principal work is "Critica Sacra," a collection of various readings and errors which he thought were crept into the copies of the Bible through the fault of the transcribers; it must have been a work of great labour, since it occupied his attention thirty-six years. He died in 1658.

Carpocrates, a heretic of Alexandria, who received and improved the Gnostic theory, about 130.

Cartwright, Thomas, a puritan of great eminence and learning, born in Hertfordshire. He was a sharp and powerful controversialist, and was much persecuted, being obliged to quit the kingdom for safety. He wrote a practical commentary on the four gospels, and on the proverbs, and died in the year 1603, in great poverty.

Casas, Bartholomi de las, a Spaniard, and bishop of Chiapa, born at Seville, 1474. At the age of nineteen he attended his father, who went with Columbus to the Indies in 1493. Upon his return he became an ecclesiastic and a curate in the isle of Cuba; but quitted his cure and his country in order to devote himself to the service of the Indians, who were then enslaved to the most ridiculous superstitions, as well as the most barbarous tyranny. The Spanish governors had long since made Christianity detested by their unheard-of cruelties, and the Indians trembled at the very name of Christian. This humane and pious missionary resolved to cross the seas, and to lay their cries and their miseries at the feet of Charles V. The affair was discussed in council, and the representations of Casas so affected the emperor, that he made ordinances as severe to the persecutors as favourable to the persecuted; but these ordinances were never executed, and the governors continued to tyrannise as usual. Casas employed above fifty years in America, labouring with incessant zeal, that the Indians might be treated with mildness, equity, and humanity; but instead of availing any thing, he drew upon himself endless persecutions from the Spaniards, and died in 1566.

Cassan, a Christian, who renounced his religion to become king of Persia, died in 1304.

Castell, Edmond, a divine of the seventeenth century, and compiler of a very learned and laborious work, called "Lexicon Heptaglotton." He was also an eminent assistant to Dr. Walton, in the celebrated edition of the "Polyglott Bible," and died in 1685.

Cave, Dr. William, a learned divine, born 1637, died

1713. He was the author of some large and learned works relating to ecclesiastical history and antiquity; particularly "The History of the Lives, Acts, Deaths, and Martyrdoms of those who were cotemporary with the Apostles, and of the principal Fathers within the first three centuries of the Church," and "Historia Literaria," &c.; in which he gives an exact account of all who had written upon Christianity, either for or against it, from Christ to the fourteenth century.

Cerinthus, a disciple of Simon Magus, about A. D. 54, a heretic who denied the divinity of Christ.

Chamier, Daniel, a French protestant professor of divinity at Montauban. He drew up the famous edict of Nantes, and was killed in 1621.

Chandler, Thomas Bradbury, D. D., an eminent episcopal minister and writer, of Elizabethtown, New Jersey, published several works in defence of episcopacy; he died in 1790.

Charles IX. ascended the throne in 1560. During his reign the fatal massacre of St. Bartholomew took place, which renders his name odious. He died in 1574.

Charlevoix, Peter Francis Xavier de, born in France in 1684; a learned Jesuit. He made a voyage to Canada by order of the French king in 1720; from thence he passed up the great lakes and descended the Mississippi to New Orleans, then to St. Domingo, and from thence he returned to France. His history of New France or Canada, wherein the manners and customs of the Indians are described, is considered valuable.

Charnock, Stephen, an eminent divine among the presbyterians and independents, who published his works in two volumes folio, and died in 1680.

Chaucer, Geoffrey, one of the greatest and most ancient of English poets; was born in London in 1328. In 1382, having given offence to the clergy by adopting many of Wickliffe's tenets, he was obliged to quit the kingdom; he died Oct. 25, 1400.

Charlemagne, king of France, was consecrated emperor of the west by pope Leo III.; his conquests spread Christianity in the north of Europe; he died in 814, in the seventy-fourth year of his age.

Chillingworth, William, a divine of the church of England, celebrated for his skill in defending the cause of protestants against papists; born at Oxford, 1602, died 1644. His most important work is, "A free Inquiry into Religion."

Christina, queen of Sweden, and daughter of Gustavus Adolphus the Great, born Dec. 8, 1626. She succeeded him in the government of the kingdom in 1633, and ruled it with great wisdom and prudence till 1654, when she resigned it in favour of her cousin, Charles Gustavus. She then changed her religion for that of the Romish church, and retired to Rome; yet upon the death of Charles Gustavus, which happened in 1660, she returned to Sweden, with an intent to resume the government. But this could not be admitted, because, by the laws and constitution of the land, Roman catholics are excluded from the crown. She died at Rome in 1689.

Chubb, Thomas, born at East Harnham, near Salisbury, Wilts, 1679. He was bred a glover, but became tolerably versed in mathematics, geography, and many other branches of science. But divinity, above all, was his favourite study; and it is said that a little society was formed at Salisbury, under the management and direction of Chubb, for the purpose of debating upon religious subjects. It appears "that he had little or no belief in revelation; indeed, he plainly rejects the Jewish revelation, and consequently the Christian, which is founded upon it; that he disclaims a future judgment, and is very uncertain as to any future state of existence; that a particular Providence is not deducible from the phenomena of the world, and, therefore, that prayer cannot be proved a duty," &c. &c. He died at Salisbury in the sixty-eighth year of his age.

Clarke, Dr. Samuel, a very celebrated English philosopher and divine, born at Norwich in 1675; died May 17, 1729. His works are very numerous.

Claude, John, a French protestant, distinguished as an orator and writer in defence of the protestant church; died in 1687. His son, Isaac Claude, published his works, settled at the Hague, and died in 1695.

Clayton, Dr. Robert, a learned prelate and writer, bishop of Cork, in 1735; of Clogher, in 1745; died in 1758.

Clemens, Romanus, a father of the church, companion of Paul, bishop of Rome, and author of an epistle to the Corinthians; died A. D. 100.

Clement VII., Julius de Medicis, an Italian, elected pope in 1523; he was besieged by Charles V., who plundered Rome; he excommunicated Henry VIII., which led to the reformation in England, and died in 1534.

Clement XIV., John Vincent Anthony Ganganelli, an Italian, raised to the popedom on the death of Clement XIII. He suppressed the Jesuits, and died, supposed by some to have been poisoned, in 1774.

Clovis I., founder of the French monarchy, was converted to Christianity, and died in 511.

Cocceius or *Cock*, John, a native of Bremen, and Hebrew professor there; afterwards removed to Leyden; he maintained that the Bible is mystical of Christ and the church: he died in 1669.

Coke, Thomas, LL.D., a leading minister of the Wesleyan Methodists, a very zealous and able divine, and a most excellent man, was born at Brecon, in Wales, educated at Jesus College, Oxford, and entered into orders in the established church. For the last twenty-eight years he discharged with unremitting diligence the extensive duties of general superintendent of the Methodist missions; which so warmly engaged his active and incessant energies, that he many times crossed the Atlantic; visiting the West India islands, and travelling through the United States. He gave to the world, among many other works, "A Commentary on the Bible," in six large vols. 4to. Dr. Coke died May 3d, 1814, on his voyage to India with six missionaries intended for Ceylon and Java.

Colet, Dr. John, a learned English divine, born in London in 1446, died in 1519. He founded and endowed St. Paul's school in London in 1512. He endowed it with lands and houses amounting then to 122*l.* 4*s.* 7*d.* per annum.

Coligni, Gaspard de, a celebrated admiral of France, who bravely supported the cause of the French protestants against the duke of Guise and his adherents; but after several victories gained over their persecutors, was at last basely assassinated by one of the domestics of the duke of Guise, in the beginning of the horrid massacre of St. Bartholomew's day, 1572.

Collins, Anthony, an eminent writer on polemical subjects, and the friend and correspondent of the great Mr. Locke, was born at Heston, near Hounslow, in Middlesex, in 1676, and died 1729. He published his celebrated "Discourse of Free-thinking" in 8vo. 1713, and his "Discourse of the grounds and reasons of the Christian religion" in 1724; and wrote, besides these, a great many books, which were warmly attacked by the orthodox writers of that time.

Colluthus, a priest of Alexandria, who maintained that God was not the author of the wicked; he was condemned as a heretic in 324.

Constantine, usually called the Great, and memorable for having been the first emperor of the Romans who established Christianity by the civil power, was born at Naissus, a town of Dardania, in 272, and died 337.

Conybeare, Dr. John, bishop of Bristol, born at Pinhoe, near Exeter, in 1692, died at Bath in 1755. His "Defence of revealed Religion," published in 1732, in answer to Tindal's "Christianity as old as the Creation," is an admirable work, and rendered eminent service to the church.

Cotton, John, one of the most distinguished early ministers of New England, born in England; he sustained a high reputation for wisdom and learning; his publications were numerous.

Cotton, John, son of the Rev. John Cotton, minister, of Plymouth, Mass., and of Charleston, South Carolina.

He was a faithful minister, and eminent for his knowledge of the Indian language. He revised and superintended the printing of Eliot's Bible. He died in 1699.

Coverdale, Miles, bishop of Exeter, in the time of Edward VI., was ejected from his see by queen Mary, and thrown into prison. Being liberated by queen Elizabeth, he attached himself to the puritans, and died in 1567, at the age of eighty-one. He assisted Tindal in the English version of the Bible, published in 1537, and afterwards revised and corrected the edition of it in a larger volume, with notes, in 1540.

Cowper, William, an excellent English poet, equally distinguished by his genius and his virtues. He was born at Berkhampstead, Herts, Nov. 1731. His poems are various; but the most celebrated of them is called "The Task;" and the tendency of all his writings is to enlarge the soul to every liberal sentiment and to improve the heart. Cowper died April 25th, 1800.

Craddock, Samuel, a learned divine, author of "A History of the Old and New Testament," an "Apostolical History," and "The Harmony of the Four Evangelists," died in 1706, aged eighty-six. The latter of these works was revised by Dr. Tillotson, who preserved it from the flames in the fire of London.

Cradock, Thomas, rector of St. Thomas, Baltimore county, Maryland, published Psalms of David in heroic verse in 1756.

Courtney, William, archbishop of Canterbury, a persecutor of Wickliffe and his followers, died in 1396.

Cox, Richard, bishop of Ely, born at Whaddon, in Buckinghamshire, in 1499, died 1581. He was the chief framer of the Liturgy, and translator of the Bible called "The Bishops' Bible," made in the reign of Elizabeth.

Cranmer, Thomas, an English archbishop, memorable for having endured martyrdom in the cause of protestantism, was born at Aslacton, in Nottinghamshire, in 1489, and burnt at Oxford, March 21st, 1555, by order of queen Mary. He was an open, generous, and honest man; a lover of truth, and an enemy of falsehood and superstition; he was gentle and moderate in his temper, and though heartily zealous in the cause of the Reformation, yet a friend to those persons who most strenuously opposed it; he was a great patron of learning and the universities, a very learned man himself, and author of several works.

Crisp, Tobias, a controversial writer on divinity, and the great champion of Antinomianism, died in 1642.

Cruden, Alexander, a corrector of the press, whose literary labours will ever entitle him to the veneration of all students of the sacred writings. His "Concordance of the Holy Scriptures of the Old and New Testament" is his chief work, and a singular instance of indefatigable labour and perseverance in the most useful employment. His private character (though naturally liberal in the extreme) was influenced by a temporary frenzy, which gave a certain colour to all his actions, and suggested to him many whimsical plans of reformation, hopes of superiority, and visionary views of ambition, which were as useless to himself as unprofitable to others. Of his singularities, however, which were many, the tendency was uniformly virtuous. He was born at Aberdeen in 1701, and was found dead on his knees, apparently in the posture of prayer, at his lodgings in Islington, on the morning of Nov. 1st, 1770.

Cudworth, Ralph, an eminent English divine, was born at Aller, in Somersetshire, 1617, and died 1688. He was a man of very extensive learning, excellently skilled in the learned languages and antiquity, a good mathematician, a subtle philosopher, and a profound metaphysician. His great work, "The True Intellectual System of the Universe," was published in folio, 1678.

Cuerenhert, Theodore Van, a native of Amsterdam, distinguished for science; but especially for maintaining that a Christian should not enter a place of worship: he died in 1590.

Cumberland, Dr. Richard, a very learned English divine, and bishop of Peterborough, born in London in 1632, died in 1718. He had studied mathematics in all its branches, and the Scriptures in their original languages. His book "De Legibus Naturæ" is his capital work, and will always be read while sound reasoning shall continue to be thought the best support of religion.

Cyprian, Thascius Cæcilius, bishop of Carthage, a principal father of the Christian church, born at Carthage, in Africa, about the beginning of the third century, and beheaded there. (See page 58.)

Cyril, of Jerusalem; one of the fathers, died in 386.

Cyril, made bishop of Alexandria in 412, died 444. His works are voluminous, and have been often printed.

Cyrill, Lurcar, bishop of Alexandria and patriarch of Constantinople, strangled for attempting to reform the clergy, in 1638.

D

Dalmatin, George, a Lutheran minister of Layback, who translated the Bible into the Sclavonian language, in the 16th century.

Dalmatius, a bishop of Cyzicum, who attended the council of Ephesus, and wrote the acts of the synod of Nice.

Damascenus, John, an illustrious father of the church, in the eighth century. He died about 750, leaving many compositions of various kinds behind him.

Davenport, John, born in Coventry, Eng., in 1597. Being a nonconformist, he was persecuted, and was obliged to retire to Holland, from whence he came to America. He was the first minister of New Haven, Connecticut, and one of the founders of the colony of that name, where he endeavoured to establish a civil and religious liberty more strictly in conformity to the word of God than he had seen exhibited in any part of the world. After remaining in New Haven about thirty years, he was invited to become the pastor of the first church in Boston; he accepted the call, and died in that place in 1670.

David, St., the patron of Wales, was a native of Bangor, where he was educated in the fifth century. He was buried at St. David's cathedral.

David, de Dinant, taught in the thirteenth century that God was originally matter.

David, George, a most extraordinary heretic, son of a waterman at Ghent, and bred a glazier, or, as some say, a glass painter. He began about 1525 to preach such whimsies as these; namely, that he was the true Messiah, the third David, nephew of God, not after the flesh, but after the spirit. A persecution being commenced against him and his followers, he fled, first to Friesland, and from thence to Basil, where he lurked under the name of John Bruck, and died in that city in 1556.

David el David, a Persian Jew in the twelfth century, who pretended to be the Messiah.

Davidis, Francis, a Hungarian, who changed his religion four times, and finally declared that no worship was due to Christ; he died in prison in 1579.

Daille, John, a minister of the church of Paris, and one of the ablest advocates the protestants ever had, was born at Chatelherault in 1594. In 1628 he wrote his celebrated work "Of the Use of the Fathers," which Bayle has pronounced a masterpiece.

Davies, Samuel, president of Princeton College, New Jersey; eminent as a preacher; published several sermons still much admired; he died in 1761.

Delaune, Thomas, wrote in 1683, "Plea for Nonconformity," which gave so much offence that he was cast into prison, where he died.

Diaz, John, a Spaniard who embraced the doctrines of Luther, for which his brother, Alphonsus, a violent Catholic, hired an assassin to dash out his brains, in 1546.

Dickinson, Jonathan, first president of New Jersey College; he published several sermons besides some miscellaneous works, and died in 1747.

Dioclesian, Caius Valerius, a Roman emperor, whose bloody persecution of the Christians forms a chronological era, called the Era of Dioclesian, or the Martyrs. It commenced August 29th, A. D. 284. Dioclesian was born 233, and died 313.

Diodati, John, a famous minister and professor of theology at Geneva, born at Lucca in 1579, died at Geneva in 1652. He is distinguished by translations of "The Bible into Italian," "The Bible into French;" and of "Father Paul's history of the Council of Trent into French."

Dionysius, bishop of Rome, condemned the heresy of the Sabellians in a full synod; died in 269.

Dodd, Dr. William, an ingenious divine of unfortunate memory, was born in 1729, at Bourne, in Lincolnshire, Eng. In 1753 he received orders; and being settled in London, soon became a popular and celebrated preacher. He obtained several lectureships, and advanced his theological character greatly by an almost uninterrupted publication of sermons and tracts of piety. In 1766 he took the degree of LL.D. at Cambridge, having been made a chaplain to the king some time before. Becoming deeply involved in debt by his extravagant manner of living, in an evil hour he signed a bond which he had forged as from his pupil, Lord Chesterfield, for the sum of 4200*l*., and upon the credit of it obtained a considerable sum of money; but detection instantly following, he was committed to prison, tried, and convicted at the Old Baily, Feb. 24th; and executed at Tyburn, June 27th, 1777.

Doddridge, Dr. Philip, an eminent dissenting minister, born in London, in 1702, died 1751. He was twenty-one years pastor of a church at Northampton; director of a flourishing academy; and author of many excellent writings; in which his pious, benevolent, and indefatigable zeal to make men wise, good, and happy, is every where manifest. He left many works behind him; the principal of which are "The Rise and Progress of Religion in the Soul, illustrated in a course of serious and practical addresses suited to persons of every character and circumstance;" and "The Family Expositor, containing a version and paraphrase of the New

Testament, with critical notes, and a practical improvement of each section," in six vols. quarto.

Dominus, Mark Anthony de, archbishop of Spalato, in Dalmatia, in the sixteenth century. He wrote against the papal power, turned protestant, then again turned Catholic. He was suspected, seized, and imprisoned. After his death, his body was dug up and burned as a heretic, in 1645.

Donatus, a bishop of a religious sect in Africa, who began to be known about the year 329, and greatly confirmed his faction by his character and writings. He was a man of great parts and learning, but withal so prodigiously haughty, that he treated all mankind with contempt. The Donatists affirmed baptism in other churches to be null and of no effect: while other churches allowed it to be valid in theirs; from which they inferred, that it was the safer to join that community where baptism was acknowledged by both parties to be valid, than that where it was allowed to be so only by one.

Doring, or *Dorink*, Matthias, a German Franciscan, who, in his writings, inveighs against the vices of the popes and cardinals. He was the forerunner of Luther, and died in 1494.

Drownham, John, an English divine, author of a well-known pious work, called "The Christian Warfare;" died in 1644.

Drelincourt, Charles, minister of the church of Paris, born at Sedan 1595, and died 1669. His "Consolations against the Fears of Death" have, of all his works, been the most frequently reprinted; having passed through above forty editions, and been translated into several languages. His "Charitable Visits," in five volumes, have served for a continual consolation to private persons, and for a source of materials and models to ministers. He published three volumes of sermons; in which, as in all the forementioned pieces, there is a wonderful vein of piety, which is very affecting to religious minds.

Drexelius, Jeremiah, a Jesuit of Augsburgh, author

of a curious poem on hell torments, in which he calculates how many souls can be contained in a given space; he died in 1638.

Duppa, Brian, bishop of Winchester, born at Lewisham, in Kent, 1588–9. This bishop is deservedly remembered for his numerous charitable institutions; among which is to be remembered an alms-house at Richmond, on the gate of which is this inscription; "I will pay my vows which I made to God in my trouble," &c. He died in 1662.

Dwight, Timothy, D.D. LL.D., was born at Northampton, Mass., 1752. "As a poet, philosopher, and divine, he had few equals; as president and professor of divinity in Yale College he stood unrivalled, both for his talents as an instructer, and for eloquence as a divine." His system of theology has been frequently republished in Europe; he died in 1817.

Dyer, William, a nonconformist of England, who turned quaker. He wrote much after the manner of Bunyan, and died in 1696.

E.

Ebion, a Stoic philosopher, father of the sect of the Ebionites, who denied the miraculous conception and divinity of Christ, flourished about A.D. 72.

Eckius, John, a learned German divine and controversial writer, born in 1483, died in 1543. He is chiefly memorable for his disputations with Luther and Melancthon.

Edwards, Jonathan, a celebrated American divine, and a most acute metaphysician, was born at East Windsor, Connecticut, Oct. 5. 1703. His uncommon genius discovered itself early, and while yet a boy he read Locke on the human understanding with a keen relish. Though he took much pleasure in examining the kingdom of nature, yet moral and theological researches yielded him the highest satisfaction. He was not only distinguished for his vigour and penetration of mind, but also for his Christian virtues. In 1727, he entered the pastoral office in Northampton, Mass. where he he preached the gospel about twenty-four years. In 1751 he succeeded the Rev. Mr. Sergeant as missionary to the Indians at Stockbridge, Mass. He continued here six years, preaching to the Indians and white people. During this time he found leisure for prosecuting his theological and metaphysical studies, and produced works which have distinguished his name. In January, 1758, he accepted the office of president of the college of New Jersey. Before he had fully entered upon the duties of his station, he was inoculated with the small pox, which was the cause of his death, March 22d, 1758. His most celebrated works are "*On Original Sin*," "*Freedom of the Will*," "*Treatise on Religious Affections*," &c. His essay on the freedom of the will is considered by many as one of the greatest efforts of the human mind.

Edwards, Jonathan, D.D., president of Union College, New York, was the son of the preceding, and was likewise distinguished as a scholar and able theologian; he died in 1801.

Egede, Paul, bishop of Greenland, was born in the year 1708, and at twelve years of age was an active assistant to his father, the celebrated Hans (or John) Egede (to whom Denmark is indebted for its colony in Greenland), having accompanied him on his voyage thither in 1720. His zeal for the conversion of the Greenlanders to Christianity, exerted with unabated ardour through the course of a long life, both during his residence in their country, and after his quitting it, is strongly displayed in his "Account of Greenland," published shortly before his death, which happened June 3d, 1789.

Eliot, John, (see page 232.)

Elliot, Caleb, a visionary enthusiast, who starved himself, near Modbury, in Devonshire, Dec. 14th, 1789. It is imagined that he meant to have fasted forty days, as he actually lived sixteen without food of any kind, having refused all sorts of sustenance.

Engelbrecht, John, a German Lutheran, of Brunswick, who maintained doctrines similar to those which Swedenborg has since promulgated; he died in 1641.

Ephrem, St., an eminent Christian writer of the fourth century. Photius tells us that he wrote above one thousand orations, and that himself had seen forty-nine of his sermons; and Sozomen observes that he composed three hundred thousand verses. His works were so highly esteemed that they were publicly read in the churches after the Scriptures. St. Ephrem was a man of the strictest severity of morals; and so strict an observer of chastity, that he avoided even the sight of a woman. He died in 378.

Erasmus, Desiderius, born at Rotterdam in 1467, died at Basil 1536. He was a most learned man, and spent his life in promoting literature and true piety. He was cotemporary with Luther, and assisted the Reformers by his writings.

Eunomius, heresiarch of the fourth century, bishop of Cyzicum, and founder of the sect that have since been called Eunomians. He died very old, about 394, after having experienced a great variety of sufferings. Eunomius wrote many things, and his writings were so highly esteemed by his followers, that they thought their authority preferable to that of the gospel. His doctrines were, that "there is one God, uncreate, and without beginning; who has nothing existing before him, for nothing can exist before what is uncreate; nor with him, for what is uncreate, must be one; nor in him, for God is a simple and uncompounded being. This one simple and eternal being is God, the creator and ordainer of all things: first, indeed, and principally of his only begotten Son, and then, through him, of all other things; for God begot, created, and made the Son only, by his own direct operation and power, before all things and every other creature; not producing, however, any other being like himself, nor imparting any of his own proper substance to the Son; for God is immortal, uniform, indivisible, and therefore cannot communicate any part of his own proper substance to another," &c.

Euphrates, a heretic, of the second century, who maintained that our first parents were deceived by Christ in the form of a serpent.

Eutychius, a Christian author, patriarch of Alexandria, was born at Cairo, in Egypt, in 876, and became eminent in the knowledge of physic. He wrote annals from the beginning of the world to the year 900; in which may be found many things which occur nowhere else; but certainly many more which were collected from lying legends, and are entirely fabulous. He died in 950.

Eutyches, an abbot of Constantinople, who maintained that Christ's body was an aerial form, and therefore not human.

Euzorius, a deacon of Alexandria, deposed and condemned by the council of Nice for adhering to Arius; he baptized Constantius, and died in 376.

F.

Farel, William, an able reformer, born 1489. Being driven from Paris, as a protestant, he went to Strasburgh, Geneva, Basil, and Neufchatel, where he preached the doctrines of the reformation with zeal, ability, and success, although opposed with ridicule and abuse. He was the associate of Calvin, and died in 1565.

Feijoo, Benedict Jerome, a Spanish benedictine, who attempted by his writings to expose the ignorance of the clergy and the inutility of pilgrimages, &c. He died in 1765.

Felix, Minutius, a father of the primitive church, who flourished in the third century, about the year 220. He wrote a very elegant dialogue in defence of the Christian religion, entitled "Octavius."

Fenelon, Francis de Salignac de la Motte, archbishop of Cambray, born at the castle of Fenelon, in the province of Perigord, 1651, died 1715. He wrote many works; but what has gained him the greatest reputation is his "Telemachus." He published another considerable work, entitled, "A demonstration of the Being of God, grounded on the knowledge of nature and suited to the meanest capacity;" which is one of the best books that is written in French upon that subject.

Ferrar, Robert, bishop of St. Davids, was burnt as a heretic in the reign of Mary, in 1555.

Finley, Samuel, D. D., a native of Ireland, and president of New Jersey College; he was much distinguished for his piety; published many sermons, and died in 1766.

Fisher, John, bishop of Rochester, and martyr to popery, born in 1459, was beheaded for denying the king's supremacy, in 1535. His death was hastened by an unseasonable honour paid him by pope Paul III., who in May, 1535, created him cardinal priest. When the king heard of it, he said, in a great passion, "Well, let the pope send him a hat when he will; Mother of God, he shall wear it on his shoulders then, for I will not leave him a head to set it on." Fisher was said to be a man of integrity, deep learning, sweetness of temper, and greatness of soul.

Fisher, Mary, an enthusiastic quakeress of the seventeenth century, who went to Constantinople to convert the grand-seignior. Mahomet, after hearing her patiently, sent her back to her own country in safety.

Flavel, John, an English divine, educated at Oxford, was ejected from his living at Dartmouth, and afterwards restored by Charles I.; he died in 1692.

Fleetwood, William, bishop of Ely, born in the tower of London in 1656; died in 1723. His most celebrated work is "An Essay upon Miracles." Bishop Fleetwood's character was great in every respect. As for his accomplishments, he was incontestably the best preacher of his time; and for occasional sermons may be considered as a model.

Flemming, Richard, prebendary of York and bishop of Lincoln, was the founder of Lincoln College, Oxford; he died in 1431.

Fletcher, John de la, vicar of Madeley, a learned and pious divine, in connexion with Mr. Wesley, the founder of Methodism, celebrated for his work entitled "*Checks to Antinomianism.*" He died in 1785

Fordyce, Dr. James, many years a very popular and eloquent preacher among the protestant dissenters; born at Aberdeen in 1720, died in 1796, leaving behind him some excellent moral and religious publications; particularly, "Sermons to Young Men and Women."

Formosus, bishop of Porto, and pope after Stephen V., in 891. His unpopularity was such, that his body was dragged from its grave by the populace and thrown into the Tyber.

Foster, Dr. James, an English dissenting minister, born in 1697. He published a "Defence of the Usefulness, Truth, and Excellency of the Christian Revelation," against Tindal's "Christianity as old as the Creation." This defence is written with great force of argument, and, as he said, was spoken of with great regard by Tindal himself. He died in 1753.

Fothergill, Samuel, was eminent as a preacher among the Quakers. He travelled over Great Britain and North America to propagate his doctrines, and died in 1773.

Fox, Edward, an eminent statesman, almoner to Henry VIII., and bishop of Hereford. He was the principal pillar of the reformation as to the politic and prudential part of it; being of more activity, and no less ability, than Cranmer himself; but he acted more secretly than Cranmer, and by that means did not bring himself into danger of suffering on that account. He was born in Gloucestershire, and died in 1538.

Fox, John, an English divine, born at Boston, in Lincolnshire, in 1517, the very year that Luther began to oppose the errors of the church of Rome; he died in 1587. He is distinguished for his "History of Christian Martyrdom," a work which cost him above eleven years' close application and study.

Fox, George, the founder of the English Quakers, was born in 1624, and died in 1690. Being, as he believed, divinely illuminated, he commenced preaching. His wife Margaret, being under the same persuasion, shared in his ministerial functions. (See page 224.)

Francis, of Paulo, a Romish saint canonized by pope Leo X., was the founder of the Minins, and celebrated for his austerities; he died in 1507.

Francis, of Assissi, a great saint of the Romish church, and founder of one of four orders of mendicant friars, born in 1182. He was the son of a merchant, whose profession he followed till 1206; at which time he became so strongly affected with religious truth that he resolved to retire from the world. He prevailed with great numbers to devote themselves, as he had done, to the poverty enjoined by the gospel; and drew up an institute, or rule for their use, which was approved by the Roman Pontiffs. Francis was canonized by pope Gregory IX. the 6th of May, 1230; and October the 4th, on which his death happened, in 1226, was appointed as his festival. His order soon rose to great splendour, and has done prodigious service to the Roman pontiffs.

Francis de Sales, a Romish saint, was bishop of Geneva and founder of the order of the visitation. It is stated by the catholics that he converted seventy thousand protestants before his death, which happened in 1662. He was canonized by pope Alexander VI.

Frederick 1st, king of Denmark, distinguished himself by his wisdom, prudence, and by the utility of his public measures, particularly in introducing Lutheranism among his subjects. He died in 1533.

Frederic, surnamed the Wise, elector of Saxony, was the friend of the emperor Maximilian, and might have succeeded him had he not declined. He was the firm and zealous friend of Luther and the reformation, and died in 1526.

Frecke, William, born in 1664. He wrote, among other things, "A Dialogue by way of question and answer, concerning the Deity," and "A brief and clear confutation of the doctrine of the Trinity;" which two pieces, being laid before the House of Commons, were voted to be burnt, as containing much blasphemy, and accordingly were so: the author being afterwards fined £500, and obliged to give security for his good behaviour for three years, and to make a recantation in the four courts in Westminster-hall.

Fust, or *Faustus*, John, a citizen of Mentz, and one of the earliest printers. He had the policy to conceal his art; and to this policy we are indebted for the tradition of "*The Devil and Dr. Faustus*," handed down to the present time. At about 1460 he associated with John of Guttenburg; their types were cut in wood, and fixed, not moveable as at present. Having printed off a considerable number of copies of the Bible, to imitate those which were commonly sold in manuscript, Fust undertook the sale of them in Paris, where the art of printing was then unknown. As he sold his printed copies for sixty crowns, while the scribes demanded five hundred, this created universal astonishment; but when he produced copies as fast as they were wanted, and lowered the price to thirty crowns, all Paris was agitated. The uniformity of the copies increased the wonder; informations were given in to the police against him as a magician; his lodgings were searched, and a great number of copies being found, they were seized: the red ink with which they were embellished was said to be his blood; it was seriously adjudged that he was in league with the devil; and if he had not fled, most probably would have shared the fate of those whom ignorant and superstitious judges condemned in those days for witchcraft. Fust died at Mentz in 1466.

G.

Gale, John, a learned divine among the Baptists, born at London in 1680. He is chiefly known for his writings against "Wall's defence of Infant Baptism," and died in 1721.

Ganganelli, John Vincent Antony, was born in 1705, the son of a physician; and from being a petty monk of the order of St. Francis, ascended to the papacy May 19th, 1769, when he assumed the name of Clement XIV. Thus becoming sovereign pontiff in the most critical and tempestuous times. In his commerce with the world, he practised the humility of a Franciscan monk; but on occasions of splendour he sustained the papal grandeur with appropriate magnificence. The most striking incident of his life was his being the instrument, under Providence, of annihilating the mighty order of the Jesuits. To the resentment of that order it is supposed he at last fell a sacrifice, his robust constitution and regularity of life seeming to promise him a much longer period than sixty-nine years; for he died in 1774, poisoned, as is supposed, in the sacrament; he himself declaring his suspicions before he died, and all the after-symptoms strongly confirming the same.

Gano, John, minister in New York, collected the first Baptist society in that city, and was ordained its minister in 1762. He distinguished himself in the American war in the capacity of a chaplain to the army. He left his society in New York in 1788, and removed to Kentucky, where he died in 1804.

Garasse, Francis, a Jesuitical writer, and author of the enmity between the Jesuits and Jansenists in the church of Rome, was born at Angouleme, in 1585, and died in 1631.

Gardiner, Stephen, bishop of Winchester and chancellor of England, was born at Bury St. Edmonds, in Suffolk, 1483. His character as a minister is to be drawn from the general histories; he had a large portion of haughtiness, boundless ambition, and deep dissimulation; for he looked on religion as an engine of state, and made use of it as such. He died in 1555.

Gastaud, Francis, an ecclesiastic of Aix; he insulted the bishop of Marseilles in his writings, and was denied the honours of sepulture; he died in 1732.

George, the Cappadocian, Arian bishop of Alexandria, was assassinated, in consequence of his oppression, in 361.

Gerard, Balthazar, the assassin of William I., prince of Orange, whom he shot through the head with a pistol as he was going out of his palace at Delft. His sentence was the same as that of Damien; and this fanatic died, in his own conceit, a martyr to the church of Rome, 1584.

Germanus, bishop of Cyzicum, made patriarch of Constantinople, and was degraded for supporting image worship; he died in 740.

Giafar, or *Sadek*, the Just, a Mussulman doctor who wrote a book on prophecies, &c., died at Medina in 764.

Giahedk, or *Large Eyed*, the head of the Montazalis, a sect who united religion and philosophy.

Gibieuf, William, a priest, who wrote a book on the liberty of God and the Creator, a work of great merit; he died in 1650.

Giles, John, or Ægidius, the first Englishman on record entered among the Dominicians; he lived in the thirteenth century.

Gill, Dr. John, an eminent English Calvinistic divine, a learned orientalist and voluminous writer on theological subjects, born 1697, and died in London 1771. His greatest work is a "Commentary on the Bible." He was a Baptist in sentiment.

Gilpin, Bernard, an eminent English divine and reformer, born in 1517, died 1583.

Giraldus, Cambrensis, an ancient British historian, who died about the latter end of the twelfth century, having written a "History of the World," in which his information respecting ecclesiastical affairs is very valuable.

Glain, N. Saint, a zealous protestant, born at Limoges about 1620, remarkable for having been, by reading of Spinoza's book, changed into as zealous an atheist.

Glass, John, a Scotch divine, who, in 1727, published a treatise to prove that the civil establishment of religion was inconsistent with Christianity; for this he was deposed, and became the father of a new sect, called in Scotland, Glassites, and in England, Sandemanians. He was born at Dundee in 1698, and died in 1773.

Glynn, Robert, a native of Cambridge, author of the Day of Judgment, a poem of great merit; he obtained the prize at Cambridge, and died in 1800

Godfrey of Bouillon, a most celebrated crusader and victorious general; he took Jerusalem from the Turks in 1099, and was proclaimed king; but his piety, as historians relate, would not permit him to wear a diadem of gold in the city where his Saviour had been crowned with thorns: he died in 1100.

Goodwin, Thomas, a puritanical divine, one of the members of the assembly of divines at Westminster, and author of theological works; he died in 1679.

Goodwin, John, a most acute and subtle controversialist of the seventeenth century. He wrote a vindication of the death of Charles I., which at the restoration was burnt by the common hangman. He was excepted out of the act of the common indemnity, and died soon after. His works are numerous, but mostly in support of Arminian doctrines.

Gratian, a monk of Tuscany, in the twelfth century; he was employed twenty-four years in reconciling the contradictory canons one to another.

Gregory IX., Ugolin, elected pope in 1227. He excited the Christian princes to undertake a crusade, and died in 1241.

Gregory X., Theobald, summoned a general council at Lyons, and endeavoured to heal all schisms in religion; he died in 1276.

Gregory, Dr. John, an eminent physician and moral writer. Those writings by which he is best known are, "A comparative View of the state of Man and other Animals," and "A Father's Legacy to his Daughters:" he died in 1773.

Gregory, Nazianzen, patriarch of Constantinople, born in 324, died in 389. He was one of the ablest champions of the orthodox faith concerning the Trinity, whence he had the title given him of "*The Divine*," by unanimous consent.

Gregory, Theodorus, bishop of Neo Cesarea, surnamed Thaumaturgus, a disciple of Origen, and famous for his conversion of the Gentiles; he died about 265.

Gua de Malves, John Paul de, a French ecclesiastic,

who first conceived the idea of an encyclopedia, which was executed by d'Alembert: he died in 1786.

Guillelma, of Bohemia, the foundress of an infamous sect which started up in Italy in the thirteenth century, and which, under the mask of devotion, used to practise all manner of lewdness. Guillelma imposed so effectually upon the world by a show of extraordinary devotion all her lifetime, that she was not only reputed holy at her death, but also revered as a saint a considerable time after it. However, her frauds, and the delusions she had employed, were at last discovered; upon which her body was dug up and burnt in 1300 She died in 1281, and had been buried in Milan.

Guise, Henry, duke of, memorable in the history of France as a gallant officer; but an imperious, turbulent, and seditious subject, who placed himself at the head of an armed force, and called his rebel band the League: the plan was formed by the cardinal, his younger brother; and, under the pretext of defending the Roman catholic religion, the king Henry III., and the freedom of the state, against the designs of the French protestants, they carried on a civil war, massacred the Huguenots, and governed the king. He was privately assassinated Dec. 23d, 1558, in the thirty-eighth year of his age, by the order of the king. His brother, the cardinal, shared the same fate the next day.

Gustavus Adolphus was the greatest king Sweden ever had. He protected the Lutherans in Germany, and by his victories greatly humbled the catholic powers. He was slain in battle, A. D. 1663, in the thirty-seventh year of his age.

H.

Hakem, the third of the Fatimite caliphs, was a violent persecutor of the Christians and Jews, and pretended to be the visible image of God. He was assassinated by the intrigues of his sister, in 1021.

Hacket, William, an English fanatic, in the reign of

Elizabeth. He was hung and quartered for blasphemy, in 1592.

Hakewell, George, a learned divine, born at Exeter in 1579, died in 1649. His principal work is "An Apology or Declaration of the Power and Providence of God in the government of the World," proving that it doth not decay, &c.

Hali-Beigh, a Polander, whose original name was Bobowski. Being taken by the Tartars while a child, he was sold to the Turks, who educated him in their religion. He acquired the knowledge of seventeen languages, and became interpreter to the grand seignior: translated into the Turkish language the catechism of the church of England, and all the Bible: composed a Turkish Grammar and Dictionary, and other things which were never printed. His principal work is "A Treatise upon the Liturgy of the Turks, their Pilgrimages to Mecca, their Circumcision and manner of visiting the sick." He died in 1675.

Hammond, Dr. Henry, a learned English divine and commentator, born at Chertsy in 1605, died in 1660. His chief works are a "Practical Catechism;" a "Paraphrase and Annotations on the New Testament;" and a "Paraphrase and Commentary on the Old Testament;" of which he only published the Psalms, and went through a third part of the book of Proverbs.

Hanifah, a saint among the Mussulmans, the head of all their sects; he died at Babylon.

Harmer, Thomas, an eminent dissenting divine and critical writer on Biblical literature, born at Norwich in 1715, was fifty-four years pastor of a congregation at Wattesfield, in Suffolk, and died in 1788.

Hawley, Gideon, many years a missionary to the Stockbridge, Mohawk, and Oneida Indians, and eminently useful to them: he died in 1807.

Heckewelder, John, a native of England, was for many years a Moravian missionary among the Delaware Indians, and author of an account of the manners and customs of the Indian tribes which once inhabited Pennsylvania; he died in 1823.

Heber, Reginald, lord bishop of Calcutta. He died suddenly at Trichinopoly, a town in Hindoostan, April 3d, 1826, aged forty-three, in the third year of his episcopate, universally lamented. He was the author of a number of beautiful poetic compositions.

Helena, St., the mother of Constantine the Great, was distinguished for her piety and Christian charity, and as the founder of several churches. She died in 328.

Heloise, the concubine, and afterwards wife of Peter Abelard; a nun, and afterwards prioress of Argentuil; and lastly, abbess of the Paraclete; she was born about the beginning of the twelfth century, and died 1163.

Henry IV., king of France, was born at Pau, in 1553. His right to the throne was disputed, because he was a protestant; but after the massacre of St. Bartholomew, he signalized himself against the leaguers; and Henry III. dying, he succeeded him in opposition to Cardinal de Bourbon. In 1589, with four thousand men he defeated thirty thousand, commanded by the duke of Mayenne, &c. He embraced the Catholic religion afterwards, and was crowned. He also defeated eighteen thousand Spaniards, in Burgundy, and reduced the leaguers to their duty, whom he pardoned. A young scholar, John Chastel, would have struck him in the mouth with a knife, but missed him; the king said, "And is it so that the Jesuits must be condemned by my mouth?" and thereupon they were banished. A protestant minister told him, "He denied God with his mouth, and therefore he was struck there; but if he denied him in his heart, the next stroke might be thereabouts, too." He concluded a peace with Spain, and an agreement with Savoy, in 1601; and was stabbed with a knife by Ravillac, in his coach at Paris, May 14th, 1610.

Henry I., king of England, and duke of Normandy, was the third son of William the Conquerer, and ascended the throne in 1100. Although absolute in power, he reigned with wisdom, opposed the encroachments of the church of Rome, abolished the curfew, regulated the weights and measures of his kingdom, and laid the foundation of that liberty of which Englishmen are so justly proud; he died in 1185.

Henry VIII., son and successor of Henry VII., ascended the throne in 1509, at the age of eighteen. Although for a short time popular, he soon, by his arbitrary and capricious conduct, proved himself a tyrant. He obtained the title of *defender of the faith* from the pope by opposing Luther. He afterwards quarrelled with the pope, who refused to divorce him from his wife, and renounced his authority, and declared himself head of the church, thus introducing the reformation into England. He was six times married; two of his wives perished on the scaffold, and two others were divorced. Although benefits resulted from his reign, he must be detested for his tyranny and oppression; he died in 1547.

Henry, Matthew, an eminent dissenting teacher and voluminous writer, born 1662, died in 1714. His best known work is his "Exposition of the Bible."

Hervey, James, an English divine, of exemplary virtue and piety, born at Hardingstone, in Northamptonshire, in 1714, died in 1758. His chief writings are "Meditations and Contemplations;" "Remarks on Lord Bolingbroke's Letters on the study and use of History;" and "Theron and Aspasia, or a series of Dialogues and Letters on the most important subjects."

Hiacoomes, the first Indian in New England converted to Christianity, and minister at Martha's Vinyard; he died in 1690.

Hicks, Elias, a preacher among the Friends or Quakers. He was the founder of the sect in that society called *Hicksites.* He was born in Hempstead, Long Island, N. Y., on the 19th of March, 1748, and died in Jericho, Long Island, February 27th, 1830.

Hieronymus, or, as he is commonly called, Jerome, a very celebrated father of the church, born about 329, died in 420. (See page 58.)

Hoadly, Benjamin, bishop of Winchester, born at

Westerham, in Kent, 1676, died in 1761. Preaching against what he considered as the inveterate errors of the clergy, among other discourses, one was upon these words, "My kingdom is not of this world;" which producing the famous "*Bangorian controversy*," as it was called, employed the press for many years. Hoadly contended that the clergy had no pretensions to temporal jurisdictions; but that temporal princes had a right to govern in ecclesiastical politics; and by this means he drew on himself the indignation of almost all the clergy. These disputes, however, have long since subsided.

Hobbes, Thomas, born at Malmsbury, in 1588, died in 1679. He published many works, but there have been few persons whose writings have had a more pernicious influence in spreading irreligion and infidelity than Hobbes; and yet none of his treatises are directly levelled against revealed religion.

Hooker, Thomas, was born in Leicestershire, England, 1586, and educated at Emanuel College, Cambridge; he preached in London and Chelmsford with great success. On account of the persecution which raged he came to New England, and was the first minister of Cambridge, Mass. He was one of the founders of the colony of Connecticut, where he removed with his people in 1636, travelling through the wilderness with no other guide but a compass. He published many sermons and treatises, which were much admired. He died July 7th, 1647. As he lay dying, one of his friends that stood by his bedside observed to him, that he now was going to receive the *reward* of all his labours; "Brother," said he, "I am going to receive *mercy*."

Hooper, John, bishop of Gloucester, was born in Somersetshire, in 1495. In the persecution under Mary, refusing to recant his opinions, he was burned in the city of Gloucester, and suffered death with admirable constancy, in 1555.

Hopkins, Samuel, D. D., a distinguished divine, was born in Waterbury, Conn., Sept. 17th, 1721. He died in Newport, R. I., Dec. 20th, 1803, where he had preached many years. He maintained in his writings that holiness consists in disinterested benevolence, and sin in selfishness. His peculiar sentiments are distinguished by the term *Hopkinsianism*.

Horne, George, bishop of Norwich, born at Otham, in Kent, 1730, and died in 1792. This divine united, in a remarkable degree, depth of learning, brightness of imagination, sanctity of manners, and sweetness of temper. Four volumes of his incomparable "Sermons" are published. His "*Commentary on the Psalms*," in two volumes, quarto, "will (as the writer of his epitaph expresses it) continue to be a companion to the closet, till the devotion of the earth shall end in the hallelujahs of heaven." Dr. Horne also wrote a celebrated piece of irony, in reply to Adam Smith's sketch of David Hume's Life.

Horsely, Samuel, bishop of St. Asaph, was born in the parish of St. Martin's in the Fields, where his father was clerk in orders, and was educated at Trinity Hall, Cambridge. He became one of the most eminent men of his day, as a theologist, a mathematician, and a profound classic. No man of his age, perhaps, possessed more of what is generally understood by the idea of recondite learning, or was more profoundly versed in classical chronology. He edited and illustrated some of the most important of sir Isaac Newton's works, in 5 vols. 4to., and was himself the author of several esteemed mathematical and theological productions. His lordship died at Brighton, October 4th, 1806.

Hospinian, Rodolphus, a learned Swiss writer, who has done prodigious service to the protestant cause, born at Altdorf, in 1547, died in 1626. He wrote an excellent work, of vast extent, called "A History of the Errors of Popery."

Howard, John. (See page 255.)

Hubbard, William, minister of Ipswich, Mass., author of a History of New England in manuscript; he died in 1704.

Hugo, of Cluni, abbot of Cluni, and a saint of the Romish calendar, died in 1609.

Hunneric, king of the African Vandals, known for his severe persecution of the Christians; died in 484.

Hunter, Dr. Henry, an eminent presbyterian divine, equally admired for his pulpit eloquence, and beloved for his benevolence, was born at Culross, in Perthshire, in 1741, and died at Bristol, in 1802. His works are numerous; but the most important are translations. His principal original publication is a course of sermons, in 6 vols. 8vo., entitled "Sacred Biography." The most distinguished of his translations is "Saurin's Sermons," and "St. Pierre's Studies of Nature."

Huntingdon, Selina, countess dowager of, was born in 1707; married, in 1728, Theophilus, earl of Huntingdon, by whom she had four sons and three daughters. She died in 1791. Her ladyship had been a widow forty-five years; and her great religious concerns, as head of a very numerous sect in Great Britain and Ireland, she left by will, in the hands of committees, for managing them in both kingdoms. Her religious principles have been long since known; and her unbounded benevolence bore the best testimony of the purity of her intentions; having in the course of her life expended above £100,000 in public and private acts of charity.

Huntington, Joseph, D.D., minister of Coventry, Conn., author of "Calvinism Improved, or the gospel illustrated as a system of real grace, issuing in the salvation of all men;" this work was published after his death in 1796, and was answered by Dr. Strong of Hartford, Conn., the same year.

Huss, John. (See page 164.)

Hutten, Jacob, a native of Silesia, founder of an anabaptist sect, called the Moravian brethren; the time of his death is not known, although it is said that he was burnt as a heretic.

Hutchinson, Ann, an artful woman in Massachusetts, whose religious opinions were heretical, and which were condemned by a council of ministers; she was banished from the colony, and was murdered by the Indians, west of New Haven, 1643.

I.

Ignatius. (See page 55.)

Innocent III., Lothaire Conti, elevated to the popedom in 1198. He persecuted the Albigenses, and raised the papal authority to its greatest height. He died in 1216.

Innocent IV., Sinibaldi de Fiesque, was elected pope in 1243, and was the first who invested the cardinals with a red hat as a mark of dignity. He died in 1254.

Innocent X., John Baptist Pamphili, was elected pope in 1644. He published a bull against the Jansenists, and died in 1655.

Irenæus. (See page 57.)

Isidore, St., surnamed Pelusiota, or Daciata, from his retiring into a solitude, near the town which bears both these names, was the most celebrated of the disciples of John Chrysostom. He died about 440; and we have remaining 2012 of his letters, in five books.

J.

Jaaphan, Eben Tophail, an Arabian philosopher, cotemporary with Averroes, who died about 1198. He composed a philosophical romance, entitled "The Life or History of Hai Ebn Yokddhan;" in which he endeavours to demonstrate how a man may, by the mere light of nature, attain the knowledge of things natural and supernatural; more particularly the knowledge of God, and the affairs of another life.

Jacob, Ben Napthali, a famous Jew rabbi in the fifth century, and inventor (with Ben Aser) of the points in Hebrew, to serve for vowels, and of the accents, to facilitate the reading of that language.

Janeway, James, educated at Oxford, was ejected for nonconformity, and died in 1674.

Jansen, Cornelius, bishop of Ypres, and principal of the sect called Jansenists, born at Leerdam, in Holland, in 1585, died in 1638.

Jenyns, Soame, born in London in 1705, and well known in the literary world as the author of "*The In-*

ternal Evidences of the Christian Religion;" an "Essay on the Origin of Evil;" and various poetical pieces. He was many years member of parliament for the town of Cambridge; he was also a commissioner for trade and plantations, and died in 1787.

Jenks, Benjamin. a pious divine, born in Shropshire in 1646, died in 1724. His best known writings are, "Prayers and Offices of Devotion for families," and Meditations on various important subjects.

Jerome of Prague. (See page 166.)

Jerome, of St. Faith, or Joshua Lavehi, a Spanish Jew of great influence, who became a convert to Christianity, and it is said 5,000 Jews followed his example. He died in the fifteenth century.

Jewel, John, bishop of Salisbury, a great polemic writer in defence of the English church against popery; he was born in 1522, and died in 1571.

Joachim, abbot of Corrazo, made a pilgrimage to the Holy Land. He pretended to be a prophet, and died in 1202, leaving a numerous sect behind him.

Joan, pope, a woman placed among the successors of St. Peter as John VIII. or John VII. This story was believed for more than two hundred years, but is now generally discredited.

Joan of Arc, commonly called the maid of Orleans, whose heroic behaviour in reanimating the expiring valour of the French nation, though by the most superstitious means (pretending to be inspired), deserved a better fate. She was burnt by the English as a sorceress in 1431, at the age of twenty-four.

John VI., a Roman, was made pope in 985. He was the first who rewarded meritorious deeds by canonization; he died in 986.

John III., king of Sweden, son of Gustavus Vasa, ascended the throne in 1568. He attempted to restore the popish religion, but was unsuccessful, and died in 1592.

Jones, sir William, one of the judges of the supreme court in Bengal, born in London in 1746. He was a celebrated oriental scholar and sincere Christian. His researches in Asia have done much to give validity to the Mosaic history of the creation. He died at the age of 48.

Johnson, Edward, an inhabitant of Massachusetts, author of a work entitled "The Wonder-working Providence of Zion's Saviour in New England, from 1628 to 1652."

Johnson, Samuel, D.D., a native of Connecticut, distinguished as the first convert to episcopacy in the colony, and afterwards as president of King's college, New York; he died in 1772.

Jortin, Dr. John, a learned English divine and ecclesiastical historian, born in London in 1698, died in 1770. His chief works are, "Discourses concerning the truth of the Christian Religion," and "Remarks upon Ecclesiastical History."

Joseph, Father, an apostate monk, who raised six thousand banditti, in 1678, to extirpate the catholic religion in Hungary.

Josephus, Flavius, the ancient historian of the Jews, born at Jerusalem, A. D. 37, died in 93. His "History of the Jewish War and the Destruction of Jerusalem," in seven books, was composed at the command of Vespasian, and is singularly interesting and affecting, as the historian was an eyewitness of all that he relates. His "Jewish Antiquities," in twenty books, written in Greek, is a very noble work; we have also "A Discourse upon the Martyrdom of the Maccabees," which is a masterpiece of eloquence; he was a great orator, as well as a great historian.

Julian, the Roman emperor, commonly styled the apostate, because he professed Christianity before he ascended the throne; after which he openly embraced paganism, and persecuted the Christians. (See page 86.)

Jovinian, a monk of Milan, who became the head of a sect, and died in consequence of his debauchery, A. D. 406.

Juliana, a singular character of Norwich, England,

who, in her zeal for mortification, confined herself between four walls; she lived in the time of Edward III.

Justin, surnamed the martyr, one of the earliest writers of the Christian church. (See page 56.)

Juxon, Wm., archbishop of Canterbury, was imprisoned by the parliament; he was reinstated in office at the restoration, and died 1663.

K.

Kam-hi, emperor of China in 1661, was a liberal patron of the literature and arts of Europe, and of Christian missions: he died in 1722.

Kempis, Thomas á, famous for his transcendant piety and devotion, was born at Kempen, in the diocess of Cologne, about 1380, and died in 1471. His well-known work, "*The Imitation of Christ*," has been translated into numerous languages.

Kirkland, Samuel, a missionary among the Seneca Indians for forty years; he died at Paris, New York, in 1808.

Kirwan, William, dean of Killala, a distinguished ornament of the church, was originally a Romish priest; but became a zealous adherent and powerful supporter of the protestant faith. He was one of the most popular orators that ever appeared in the pulpit, and no man ever made a more powerful impression on his audience. He was at all times ready to exert his great powers in forwarding the objects of benevolence. He was born about 1754, and died near Dublin in 1805.

Klopstock, Frederic Theophilus, a very celebrated German poet, born in 1724, died in 1803. His "Messiah," by which his name is chiefly immortalized, was published at Halle, in 1751. He was likewise the author of three tragedies, called the "The death of Adam," "Solomon," and "David." His funeral was conducted with extraordinary pomp, being attended by the senate of Hamburg.

Knox, John, an eminent Scottish minister, a chief instrument and promoter of the reformation in that country, and a steady and undaunted patriot in the worst of times; born in 1505, and died in 1572. As to his character, he was, like Luther, one of those extraordinary persons of whom few, if any, are observed to speak with sufficient temper; all is either extravagant encomium, or senseless invective. After his death came out a "History of the Reformation in the realm of Scotland," &c. to which are subjoined all his other works.

Knox, Vicesimus, D.D., a learned divine and miscellaneous writer, born in 1752. He was master of Tunbridge school, where he presided thirty-three years. The duties of a parish priest he discharged for nearly forty years, with a zeal and ability perhaps never surpassed; he died in 1821. His principal works are "Essays, Moral and Literary;" "Christian Philosophy;" "Sermons;" "Domestic Divinity;" "Elegant Extracts;" "Elegant Epistles;" "Winter Evenings;" "Liberal Education;" "Personal Nobility," &c.

Knuzen, Matthias, a celebrated atheist, born in Holstein about 1650. He was the only person on record who openly taught atheism: and he undertook long journeys on purpose to make proselytes. His followers were called consciencIaries, because they asserted that there was no other god, no other religion, no other lawful magistracy, than conscience.

Kotterus, Christopher, a tanner, of Silesia, and one of the three fanatics whose visions were published at Amsterdam in 1657, with the following title, "Lux in Tenebris." He died in 1647.

Kuick, John Van, a painter of Dordt, accused of heresy, was cruelly burnt by the Jesuits in 1572.

L.

Labat, John Baptist, a celebrated traveller and missionary of the order of St. Dominic, born at Paris in 1663, died in 1738. His "Voyages and Travels" into different kingdoms are works of much amusement, and of good reputation.

Laidlie, Archibald, D.D., the first minister of the Dutch church in America who officiated in the English language. He was a native of Scotland, arrived in New York in 1764, and died in 1778.

Lardner, Dr. Nathaniel, a very eminent dissenting divine, author of "The Credibility of the Gospel History;" "The Testimonies of the ancient Jews and Pagans in favour of Christianity;" "The History of the Heretics," &c. He was born in 1684, and died in 1768.

Latimer, Hugh, bishop of Worcester, one of the first reformers of the church of England, born in 1470. From being a papist he became a zealous protestant, active in supporting the reformed doctrine, and assiduous to make converts. For his zeal, however, in the protestant faith, he was, with Ridley, bishop of London, burnt at Oxford, 1555. (See page 192.)

Laud, William, archbishop of Canterbury in the reign of Charles I., was born in 1573, and beheaded in 1645 for high treason; he fell a sacrifice to party violence.

Lavater, John Gaspar Christian, a Swiss divine, of warm fancy and natural acuteness, by which he was led to turn his attention to the expression of human sentiment and character. He perceived that not only transient passion, but even the more permanent qualities of character, are often very distinctly expressed; but carried his observation on this subject much farther than any other person had before advanced. Success inflamed his imagination, and he became an enthusiast in the study of physiognomy. The opinions relative to it which he propagated, were a medley of acute observation, ingenious conjecture, and wild revery. His books, published in the German language, were multiplied by many editions and translations. This amiable clergyman (for such he was) was born at Zurich in 1431, and died there in 1801, in consequence of a wound which he received from a French soldier a twelvemonth before.

Leese, Anna, founder of the sect of Shakers, was

born in England. She was of low parentage, and of doubtful character. She first divulged her extraordinary pretensions in 1770, assuming the name of the "*elect lady*," but being more generally denominated the "Mother." She came to America with five of her followers in 1774, and settled near Albany, N.Y. About the year 1780 she declared herself to be the woman clothed with the sun, mentioned in the twelfth chapter of Revelations, claimed the power of ministering the Holy Spirit to whom she pleased, asserted that she was daily judging the dead of all nations, &c. These impious pretensions she enforced upon persons by the magical charms of wry looks, whimsical gestures, unintelligible muttering, alternate groans and laughter, the ceremony of dancing, whirling, &c. By these means she succeeded in obtaining a considerable number of followers. One of these was Mr. Rathbun, a Baptist minister, who, however, in about three months recovered his senses, and published a pamphlet against the impostor. He says that there attended this infatuation an inexplicable agency upon the body, to which he himself was subjected, that affected the nerves suddenly and forcibly like the electric fluid, and was followed by tremblings and the complete deprivation of strength. "Mother Anna" asserted that she was not liable to death, but when she should leave this world, she should ascend in the twinkling of an eye to heaven. She died in 1784, and her sect has experienced a number of revolutions.

Leland, Dr. John, a celebrated English dissenting divine, settled in Dublin, distinguished himself by some very estimable and laborious publications, particularly "A View of the Deistical Writers of England," and "The Advantage and Necessity of the Christian Revelation." He was born in 1691, died 1766.

L'Enfant, James, an eminent French protestant minister, born in 1691, died in 1728. He was author of three capital works, viz. "Histories of the Council of Constance, Basil, and Pisa." Besides these, he published the New Testament, translated into French from the original Greek, with notes, in conjunction with Beausobre; which version was much esteemed by the protestants.

Leo II., pope, was an able and resolute pontiff. He first established the kiss of peace at the mass, and the use of holy water; he died in 683.

Leo X., pope of Rome, ever to be remembered by the protestants, as having been the cause of the Reformation begun by Luther, was born at Florence in 1475, and died in 1521. He was a lover and patron of learning and learned men, and equally favoured arts and sciences, being himself a man of taste.

Leovitius, Cyprian, a noble Bohemian, author of a collection of astrological productions and incoherent reveries. He prophesied that the world would end in 1584: he died in 1574.

Leslie, Charles, studied law, which he afterwards forsook for divinity, and became a famous theological disputant. His tracts on religion and politics amount to fifty. He left also two folio volumes of theological works, and was a man of great talents; he died in 1722.

Lightfoot, John, a most eminent divine, born in Staffordshire. He was one of the most learned rabbinnical scholars that England ever produced. His works are published in two volumes folio; he died in 1675.

Lilburne, John, a famous English enthusiast, born in 1618, died in 1657. He was the chief ringleader of the levellers, a modeller of state, and publisher of several seditious pamphlets; and of so quarrelsome a disposition as to have it appositely said of him, that if there were none living but him, John would be against Lilburne, and Lilburne against John.

Lilly, William, a famous English astrologer, born in 1602, died in 1681. In him we have an instance of the general superstition and ignorance that prevailed in the time of the civil war between Charles I. and his parliament; for the king consulted this astrologer to know in what quarter he should conceal himself if he could escape from Hampton court; and general Fairfax, on the other side, sent for him to his army, to ask him if he could tell by his art whether God was with them and their cause. Lilly, who made his fortune by favourable predictions to both parties, assured the general that God would be with him and his army. His almanacs were in repute upwards of thirty-six years, and to be found in almost every family in England.

Lodbrok, Regner, a celebrated king of Denmark at the beginning of the ninth century. He was a warrior and poet, full of fanaticism and religious frenzy. (See p. 94.)

Lollard, Walter. (See page 158.)

Louis VII., the Young, king of France, was early engaged in a quarrel with the pope, and was excommunicated by him. He made a crusade with an army consisting of eighty thousand men to Palestine, but was defeated by the Saracens; he died at Paris in 1180.

Louis IX., called the Saint. He made two crusades, during the last of which he died at Tunis, in 1270, and was canonized by Boniface VIII.

Lowth, Dr. Robert, bishop of London, &c., born in 1710, died in 1787. His literary character is well known by his "Translation of Isaiah;" a sublime poetic composition.

Loyola, Ignatius of, the founder of the order of the Jesuits, born in 1491, at the castle of Loyola, in Spain, was first page to Ferdinand V., king of Spain, and then an officer in his army; in which he signalized himself by his valour, and was wounded in both legs at the siege of Pampeluna, in 1521. To this circumstance the Jesuits owe their origin; for while he was under cure of his wounds, a Life of the Saints was put into his hands, which determined him to forsake the military for an ecclesiastical profession. His first devout exercise was to dedicate himself to the blessed virgin as her knight; he then went a pilgrimage to the Holy Land; and on his return to Europe, he continued his theological studies in the universities of Spain, though he was then thirty-three years of age. After this he went to Paris, and in France laid the foundation of this new order, the institutes of which he presented to pope Paul III., who made many objections to them; but Loyola adding to the three vows of chastity, poverty, and obedience a fourth, of implicit submission to the holy see, the institution was confirmed in 1540. Loyola died in 1555. (See p. 177.)

Lucifer, bishop of Cagliari, in Sardinia; author of a new schism called Luciferians; he died in 370.

Lucius III., Humbaldo Allineigoli, a native of Lucca, elected pope in 1181. The inquisition originated under this pontiff.

Lugo, John, a Spanish Jesuit, born at Madrid, a professor of theology at Rome. He was made cardinal by pope Urban, introduced Jesuits' bark into France, wrote seven volumes folio, and died in 1660.

Luther, Martin. (See page 167.)

M.

Macedonius, Arian, bishop of Constantinople, in 341. He was deposed by a council, and caused great commotion and trouble in his diocess.

Macknight, Dr. James, an eminent clergyman of the church of Scotland, distinguished by his learned and useful labours in illustration and defence of the New Testament, was born in 1721, and died at Edinburgh in 1800. Of his various works, the most distinguished are, "The harmony of the Four Gospels," and his "Translation of the Epistles."

Mahomet, or *Mohammed*. (See page 102.)

Mailla, Joseph Anne Maria de Mayrice de, a Jesuit born in Savoy, a most learned and amiable man, who spent forty-five years as a missionary in China. He translated the "Great Annals of China," published in twelve volumes quarto, and died at Pekin in 1748.

Malagrida, Gabriel, an Italian Jesuit, for a long time regarded as a saint, and consulted as an oracle. He was burnt alive in 1761, at the age of seventy-five, as a false prophet.

Malebranche, Nicholas, a celebrated French divine and philosopher, born in 1638, died in 1715. He wrote several works; of which the first and principal, as indeed it gave rise to almost all that followed, was his

"Search after Truth." His design in this book is to point out to us the errors into which we are daily led by our senses, imagination, and passions; and to prescribe a method for discovering the truth, which he does by starting the notion of seeing all things in God.

Manning, James, D.D., a distinguished Baptist clergyman, who was the first president of the college at Providence, R. I., and a member of congress from that state; he died in 1791.

Manton, Thomas, D.D., a popular preacher in London, and before parliament. At the restoration he was chaplain to the king. He wrote sermons and Calvinistic tracts, and died in 1677.

Martin, St., was converted to Christianity, and became bishop of Taurus. He is regarded as the apostle of Gaul. His confession of faith is still extant; he died in 397.

Mary, queen of England, eldest daughter of Henry VIII. and Catharine of Arragon. She was a learned woman, but bigoted in the popish superstition, exceedingly jealous, and violent and sanguinary in her resentments. During her reign, fire, fagots, and the stake were the horrid means used to make proselytes to the Romish church. The sacrifice of the innocent lady Jane Grey and her husband to a mean fit of jealousy, showed a degree of barbarity rarely equalled in civilized life. She married Philip of Spain, whose coldness towards her, together with the loss of Calais, is said to have so preyed on her mind, that she fell into a fever, of which she died in 1558.

Mason, John, a learned and pious dissenting minister, author of "Self Knowledge," "Practical Discourses for Families," and other works. He died in 1763.

Mascaron, Julius, bishop of Agen, and a most eminent French preacher, born in 1634, died in 1703. His eloquence was astonishing; and it is related that his preaching had such an effect upon the Huguenots, that, of thirty thousand Calvinists, which he found at his coming to the see of Agen, twenty-eight thousand forsook their church.

Massillon, John Baptiste, a celebrated French preacher, and considered as a consummate master of eloquence, born in 1663, died in 1742.

Mather, Increase, D.D., a clergyman of Boston, and afterwards president of Harvard College, and author of several works. He died in 1723.

Mather, Cotton, D.D., F.R.S., son of the preceding, distinguished for his great learning and piety, and was the most eminent clergyman of his day in New England. His writings on various subjects were very numerous; his publications amounted to three hundred and eighty-two. He died at Boston, 1728.

Mayhew, Thomas, governor of Martha's Vineyard, and distinguished for his regard for the spiritual and temporal welfare of the Indians. He died in 1681. A number of descendants of his name were distinguished for their ministerial labours among the Indians on Martha's Vineyard.

Mills, Samuel J., an American clergyman, distinguished for his piety and zeal in promoting the missionary cause. He died in 1818, on his return from Africa, whither he had gone as an agent of the American Colonization Society.

Melancthon, Philip, a celebrated German divine, coadjutor with Luther in the reformation, and one of the wisest and greatest men of his age, born at Bretten, Feb. 16th, 1497, died in 1560.

Menno, Simonis, an ecclesiastic of Friesland, and an anabaptist leader. His followers are still to be found in the Low Countries by the name of Mennonites. He died in 1565.

Michael Cerularius, patriarch of Constantinople, in 1043; he prevented the union of the eastern and western churches, and was banished in 1059.

Michaelis, John David, a very learned German writer on divinity, and the oriental languages, was born in 1717, and died in 1791. His works are numerous, but his most celebrated is an "Introduction to the New Testament," a translation of which was published in English in 1761.

Middleton, Thomas Fanshaw, D.D., a distinguished English clergyman, and bishop of Calcutta; he was the first English bishop in India, appointed in 1814, and died in 1822.

Milner, Joseph, a divine, born in 1744. He became vicar of a church at *Hull*; was author of "An answer to Gibbon's attack of Christianity," and "A History of the Church of Christ."

Milner, Dr. Isaac, brother of Joseph, was a mathematical tutor at the university of Cambridge. Mr. Wilberforce and Mr. Pitt were among his pupils. He afterwards became dean of Carlisle, continued his brother's "History of the Church of Christ," and died in 1820.

Milton, John, a most illustrious English poet, was born in London in 1608, and died of the gout in 1674. His most celebrated poems are "*Paradise Lost*," which he published in 1667, and his "Paradise Regained," published in 1670.

Molay, James de, the last grand master of the Templars. Philip the Fair summoned him to Paris, where he came with sixty knights, who were seized and burnt alive in 1314.

Molinos, Michael de, a Spanish ecclesiastic, who caused great controversy in the church. He was the founder of the sect called Quietists, and died in 1696.

Montanus, an ancient heresiarch among the Christians, and founder of a sect in the second century called Montanists. They pretended to the gift of prophecy, and prohibited second marriages.

Morin, Simon, a celebrated French fanatic, burnt alive at Paris in 1663, for having assumed the title of the Son of God.

Morin, Stephen, a learned French theological and biblical writer, born in 1625, died in 1700. In one of his works he endeavours to prove that the Hebrew language is as old as the creation, and that God himself inspired it into Adam.

More, Hannah, one of the most distinguished female writers of the age, was born near Bristol, Eng., and was the youngest of five sisters. Early in life she was distinguished by her literary talents, and was honoured with the intimate acquaintance of Dr. Johnson, Burke, and other distinguished persons. Imbued with a spirit of piety, she devoted herself to a life of Christian benevolence, and the composition of various works, having for their object the religious improvement of mankind. This venerable lady died at her residence in Windsor Terrace, Clifton, Sept. 7th, 1833, in the eighty-sixth year of her age.

Morton, Nathaniel, one of the early settlers of Plymouth, author of a History of the Church of that colony, and of "New England's Memorial," published in 1699.

Mosheim, John Lawrence, an illustrious German divine, ecclesiastical historian, and critic, born in 1695, died in 1755. His "Ecclesiastical History, from the birth of Christ to the beginning of the eighteenth century," is unquestionably the best that is extant.

Muggleton, Lodowick, an English tailor of notorious fame as a schismatic, who damned all the world that differed from his strange mode of faith. He was born in 1607; his books were burnt by the hangman, himself pilloried and imprisoned, and he died in 1697.

Munscer or *Muntzer*, Thomas, a Saxon divine, one of the disciples of Luther, and chief of the German anabaptists. In conjunction with Stork, he pulled down all the images in the churches which Luther had left standing; and then, finding an army in his followers, he commenced leveller, and openly taught that all distinctions of rank were usurpations on the rights of mankind. At the head of 40,000 men he ravaged the country. The Landgrave of Hesse at length defeated him; 7000 of the enthusiasts fell in battle, and the rest, with their leader, fled; he was taken and beheaded at Mulhausen, in 1525.

N.

Nayler, James, a remarkable enthusiast, born in 1616; he became a convert of the famous George Fox to quakerism, and commencing preaching, he set out for Bristol, attended by a numerous cavalcade, singing, "Holy, holy, holy, Lord God of Sabaoth; Hosannah in the highest; Holy, holy, holy, Lord God of Israel." He was brought before parliament, tried and condemned as guilty of blasphemy, and sentenced to imprisonment for life. But two years after he was liberated, and died in 1666.

Neal, Daniel, a nonconformist divine, born in 1678. In 1706 he was chosen pastor of an independent congregation in London. As a writer, his principal production is, "A History of the Puritans." He died in 1743.

Nelson, Robert, a learned and eminently pious English gentleman, born in 1656, died in 1715. He published several works of piety, and left his whole estate for charitable uses. There is a great degree of excellence in all his writings; but his "Companion for the Festivals and Fasts," &c. will perpetuate his memory.

Nestorius, a Syrian, bishop of Constantinople in 431. He was deposed for denying the incarnation of the Redeemer.

Newell, Samuel, one of the first American missionaries to India; he died at Bombay in 1821. His wife, *Harriet*, who accompanied him, died at the Isle of France, in 1812.

Newton, John, an English divine, author of sermons, and other valuable religious works; he died in 1807.

Newton, Dr. Thomas, bishop of Bristol, and dean of St. Paul's, born in 1703, died in 1782, having distinguished himself by publishing an edition, with annotations, of "Milton's Paradise Lost" and "Paradise Regained;" but more by his learned and valuable "Dissertations on the Prophecies."

Nicephorus, Callistus, a Greek historian, who flourished in the fourteenth century, and wrote an "Ecclesiastical History," in twenty-three books, eighteen of which are still extant, containing the transactions of the church from the birth of Christ to the death of the emperor Phocas, in 610.

Nicholas I., surnamed the Great, was elected pope in 858. He was the cause of the schism between the Greek and Latin churches, and died 867.

Nicholas III., John Gaetan, was elected pope in 1277. He sent missionaries to Tartary; died 1280.

Novatian, a pagan philosopher of the third century,

who was converted to Christianity, but founded a new heresy. His followers were called Novatians.

O.

Occum, Samson, a Mohegan Indian, converted to Christianity, and became a missionary among the western Indians; he died in 1792.

Olaf, a king of Norway in the tenth century, sent missionaries to Greenland to convert the natives.

Oldcastle, Sir John, called the good lord *Cobham*, (see page 160.)

O'Leary, Arthur, a native of Ireland, who entered into the Franciscan order of Capuchins. Returning to Ireland, he soon distinguished himself by his writings, both on religious and political subjects, by which he gained the esteem of all parties, as a friend to freedom, liberality, and toleration. His addresses to the catholics gained him the most flattering notice of the Irish government; he died in London in 1802, aged 73.

Omar I., caliph of the Saracens, the second after Mahomet, and one of the most rapid conquerers of modern history. He drove the Greeks from Syria and Phenicia; Jerusalem was surrendered to him; his generals took the capital of Persia; and soon after Memphis and Alexandria submitted to his victorious troops; and in this conquest, the famous Alexandrian library was burnt by these savages, who heated their stoves with its valuable books. He was assassinated by a Persian slave in 643, the tenth year of his reign, and sixty-third of his age.

Orono, an Indian chief of the Penobscot tribe, was faithful in his attachment to the white people, and laboured to promote Christianity among his own. He died in 1801, aged 113. His wife died in 1809, aged 115.

Orton, Job, a dissenting minister, born at Shrewsbury in 1717, and died in 1783. He wrote "Memoirs of Dr. Doddridge," "Letters to a Young Clergyman," and "An Exposition of the Old Testament."

Osterwald, John Frederic, a celebrated Swiss protestant minister, born in 1663, and died in 1747. He was the author of many excellent works, the best of which is his "Instructions in the Christian Religion."

Owen, Dr. Henry, a very celebrated English divine, whose biblical knowledge was perhaps superior to any of his cotemporaries. He was born in 1715, published many excellent works of divinity, and died in 1795.

Owen, Dr. John, an eminent English divine among the Independents, and sometimes styled the oracle and metropolitan of that sect, was born 1616, and died in 1683. He was a very voluminous writer.

P.

Paine, Thomas, (see page 264.)

Paley, Dr. William, archdeacon of Carlisle, an elegant writer on ethics, author of "Natural Theology," "Moral Philosophy," &c.; born in 1743, died in 1805.

Parkhurst, John, a learned divine, born in 1728. He died at Epsom in 1797, leaving, among other works, "A Greek and English Lexicon to the New Testament."

Patrick, St., the apostle and guardian saint of Ireland, was, as is supposed, a native of Wales, or of Cornwall, who was seized by pirates and carried to Ireland, where he converted the inhabitants to Christianity: he died about 460.

Paul, a celebrated heresiarch of Samosata, a city on the Euphrates. He was bishop of Antioch in 260; but avowing his belief that Jesus Christ was only a good man endowed with great wisdom, he was deposed by the synod of Antioch in 270.

Paul, Father, a most illustrious person, and universal scholar, but particularly skilled in the canon and civil law, and in physic. He wrote many works, and is principally celebrated for his "History of the Council of Trent," the rarest piece of history the world ever saw.

Pelagius, (see page 91.)

Penn, William, the founder and legislator of the colony of Pennsylvania, was born in London, in 1644. He was a member of the society of Friends, or Quakers, and became a preacher of that order at the age of twenty-four. He died in England in 1718.

Peter the *Hermit*, a French officer of Amiens, who, quitting the military profession, commenced hermit and pilgrim. He travelled to the Holy Land in 1093; after which he received a commission from pope Urban II. to excite all Christian princes to a general crusade against the Turks and Saracens. He died about 1100.

Peter III., king of Arragon, married Constance, daughter of the king of Sicily, and having formed the plan of seizing that kingdom, against the pretensions of Charles of Anjou, he caused all the French in that island to be assassinated at the same time, which was done on Easter day, 1282. This massacre has been since called the *Sicilian Vespers.*

Peter Nolasque, a native of Languedoc, in the service of James, king of Arragon. He established the "order of mercy," whose sole business was the redemption of Christian slaves from the power of infidels. He died in 1256.

Peter de Osma, a Spanish ecclesiastic in the fifteenth century, who was, perhaps, the forerunner of the reformation, as he wrote and preached against the infallibility of the church of Rome.

Philip II., surnamed Augustus, king of France. In conjunction with Richard I. of England, he made a crusade to the Holy Land, with 300,000 men, but, though victorious, returned with little glory. He died in 1223.

Philip III., or the Hardy, was proclaimed king of France in 1270, while in Africa on a crusade with his father, Lewis IX. He defeated the Saracens, and made a truce with them for ten years; he died in 1285.

Philip V., surnamed the Long, king of France. He banished the Jews from the kingdom; he permitted great cruelties against lepers, who were either put to death or confined; he died in 1531.

Philpot, John, a native of Hampshire, a warm advocate for the reformation, was made archdeacon of Winchester by Edward VI., but in the next reign was convicted of heresy, and burnt at Smithfield in 1555.

Photinus, bishop of Sirmium, was deposed for supporting that Christ was only a man; he died in 376.

Photius, patriarch of Constantinople, in the ninth century, and the greatest man of the age in which he lived. Of his works the greatest is his "Bibliotheca." He died 886.

Piazzi, Jerome Bartholomew, a historian of the "Inquisition in Italy," of which court he was formerly a judge; but became afterwards a convert to the church of England, and died at Cambridge in 1745.

Polycarp, bishop of Smyrna, (see page 56.)

Pompignan, John James Le Franc, marquis of, a French poet, little inferior to Racine. He pronounced a discourse in favour of Christianity, before the French academy in 1760, which drew upon him the ridicule of his associates. He died in 1784, highly esteemed.

Porteus, Dr. Beilby, bishop of London, was born in 1731, and died in 1809. His single sermons and charges are numerous, and his "Lectures" at St. James' church are well known.

Priestley, Joseph, a distinguished polemical and philosophical English writer, who, having embraced the Unitarian faith, and meeting with opposition in England removed to America, where he died in 1804.

Prince, Thomas, an eminent American clergyman, settled at Boston; he was author of a chronological history of New England, and made large collections for a history of the country He died in 1758.

Pucci, Francis, a noble Florentine. After changing his religious opinions several times, he was taken while a protestant, and burnt at Rome as a heretic in 1600.

Q.

Quadratus, a disciple of the apostles and bishop of Athens, who composed an "Apology for the Christian Faith," and presented it to the emperor, who stopped the persecution against the Christians, A. D. 125.

Quarles, Francis, an English poet who wrote a number of religious works. He was born in 1592, and died in 1644.

Quesnel, Pasquier, a celebrated priest of the oratory, in France, born at Paris in 1634: he became the head of the sect of the Jansenists, wrote many polemical books, and died at Amsterdam in 1719

R.

Radegonde, St., a German princess, renowned for her personal charms and devotedness to religious duties. At the age of ten she renounced paganism for the Christian faith by direction of Clotaire, who afterwards married her, and then, yielding to her wishes, permitted her to retire to the seclusion of a monastery; she died 587.

Raikes, Robert, a printer and philanthropist, founder of Sunday-schools, born in Gloucester, Eng., in 1735, died in 1811.

Rantzan, Josias, a Danish nobleman in the French service, died 1645. Chiefly known as the active agent by whom the protestant religion was introduced into Denmark.

Rasles, or *Ralle*, Sebastian, a French Jesuit, who was a missionary among the Indians, and acquired great influence over them. The last twenty-six years of his life he spent among the Indians at Norridgewok, on the Kennebec river. He was a man of learning, and wrote "A Dictionary of the Indian Language," which is still preserved in Harvard College. He was killed in an attack of the English in 1724, in the sixty-seventh year of his age.

Richard I., king of England, left his country for a crusade to the Holy Land, where, after displaying great bravery, he defeated the infidels under Saladin, and embarked for Europe. He was killed while besieging Chalus, 1199.

Richmond, Legh, rector of Turvey, Bedfordshire, Eng., was born at Liverpool Jan. 29th, 1772, died May 8th, 1827. He was the author of the "Dairyman's Daughter," "Young Cottager," &c., works which are highly esteemed throughout the Christian world.

Ridley, Nicholas, bishop of London, one of the principal instruments of the reformation, who suffered martyrdom for it in the reign of queen Mary, was born in 1500, and burnt at Oxford in 1555. (See page 192.)

Robinson, John, a distinguished English clergyman, pastor of the English church at Amsterdam, and afterwards at Leyden, and died there in 1625.

S.

Sabatai Sevi. (See page 235.)

Sabellius, a noted African, founder of a sect in the third century, which denied distinction in the trinity.

Sandeman, Robert, founder of the sect of the Sandemanians, was born at Perth, in Scotland, about the year 1718. He represented faith as the mere operation of intellect, and maintained that men were justified merely on speculative belief. He came to New England and gathered a church in Danbury, Conn., in 1765, where he died April 2d, 1771.

Saturninus, a heretic of the second century. He supposed that the world was created by angels and regarded the connexion of the sexes as criminal.

Saurin, James, an eminent Flemish divine and theological writer, died in 1730.

Scott, Thomas, D. D., an English divine, and chaplain to the Lock Hospital, and Rector of Aston Sanford, Bucks, distinguished for his "Commentary on the Bible," and other works; he died in 1821.

Scudder, Henry, a presbyterian clergyman of England, author of "The Christian's Daily Walk." He died before the restoration of Charles II.

Seabury, Samuel, D. D., an episcopal clergyman, bishop of Connecticut, and the first diocesan in the United States, published two volumes of his sermons, and died in 1796.

Secker, Thomas, archbishop of Canterbury, born 1693, and died 1768. His catechetical lectures and sermons, published after his death, are masterly compositions.

Seneca, a celebrated Stoic philosopher, born in Spain, at Corduba, A. D. 12. He was put to death in A. D. 65, by order of the tyrant Nero, to whom he had been a preceptor.

Sergeant, John, a missionary to the Stockbridge Indians; he translated part of the Bible into the Indian tongue; born at Newark, N. J., and died at Stockbridge in 1749. His son of the same name afterwards engaged in the same cause.

Sergius, a Syrian, patriarch of Constantinople, and head of a sect called the Monothelite: died in 638.

Servetus, Michael, a most ingenious and learned Spaniard, was burnt at the stake in Geneva for his heretical and blasphemous opinions in 1553, aged forty-four. He was first a physician and then a divine.

Severus, a heretic of the second century, who maintained the existence of a good and evil principle.

Shepard, Thomas, an English nonconforming divine, became minister of Cambridge, Mass., and was author of many useful works: he died in 1649.

Sherlock, Dr. Thomas, bishop of London, a controversial writer, died in 1761, aged eighty-three.

Sigismond, son of Charles IV., king of Hungary in 1386, and emperor of Germany in 1410. He prevailed upon the pope to call the council of Constance, in 1414, to settle the difficulties of the church, at which he presided, and at which were present eighteen thousand ecclesiastics and sixteen thousand nobles; he suffered that council to burn John Huss and Jerome of Prague, after he had given them a safe passport.

Simeon Stylites, the founder of a sect of devotees called Stylites. He died in 461, aged sixty-nine, after having spent forty-seven years on the top of a column sixty feet high, exposed to the inclemencies of the season, and often supporting himself for days on one foot.

Simpson, John, a Scottish divine and divinity professor at Glasgow; he was deposed and excommunicated for denying the doctrine of the Trinity, and died in Edinburg, in 1744.

Smith, Samuel Stanhope, D.D., LL.D., an eminent presbyterian clergyman, who was the founder and first president of Hampden Sidney college, Virginia, and afterwards professor of moral philosophy and theology at Princeton college, and president of that institution; he died in 1819.

Southcot, Joanna. (See page 275.)

Spener, a Lutheran divine, founder of the sect called Pietists, held some ecclesiastical dignities at Berlin, and died in 1705, aged seventy-six.

Spinoza, Benedict de, was born at Amsterdam in 1638 was first a Jew, then a Christian, and lastly an atheist. He died in 1677.

Spira, Francis, an eminent Venetian lawyer in the sixteenth century; he favoured the tenets of the reformation, and was compelled to make a recantation to save his life, which had such an effect upon his spirits as to hasten his death. He died in 1548.

Stephen II. was chosen pope in 752. Being attacked by the king of Lombardy, he appealed for assistance to Pepin, king of France, who defeated the Lombards, and took from them twenty-five towns, which he gave to the pope, and thus laid the foundation of the temporal power of the holy see. Stephen died in 757.

Sternhold, Thomas, an English poet, celebrated for his version of the Psalms of David in conjunction with *Hopkins*; he died in 1549.

Stifelius, Michael, a protestant divine of Germany, died in 1567. He predicted that the destruction of the world would happen in 1553, but lived to witness the fallacy of his prediction.

Stillingfleet, Dr. Edward, bishop of Worcester, died in 1699, greatly distinguished by his numerous writings, particularly by his "Origines Sacræ," or a rational account of natural and revealed religion.

Stoddard, Solomon, an eminent clergyman of New England, settled for nearly sixty years at Northampton, Mass., and died in 1729.

Summerfield, John, A. M., a very eloquent and popular preacher of the methodist episcopal church, died at New York in 1825, aged twenty-seven, having been a preacher eight years.

Swartz, Christian F. (See page 245.)

Swedenborg, Emanuel. (See page 230.)

Swift, Dr. Jonathan, dean of St. Patrick's, Dublin, an illustrious political, satirical, and miscellaneous writer and poet, died in 1745, aged seventy-eight. He was the author of several singular books.

T.

Taylor, Dr. Jeremy, bishop of Down and Connor, in Ireland, and a very eminent theological writer and controversialist, died in 1667, aged fifty-four.

Tetzel, John, a Dominican, of Germany. He was commissioned to publish the indulgences of the holy see; and the zeal with which he executed the office caused the animadversion of Luther, and consequently the reformation. When charged with being the author of the disasters of the church, he was so afflicted with the imputation, that he died of a broken heart in 1519.

Theodorus, a bishop of Cilicia, who died in 428. His works, some of which are extant, were condemned as heretical by a general council.

Theodosius the Great, the last Roman emperor, a convert to Christianity and renowned general and legislator, died in 395. His sons, Arcadius and Honorius, made a division of the empire into East and West; Arcadius being first emperor of the East, and Honorius of the West.

Theodotus, a tanner of Byzantium, who apostatized from the Christian faith to save his life, and founded a new sect which denied the divinity of Christ. Another of the same name was the head of a sect which maintained that the Messiah was inferior to Melchisedec.

Tillotson, Dr. John, archbishop of Canterbury, was the son of a clothier, and died in 1694. He published many valuable sermons.

Titus, Vespasian, a Roman emperor, son of Vespasian, distinguished for his conquest of Jerusalem. The "triumphal arch of Titus," built at Rome to commemorate this event, is still remaining. He died A. D. 81. in the forty-first year of his age.

Trimmer, Sarah, an English lady, eminent for her exertions in support of Sunday-schools and other religious institutions, died in 1810.

Tyndall or *Tindal*, William, an English reformer, memorable for having made the first English version of the Bible. He suffered death as a heretic in 1536.

U.

Urban V., William, de Grimoald, elected pope in 1302, after Innocent VI. He was the first pope who resided at Rome, and was the patron of learned and religious bodies, founded churches and colleges, and corrected abuses. He died at Avignon, in 1370.

V.

Vanini, Lucilio, a most determined atheist, who settled in France, and was burnt for blasphemy in 1619.

Vanderkempt, J. T., D. D., missionary to South Africa. He laboured with success among the Hottentots and Caffres, and died in Cape Town in 1811.

Varenius, Augustus, an eminent Lutheran divine of Lunenburg, celebrated for his profound knowledge of the Hebrew. It is said that he could repeat the Hebrew Bible by heart. He died in 1684.

Veil, Charles Maria de, a Jew of Metz, was converted to Christianity by Bossuet, and made canon of St. Genevieve. After lecturing on theology at Angers he went to England, where he joined the anabaptists, and became a preacher of that persuasion. He wrote commentaries on the Scriptures, and died about 1700.

Venner, Thomas, a noted fanatic in the time of Cromwell and Charles II., was originally a wine cooper. His followers were called fifth monarchy men. He was executed, with twelve of his associates, in 1661.

Vincent, Thomas, an English nonconformist divine, author of "Explanation of the Catechism," and other religious tracts, died in 1671.

Voltaire, Marie Francis Aruet de, gentleman of the bedchamber, and historiographer to the king of France, a celebrated historian, philosopher, dramatic writer, and epic poet; died in 1788. He is also distinguished as a champion of infidelity. (See page 256.)

W.

Waldo, Peter, a merchant of Lyons, was the founder of a sect called the Waldenses, in the twelfth century.

Warburton, William, bishop of Gloucester, a very eminent theological writer, critic, and controversialist; he died in 1779, leaving behind him numerous valuable works.

Ward, William, D.D., baptist missionary to Serampore, in Hindostan. He died in 1823.

Watson, Richard, a celebrated English prelate, who became bishop of Llandaff; he wrote, among other works, an answer to Paine's Age of Reason, called an Apology for the Bible, and died in 1816.

Watts, Isaac, a dissenting divine, philosopher, poet, and mathematician, of uncommon genius and celebrity; died in 1748.

Wesley, John. (See page 252.)

Westfield, Thomas, a native of Ely, was made archbishop of St. Alban's, and soon after bishop of Bristol. He was so eloquent and pathetic a preacher, that he was called the weeping prophet; he died in 1644.

Wheelock, Eleazer, D.D., first president of Dartmouth College; he formed at Lebanon, Conn., a school for the purpose of educating Indian youth for missionaries. He removed to Hanover, N. H., and founded Dartmouth College in 1770. He died in 1774, aged sixty-eight.

Whitehead, John, was first a methodist preacher, and then a quaker, and at last applied himself to physic in London. He published a Life of Wesley, and died in 1804.

Whitgift, Dr. John, archbishop of Canterbury, died in 1604.

Whitefield, George. (See page 252.)

Wickliffe, John. (See page 153.)

Wilkinson, Jemima, a religious enthusiast, was born in Cumberland, in America, and died in 1819. She claimed that she had been raised from the dead, and that she was invested by divine authority with the power of working miracles, and the authority of teaching in religion.

Williams, Roger, the founder of the colony of Rhode Island, of which he became president; he was an eminent clergyman of great learning and uncommon energy. He was born in Wales in 1599. After having been for some time a minister of the church of England, his nonconformity induced him to seek religious liberty in America. He arrived in Boston in 1631. His peculiar sentiments soon brought him before the magistrates. He asserted that an oath ought not to be tendered to an unregenerate man; that a Christian should not pray with the unregenerate, &c. Persisting in these sentiments, he was banished. He went with a number of his friends to a place which he named Providence, in acknowledgment of God's mercies. He embraced the sentiments of the baptists; he was baptized by one of his brethren, and he then baptized about ten others. He died in April, 1683. His memory is deserving of lasting honour, for the liberty of conscience and generous toleration which he established.

Williams, John, a clergyman of Deerfield, Mass. He, with his family, and many of his parishioners, were taken prisoners by the Indians in 1704; his wife and two children were murdered, and the remainder of the party carried to Canada, and after two years of suffering, were ransomed. He returned to Deerfield, and died in 1729.

Winchester, Elhanan, an itinerant preacher of the doctrine of universal restoration, was born in Brookline, Mass., in 1751. In 1778 he was a baptist minister on Pedee river, South Carolina, zealously teaching the Calvinistic doctrines as explained by Dr. Gill. In 1781 he became a preacher of universal salvation in Philadelphia. He preached in various parts of America and England, and died in Hartford, Conn., in 1797.

Wolsey, Thomas, prime minister of Henry VIII., who, from being the son of a butcher, rose to be archbishop of York, chancellor of England, cardinal of St. Cicily, and legate a latere. He died in 1530.

Woolston, Thomas, an English divine, author of several works filled with heterodox sentiments and absurdities. He died in prison in 1733, where he had been sentenced for publishing a blasphemous work.

Worcester, Samuel, D.D., an American clergyman settled in Massachusetts, distinguished for his zeal in promoting the missionary cause. He died in 1821.

Wyatt, Sir Thomas, one of the most learned and accomplished persons of his time. He wrote poetry, and was the first Englishman who versified any part of the book of Psalms. He died in 1541, aged thirty-eight.

X.

Xavier, Francis, the great coadjutor of Ignatius Loyola, was born at Xavier, at the foot of the Pyrenees, in 1506; and was sent one of the earliest missionaries to the East Indies; for his zeal and ability in this undertaking, he obtained the appellation of the "Apostle of the Indies." He died in 1552, and was canonized in 1622 by Gregory XV.

Y.

Young, Edward, an English poet and divine, died in 1765. He wrote "Night Thoughts," and other works.

Z.

Zanzalus, James, an obscure monk in the sixth century, who became founder of the sect of the Jacobites. They hold the perfection of the gospel to be the strict observance of fasts.

Zeigenbalg, Bartholomew, (see page 244.)

Zegeden, Stephen, of Hungary, was one of the first disciples of Luther, and wrote several theological works; he died in 1572.

Zuinglius, Ulric, (see page 170.)

A CHRONOLOGICAL TABLE

OF IMPORTANT AND INTERESTING RELIGIOUS EVENTS, WHICH HAVE OCCURRED SINCE THE COMMENCEMENT OF THE CHRISTIAN ERA TO THE PRESENT TIME.

A. D.

Jesus Christ, the Saviour of mankind, was born four years before the commencement of the Christian era.

26. John the Baptist preaches in Judea the coming of the Messiah.
29. Jesus Christ is crucified.
35. Conversion of St. Paul to Christianity.
39. St. Matthew writes his gospel.
40. The name of Christians first given to the disciples of Christ at Antioch.
41. Herod persecutes the Christians, and imprisons Peter.
42. Sergius Paulus, proconsul, converted by St. Paul.
44. St. Mark writes his gospel.
50. St. Paul preaches in the Areopagus at Athens.
60. Christian religion published in England.
64. The first persecution raised by Nero.
67. St. Peter and St. Paul put to death.
70. *Titus destroys Jerusalem.* The lands of Judea sold.
95. Dreadful persecutions of the Christians at Rome and in the provinces.
95. St. John writes his Apocalypse.
    writes his gospel.
98. Trajan forbids the Christian assemblies.
108. St. Ignatius was devoured by wild beasts at Rome.
118. Persecution of the Christians renewed by Adrian, but afterwards suspended.
137. Adrian rebuilds Jerusalem by the name of Elia Capitolina.
139. Justin Martyr writes his first apology for the Christians.
167. Polycarp and Pionicusus suffered martyrdom at Asia.
177. Persecution of the Christians at Lyons.

In the *second century* Christian assemblies are held on Sunday, and other stated days, in private houses, and in the burying places of martyrs.

Infant baptism and sponsors used in this century.

Various festivals and fasts established.

A distinction formed between the bishops and presbyters, who with the deacons and readers are the only orders of ecclesiastics known in this century.

The sign of the cross and anointing used.

The custom of praying towards the east introduced.

A. D.

202. The fifth persecution of the Christians, principally in Egypt.

203. The Scots converted to Christianity by the preaching of Marcus and Dionysius.

236. The sixth persecution of the Christians.

250. The seventh persecution of the Christians under Decius.

257. The eighth persecution of the Christians.

260. The temple of Diana of Ephesus burned.

272. The ninth persecution of the Christians.

The Jewish Talmud and Targum composed in the *third century.*

The Jews are allowed to return into Palestine.

Many illustrious men and Roman senators converted to Christianity

Religious rites greatly multiplied in this century; altars used; wax tapers employed.

Public churches built for the celebration of Divine worship.

The pagan mysteries injudiciously imitated in many respects by the Christians.

The tasting of milk and honey previous to baptism, and the person anointed before and after that holy rite receives a crown, and goes arrayed in white some time after.

302. The tenth persecution of the Christians.

306. *Constantine the Great,* emperor of Rome, stops the persecution of the Christians.

313. Edict of Milan published by Constantine—Christianity tolerated throughout the empire.

325. Constantine assembles the first general council at Nice, where the doctrines of Arius are condemned.

326. St. Athanasius, bishop of Alexandria, introduced monarchism into the Roman empire.

361. Julian, emperor of Rome, abjures Christianity, and is elected Pontifex Maximus. Attempts fruitlessly to rebuild the temple of Jerusalem.

381. Second general council held at Constantinople.

387. St. Jerome dies, aged seventy-eight.

397. St. Chrysostom chosen patriarch of Constantinople.

In the *fourth century* the Athanasians or Orthodox persecuted by Constantius, who was an Arian, and by Valens, who ordered eighty of their deputies, all ecclesiastics, to be put on board a ship, which was set on fire as soon as it was got clear of the coast.

Remarkable progress in this century of the Christian religion among the Indians, Goths, Marcomanni, and Iberians.

Theodosius the Great is obliged by Ambrose, bishop of Milan, to do public penance for the slaughter of the Thessalonians.

The Eucharist was during this century administered in some places to infants and persons deceased.

Something like the doctrine of transubstantiation is held,

A.D.

and the ceremony of the elevation used in the celebration of the eucharist. The use of incense, and of the censor, with several other superstitious rites, introduced.—The churches are considered as externally holy, the saints are invoked, images used, and the cross worshipped. The clerical order augmented by new ranks of ecclesiastics, such as archdeacons, country bishops, archbishops, metropolitans, exarchs, &c.

412. The Pelagian heresy condemned by the bishops of Africa.

432. The conversion of the Irish to the Christian faith effected by St. Patrick, whose original name was Succathus.

451. The fourth general council held at Chalcedon.

497. Clovis and the Franks converted to Christianity.

During the *fifth century* terrible persecutions were carried on against the Christians in Britain by the Picts, Scots, and Anglo-Saxons—in Spain, Gaul, and Africa, by the Vandals—in Italy and Pannania, by the Visigoths—in Africa by the Donatists and Circumcellians—in Persia by the Isdegerdes—besides the particular persecutions carried on alternately against the Arians and Anathasians.

Felix III., bishop of Rome, is excommunicated, and his name struck out of the dyptycs, or sacred registers, by Acacius, bishop of Constantinople.

Many ridiculous fables invented during this century; such as the story of the phial of oil brought from heaven by a pigeon at the baptism of Clovis—the vision of Attiala, &c.

516. The computation of time by the Christian era introduced by Dyonisius the monk.

519. Justin restores the orthodox bishops, and condemns the Eutychians.

525. The emperor Justin deposes the Arian bishops.

565. The Picts converted to Christianity by St. Columbia.

569. *Birth of Mahomet*, the false prophet.

580. The Latin tongue ceases to be spoken.

596. Forty Benedictine monks, with Augustine at their head, sent into Britain by Gregory the Great to convert Ethelbert, king of Kent, to the Christian faith.

In the *sixth century* the orthodox Christians are oppressed by the emperor Anstatius Thrasemond, king of the Vandals, Theodoric, king of the Ostrogoths, &c.

Benedictine order founded, and the canon of mass established by Gregory the Great.

Augustine the monk converts the Saxons to Christianity.

Female converts are greatly multiplied in this century.

Litanies introduced into the church of France.

The Arians are driven out of Spain.

The Christian era formed by Dionysius the Little, who first began to count the course of time, from the birth of Christ.

A. D.

The Justinian Code Pandects, Institutions and Novellæ, collected and formed into a body.

609. The Jews of Antioch massacre the Christians.

611. The church and abbey of Westminster founded.

612. Mahomet begins to publish the Koran.

In the *seventh century* the archbishoprics of London and York are founded, with each twelve bishoprics under its jurisdiction.

Boniface IV. receives from the tyrant Phocas (who was the great patron of popes, and the chief promoter of their grandeur) the famous Pantheon, which is converted into a church. Here Cybele was succeeded by the Virgin Mary, and the pagan deities by Christian martyrs. Idolatry still subsisted, but the objects of it were changed.

Ina, king of West Saxony, resigns his crown and assumes the monastic habit in a convent at Rome. During the heptarchy, many Saxon kings took the same course. Pope Agatho ceases to pay the tribute which the see of Rome was accustomed to pay the emperor at the election of its pontiff.

726. Leo forbids the worship of images, which occasions a great rebellion of his subjects, the pope defending the practice.

728. Leo orders pope Gregory to be seized and sent to Constantinople, but the order is frustrated, and Leo confiscates the imperial dominions of Sicily and Calabria.

736. Leo persecutes the monks.

737. Death of Pelagius, who preserved the Christian monarchy in Austria.

753. Astolphus, king of the Lombards, erects the dukedom of Ravenna, and claims from the pope the dukedom of Rome.

754. Pepin invades Italy, and strips Astolphus of his new possessions, conferring them on the pope as a temporal sovereignty.

770. Constantine dissolves the monasteries in the east.

781. Irene re-establishes the worship of images.

787. The seventh general council, or second of Nice, is held.

In the *eighth century* the ceremony of kissing the pope's toe is introduced.

The Saxons, with Witekind their monarch, converted to Christianity.

The Christians persecuted by the Saracens, who massacre five hundred monks in the abbey of Lerins.

Controversy between the Greek and Latin churches, concerning the Holy Ghost's proceeding from the Son.

Gospel propagated in Hyrcania and Tartary.

The reading of the epistle and gospel introduced into the service of the church.

Churches built in honour of saints.

Solitary and private masses instituted.

829. Missionaries sent from France to Sweden.

A. D.

851. Pope Joan supposed to have filled the papal chair for two years.

867. Photius, patriarch of Constantinople, excommunicates pope Adrian.

886. The university of Oxford founded by Alfred.

In the *ninth century* the conversion of the Swedes, Danes, Saxons, Huns, Bohemians, Moravians, Sclavonians, Russians, Indians, and Bulgarians, which latter occasions a controversy between the Greek and Latin churches.

The power of the pontiffs increase; that of the bishops diminishes; and the emperors are vested of their ecclesiastical authority.

The fictitious relics of St. Mark, St. James, and St. Bartholomew are imposed upon the credulity of the people.

Monks and abbots now first employed in civil affairs, and called to the courts of princes.

The superstitious festival of the assumption of the Virgin Mary, instituted by the council of Mentz, and confirmed by pope Nicholas I., and afterwards by Leo X.

The legends or lives of the saints began to be composed in this century.

The apostles' creed is sung in the churches; organs, bells, and vocal music introduced in many places—Festivals multiplied.

The order of St. Andrew, or the knights of the Thistle, in Scotland.

The canonization of saints introduced by Leo II.

Theophilus, from his abhorrence of images, banishes the painters from the eastern empire.

Harold, king of Denmark, is dethroned by his subjects, on account of his attachment to Christianity.

915. The university of Cambridge founded by Edward the elder.

965. The Poles are converted to Christianity.

In the *tenth century* the Christian religion is established in Muscovy, Denmark, and Norway.

The baptism of bells; the festival in remembrance of departed souls, and a multitude of other superstitious rites were introduced in the tenth century.

Fire ordeal introduced.

The influence of monks greatly increased in England.

1015. The Manichean doctrines prevalent in France and Italy.

1061. Henry IV. of Germany, on his knees asks pardon of the pope.

1065. The Turks take Jerusalem from the Saracens.

1076. The emperor Henry IV. excommunicated and deposed by the pope.

1079. Doomsday-book begun by William the Conqueror.

1095. *The first crusade* to the Holy Land. The crusaders take Antioch.

A. D.

1099. Jerusalem taken by Godfrey, of Boulogne. The knights of St. John instituted.

In the *eleventh century*, the office of cardinal instituted.—A contest between the emperors and popes.—Several of the popes are looked upon as magicians, and learning was considered magic.—The tyranny of the popes opposed by the emperors Henry I., II., and III. of England, and other monarchs of that nation; by Philip, king of France, and by the English and German schools.

Baptism performed by triple immersion.

Sabbath fasts introduced by Gregory VII.

The Cistersian, Carthusian, and whipping orders, with many others, are founded in this century.

1147. The second crusade excited by St. Bernard.

1160. The Albigenses maintain heretical doctrines.

1171. T. Becket murdered at Canterbury.

1187. The city of Jerusalem taken by Saladin.

1189. The third crusade under Richard I. and Philip Augustus.

In the *twelfth century* the three military orders of the knights of St. John, of Jerusalem, the knight templars, and the Teutonic knights of St. Mary, were instituted.

Sale of indulgences begun by the bishops, soon after monopolized by the popes.

The scholastic theology, whose jargon did such mischief in the church, took its rise in this century.

Pope Paschal II. orders the Lord's supper to be administered only in one kind, and retrenches the cup.

1202. The fourth crusade sets out from Venice.

1204. *The Inquisition established* by pope Innocent III.

1210. Crusade against the Albigenses, under Simon de Montfort.

1226. Institution of the orders of St. Dominic and St. Francis.

1234. The Inquisition committed to the Dominican monks.

1248. The fifth crusade, under St. Louis.

1260. Flagellants preach baptism with blood.

1282. The Sicilian's vespers, when 8,000 Frenchmen were massacred in one night.

1291. Ptolemais taken by the Turks. End of the crusades.

1293. Jubilee first celebrated at Rome.

1299. Ottoman, or Othoman, first sultan, and founder of the Turkish empire.

In the *thirteenth century* the knights of the Teutonic order, under the command of Herman de Saliza, conquer and convert to Christianity the Prussians.

The power of creating bishops, abbots, &c. claimed by the Roman pontiff.

John, king of England, excommunicated by pope Innocent III., and through fear of that pontiff, is guilty of the most degrading compliances.

A. D.

Jubilees instituted by Boniface VIII.

The Jews driven out of France by Lewis IX., and their Talmud burnt.

The associations of Hans-Towns, Dominicans, Franciscans, Servites, Mendicants, and the hermits of St. Augustine, date the origin of their orders from this century.

The festivals of the nativity of the blessed Virgin, and of the holy sacrament, or body of Christ instituted.

1308. The seat of the popes transferred to Avignon for seventy years.

1310. Rhodes taken by the knights of St. John to Jerusalem.

1377. *Wickliffe's doctrines* propagated in England.

1378. The schisms of the double popes at Rome and Avignon begins and continues thirty-eight years.

1386. Christianity encouraged in Tartary and China; the Lithuanians and Jagello, their prince, converted to the Christian faith.

In the *fourteenth century* pope Clement V. orders the jubilee, which Boniface had appointed to be held every hundredth year, to be celebrated twice in that space of time.

The knight templars are seized and imprisoned; many of them put to death, and the order suppressed.

The Bible is translated into French by the order of Charles V.

The festival of the holy lance and nails that pierced Jesus Christ, instituted by Clement V., in this century. Such was this pontiff's arrogance, that once while he was dining he ordered Dandalus, the Venetian ambassador, to be chained under his table, like a dog.

1409. Council of Pisa, where pope Gregory is deposed.

1414. Council of Constance, in which two popes were deposed, and the popedom remained vacant near three years.

1415. John Huss condemned by the council of Constance for heresy, and burnt.

1416. Jerome of Prague condemned by the same council, and burnt.

1439. Reunion of the Greek and Latin churches.

1450. The first book printed with types of metal; which was the Vulgate Bible published at Mentz.

1453. Constantinople taken by the Turks.

1471. Thomas a'Kempis died.

1492. America discovered by Columbus.

1498. Savanazola, burnt by pope Alexander VI. for preaching against the vices of the clergy.

In the *fifteenth century* the Moors of Spain are converted to the Christian faith by force.

The council of Constance remove the sacramental cup from

A. D.

the laity, and declare it lawful to violate the most solemn engagements, when made by heretics.

1517. The *Reformation* in Germany begun by Luther.

1518. Leo X. condemns Luther's doctrines.

1520. Massacre of Stockholm by Christiern II. and archbishop Trollo.

1521. Gustavus Eriscon introduces the reformation into Sweden by the ministry of Olaus Petri.

1524. Sweden and Denmark embrace the protestant faith.

1529. Diet of Spires against the Huguenots, then first termed protestants.

1530. The league of Smalcand between the protestants.

1531. Michael Servetus burnt for heresy at Geneva.

1534. The reformation takes place in England.

1535. The society of the jesuits instituted by Ignatius Loyola.

1538. The Bible in English appointed to be read in the churches in England.

1540. Dissolution of the monasteries in England by Henry VIII.

1545. The council of Trent begins, which continued eighteen years.

1548. The interim granted by Charles V. to the protestants.

1552. The treaty of Passau between Charles V. and the elector of Saxony, for the establishment of Lutheranism.

1555. A number of bishops in England burnt by queen Mary.

1560. The reformation completed in Scotland by John Knox, and the papal authority abolished.

1564. John Calvin, a celebrated theologian, died.

1572. The massacre of St. Bartholomew's, August 24th.

1576. The league formed in France against the protestants.

1587. The second settlement in Virginia. Manteo, an Indian, received Christian baptism. Virginia Dare born, the first child of Christian parents born in the United States.

1592. Presbyterian church government established in Scotland.

1598. Edict of Nantes, tolerating the protestants in France.

In the *sixteenth century* pope Julius bestows the cardinal's hat upon the keeper of his monkeys.

1608. Arminius propagates his opinions; the Socinians publish their catechism at Cracow.

1610. The protestants form a confederacy at Heilbron.

1618. The synod of Dort, in Holland.

1619. Vanini burnt at Thoulouse for atheism.

1620. Settlement of Plymouth by the puritans.

1622. The congregation de propaganda, &c. founded at Rome by pope Gregory XV.

1626. League of the protestant princes against the emperor.

1638. The solemn league and covenant established in Scotland.

1639. First baptist church in America formed at Providence.

1640. New England psalm-book first published.

1641. The Irish rebellion and massacre of the protestants, Oct. 33.

A. D.

1656. The friends or quakers first came to Massachusetts. Four executed in 1659.

1664. *Mr. Eliot's Indian Bible* printed at Cambridge, Mass. The *first Bible* printed in America.

1674. John Milton, a celebrated poet, died.

1685. Revocation of the edict of Nantes by Lewis XIV.

1690. Rev. J. Eliot, "apostle of the Indians," died.
Episcopacy abolished in Scotland by king William.

1708. Saybrook platform formed by a synod of ministers under the authority of the state of Connecticut.

1731. Rev. Solomon Stoddard, a theological writer, died.

1740. George Whitfield, a celebrated preacher, first arrives in America; he dies at Newburyport, Mass., Sept. 30, 1770, on his seventh visit to America.

1748. Dr. Watts, a celebrated poet and divine, died, aged 75.

1751. Dr. Doddridge, a celebrated divine, died.

1758. President Edwards, a celebrated divine, died.

1772. Swedenborg, the founder of the New Jerusalem church, died.

1773. The society of the jesuits suppressed by the pope's bull August 25.

1774. The Shakers first arrived from England; they settled near Albany.

1782. *First English Bible* printed in America by Robert Aiken, of Philadelphia.

1788. Voltaire, a celebrated infidel philosopher, died

1790. Howard, the philanthropist, died.

1791. John Wesley, the founder of methodism, died, aged 87.

1793. Triumph of infidelity in France. The national convention decreed that "*death is an eternal sleep.*"

1796. The London missionary society sent out a number of missionaries to the Society islands.

1798. The papal government suppressed by the French.—The pope quits Rome Feb. 26th.

1804. British and foreign Bible society instituted.

1806. The slave-trade abolished by act of parliament, February.

1812. Pomare, king of Otaheite, baptized.

1813. Russian Bible society formed at St. Petersburg.

1815. Idolatry abolished in the Society islands.

1816. The American Bible society instituted at New York.

1818. Paris protestant Bible society formed.

1820. First mariner's church erected at New-York.

1821. Monrovia settled by the American colonization society.

1823. American missionaries arrived at the Sandwich islands.

1826. American temperance society formed at Boston, Mass.

THE END.

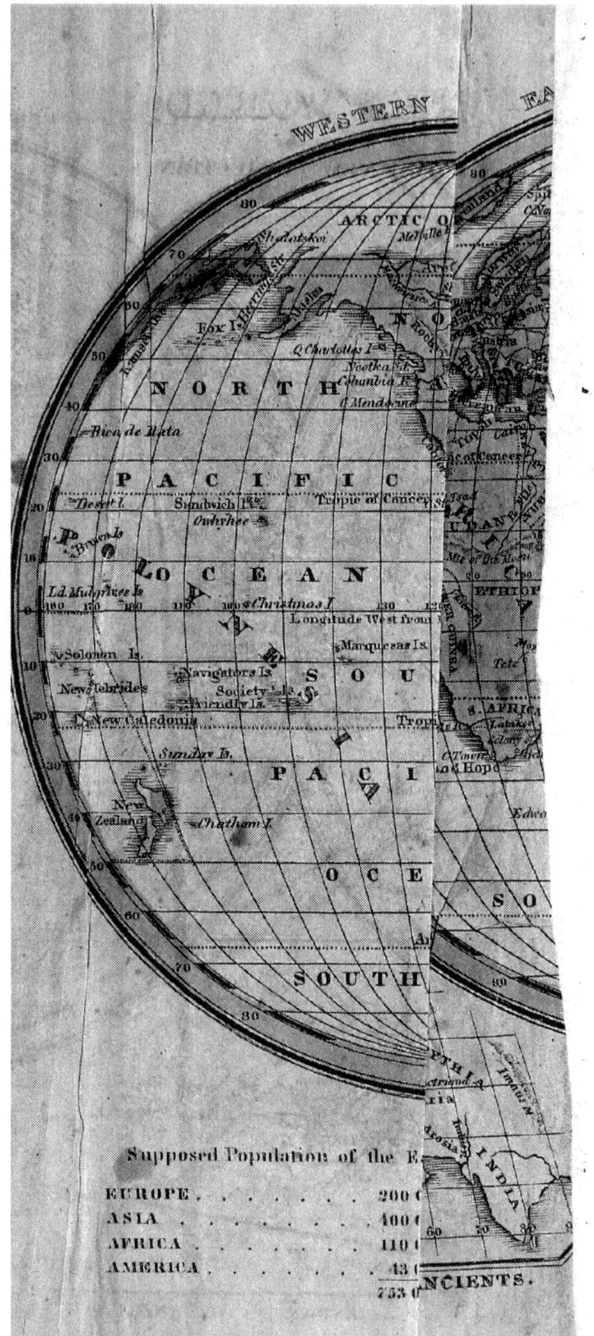
WESTERN
ARCTIC
Fox I.
Q. Charlottes I.
Nootka Sd.
Columbia R.
C. Mendocino
N O R T H
Rica de Plata
P A C I F I C
Desert I.
Sandwich Is.
Owhyhee
Tropic of Cancer
O C E A N
Ld. Mulgraves Is.
Christmas I.
Longitude West from
Marquesas Is.
Solomon Is.
Navigators Is.
New Hebrides
Society Is.
Friendly Is.
New Caledonia
S O U
Sunday Is.
P A C I
New Zealand
Chatham I.
O C E
S O U T H
S O
C. of Good Hope
ETHIOP
S. AFRICA
INDIA
Supposed Population of the
EUROPE 200
ASIA 400
AFRICA 110
AMERICA 43
753
NCIENTS.
1500

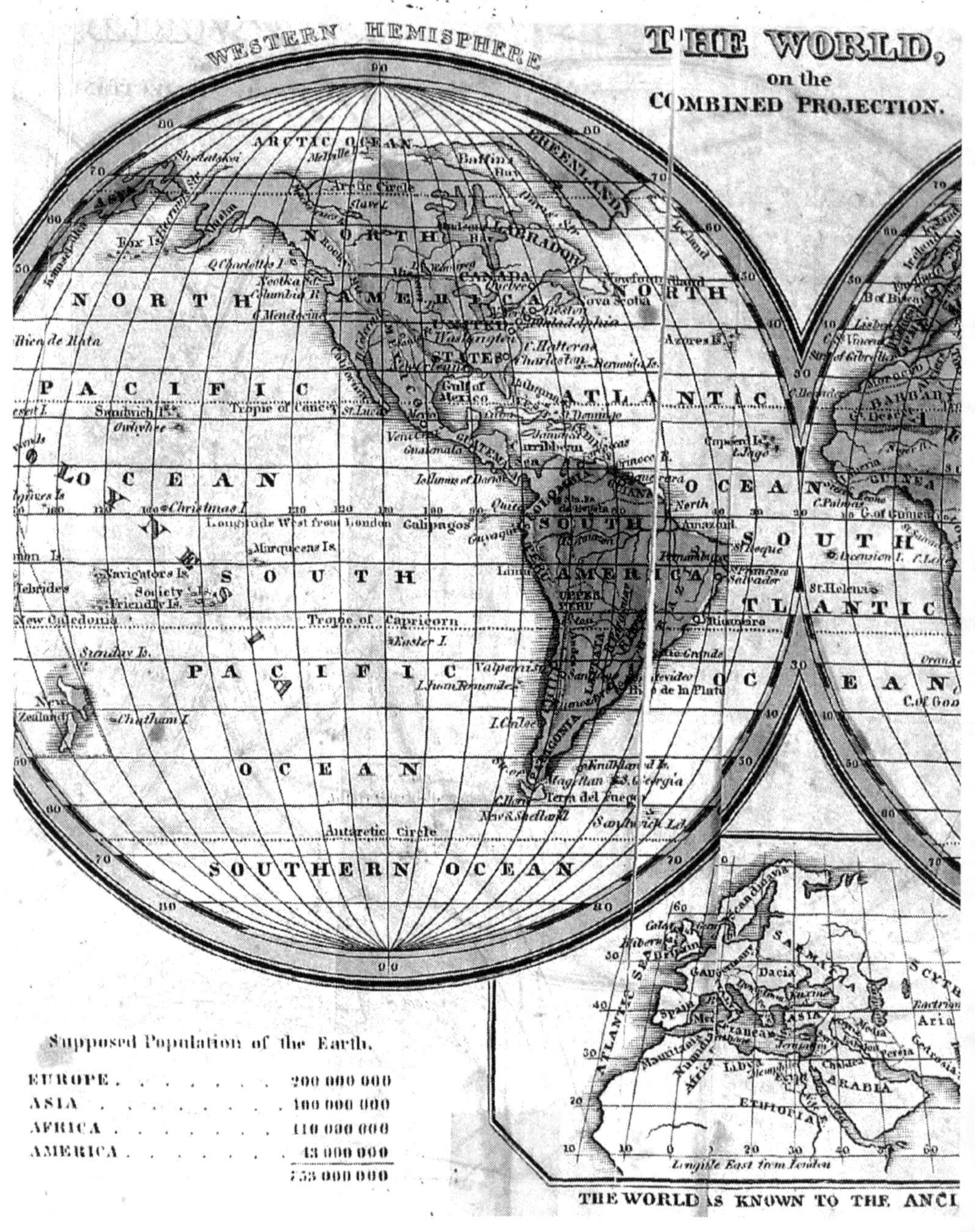

Supposed Population of the Earth.

EUROPE	200 000 000
ASIA	400 000 000
AFRICA	110 000 000
AMERICA	43 000 000
	753 000 000

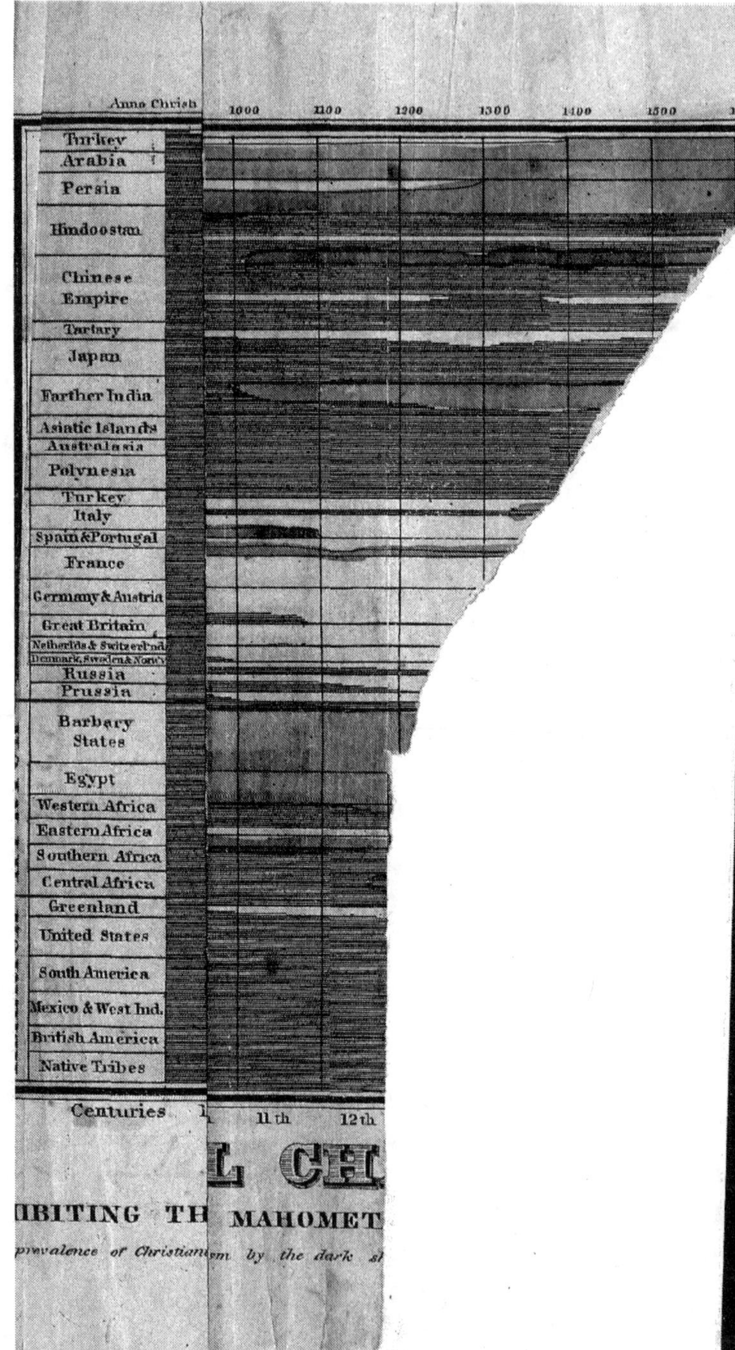

Anno Christi
1000
1100
1200
1300
1400
1500
Turkey
Arabia
Persia
Hindoostan
Chinese Empire
Tartary
Japan
Farther India
Asiatic Islands
Australasia
Polynesia
Turkey
Italy
Spain & Portugal
France
Germany & Austria
Great Britain
Netherlds & Switzerlnd
Denmark, Sweden & Norwy
Russia
Prussia
Barbary States
Egypt
Western Africa
Eastern Africa
Southern Africa
Central Africa
Greenland
United States
South America
Mexico & West Ind.
British America
Native Tribes
Centuries
11th
12th
L CH
IBITING TH MAHOMET
prevalence of Christianism by the dark

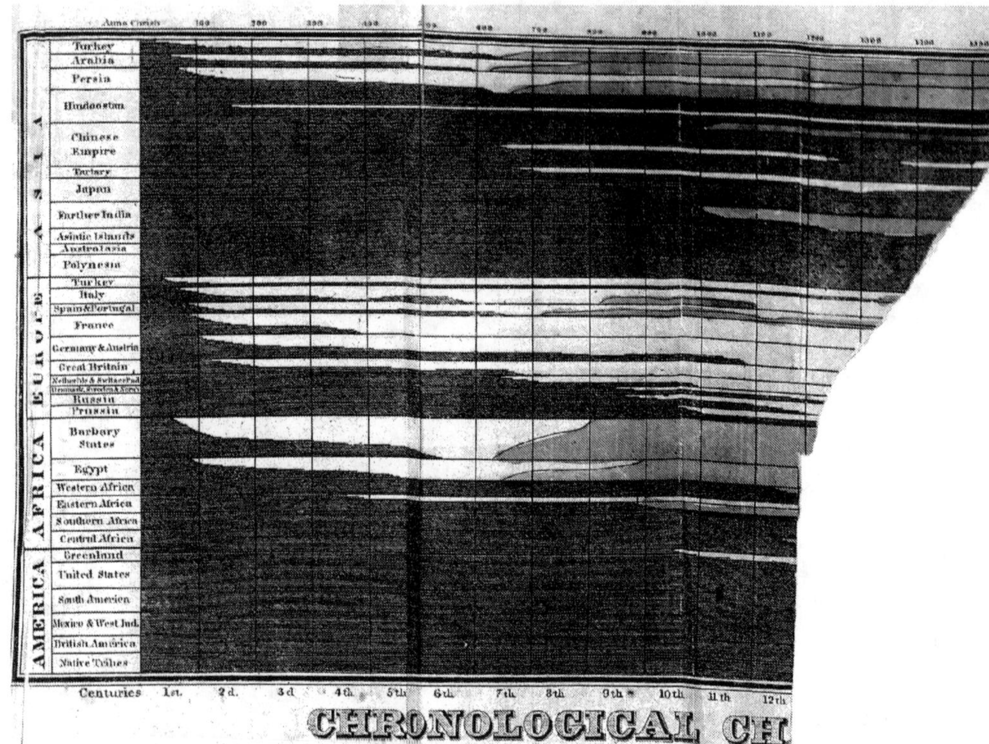

CHRONOLOGICAL CH

EXHIBITING THE RISE AND PROGRESS OF CHRISTIANITY AND MAHOMET

The prevalence of Christianity is denoted by the white space, that of Mahometanism by the red, and Paganism by the dark

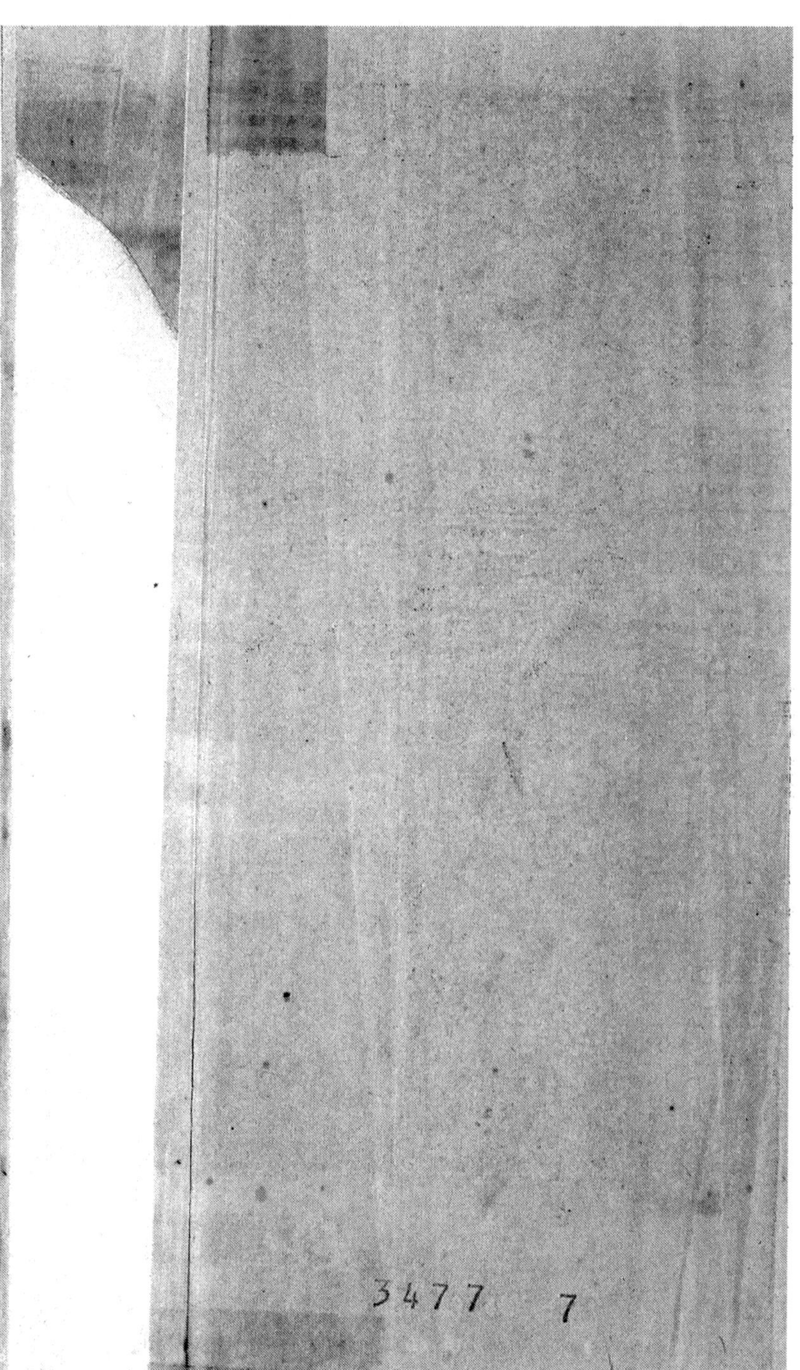

www.ingramcontent.com/pod-product-compliance
Lightning Source LLC
LaVergne TN
LVHW012207040326
832903LV00003B/169

* 9 7 8 1 0 1 6 9 0 7 0 1 9 *